A Birder's Guide To Minnesota

By Kim R. Eckert

Fourth Edition
2002

A county-by-county guide to over 1,000 birding locations,
including references and resources,
an annotated list of 427 Minnesota birds,
selected identification hints,
and over 200 maps.

"Embrace the joy of not knowing where you are going."

Author's horoscope for February 1992 from *American Way* in-flight magazine, which he found en route to leading a birding tour in South Texas.

"Must be old age creeping up. Be careful, Kim."

October 1991 message left on the Duluth Birding Report recording by Bill Litkey, who was calling to correct his earlier report involving a misidentified bird.

PUBLISHED BY GAVIAN GUIDES

8255 CONGDON BOULEVARD

DULUTH, MINNESOTA 55804

TELEPHONE (218) 525-6930

E-MAIL <KRECKERT@CPINTERNET.COM>

ISBN 0-9719902-0-4

Distributed by American Birding Association Sales
P. O. Box 6599
Colorado Springs, CO 80934
Telephone 800-634-7736
E-mail <abasales@abasales.com>
Website <www.americanbirding.org>

Printed in the USA by University of Minnesota Printing Services, 2818 Como Avenue S.E., Minneapolis, MN 55414.

Table of Contents

PHOTO CREDITS

Cover / Great Gray Owl / ©Dudley Edmondson,
       Raptor Works (website <raptorworks.com>)
Title Page / Great Gray Owl / Dudley Edmondson
Table of Contents / Northern Hawk Owl / Warren Nelson
Acknowledgments / Panda (1975-1992) / Carol Copeland
page 17 / Yellow-crowned Night-Heron / Warren Nelson
page 20 / Northern Goshawk / Dudley Edmondson
page 24 / Yellow Rail / Warren Nelson
page 29 / Red Phalarope / Denny Martin
page 32 / Boreal Owl / Terry Brashear
page 36 / Three-toed Woodpecker / Anthony Hertzel
page 40 / Northern Wheatear / Terry Brashear
page 45 / Le Conte's Sparrow / Warren Nelson
page 49 / Lapland Longspur / Vija Kelly
page 52 / Northern Hawk Owl / Dudley Edmondson
page 124 / Upland Sandpiper / Vija Kelly
page 191 / Sharp-tailed Grouse / Vija Kelly
page 246 / Boreal Owl / Warren Nelson

ACKNOWLEDGMENTS

Several individuals deserve recognition for their direct contributions to this book. Foremost among them certainly is Tony Hertzel, whose assistance and expertise at the computer screen was instrumental in solving all the technical difficulties I faced with the text and maps. Without compensation, Tony donated countless hours transforming the manuscript into its final form for the printer.

My appreciation is extended to Parker Backstrom, Dave Benson, Paul Egeland, Tony Hertzel, Allison Jensen, Craig Mandel, and Barb and Denny Martin who helped proofread much or all of the manuscript. Thanks also is due to Barb Akre, Dave Benson, Molly Evans, Mary Gabrys, Mike Hendrickson, Sarah Grosshuesch, Jim and Sharon Lind, and Peder Svingen, who assisted with the tedious task of indexing the text.

Several persons provided answers to my questions about specific birding areas and other information presented in the book: Mark Alt, Al Batt, Betsy Beneke, Jo Blanich, Brad Bolduan, Paul Budde, Steve Carlson, Herb Dingmann, Paul Egeland, Bob Ekblad, Audrey Evers, Bruce Fall, Randy Frederickson, Merrill Frydendall, Doug Jenness, Doug Johnson, Jeanie Joppru, Martin Kehoe, Cindy Krienke, Fred Lesher, Craig Menze, Steve Millard, Warren Nelson, Gerda Nordquist, Mark Ochs, Bob O'Connor, Bob Russell, Roger Schroeder, Dick Smaby, Shelley Steva, Jeff Stephenson, and Peder Svingen. My apologies to those whom I undoubtedly forgot to acknowledge.

Terry Brashear, Carol Copeland, Dudley Edmondson, Tony Hertzel, Vija Kelly, Denny Martin, and Warren Nelson generously donated photographs for use in these pages. Rick and Bonnie of Kollath Graphic Design produced the finished versions of the maps on pages 2, 53, 125, and 192. Jann Jarvis of University of Minnesota Printing Services and Terry O'Nele of American Birding Association Sales also provided advice and assistance with this book's final preparation, printing, and distribution.

As I reminisce after 40 years of birding (it all started in April, 1962, with 10th grade Biology class), some names of those I used to bird with come to mind: Ed Hibbard, Ray Glassel, Leata Pearson, Bill Pieper, Dick Ruhme, and Terry Savaloja. Sadly, they are no longer still around to read this. Bob Russell, though, is very much alive and still in touch — it was Bob who had kept my initial interest in birding alive four decades ago. And it was Ed Hibbard and Bob who first introduced me to the subtle wonders along the back roads of Stearns County when I first came to Minnesota back in 1964. I remember especially an aimless but wonderful search with them for non-existent prairie-chickens near St. Cloud, and my first prairie birding experience in the Dakotas in Ed's Studebaker with only a 1950 road map as our guide.

From Bob and Ed I learned that birding involves more than stake-outs, life lists, ornithological sciences, and the alleged beauty of Wood Ducks. It is a reason to wander and explore, to appreciate the unplanned more than the predictable, to not take too much too seriously. To even enjoy a birding trip with no birds, and not necessarily mind getting stuck or lost miles from nowhere -- just as we used to in Stearns County. Regretfully, those years are gone now, a time before there were birding hotlines, internet listserves, and finding guides such as this telling you where to go. It sometimes seems no one is interested in finding their own birds and birding places any more. I actually hope this guide is not too comprehensive — that there are still places left to discover and birds to find on your own.

And, for nearly 17 years, Panda was always along on my trips and tours throughout the state. One of those tours was to Blue Mounds, a place with lots of cactus to step on, but a place where Panda had learned where not to step when we lived there in the 1970s. Years later, as my birding group hiked along the park's escarpment, many learned to fall in line behind him as he led the way around the cactus without mishap. Panda was also a daily fixture at Hawk Ridge each fall for 14 years, with a special fondness for perching atop this one rock, the highest one along the road at the Main Overlook, where he spent much of the day. Indeed, he became part of the "skyline" of the ridge, the first sight many visitors noticed upon their arrival. It seemed almost every Minnesota birder and hawk watcher came to know Panda. Many may have come to think of him as their dog as well and perhaps also lost something when he died. For one thing, the landscape of Hawk Ridge now seems diminished — that highest rock stands not quite as tall as it did before.

This book is dedicated to Bob's inspiration, and to the memory of Ed, Ray, Leata, Bill, Dick, Terry, and Panda.

INTRODUCTION

MINNESOTA GEOGRAPHY

With eighty-four thousand square miles within its borders, Minnesota is second only to Texas as the largest state east of the Rockies. Indeed, just one of its counties, St. Louis, at 6,711 square miles, could qualify for statehood. It is, after all, larger than Connecticut, Delaware, Hawaii, and Rhode Island. Over 400 miles separate the Minnesota-Iowa border from the Northwest Angle peninsula up on Lake of the Woods, the northernmost point in the 48 contiguous United States.

The four corners of the state are even more remote from each other. Standing among aspen groves and magpies in northwestern Kittson County, you would be closer to the Canadian outposts of Saskatoon or Flin Flon than to the southeastern corner of Houston County. In turn, the moorhens and Prothonotaries of Houston County's Mississippi River backwaters are nearer to Louisville or Cincinnati than they are to Kittson County.

At the same time, a Blue Grosbeak nest in the southwestern corner of Rock County lies closer to Cheyenne, Wyoming, or the northern Oklahoma border than to Grand Portage in Cook County. Meanwhile, Grand Portage is about as close to the James Bay portion of cold Hudson Bay as it is to Rock County.

As for its population, Minnesota's statistics are more modest. More than four million people live in the state, but, because of its size and since roughly half its residents are concentrated in the Twin Cities metropolitan area, Minnesota remains for the most part a land of wide open spaces, small towns, and, as the beer commercials used to say, Sky Blue Waters.

Minnesotans do consider Minneapolis and St. Paul as big-time cities. In fact, these must be the only cities in their world, since most simply call them "the Cities." But their combined human population is a relatively modest 650,000, and they have enough room within their corporate limits and more populous suburbs for dozens of lakes, three major river valleys, and a large avian population.

Minnesota is not only large in area but also in its variety of habitats. Most characteristic of these would be the coniferous forest of the boreal zone which spills over the Canadian border and reaches its southern limit in the predominantly wooded Northeast Region. Deciduous riverbottom woods of a more southern flavor come as far north as the Mississippi River watershed which covers the Southeast Region, a mixed landscape of farms and woodlands. The Great Plains of the Dakotas spill over into the West Region, mostly open country with extensive farmlands and a few remnant prairie grasslands. And the Great Lakes extend a marine component inland as far as Lake Superior, the largest freshwater lake in the world.

Superior may be Minnesota's largest lake, but there are thousands of others here (this is, after all, the Land of Ten Thousand Lakes), and lakes and other wetlands represent another facet of this state's mosaic of habitats. Depending on how one defines a lake, there are actually 12,000 or more of them in Minnesota, and this state has more surface water area than any other. These wetlands are distributed through most of the state, although some counties along the western border and the eight counties in the southeastern corner are practically devoid of lakes.

Rivers form another integral part of Minnesota's landscape, and their wooded valleys provide important corridors for migrants. The Mississippi River, the longest river with the largest drainage area in the U.S., flows some 500 miles through the state from its source at Lake Itasca in Clearwater County. Along with its two major tributaries, the St. Croix and Minnesota rivers, its watershed includes about two-thirds of Minnesota.

Most of northern Minnesota is part of the Hudson Bay watershed, drained by the Red River along the North Dakota border and by a maze of lakes and rivers along the Canadian border. Lake Superior drains the southern halves of St. Louis, Lake, and Cook counties, while the opposite southwestern corner of the state is part of the Missouri River watershed.

These rivers and lakes provide most of the relief in Minnesota's relatively level terrain. From Lake Superior, the state's lowest elevation at 602 feet, the hills rise from its North Shore and reach their peak at 2,301-foot Eagle Mountain in Cook County. This highest point in Minnesota is only 13 miles from lowly Lake Superior.

Equally scenic and hilly is the broadly wooded and bluff-lined Mississippi River valley from the Twin Cities southeast to the Iowa border; north of the Twin Cities, the Mississippi forms a less significant valley and migration corridor. The valley carved by the St. Croix River along the Wisconsin border east of the Twin Cities is similarly lined with deeply wooded hillsides and scattered rocky bluffs.

Although the Minnesota River valley from the Twin Cities southwest to Mankato is less dramatic, its extensive woodlands form an important route for migrants. West of Mankato the valley gradually opens up into hillsides dotted with a unique mixture of rock outcrops, tracts of virgin prairie, and stands of junipers.

The last "valley" is formed by the narrowly wooded Red River, which resembles more an irrigation ditch as it stretches (and yawns) its way through the intensively farmed "black desert" along the North Dakota border en route to Canada.

MINNESOTA WEATHER

Certainly, no description of Minnesota would be complete without a word about its weather, especially in winter. While the state gets its share of snow, the amounts are moderate when compared to places like Michigan's Upper Peninsula or northern New York State. Duluth does have about 80 inches over a normal winter, but the Twin Cities has an

STATE OF MINNESOTA:
Counties and County Seats, Principal Lakes and Rivers, Biomes and Other Natural Areas

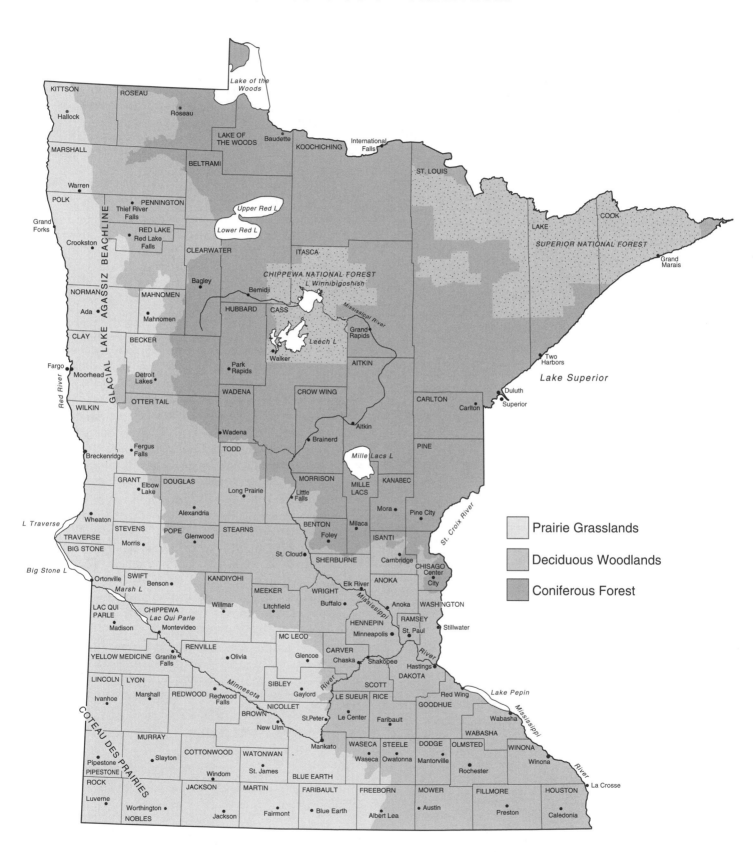

Legend:
- Prairie Grasslands
- Deciduous Woodlands
- Coniferous Forest

average of 50 inches or so (about the same as Chicago), while the West Region averages less than 40.

Continuous snow cover usually starts during November and has ended by late March or early April, but it is not unusual for the ground in the Southeast or West region still to be free of snow by Christmas Bird Count time, or for the snow pack to disappear in February.

The real news in winter is the cold, as northern Minnesota has the nation's coldest temperatures south of Alaska. It is not unusual for a day's low to be in the -20s (or even the -30s along the Canadian border), for its "high" to remain below zero, or with readings in the -50s or -60s once you factor in the wind chill. By the way, Minnesota's all-time record low is 60 below zero, recorded at the town of Tower on February 2, 1996 — and that was the actual air temperature, not a wind-chill factor!

But a winter's birding trip to northern Minnesota is a must for several sought-after species, and native Minnesotans and visiting birders alike have managed to survive such weather. Normal January highs in Duluth are in the mid-teens with lows averaging a few degrees below zero (normal highs in southern Minnesota are in the low 20s; average lows just above zero). Actually, a sunny winter afternoon with average temperatures and minimal winds can actually be described as pleasant.

The summers are less newsworthy: an average July day would have highs from the pleasant mid-70s in the Northeast to the low 80s elsewhere. But hot and humid days in the 90s do occur, at least away from cold Lake Superior, and it might hit 100 degrees a time or two each summer. On the other hand, when an east wind blows in off Lake Superior, Duluth and its North Shore could have mid-summer highs only in the 60s, 20 or even 30 degrees cooler than the rest of the state.

Spring and fall are highly unpredictable. April and early May sometimes resemble winter more than summer, especially in the Northeast Region where warmer weather (along with warblers and other such migrants) cannot be expected to arrive until late May. Autumn, however, is generally more pleasant, even in the Northeast where seriously cold temperatures and significant snowfalls generally hold off until November.

MINNESOTA BIRDS

When birders contemplate a trip to add birds to their life lists, states like Alaska, California, Arizona, and Texas initially come to mind. But several of the most sought-after species in North America are regularly found in Minnesota: e.g., Gyrfalcon, Spruce and Sharp-tailed grouse, Yellow Rail, Snowy, Northern Hawk, Great Gray and Boreal owls, Three-toed and Black-backed woodpeckers, Northern Shrike, Boreal Chickadee, Bohemian Waxwing, Connecticut and Mourning warblers, Henslow's and Le Conte's sparrows, Chestnut-collared Longspur, all the winter finches, plus many others. Certainly only one or two other states could include as many highly-sought species on their official lists.

Because of its geographical position in North America and its variety of habitats, Minnesota is also a key state for finding birds at the limits of their ranges. Thus, no matter from which direction the birder comes, a trip here should result in some additions to one's list.

For example, several species occur regularly in western Minnesota but only rarely so east of the Mississippi: these include Eared, Western and Clark's grebes, Ross's Goose, Swainson's Hawk, Greater Prairie-Chicken, Franklin's Gull, Western Kingbird, Black-billed Magpie, Spotted Towhee, Harris's Sparrow, and Chestnut-collared Longspur.

Conversely, visitors from the West might encounter a few birds for the first time if this were their first eastern trip: e.g., American Black Duck, American Woodcock, Yellow-throated Vireo, Wood Thrush, Golden-winged, Black-throated Blue and Pine warblers, Northern Parula, Scarlet Tanager, and Eastern Towhee.

There is also a large assortment of typically southern birds which reach their breeding range limits in southern Minnesota and are mostly absent farther north: Great Egret, Red-shouldered Hawk, Wild Turkey, Common Moorhen, Yellow-billed Cuckoo, Eastern Screech-Owl, Red-bellied Woodpecker, Acadian and Willow flycatchers, Bell's Vireo, Tufted Titmouse, Blue-gray Gnatcatcher, Blue-winged, Cerulean, Prothonotary and Hooded warblers, Louisiana Waterthrush, Field and Henslow's sparrows, Northern Cardinal, Blue Grosbeak, and Dickcissel.

In addition to the long list of species which breed at their southern range limits in the boreal forest, these permanent and winter residents of the Northeast Region tend to be absent or rare farther south: Gyrfalcon, Spruce and Sharp-tailed grouse, Snowy, Northern Hawk, Great Gray and Boreal owls, Three-toed and Black-backed woodpeckers, Gray Jay, Common Raven, Boreal Chickadee, Bohemian Waxwing, Pine Grosbeak, White-winged Crossbill, and Hoary Redpoll.

And, finally, birders regularly find several Great Lakes specialties on and along Lake Superior, more so than farther west or south elsewhere in Minnesota: Red-throated and Pacific loons, Harlequin and Long-tailed ducks, Surf, White-winged and Black scoters, Whimbrel, Red Knot, Parasitic Jaeger, and Little, Thayer's, Iceland, Glaucous and Great Black-backed gulls.

Minnesota's birds are also notable for their quantity as well as their quality. Besides rarities of the most-wanted variety and those birds from all directions at the periphery of their ranges, this is a state in which to find significant numbers of many species.

Flocks of Common Loons, often by the hundreds, congregate on Lake Winnibigoshish and Mille Lacs in October. Also in fall, but of dubious merit, as many as 100,000 Canada Geese have been counted in late fall/early winter in the vicinity of Lac Qui Parle Lake. In fall as well, the concentration of thousands of Common Mergansers and other ducks along the Mississippi River from Goodhue County downstream to the Iowa border is especially impressive, as is the possibility of seeing a few hundred Bald Eagles on a single day.

The fame of Hawk Ridge in Duluth as one of this continent's premier sites for fall raptor migration is well deserved. Some 80,000 hawks is a season's average total (148,000-plus in 1993 is the record), and on just one September day in 1993 nearly 50,000 hawks (mostly Broad-wingeds) were counted. Other statistics of note: over 4,300 Bald Eagles counted in 1994; nearly 4,000 Red-taileds seen on a single day the same year; and 5,800-plus Northern Goshawks in 1982, no fewer than 1,229 of these on one October day! The activity even continues after sunset: on a single October night in 1989 nearly 300 Northern Saw-whet Owls were banded, and the 1995 season total was 1,400 saw-whets in the nets.

There are days in some years in late May when the fog and rain ground hundreds of warblers and other passerines at Park Point in Duluth. When the weather is right, it can resemble such famed migrant traps as Point Pelee, Ontario, or High Island, Texas.

And finally, numbers of much greater proportions were documented in past years during fall counts of passerines in Duluth along the shore of Lake Superior. These daily August-October censuses (with nighthawks, jays, crows, robins, waxwings, warblers, and blackbirds predominating) averaged around a quarter million birds each season, with some single-morning bird counts recording totals in the tens of thousands.

Suggestions to the Birder

SUMMER BIRDING

To see the most sought-after species, out-of-state birders tend to come to Minnesota in summer or winter. The summer nesting season may begin as early as March or April for some species and extend into August for others, but it's best to visit between late May and early July when most birds will be singing on their breeding grounds. If you arrive in mid-May or earlier, some later migrants (mainly cuckoos, flycatchers, and warblers) may not be on territory yet; by mid-July, most passerines have stopped singing and are thus harder to find. And it is certainly suggested that birders learn the vocalizations of the species they seek: most woods birds are difficult to see unless they first are heard.

However, note that some breeding species are mostly silent in June but more vocal and easier to find in spring: e.g., Ruffed and Sharp-tailed grouse, Greater Prairie-Chicken, Wild Turkey, American Woodcock, Great Gray, Long-eared, Boreal and Northern Saw-whet owls, and Boreal Chickadee. For other reasons, summer is not the best time to find the permanent resident Northern Goshawk (easier in fall), Gray Partridge (best looked for in fall or winter), or

Spruce Grouse (you'd have better chances almost any other time of year).

A visit to the Northeast Region is needed to see the most sought-after breeding species, with a side trip to the West adding a few prairie-type specialties. Unless in search of Henslow's Sparrows, out-of-state birders spend relatively little time in the Southeast, a region attractive mostly to resident Minnesota birders.

WINTER BIRDING

In spite of the weather, winter is also a popular season for visiting birders, the best or only time to look for many of Minnesota's specialties: Gyrfalcon, Spruce and Ruffed grouse, Snowy, Northern Hawk and Great Gray owls, Bohemian Waxwing, Northern Shrike, Pine Grosbeak, Red and White-winged crossbills, Common and Hoary redpolls. Other annual winter possibilities include Harlequin and Long-tailed ducks, Northern Goshawk, Sharp-tailed Grouse, Thayer's and Glaucous gulls, Boreal Owl, Three-toed and Black-backed woodpeckers, Gray Jay, Boreal Chickadee, Varied Thrush, Snow Bunting, and Evening Grosbeak.

The first winter residents arrive in late October or early November and the last gradually depart in March, but it is difficult to predict the best month for a winter's trip. If one comes in January or February, it might be difficult to find ducks and gulls on Lake Superior if the ice has blown in on east winds. (The lake hardly ever freezes entirely, but in late winter a solid ice pack sometimes forms over the west end of the lake.) In some winters, Bohemian Waxwings and crossbills might become scarce or disappear altogether after December if they have exhausted their food supply.

On the other hand, the visiting birder in November or December might miss something like the Gyr that waits until January to settle into a winter hunting territory, some owl invasions do not develop until January or February, and Three-toed and Black-backed woodpeckers tend to drum more and be more responsive to recordings in February. It may be hard to pick the correct month for a winter birding trip, but it's easy to advise where to go. As in summer, almost all of the species of interest are best looked for in the Northeast Region, and most birders use Duluth as the base for their trip.

Note that many out-of-state birders have a misconception of what birding is like here is winter, assuming it is synonymous with looking at owls. Yes, the birding can be exciting most years, but there are some relatively owl-free winters with Great Gray and Northern Hawk owls difficult or impossible to find. Also be prepared to find quality, not quantity. It is easy to drive or hike through the boreal forests and meadows for a half hour or more without seeing a single bird, and at day's end in mid-winter your list may only include 20 or so species.

Speaking of misconceptions, if you are fortunate enough to be here when there are lots of owls around, don't call it a good winter for owls. When northern owls are especially visible and approachable, it generally means they are stressed from starvation, forced to be out hunting longer after dawn and before dusk, and attracted to residential yards and roadsides where small mammals tend to be easier to find. Many starve to death. Such winters may be good for owl-watchers, but obviously not for the owls.

SPRING AND FALL BIRDING

Like other states, Minnesota has its greatest variety of birds present during migration, but, since birds are on the move and as unpredictable as the weather, spring and fall are generally not the best times to look for most sought-after species at particular places and times. As mentioned earlier, however, there are some specialties best looked for during spring or fall.

The earliest spring migrants (waterfowl, hawks, blackbirds, etc.) begin to appear in southern Minnesota during March, peak waterfowl movements normally occur from late March through mid-April, most shorebirds pass through during May, while warblers and the like peak during mid- and late May. Even into mid-June, some shorebirds, flycatchers, warblers, and other late migrants are still moving north.

While a day's birding during the peak of spring migration will turn up more species than on a good fall day, it is during fall migration that most vagrants and other rarities appear, with most of them turning up in Duluth and along the North Shore. Fall actually begins as early as late June and early July when the first southbound shorebirds appear; peak shorebird numbers are usually seen between mid-July and late August. In late July, a few warblers and other passerines begin migrating south from the boreal forest, with the greatest movement of warblers from late August through mid-September.

Many passerines continue to migrate south in numbers into mid-October, as do hawks which mostly pass over Hawk Ridge in Duluth between mid-September and late October. By the end of October, many winter residents have begun to arrive from Canada, and, during November, the peak influx of waterfowl occurs along the Mississippi southeast of the Twin Cities. Some migration is still going on during Christmas Bird Count time, especially during milder Decembers.

SHOREBIRDS AND SEWAGE PONDS

Finding shorebirds in Minnesota is always a challenge and mostly a matter of luck. Good shorebirding locations typically result from rains briefly flooding some field, from dry conditions exposing mudflats temporarily at an otherwise ordinary lake, or from a lake's water levels unpredictably drawn down for various reasons. But one year's (or week's) mudflats are usually gone the next, either overgrown with weeds or under water, and few shorebirding places are good every year. Recently, however, national wildlife refuges like Agassiz and Big Stone have been drawing down a pool or two annually to attract migrant shorebirds.

Of course, shorebirds are often associated with sewage ponds, but in Minnesota virtually all of these have riprapped shorelines with little or no mud, and many are too small to attract much. Any ponds can be worthwhile, however, especially those in the open country of the West and Southeast regions, and especially where natural wetlands are scarce with shorebirds and other water birds having little habitat from which to choose.

Almost all Minnesota sewage ponds are fenced off and posted with "No Trespassing" signs, but usually the ponds can be scanned from the road. And note that at most sewage ponds no one seems to mind when birders climb through gates and fences for a better look; the condition of the gate/fence typically indicates if others have entered before. However, especially when confronted with ponds behind serious-looking signs and fences, it's always safest to try to find someone in town who can grant you permission to gain access.

NATIONAL AND STATE FORESTS

For those birders who (for reasons unknown) prefer national and state forests to sewage ponds, always pay close attention when trying to navigate along their back roads. No matter which maps you use, including those insets in this book, new forest roads not on your map will appear (and old ones on the map will disappear) unpredictably. Forest road numbers are also changed sometimes for no apparent reason. Accordingly, birders with a taste for back roads and the unknown might want to inquire locally for directions to avoid getting lost. (Or, on second thought, avoiding directions and not knowing where you're headed might well be the whole point of your trip.)

Also beware of logging trucks speeding down that road you're trying to bird along. Some loggers are unable, unprepared, or unwilling to slow down for birders parked or walking along "their" road.

GAS, FOOD, LODGING

Once the birder has decided where and when to bird, some further advice might be useful. While Minnesota gas stations, restaurants, and motels are about the same as anywhere else, it is important to be aware of a few things. Note first the large unpopulated areas in the Northeast with facilities few and far between. Especially in winter or at night, therefore, a gas station may be more important to find than any owl.

Like everyone else, Minnesotans are addicted to fast-food and other restaurant chains, but, if you're not in a hurry and not locked into the security of a predictable menu at the nearest franchise place, take the time to find that downtown cafe or rural supper club where the food and prices are usually better than those places along the interstate. Besides, to discover the character (and characters) of Minnesota, as well as its birds, you have to travel the back roads and visit the small towns.

Motel reservations are always a good idea, especially on weekends, since some local event or vacationing travelers may fill up every available room in town. Since Duluth is frequently the base for many birding trips, be especially aware that every motel room there on many weekends from June through mid-October is reserved by non-birding tourists weeks in advance.

If you prefer camping to motel rooms, the best places are national and state forest campgrounds which are usually pleasant settings, good birding spots, and inexpensive. Most of these, however, are only located in the Northeast Region. More evenly distributed statewide are state park campgrounds. Their settings and birding are usually just as good, and their facilities better, although they are more expensive. Also scattered around the state, but harder to find on maps, are municipal and county campgrounds. They are often free, but many are only marginally maintained, and some are noisy sites for weekend beer parties.

Of course, there are always those expensive private campgrounds which mostly cater to motor homes and trailers looking for a place to plug in TVs and drain septic systems. Camping used to mean getting away from it all with tent and sleeping bag, but today's modern "campgrounds" look more like a parking lot for an amusement park and charge as much as a motel.

CAVEATS

Minnesota birding can involve some difficulties, but most are not all that serious, and many should already be familiar to both visiting and resident birders.

• WINTER. The most serious problem that might require special precautions is the potential for severe winter weather from November through March. Since temperatures well below zero are common, you obviously want to dress as warmly as possible, preferably in layers. Toes, fingers, and ears are most vulnerable. Most persons have special trouble keeping their feet warm, so insulated boots are a must, and those with felt liners are of adequate warmth and most popular. Also note that mukluks, I am told, will keep feet warmer than anything else, though a pair can cost $200 or more. Warm mittens also are recommended and work better than gloves in keeping fingers warm. A hat covering the ears is of obvious importance.

Preparing your car is as important as choosing what to wear. Make sure the radiator is winterized to at least 30 below. A shovel in the trunk is a must in case you slide into the ditch and need to dig your way out. And use special care when pulling to the side of the road to park: it is often difficult to see where the solid shoulder ends and the snow-filled ditch begins, and thus very easy to become stuck.

Jumper cables should also be in the trunk in case your battery dies after a night of 30 below.

Snow tires or four-wheel-drive vehicles would prove useful on an unplowed road but are not necessary on most trips. Radial tires on a front-wheel-drive car are entirely adequate on plowed roads and actually work better than snow tires on ice. If you drive a rear-wheel-drive vehicle, you might want to add extra weight in the trunk for traction (e.g., 50-pound bags of sunflower seeds).

Two final words of advice about winter. First, don't let the weather scare you off. Most days are quite tolerable and some are even pleasant. The main highways and back roads alike are generally well maintained and promptly plowed, and most winter birding can be done along roadsides from or near the warmth of your car. Or even from the warmth of the living room of someone you've never met before who invites you in for a better look at their feeders.

And second, don't panic if your car stalls or gets stuck miles from town. It's usually best to stay in your car and wait for help, especially during blowing snow or extreme cold. It's common practice for Minnesotans to stop, without being asked, to pull you out of the ditch with a tow chain, jump start your car, or give you a ride. What's also common is for them to refuse any payment you try to offer in return.

• INSECTS AND OTHER PESTS. During warmer months there are other potential problems: mosquitoes, black and deer flies, wood and deer ticks, and even a few rattlesnakes. Yes, there are mosquitoes in Minnesota, but, no, they aren't any worse than other places; just bring along your favorite repellent.

Less familiar to visitors are black flies, which are small, silent, inactive at night, and curiously harmless when indoors or in a car. They are most active in May and June, mostly in the boreal forest of the Northeast Region. You don't feel anything when they bite, and you may not know they were even there until the next day when bites become welts and start itching. Unfortunately, some persons get allergic-type reactions when bitten too severely, but insect repellent does work on this pest. The much larger deer and horse flies will sometimes bite, but they usually just delight in buzzing around your head and driving you crazy.

Wood ticks are present April through July, especially in brushy terrain and long grass. They might be a problem if they were smarter and attached themselves to you right away. Instead, they tend to crawl around awhile first, and you can usually feel them in time to pluck them off. Just check yourself over at the end of the day, and if one is attached to your skin simply pry it off with your fingernail (there is no need to overreact with fingernail polish or burnt matches, as some would advise).

Potentially more serious are deer ticks and Lyme's disease. These tiny ticks are harder to detect, active well into the fall, and most prevalent in east-central Minnesota between the Twin Cities and Duluth. If possible, avoid brush and long grass and meticulously search yourself for ticks at day's end. Several birders have found Duranon and other tick repellents to be very effective.

And, yes, there are a few Timber Rattlesnakes in the southeastern corner of Minnesota, especially on rocky slopes and ledges along rivers and creeks. But, like rattlesnakes everywhere, they are seldom encountered unless you go looking for them and generally harmless unless provoked. Finding a rattlesnake in Minnesota is something to look forward to, not dread.

• PREDATORS. There is one mammal which poses a potential threat at certain times and places. No, not the Gray Wolf or Black Bear: yes, both do occur in Minnesota, but, no, neither is generally any threat to humans. I refer to *Homo sapiens*. As in other metropolitan areas, crime does exist in Minneapolis-St. Paul and less often elsewhere in the state. Since there are several good birding spots in the Twin Cities, birders with their expensive optics in more remote sections of parks and woodlands are potential targets and should use common sense. (On the other hand, many small-town Minnesotans still leave houses unlocked when away from home and ignition keys in cars parked in their driveways.)

• TRAFFIC. Highway congestion is another problem, and not just during weekday rush hours in the Twin Cities. If possible, time your birding trip to avoid highways such as U.S. 169 and Interstates 94 and 35 which can be bumper-to-bumper for miles north of the Cities on Friday and Sunday evenings from May through September. Everyone then, it seems, is heading north in their SUV with boat trailer in tow for the weekend to The Cabin On The Lake to catch The Walleye. (*Homo sapiens?* I use the term loosely. I, for one, would prefer the company of Timber Rattlesnakes on a remote bluff overlooking a Houston County creek.)

• TRESPASSING. There are states (Texas, for one) where straying onto private property is generally taken very seriously. While Minnesota property owners aren't usually of the mind to shoot first and ask questions later, it's obvious that "No Trespassing" signs mean the same here as elsewhere. Some are enforced; others (like those at most sewage ponds) are not. Be aware, however, in Minnesota it is illegal to venture onto any agricultural lands, even those not posted. When in doubt, ask permission before chasing off across some field after birds. You'll find most farmers are interested in birds, tolerant of birders, and willing to grant your request.

References and Resources

BOOKS

• *Birds in Minnesota* by Bob Janssen (University of Minnesota Press, 1987; $18) is still available at bookstores and is still the standard reference giving the status and distribution of all species recorded in the state, at least as of 15 years ago. Despite some outdated information, until a new edition is written, this remains a recommended reference.

• The booklet *Minnesota Birds: Status and Occurrence* briefly updates the status of all Minnesota birds (as does the anno-

tated list section of this book) as of October 2000. It is available for $6 postpaid from Peder Svingen (see birding contacts section, p. 10).

• Some of the best birding areas in this guide are state Scientific and Natural Areas, and *A Guide to Minnesota's Scientific and Natural Areas* (Second Edition, 1999; $15) has maps and complete information on all 129 of them. It is available in bookstores, or an on-line version of each area can be downloaded from the Minnesota Department of Natural Resources (DNR) website, <www.dnr.state.mn.us>.

• *A Guide to The Nature Conservancy's Preserves in Minnesota* ($15) is a similar but smaller guidebook to 38 of the Conservancy's preserves in the state; note that many of these are also designated as Scientific and Natural Areas. Order from The Nature Conservancy of Minnesota (1313 5th St. S.E., Minneapolis 55414) or from Minnesota's Bookstore (117 University Ave., St. Paul 55155; telephone 651-297-3000 or 800-657-3757).

• A nice guide to general wildlife-watching sites includes many areas not found in this book. *Traveler's Guide to Wildlife in Minnesota* (1997; $20) is published by the DNR and is available in bookstores.

• Though long out of print, way out-of-date, and available only in libraries and some second-hand bookstores, Thomas S. Roberts' monumental *The Birds of Minnesota* (University of Minnesota Press, 1932; revised 1936) is well worth paging through. This two-volume work is justifiably regarded as one of the finest state bird books ever written. If you find a set of Roberts' for sale somewhere at $100 or so, buy it.

MAPS

• Leave your Rand McNally atlas at home. Without question, the most useful state map for birding purposes (and the one used in fragments for the key maps for each chapter in this book) is the official Minnesota highway map published by the state Department of Transportation (DOT). It is free (some stores try to sell it, however) and available from the Minnesota Office of Tourism (121 7th Place E., St. Paul 55101; telephone 651-296-5029 or 800-657-3700), at some state parks and other tourist attractions, and at the state's Travel Information Centers (located at the state lines on Interstates 35, 90, and 94, U.S. Highways 53, 2, and 59, and Minnesota Highway 61).

• Any birder planning on doing a lot of birding here eventually will want to acquire a set of county highway maps prepared by the DOT (the detailed inset maps in this guide are portions of these maps). A set of 126 maps is needed to cover all 87 counties (several counties have more than one sheet), and each sheet costs 50 cents. Either write for an order form or buy them in person at the DOT, Room G-19, 395 John Ireland Blvd., St. Paul 55155; telephone 651-296-2216.

• A cheaper way to obtain a set of DOT county maps (printed at a smaller scale, however, which some find difficult to read) is to purchase the *Minnesota Atlas: A Sportsman's Guide to Public Lands and Water Accesses* (Adventure Publications, 1997). It is available at many bookstores for $25.

• Another collection of detailed maps of the entire state is DeLorme's *Minnesota Atlas and Gazetteer*, widely available at many stores for $20. There are fewer map sections spread over 77 pages (not divided along county lines), and, unlike the DOT's county maps, they are in color, are more detailed within city limits, show most of the state's sewage ponds (!), and plot wooded areas and topography. However, navigating with this atlas on back county roads is more difficult since many roads are not clearly numbered, some don't even exist, and litle distinction is shown between larger paved roads and minor gravel/dirt roads.

• Since state and national forests have some of the best birding Minnesota has to offer, maps of these areas may be useful in providing more detail than the county maps. A Superior National Forest map costs $6 and is available from forest headquarters in Duluth (8901 Grand Avenue Pl., Duluth 55808; telephone 218-626-4300), at Minnesota's Bookstore (see The Nature Conservancy guide), and at district ranger stations in Aurora, Cook, Ely, Grand Marais, Isabella, and Tofte.

The Chippewa National Forest map ($4) is also available at Minnesota's Bookstore and at national forest headquarters (U.S. Highway 2, Cass Lake 56633).

Free maps for some of the state forests are available from the Minnesota Department of Natural Resources (DNR), Division of Forestry, 500 Lafayette Rd., St. Paul 55155; telephone 651-296-6157 or 888-646-6367.

• Detailed on-line maps of all Minnesota state parks are available for free downloading at the DNR website (www.dnr.state.mn.us).

• Expensive but nicely detailed DNR Public Recreation Information Maps cost $5 each + shipping, 51 maps cover the state, and they are sold at Minnesota's Bookstore (see The Nature Conservancy guide). For a map sample and the areas covered by each map, see the DNR's website (www.dnr.state.mn.us).

• And the DNR has free, large-scale County Biological Survey maps showing woodlands, grasslands, wetlands, and other intact natural communities for the 24 counties surveyed so far. They are available from the DNR (500 Lafayette Rd., St. Paul 55155; telephone 651-296-8324 or 888-646-6367); the DNR website lists the counties available.

• The set of six "Great River Birding Trail" maps includes lots of information on birding sites along the Mississippi River, many of which are not in this book. The maps are free and available from Audubon - Upper Mississippi River Campaign, 26 E. Exchange St., Suite 110, St. Paul 55101; telephone 651-290-1695.

CHECKLISTS

• The best Minnesota field checklist, which includes all Regular and Casual species, is an 8.5 x 11" card with columns for seven entries. Ten lists cost $5 postpaid (50 for $15; 100 for $20), and they are available from Bob Ekblad, 5737 Sherri Dr NW, Byron MN 55920; his website is <home.rconnect.com/~ekblad>.

• The *Checklist of the Birds of Minnesota* booklet includes status definitions and the procedures of the Minnesota Ornithologists' Union Records Committee, is updated every five years, and is available for $6 postpaid from the Minnesota Ornithologists' Union (see Bird Clubs below).

HOTLINES

Some call them Rare Bird Alerts, some call them Birding Reports, but some just call them, and there are three telephone numbers in Minnesota with taped reports of bird sightings. Callers can also leave messages with their sightings. The Twin Cities tape (763-780-8890 or 800-657-3700) reports on observations statewide, the Duluth tape (218-525-5952; note this number may change in 2002) includes sightings in the Northeast Region, and the Detroit Lakes tape (800-433-1888) reports on northwestern Minnesota. All three tapes are transcribed and posted on the Minnesota Ornithologists' Union website and listserve (see Bird Clubs).

BIRD CLUBS

• Our state organization is the Minnesota Ornithologists' Union (MOU), an especially active group which publishes *The Loon*, a quarterly journal on Minnesota birdlife, which is justly recognized as one of the best state birding magazines; it is virtually required reading for all Minnesota birders. Annual dues are currently $25 ($35 family membership): make your checks payable to MOU, and mail to 10 Church St. S.E., Minneapolis 55455.

The MOU's website, <mou.mn.org>, includes the transcripts for the state's three hotlines. These transcripts are also posted on the MOU's listserve, MOU-net <mou-net@biosci.umn.edu>, where you can also e-mail your sightings. To subscribe to MOU-net, send an e-mail to <majordomo@biosci.umn.edu>, leave the subject line blank, and in the text of the message put "subscribe mou-net".

• Currently, there are 21 local bird clubs or Audubon chapters in Minnesota affiliated with the MOU. Some are especially active birding groups; others have little emphasis on birding. For a list of these clubs and a contact person, consult *The Loon* or the MOU website.

BIRDING TOURS

• Minnesota Birding Weekends, in cooperation with the MOU, has been scheduling weekend tours throughout the state since 1986. For information, see the MOU's website, or contact Kim Eckert, 8255 Congdon Blvd., Duluth 55804; e-mail <kreckert@cpinternet.com>.

• Two tour companies include Minnesota on their schedules. Victor Emanuel Nature Tours (telephone 800-328-8368; website <www.ventbird.com>) has tours in January and June guided by the author. WINGS (telephone 888-293-6443; website <www.wingsbirds.com>) has tours here in January, June, and October.

UNIVERSITY OF MINNESOTA

There are three University facilities of potential interest to birders: The Raptor Center and the Department of Ecology on the St. Paul campus, and the Bell Museum of Natural History on the Minneapolis campus.

• Birders sometimes find injured birds in the wild, and many of these are raptors. If you find one in the Twin Cities area, call or bring it to The Raptor Center (1920 Fitch Ave., St. Paul 55108; telephone 612-624-4745). If The Raptor Center is closed, the Veterinary Hospital's Small Animal Clinic across the street (612-625-9711) is open 24 hours. Both facilities will sometimes accept non-raptors for treatment.

• The largest collection of bird specimens in the state is in the Department of Ecology (1987 Upper Buford Cir., St. Paul 55108; telephone 612-625-5700). This resource is accessible to birders who contact them in advance to arrange a visit.

• The Bell Museum of Natural History, 10 Church St. S.E., Minneapolis 55455, houses the MOU's permanent file of Minnesota bird records. For access to this resource, contact Anthony Hertzel or Bob Janssen (see list of birding contacts below).

HAWK RIDGE NATURE RESERVE

Besides maintaining the fall hawk count and a raptor banding station, Hawk Ridge (see St. Louis County chapter) annually publishes the booklet, "A Visitor's Guide to the Fall Migration" ($2 postpaid). It includes count totals, dates, and other information on the fall raptor migration. Hawk Ridge also sponsors two raptor-oriented weekend programs, and Hawk Ridge members have access to the banding station observation blind, among other benefits. Memberships are $20 annually, checks payable to Duluth Audubon Society, c/o Biology Department, UMD, Duluth 55812. The Hawk Ridge website, <www.hawkridge.org>, includes the daily hawk counts August-November.

Also, if you find an injured raptor near Duluth from mid-August to mid-November, bring it to Hawk Ridge, where temporary care and transport to The Raptor Center will be arranged. At other times of year, call Dave or Molly Evans, 218-724-0261.

A BIRDER'S GUIDE TO BIRDERS

A local birding contact can be an invaluable source of current information on what you're looking for or someone to whom you can report your significant sightings. Those listed here are either in the Twin Cities (where out-of-state birders spend time on business or at the airport) or in the Northeast Region (where most of Minnesota's specialties occur).

Not included are several active and excellent birders residing elsewhere in Minnesota, who can be found on the MOU's listserve and membership directory. The birders below can put you in touch with them as well, and they are also mostly familiar with areas statewide. Some good birders in the Twin Cities are also excluded from this list; the few chosen are relatively easy to reach, are usually aware of what is being seen, and are conscientious about calling others when rarities appear.

Don't feel obligated, though, to seek out their birding advice, especially if you're one of that special and vanishing breed who prefers to choose and explore your own back roads and to discover your own birds. Following directions to merely check off some staked-out rarity requires little skill and adds nothing to our knowledge of that bird in particular or of Minnesota bird distribution in general.

However, it is recommended you do contact someone on the list, or any of the hotlines mentioned earlier, or the MOU's listserve (mou-net@biosci.umn.edu) should you find a rarity which others would want to know about. And should your rarity be a Casual or Accidental species (see the Annotated List section), the records committee of the MOU would appreciate documentation for your record. A documentation form for your convenience appears elsewhere in this book, or you can download this form from the MOU's website (mou.mn.org).

It's also a good idea to report the dates and locations of what you saw after your trip, so your more significant observations can be included in this region's report in *North American Birds* and the seasonal report in *The Loon*. Currently, the Minnesota compiler for these reports is Peder Svingen. The author also would greatly appreciate receiving both additional birding information not included in this guide and corrections to erroneous information that does appear.

Please use common sense and courtesy when contacting birders. When requesting information, keep your questions brief and reasonable: don't recite an endless list of birds and expect detailed directions to everything. When phoning, do so at a reasonable hour, generally not before 9 A.M. or after 9 P.M. (Central Time), and never stop by someone's residence unless you are expected or unless you know the person. And have appropriate maps in front of you: it is unreasonable, for example, to expect directions along the Sax-Zim Bog's back roads if all you have is a Rand McNally road atlas for reference.

Twin Cities

Anthony Hertzel
8461 Pleasant View Dr.
Mounds View 55112
(763) 780-7149
e-mail <axhertzel@sihope.com>

Bob Janssen
162 Lakeview Rd. E.
Chanhassen 55317
(952) 974-9735
e-mail <rbjanssen@aol.com>

Craig Mandel
10211 Cedar Lake Rd. #120
Minnetonka 55305
(952) 546-3407
e-mail <egretcman@aol.com>

Barb and Denny Martin
20185 Excelsior Blvd.
Shorewood 55331
(952) 474-4371
e-mail <dbmartin@skypoint.com>

Northeast Region

Dave Benson
427 N. 16th Ave. E.
Duluth 55812
(218) 728-5812
e-mail <drbenson@cpinternet.com>

Kim Eckert
8255 Congdon Blvd.
Duluth 55804
(218) 525-6930
e-mail <kreckert@cpinternet.com>

Mike Hendrickson
9005 Lenroot St.
Duluth 55808
(218) 626-2268
e-mail <smithville4@email.msn.com>

Jim Lind
320 2nd Ave.
Two Harbors 55616
(218) 834-3199
e-mail <jimlind@lakenet.com>

Warren Nelson
603 2nd St. N.W.
Aitkin 56431
(218) 927-2458
e-mail <wenelson@mlecmn.net>

Peder Svingen
2602 E. 4th St.
Duluth 55812
(218) 728-0105
e-mail <psvingen@d.umn.edu>

Format and Maps

W / SE / NE REGIONS

This book is divided into three sections: the West, Southeast, and Northeast regions of the state, which are shown on the inside front and back covers. Although the boundaries of these regions, drawn along county lines, are some-

what arbitrary, each region represents one of the three major habitats in Minnesota.

Prairie farmlands, pastures, some shallow wetlands and a few remnant grasslands characterize the West Region. This region is relatively flat and treeless, although good wooded stands exist along some rivers, lakeshores, and in farm shelterbelts, and extensive woodlands cover much of the region's eastern edge.

The Southeast Region is characterized by deciduous woods, especially in the Mississippi, Minnesota, and St. Croix river valleys. Though much of this region is farmed open country like the West, the Southeast has a more rolling topography, prairie grasslands are virtually nonexistent, and more of this region's wetlands have wooded shorelines.

Almost all of the state's coniferous forests of spruce, pine, tamarack, balsam fir, and white cedar are found in the Northeast Region, although in most of this region mixed or deciduous woods predominate. Most of Minnesota's lakes are located here, agriculture is limited (except in those government-subsidized tree farms known euphemistically as state and national forests), and, unlike the West and Southeast, there are no significant river valleys serving as migration corridors.

COUNTY CHAPTERS

Each chapter generally covers a single county, except for the Twin Cities section which includes all of Hennepin, Ramsey, and Washington counties, plus portions of Dakota, Scott, Carver, and Anoka counties. The sequence and page numbers of these chapters are indexed on the inside front and back covers.

Each county chapter includes a key map of the county, reproduced from the Minnesota Department of Transportation's state highway map. Most chapters also include one or more inset maps, which are normally segments from official county highway maps, to depict birding areas in more detail.

Boldface type in the text indicates a significant birding area, which corresponds to either a circled number on a map or to an inset map; these map numbers and inset map letters are also boldfaced. Several birding areas are found on both sides of a county line, and these are either included in the county chapter which appears first in the book or with the county in which most of the area is located.

COUNTY KEY MAPS

The legend of the county key maps is shown on page 11. Note the scale of all the key maps is 10 miles to the inch, and that north is always towards the top of the page. Also, where appropriate, these maps have been annotated with seven additional symbols:

 = lake

= sewage pond or other water impoundment (e.g., wild rice paddy or fish hatchery pond)

M = marsh

P = prairie grassland or pasture

W = wooded area (generally indicating a deciduous woodland or coniferous plantation in the West or Southeast regions)

BOG = coniferous forest bog (also includes upland stands of white spruce, balsam fir, and jack pine)

– – – – – = hiking trail (or a road usually closed to motor vehicles)

Outlines or arrows indicating the extent of larger marshes, prairie tracts, woodlands, and bogs also may be shown; e.g.:

The borders of inset maps are outlined on the key maps, and most are identified by an accompanying letter in a black circle; e.g.:

Some inset maps are identified by a letter in a white circle; e.g.: (A) This indicates the inset includes an adjacent county, and its birding information is discussed in that county's chapter.

And some of the better birding locations, especially those not clearly visible on the key maps, are indicated by numbers; e.g.: **1**

INSET MAPS

The legend of the Department of Transportation inset maps appears on page 12; note that a few inset maps were reproduced from other sources. The scale of these maps is 1 inch = 2 miles, except for the Dakota, Scott, and Carver county insets which are 1 inch = 1 mile. As on the county key maps, north is always towards the top of the page, and the same seven annotations explained earlier also are added to inset maps.

As shown earlier, each inset map is identified by letter and outlined on the county key map. Circled numbers to indicate some birding locations also appear on inset maps as they do on the key maps. When these locations are referred to in the text, the inset map's letter precedes the number: e.g., birding location 3 on inset B is referred to as B3.

� STATE HISTORICAL SITE

♦ STATE HISTORICAL MARKER

♠ STATE PARKS

♤ STATE WAYSIDE PARKS

Ⓐ REST AREA – Complete facilities (Includes Facilities for Persons With Mobility Impairments.)

▲ REST AREA (Limited Facilities)

✗ CAMPGROUND (State and National Forests)

☐ BOUNDARY WATERS CANOE AREA

☐ NATIONAL FOREST

■ INDIAN RESERVATION

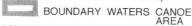 WILDLIFE MANAGEMENT AREA

POPULATIONS OF CITIES

○ Unincorporated	◉ 5,000 To 25,000
○ Under 1,000	☐ 25,000 To 50,000
◎ 1,000 To 5,000	☐ 50,000 And Over

⊛ State Capitol

Population Symbols Enclosed By ◇ Indicates County Seats

⚓ U.S. PORT OF ENTRY

♦ U.S. NATIONAL MONUMENT

 Mileage Between Junctions of Trunk Highways

🛡94 INTERSTATE HIGHWAY MARKER

🛡12 U.S. ROUTE MARKER

24 STATE HIGHWAY ROUTE MARKER

✸ GREAT RIVER ROAD MARKER

▬▬▬ INTERSTATE COMPLETED

▬ ▬ ▬ UNDER CONSTRUCTION

═══════ PROJECTED ROUTE

═══ MULTILANE DIVIDED HIGHWAY

▬▬ MULTILANE UNDIVIDED HIGHWAY

▬▬ PAVED HIGHWAY

▭▭▭▭ GRAVEL SURFACED

+–+–+ RAILROAD

 SECONDARY ROAD-HARD SURFACED

 SECONDARY ROAD-GRAVEL

 FULL TRAFFIC INTERCHANGE WITH EXIT NUMBERS

 PARTIAL TRAFFIC INTERCHANGES ACCESS DENIED

11

Following are a few additional comments on some of the symbols included on this legend; they implicitly provide some valuable bird-finding and navigation hints in many cases. (Be aware that, for the sake of clarity, some extraneous symbols and other material have been removed from virtually every inset.)

• ROAD AND ROADWAY FEATURES. Primitive, unimproved, graded-and-drained, and soil-surface roads tend to be muddy and impassable after a rain or during early spring snowmelt, and most are not plowed in winter. Most gravel/stone roads are passable in wet weather and plowed in winter, but some may not be after prolonged rains.

When you're looking for a back road that might be productive for birding, a useful hint is to simply note whether it is straight or curved on the map. In the farmlands of the West Region, for example, where roads are mostly straight, a road with a curve or jog in it often means there is a wetland or woodland in the way, so check it out. In the Southeast, when looking for good roads in the Mississippi River valley for woods birds, try the winding ones first; straight roads tend to be in more sterile open farmland. But if you're in the Northeast looking for a spruce bog, use the opposite strategy: curvy forest roads on the map often indicate mixed or deciduous woods, but when a road is built through a bog it usually goes in a straight line.

And note where roads of any kind are conspicuous by their absence: such an area suggests a section of unplowed lands or a region of undisturbed bogs.

• PUBLIC SERVICE FACILITIES. This symbol occasionally marks the locations of sewage ponds, especially when 1-3 miles from a town. Note on some maps they are marked with an "S" rather than a dot. (Also note the previously mentioned DeLorme atlas is a better set of maps for locating these ponds.)

• CONSERVATION. Some fish hatcheries are outdoor ponds which can be good for shorebirds when drained, usually in fall. Most small state and county parks are good birding spots, but municipal and wayside parks are usually just places to, well, park. Public access points are places from which to launch a boat; most are good vantage points from which to scan a lake, and they usually are clearly signed from the nearest road.

• FARM AND DWELLING UNITS. These normally indicate older farmhouses, many now abandoned, rather than newer houses, and this symbol is often helpful to the birder. Many farmhouses, including those abandoned, have shelterbelts with good habitat for nesting and migrant woods birds. And note those lakes with houses built around them. These tend to lack marshes or mudflats for water birds along their usually wooded shoreline (which, however, might be attractive to migrant passerines).

• RAILROADS. Many tracks shown on the map have since been abandoned and removed, and some have been converted into trails for hiking or bicycling (or, alas,

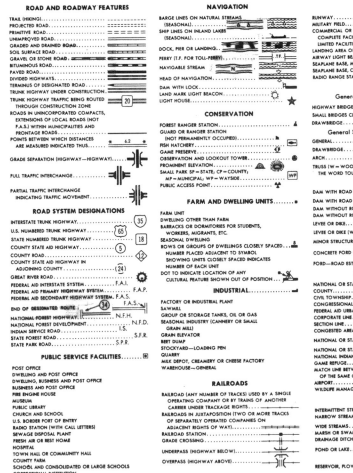

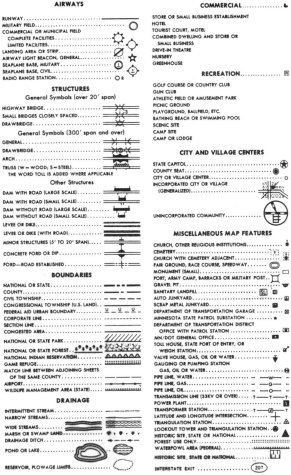

snowmobiling). Such trails might offer access to good areas otherwise inaccessible from regular roads, and some are remnant strips of native prairie grasslands long inaccessible to the farmer's plow.

• AIRWAYS. Some airports provide an island of habitat for hunting raptors and other open-country birds in the fields surrounding their runways, especially in the more wooded parts of the state. And the mown grassy edges along runways sometimes attract Buff-breasted Sandpipers in fall.

• STRUCTURES. Dams often indicate the presence of open water downstream in winter which might attract water birds. Levees sometimes have a road on them, usually closed to vehicles, but they at least provide good hiking access to adjacent wetlands.

• BOUNDARIES. Section lines occur at one-mile intervals and come in handy when measuring distances. It also helps to know that roads in open farm country are typically in one-mile increments.

Boundary lines of congested areas are very important to be aware of when navigating, since roads within them are much harder to see. In the example shown here, at first glance one might miss the road to the east side of Island Lake.

Unless a game refuge is a state area, it probably is not worth a special visit, since municipal and county game refuges generally look no different than their surroundings. In most cases, state wildlife management areas and federal waterfowl production areas are good birding spots. They usually indicate the presence of wetlands, but some also include grasslands, thickets, woodlands, and sometimes planted conifers. Note, however, these are not wildlife refuges, and they are open to public hunting in the fall.

• DRAINAGE. The symbol for marsh or swamp land can mean any number of things. In the West or Southeast regions it usually indicates a treeless cattail or sedge marsh for rails and bitterns (which in wetter years may turn into an actual lake, or become a grassland in dry years). But in the Northeast it often refers to bogs wooded with spruce, tamarack, white cedar, alder, or black ash. Therefore, unless described in this book, it's often hard to tell from the map alone if these spots have the kinds of birds and habitat you're looking for.

• RECREATION. Unless you're looking for a campsite, this symbol usually is of little interest to birders. (Apparently, recreation refers more to activities making use of golf clubs and shotguns, not binoculars.)

• MISCELLANEOUS MAP FEATURES. Many rural cemeteries are planted with conifers and might be worth checking for roosting owls, crossbills, and the like, especially in the West and Southeast regions where coniferous trees are few and far between.

Some gravel pits marked on the map are now abandoned, have since filled with water, and can be good spots for water birds, especially in areas with no other nearby wetlands.

The dump/sanitary landfill symbol (indicated on some maps with SL rather than D) might mark a place attractive not only to gulls (and bears in the Northeast Region) but also to raptors in search of rats and mice.

Power plants located on lakes and rivers, like dams, often result in open water for waterfowl in winter. (Another man-made device on some bodies of water that might attract wintering water birds is the aerator. However, none of these is indicated on a map, most keep only a relatively small area ice-free, and their presence varies from winter to winter depending on whether there are local efforts to maintain oxygen levels for fish.)

Finally, though they may not look it on the map, some "forest use only" roads are wide and passable, and unexpectedly plowed in winter, so don't overlook them when exploring an area. (As mentioned previously, however, it is easy to get lost on these back roads.)

Annotated List of Minnesota Birds

At the time of this writing, January 2002, a total of 427 species has been officially recorded in Minnesota, according to the Minnesota Ornithologists' Union Records Committee (MOURC). All are listed here and annotated so birders know what species are likely or unlikely in the places they visit. The taxonomy, nomenclature, and sequence of species follow the seventh edition of the American Ornithologists' Union *Check-list of North American Birds* (1998).

The following information is included: the species' status on the Minnesota list; its season, range, and relative abundance in the state; habitat, behavior, and selected birding locations of Minnesota specialties; and selected identification hints. These annotations are only intended to be brief and general in nature, and not all of them are included with each species, especially those which are more common and widespread.

A species' **Minnesota status** is defined as follows (if no status is given, assume it to be Regular):

• Regular (313 species) = species recorded in 8 to 10 years during MOURC's most recent 10-year base period (1989-1998);

• Casual (26) = recorded in 3-8 years of the past 10;

(Species in the 8- and 3-year categories are discussed and classified by MOURC on an individual basis.)

• Accidental (86) = recorded in 0-3 years of the past 10;

• Extirpated (1) = formerly Regular, but disappeared and not expected to recur;

• Extinct (1) = none left anywhere.

For all Regular species, **season of occurrence** is given as permanent, summer (or breeding/nesting), winter, or migration (or spring/fall). Again, such information is not intended to be thorough. Migration status is not usually included for summer and winter residents which migrate throughout most of the state or within their summer or winter ranges. Nor is it usually mentioned if a species is present but rare at a time other than during its principal season: e.g., many species of waterfowl sometimes linger into winter wherever there is open water, and some passerines that normally winter south of the state often overwinter at feeders.

Range is also given for all Regular species, and the following abbreviations are used:

• W = West Region;

• SE = Southeast Region;

• NE = Northeast Region;

• NW = north half of the West Region (from Wilkin and Otter Tail counties north);

• SW = south half of the West Region (from Traverse, Grant, and Douglas counties south);

• E or E half = Northeast plus Southeast regions;

• N or N half = NW plus Northeast Region;

• S or S half = SW plus Southeast Region.

As with season information, ranges are also only brief and approximate: for example, "throughout" for some species may mean almost all of Minnesota and absent from a few peripheral counties; or one with a range of "NE" might also occur in some adjacent NW or SE counties.

Relative abundance is indicated for most Regular species (if none is given, assume it to be common):

• common = relatively easy for most birders to see or hear in habitat and in season without directions or guidance;

• uncommon = more difficult to see or hear unless the birder has directions or is experienced with the species' behavior, habitat, and calls;

• rare = normally difficult for all birders to find unless a "staked-out" individual is present or unless the species is present in unusually high numbers in an invasion year.

• local = not evenly distributed through its range or habitat; tends to be found at certain favored sites or found unpredictably at random locations.

Additional information is also given for those **Minnesota specialties** which are rarer, have a limited range, or are frequently sought by visiting birders. Such information may include notes on behavior or habitat, or it may be a list of locations where the species is most consistently found.

Finally, **identification information (ID)** is included for those species that are difficult for most birders to identify, are frequently involved in misidentifications, or are inadequately covered in some of the standard field guides. These ID hints are not intended to be complete analyses, and they only discuss those plumages, races, and similar species normally seen in Minnesota.

For several species, the reader is referred to articles in these periodicals for additional information:

• *Birders Journal* (bimonthly Canadian journal);

• *Birding* (journal of the American Birding Association);

• *Birding World* (monthly British journal; not to be confused with *Birder's World*);

• *The Loon* (quarterly journal of the Minnesota Ornithologists' Union);

• *North American Birds* (currently published by the American Birding Association); formerly published as *American Birds* (1971-94) and *Field Notes* (1994-98).

Also recommended as identification references are the following books; in most cases, these are not mentioned as ID references in the species accounts:

- *The Sibley Guide to Birds* by David Sibley;
- National Geographic Society's *Field Guide to the Birds of North America* (3rd edition);
- *A Field Guide to Advanced Birding* by Kenn Kaufman;
- *Waterfowl: An Identification Guide* by Steve Madge and Hilary Burn;
- *A Field Guide to Hawks of North America* (2nd edition) by William Clark and Brian Wheeler;
- *A Photographic Guide to North American Raptors* (2nd edition) by Brian Wheeler and William Clark;
- *Shorebirds: An Identification Guide* by Peter Hayman, John Marchant and Tony Prater;
- *Shorebirds of the Pacific Northwest* by Dennis Paulson;
- *Skuas and Jaegers* by Klaus Olsen and Hans Larsson;
- *Gulls: A Guide to Identification* (2nd edition) by P. J. Grant;
- *Terns of Europe and North America* by Klaus Olsen and Hans Larsson;
- *Hummingbirds of North America: The Photographic Guide* by Steve Howell;
- *A Field Guide to Warblers of North America* by Jon Dunn and Kimball Garrett;
- *The Sparrows of the United States and Canada* by James Rising.

FAMILY GAVIIDAE: LOONS

Red-throated Loon — Rare and barely Regular migrant on Lake Superior with most records in spring from Duluth, especially in May. Only seen casually elsewhere in the state; also only casually in Duluth in fall. Frequently dives, remains underwater for long periods, seldom stays long in one place, and often not relocated later after the initial find.

- ID: Cormorants also swim with up-tilted bills and at a distance strongly suggest Red-throated Loons. Pacific Loons also frequently swim with bills pointed above the horizontal, and Red-throateds can swim with bills held level. Note the bottom edge of lower mandible itself curves up on this species; top edge of upper mandible (culmen) is straight, and crown profile appears lower and flatter than other loons. Fall/winter adults extensively whiter on sides of face and neck than other loons and appear extensively spotted on the back/wings; juveniles are dusky on the face/neck and may lack distinctive bill shape. References: see Pacific Loon.

Pacific Loon — Now a rare but Regular fall migrant, with most records mid-September to November on Lake Superior; only casually there in spring. Also probably rare-Regular in fall on Mille Lacs and other large NE lakes; casually elsewhere in migration. It is only an assumption that all reports of this species actually refer to Pacifics, that an Arctic Loon could "never" occur in Minnesota.

- ID: Most basic-plumaged adults and some juveniles show diagnostic "chinstrap" or narrow line across top of foreneck. Pacifics have paler gray crown and hindneck contrasting with darker back; beware of some Commons which in some light conditions also appear pale gray on hindneck. Sides of neck have a clean-cut straight or smoothly curved line separating white foreneck from gray hindneck, unlike Common Loon which shows an irregular pattern along sides of lower neck. Eyes normally surrounded by gray, but this area can be white as in most Commons or Red-throateds. Often holds bill up-tilted like Red-throated, but lacks its distinctive bill shape. Crown usually rounder than Red-throated (head flatter with lower profile) or Common (crown profile more rectangular). Back/wings of juveniles have more "scaly" or "wavy" pattern than Red-throateds. Swimming Pacific, Red-throated, and Common loons can all show white on their sides/flanks; consistently and extensively white flanks, however, might indicate a first-state-record Arctic Loon. References: *Birding* 20:12-28, 21:154-158, 22:70-73 and 29:106-115, *Birding World* 8:458-466, and *Advanced Birding* guide.

Common Loon — Common in summer N half and northern SE in Minnesota's wooded lake country; more widespread on larger lakes during migration, especially on Mille Lacs and Lake Winnibigoshish where hundreds congregate in October. With an estimated breeding population of 12,000, the largest in the U.S., a thoroughly appropriate official state bird (and would be an even classier choice if the British name Great Northern Diver were used here).

- ID: See Pacific and Yellow-billed loons.

Yellow-billed Loon — Accidental; five late fall records in the NE: on Lake Superior (twice), Mille Lacs (twice), and Lake Winnibigoshish.

- ID: Bill shape and presence of yellow on bill variable and of limited use in identifying juveniles. Instead, note paler sides of face/neck and especially, unlike Common Loon, lack of black on distal half of upper mandible. Usually shows a clearly delineated dark smudge on ear coverts which is diagnostic if present; this smudge often connected to crown with a dark vertical line (some Commons also vaguely darker on ear coverts but they lack clearly outlined smudge). References: see Pacific Loon.

FAMILY PODICIPEDIDAE: GREBES

Pied-billed Grebe — Common in summer throughout, except local or absent eastern NE.

Horned Grebe — Now rare and local in summer northern NW, and entirely absent some summers. Much more widespread in migration throughout, especially on Lake Superior where a few also have overwintered.

- ID: Fall/winter birds usually, but not always, have whitish spot on lores (lores always dark on Eared Grebe), are cleaner white on lower face and foreneck than most Eareds, and have flatter crown shape (Eareds usually have a more peaked or rounded crown). Horneds show clean-cut horizontal line behind the eye separating dark cap from white face; this line not as straight or clean-cut on Eareds. Bill shape of little use in identification. Horned and Eared grebes molting into or out of alternate (breeding) plumage can be difficult to ID. Reference: *American Birds* 46:1187-1190.

Red-necked Grebe — Uncommon but widespread in summer on medium-size or larger lakes with nesting cover NW, western NE and northern SE, often nesting on lakes overpopulated with summer cabins and fishermen. Uncommon migrant throughout, sometimes common on Lake Superior, but mostly rare or absent SW.

Eared Grebe — Common but local in summer mostly W, with a curious attraction to sewage ponds. Well-known locations include Agassiz National Wildlife Refuge (Marshall County) and Salt Lake (Lac Qui Parle County).

  • ID: See Horned Grebe.

Western Grebe — Locally common in summer W and western SE; consistent areas include Agassiz (Marshall County) and Lake Osakis (Douglas/Todd counties). Like Red-necked Grebe, often seen on lakes overrun with boaters and jet skiers.

  • ID: See Clark's Grebe.

Clark's Grebe — Now rare but Regular in summer, mostly W, and best looked for wherever Westerns occur; probable hybrids also occur.

  • ID: Brighter orange-yellow bill color this grebe's most consistent and diagnostic field mark; Western's bill duller greenish-yellow. Facial difference diagnostic only on individuals with typical patterns, but many Clark's and Westerns are intermediate and puzzling. Whiter flanks on Clark's usually useful, but there is overlap, and this feature depends on how high/low the grebe is swimming and on position of the wings. Many Clark's also have thinner hindneck stripe than Western; when present, this mark seems diagnostic and is visible from side, with Clark's showing less black on sides of neck than Western Grebes. Clark's call one-syllabled; Western's usually two-syllabled, but there may be overlap. Intermediate (hybrid?) grebes are not unusual and not easily identified: some have shown Western-like bill color and face pattern on one side and then turned around to show Clark's-like features on the other! References: *The Loon* 61:99-108 (reprinted in *Birding* 25:304-310), *Birding* 27:54-55, and *Advanced Birding* guide.

FAMILY PELECANIDAE: PELICANS

American White Pelican — Consistently nests only on Lake of the Woods and on Marsh Lake (Lac Qui Parle County), but non-breeders can be common in summer and in migration throughout except eastern NE, with flocks often numbering in the hundreds.

  • ID: See Whooping Crane.

FAMILY PHALACROCORACIDAE: CORMORANTS

Neotropic Cormorant — Accidental; one summer 1992 record from the Twin Cities.

  • ID: See Double-crested Cormorant.

Double-crested Cormorant — Common in summer throughout, though its nesting colonies are only local and are mostly absent NE.

  • ID: Even many veteran birders are unaware that cormorants can soar at high altitudes with necks stretched straight and tails fanned, and they are easily mistaken for Anhingas. Beware of some Double-cresteds with white lower edge on throat pouch which might be confused with Neotropic Cormorants; this white does not continue up along base of upper mandible (as on Neotropics) nor form sharply-pointed white "V" at base of bill (as on Neotropics). Double-cresteds have larger, brighter, rounder orange throat pouch with diagnostic orange spot on lores; Also see Red-throated Loon.

FAMILY FREGATIDAE: FRIGATEBIRDS

Magnificent Frigatebird — Accidental; two sight records, in the Twin Cities and Clearwater County, both in fall of 1988 as a result of Hurricane Gilbert.

FAMILY ARDEIDAE: BITTERNS, HERONS, AND EGRETS

American Bittern — Uncommon in summer in marshes throughout, mostly W and western NE.

Least Bittern — Uncommon and local in larger marshes in summer mostly W and SE; seldom seen during migration. Most often seen (or heard) at dawn/dusk in the SW, at La Crescent and Mound Prairie Marsh (Houston County), and in the Twin Cities at Wood Lake Nature Center. More often heard than seen, but its call is soft and infrequently given, and its response to recordings is limited.

Great Blue Heron — Common in summer throughout; a few sometimes linger into early winter.

Great Egret — Common in summer S half, but only uncommon in some areas, with its nesting colonies only locally distributed.

Snowy Egret — Rare but Regular in spring-summer, mostly S half. No known current nesting sites, but breeding formerly occurred at such rookeries as Pelican Lake (Grant County), Big Stone National Wildlife Refuge (Lac Qui Parle County), and Long Lake (Kandiyohi County).

  • ID: Juveniles do not have all-black legs; they are mostly or entirely yellowish-green like Little Blue Heron. juvenile Little Blues, however, have bicolored bills with black tip and grayish or bluish base, unlike Snowys which have all-black bills (but beware sometimes yellowish-based bills on younger juveniles). Juvenile Little Blues can have greenish or even yellowish lores and are easily misidentified as Snowy Egrets if bill color is not noted. Snowy Egret vs. Little Blue Heron is an under-appreciated ID problem. Also see Cattle Egret. References: *American Birds* 45:330-333 and *Advanced Birding* guide.

Little Blue Heron — About the same status as Snowy Egret, though usually harder to find than Snowys most years. Also formerly found at the Pelican Lake and Big Stone rookeries and at Lake Johanna (Pope County).

• ID: See Snowy Egret.

Tricolored Heron — Casual; more than a dozen records, mostly in spring in the SE.

Cattle Egret — Rare and local in summer and migration mostly in pastures S half, but usually easier to find than Snowys and Little Blues. Migrants sometimes stray to the N half. Former breeding records at the Big Stone and Lake Johanna rookeries, and possibly still breeds at Pelican Lake (Grant County), with some sightings in pastures on its south side; also several sightings in pastures near Hokah (Houston County).

• ID: Bill of juvenile may appear all-dark and lead to confusion with Snowy Egret.

Green Heron — Common in summer throughout except northern NE.

Black-crowned Night-Heron — Uncommon and local in summer mostly W and SE, with its nesting colonies few and far between and declining in number. Status in Minnesota is generally unclear.

• ID: Juvenile night-herons are hard to separate by leg length; more useful is Black-crowned's thinner and usually bicolored bill, larger and more elongated spots on back/wings, and shorter, thicker-necked profile (Yellow-crowneds have a thicker and all-black bill, smaller/rounder white spots on upperparts, and longer, thinner neck). References: *American Birds* 42:169-171 and *Birding* 31:410-415.

Yellow-crowned Night-Heron — Rare, local, and barely Regular in spring-summer, mostly SE. One of the hardest "Regular" species to find, but probably best looked for at La Crescent in Houston County (where it bred years ago) or in the Twin Cities (where there are lots of resident birders to turn one up).

• ID: See Black-crowned Night-Heron.

FAMILY THRESKIORNITHIDAE: IBISES

White Ibis — Accidental; one photographed in May 1995 in Winona.

Glossy Ibis — Accidental; one photograph record in May 1991 at Heron Lake.

• ID: See White-faced Ibis.

White-faced Ibis — Currently on the Casual list, but probably Regular, mostly in the W and SE in spring. There are also many records of unidentified ibis, especially in fall, most of them presumably White-faced.

• ID: Adult White-faceds in fall still have red eyes and facial skin and are thus identifiable; brown-eyed juve-

nile ibis generally not separable. Spring White-faceds also have red eyes and facial skin but often lack white facial border and may be mistaken for Glossys. Differences in overall size and in bill and leg colors are probably not diagnostic. References: *Birders Journal* 1:241-256, *Birding* 8:1-5, *The Loon* 67:123-129, *North American Birds* 54:241-247, and *Advanced Birding* guide.

FAMILY CATHARTIDAE: NEW WORLD VULTURES

Black Vulture — Accidental; one record from Hawk Ridge in Duluth in August 2001.

• ID: See Turkey Vulture.

Turkey Vulture — Mostly uncommon throughout in summer, more common southern SE; seen almost daily at Hawk Ridge in Duluth September to mid-October. Occasionally reported in winter, but valid records then are almost nonexistent.

• ID: Combination of white primary shafts and paler brown upper surface of outer primaries is evident in good light and can suggest Black Vulture's wing pattern. And, field guide statements to the contrary, Black Vultures often soar with Turkey Vulture-like dihedrals. Best distinction in flight is Black's more rapid flapping. Also see Golden Eagle.

Family Anatidae: Ducks, Geese, and Swans

Black-bellied Whistling-Duck — Accidental; six scattered records, all of birds possibly escaped/released from captivity.

Fulvous Whistling-Duck — Accidental; two old records, both possibly involving escaped/released birds: May 1929 in Lincoln County and October 1950 in Mille Lacs County.

Greater White-fronted Goose — Uncommon early spring migrant (March to mid-April) W; rare E half in spring, also rare throughout in fall.

Snow Goose — Common early spring migrant mostly SW; uncommon elsewhere in spring, also uncommon throughout in fall.

- ID: See Ross's Goose. Birders unfamiliar with all-dark blue-morph juveniles have misidentified these as Brant.

Ross's Goose — Rare but Regular migrant mostly W and mostly in spring (March-April), almost always in company with Snow Geese. Probably about 1% of all migrant "white" geese in the state are actually Ross's, though some estimates suggest the proportion is 4 or 5%, and flocks of Snows with dozens of Ross's among them have occurred.

- ID: Identifying a Ross's by overall size alone is risky: smallest female Snows can overlap largest male Ross's, and intermediates (hybrids?) frequently occur. Concentrate on the bill: Ross's has stubbier bill (its length about equal to its height at the base), its base meets face in a straighter line, there is little or no black along cutting edges, and basal half is bluish-gray with "warty" rough texture visible at close range. Snow Goose's bill is longer than it is high, its base meets face in a more curved line, there is a narrow black oval along cutting edges, and basal half is same color as distal half. However, some geese have intermediate bill features and are unidentifiable. Typical Ross's have higher/rounder crowns and shorter necks than Snows. Plumage of Ross's of all ages often appears whiter when in a flock of Snows. Reference: *Birding* 25:50-53.

Canada Goose — Common (too common, most would agree) in summer throughout; winters locally S half, especially at Fergus Falls (Otter Tail County), Lac Qui Parle Lake, the Twin Cities, and Rochester (Olmsted County). Late fall/early winter concentrations approach 100,000 at Lac Qui Parle and 30,000 at Rochester.

Brant — Currently listed as Accidental; formerly considered Casual, with about a dozen scattered records.

- ID: See Snow Goose.

Mute Swan — Currently listed as Regular, with a presumed stray or two from "established" introduced populations in Wisconsin or Michigan seen almost annually, mostly SE. However, the origin of all Mute Swans is suspect, and records of genuine "countable" vagrants will probably decrease, as Mute Swans are now considered a threat to Trumpeters and their numbers are now being controlled.

- ID: See Tundra Swan.

Trumpeter Swan — Formerly bred in the state in the 19th century, but reintroduced widely in Minnesota and vicinity since the late 1980s; now considered established as a Regular species. Through the mid-1990s, most were released in and around Becker County; since then, releases have been limited to southwestern Minnesota. Dozens of pairs have bred in recent years, with the total population now approaching 1,000; one consistent breeding location is Tamarac National Wildlife Refuge (Becker County). A few leave the state in winter, but most overwinter, especially at the Monticello power plant (Wright County) and Fergus Falls (Otter Tail County). This population may not yet be fully viable since it is still being augmented by introductions and is often locally reliant on hand-outs from humans.

- ID: See Tundra Swan.

Tundra Swan — Locally common migrant throughout, especially W, along the Mississippi River in the southern SE, and in spring on western NE wild rice paddies. Thousands formerly concentrated in November on the Mississippi at Weaver (Wabasha County) and in Houston County, where peak counts had been 10,000-plus; now seen there only by the hundreds. Stray individuals possible in summer or winter, but Trumpeters are more likely then.

- ID: Many adults lack yellow lores and are difficult to separate from Trumpeters, even with direct size comparison. Look for narrower line between bill and eyes, shallower "U" shape at top of bill on the forehead, higher and rounder crown shape, and concave shape on upper mandible (culmen). Trumpeters usually have broader black area on lores that envelops and encircles the eyes (Tundra Swan's eyes typically more separate and visible), more pointed "V" shape at top of bill, lower and flatter crown, and straighter culmen. Juvenile Tundras and Trumpeters both have similar pink-and-black bills, and the "U" vs. "V" difference at top of bill may not be present. Juvenile Mute Swan in winter also has pink-and-black bill, but in fall its bill is often grayer than on juvenile Tundra or Trumpeter. Juvenile Tundras from mid-winter to spring have whiter overall plumage than Trumpeter or Mute swans. References: *Birding* 23:88-91 and 26:306-318.

Wood Duck — Common in summer throughout.

Gadwall — Common in summer mostly W. A few winter annually at Shakopee (Scott County) for reasons unknown.

- ID: Female's black-and-orange bill pattern similar to female Mallard. Note Gadwall's faint or nonexistent eye line (bolder on female Mallard, especially in front of eye) and its steeper forehead profile (more sloping on Mallard).

Eurasian Wigeon — Casual; over a dozen records, mostly in spring during peak duck migration in the SE.

- ID: See American Wigeon.

American Wigeon — Uncommon in summer mostly N half; more common in migration throughout.

- ID: Flying wigeons show moderately pointed tails

and thus suggest female pintails. Note pintail's longer, thinner neck and grayish-buff overall plumage (female American Wigeon has grayish head contrasting with buffy-brown sides). Typical female Eurasian Wigeon has richer brown head, but some have grayer heads like Americans and are identifiable only if duller gray axillaries visible (white on American). Difficult-to-identify hybrid wigeon also occur.

American Black Duck — Uncommon in summer NE and in winter mostly SE; most often found wherever Mallard flocks occur in migration and winter.

- ID: See Mallard.

Mallard — Common in summer and local in winter throughout.

- ID: Beware of males in summer/fall in eclipse plumage which have dark brown body and relatively pale brown head; these strongly resemble black ducks. Also see Gadwall.

Blue-winged Teal — Common in summer throughout.

- ID: See Green-winged and Cinnamon teals.

Cinnamon Teal — Rare and barely Regular spring migrant W, mostly in April, with only a sighting or two most years. Prefers smaller or temporary wetlands, and is one of the hardest Regular species to find.

- ID: Females are usually richer brown overall with plainer face pattern and larger bill; female Blue-winged usually more grayish-brown overall, with obvious eye line and pale spot at base of smaller bill. These differences are generally lacking on juveniles. Reference: *Birding* 23:124-133.

Northern Shoveler — Common in summer mostly W.

Northern Pintail — Common in summer mostly W.

- ID: See American Wigeon.

Garganey — Accidental; two spring records: Waseca County in 1987 and Jackson County in 1993.

Green-winged Teal — Uncommon in summer throughout, and relatively few actual nesting records; much more widespread and common in migration.

- ID: A swimming female/juvenile teal with green visible on the wing is not necessarily a Green-winged: both female Blue-winged and Cinnamon teal also have green secondary patches. With direct comparison, Green-winged has smaller bill and steeper forehead than Blue-winged; some (but not all) also show a pale streak along sides of the tail, not found on Blue-winged. Reference: *Birding* 23:124-133.

Canvasback — Locally common in summer mostly W; especially common in fall along the Mississippi River in southern SE.

- ID: Plumage coloration often easier to see than bill/head shape: male has white back/sides (male Redhead dingy gray); female has buffy head/neck and pale gray back/sides (female Redhead darker, more uniform brown plumage).

Redhead — Locally common in summer mostly W; generally more widespread than Canvasback in migration, except in fall on the Mississippi River.

- ID: Females/juveniles can have ringed bills and eye rings and thus can be confused with Ring-neckeds. Redheads have rounder head shape and are more uniformly brown overall; Ring-neckeds have peaked head shape and are two-toned with upperparts darker than face, neck, and sides. Birders unfamiliar with female goldeneyes (dark reddish-brown head and gray body) sometimes mistake these for male Redheads. Also see Canvasback.

Ring-necked Duck — Common in summer throughout, mostly on wetlands in wooded areas. Congregates in October by the thousands at Rice Lake National Wildlife Refuge

- ID: See Redhead.

Greater Scaup — Uncommon migrant throughout, mostly on larger bodies of water (e.g., Lake Superior, Mille Lacs Lake, and the lower Mississippi River); more local or absent where smaller and shallower wetlands (and Lesser Scaup) predominate in the W and SE.

- ID: Many females show obvious white spot on ear coverts, similar to Surf and White-winged scoters, but note, however, some female Lessers also have a similar spot. Iridescent head colors on male scaup unreliable and dependent on sun angle and light conditions; bill size/shape and wing stripe length also often hard to determine. Best mark is usually head shape; however, beware of actively diving Lessers which can appear quite round-headed. An under-appreciated ID problem. Reference: *Advanced Birding* guide.

Lesser Scaup — Uncommon in summer NW; more common and widespread and outnumbers Greater Scaup throughout during migration.

- ID: See Greater Scaup.

King Eider — Casual; about 15 records, almost all in fall/winter, plus two or three sight records of unidentified eiders which were most likely Kings; in recent years records of females/immatures almost annual in late fall in Cook County.

- ID: Female/immature eiders can be tricky to separate, with head shape differences not as evident as shown in field guides; their overall plumage and bill colors are also variable. Best mark is King's rounder shape of feathering at base of bill which stops short of nostril; Common's feathering has more pointed shape and extends up to nostril. On female Kings, also note shorter, V-shaped barring on underparts; Commons have longer, straighter vertical lines.

Common Eider — Accidental; five or six scattered late fall records.

- ID: See King Eider.

Harlequin Duck — Rare but Regular mostly in fall and early winter on Lake Superior, especially at Duluth, Two Harbors, and Grand Marais. Only casually seen in spring here and elsewhere in the state at any time. Females and juveniles are most often seen, they typically stay close to rocky shorelines and breakwaters, and therefore are inconspicuous and easy to overlook.

- ID: Contrary to most field guide illustrations, juveniles/females appear to have two, not three, head spots, and they are sometimes mistaken for scoters.

Surf Scoter — Uncommon Lake Superior migrant; see Black Scoter.

White-winged Scoter — Uncommon Lake Superior migrant; see Black Scoter.

Black Scoter — All three scoters are uncommon to rare migrants on Lake Superior, more often in fall (October-November) than spring; most often seen in Cook County, especially at Paradise Beach, Grand Marais, and Good Harbor Bay. White-winged Scoter is usually the most common of the three; all three scoters are rare elsewhere on larger lakes throughout in fall migration.

- ID: Female/immature Surf Scoter's crown blacker than sides of head, unlike White-winged; however, at a distance this suggests female/immature Black Scoter. Also note bill differences: thinnest on Black, thicker on White-winged with eider-like feathering extending toward nostril, and thickest on Surf with vertical shape of feathering at base. Also see Greater Scaup, Long-tailed Duck, and Harlequin Duck. Reference: *Advanced Birding* guide.

Long-tailed Duck — Uncommon in migration and winter on Lake Superior, October to April, especially in Cook County (e.g., Good Harbor Bay, Grand Marais, and Paradise Beach). For reasons unknown, tends to be rare in the Lake and St. Louis counties portions of the lake; only casually seen elsewhere in the state. Typically seen in tight flocks swimming far from shore; when diving, individuals tend to submerge and surface simultaneously.

- ID: Immatures are darker than shown in most guides and thus easily mistaken for scoters.

Bufflehead — Common migrant throughout; also uncommon and local northern NW in summer. A few sometimes overwinter SE and on Lake Superior.

- ID: See Hooded Merganser.

Common Goldeneye — Uncommon in summer N half; common throughout in migration; local in winter throughout on open water, mostly on SE rivers and Lake Superior.

- ID: See Redhead and Barrow's Goldeneye. Courting males in winter/spring give a raspy, buzzy call note similar to Common Nighthawks; this results in erroneous nighthawk reports, especially in April.

Barrow's Goldeneye — Casual; most records from late fall through early spring, especially in the Twin Cities among Common Goldeneyes; also possible in the W, but relatively few Duluth/North Shore records.

- ID: Contrary to some published information, there is no useful difference between female/juvenile goldeneyes in the amount of white visible on folded wing;

variation depends mostly on how an individual arranges its feathers. Never use bill color alone to identify female Barrow's since a few female Commons have bills which appear almost entirely orange. Bill and head shape differences on goldeneyes only reliable on adults (which have golden eyes); beware of juveniles (browner eyes) whose bill/head shapes may yet to have developed. Darker brown head color of female Barrow's (more reddish-brown on Common) usually difficult to determine. Reference: *Birding* 18:17-27.

Smew — Accidental; one March 1999 record from Jackson County.

Hooded Merganser — Uncommon in summer throughout; more common in spring migration.

- ID: First-spring males may have a small white head patch and resemble female Buffleheads.

Common Merganser — Uncommon in summer NE; uncommon and local in winter on open rivers SE and on Lake Superior. Migrant throughout and especially common in late fall along the Mississippi River in the southern SE, especially on Lake Pepin (Goodhue/Wabasha counties) where thousands typically occur.

- ID: Female's clean contrast between white and reddish-brown areas on head and neck usually easy to see in flight or at a distance. However, juveniles and birds in eclipse plumage can be more obscure and resemble female Red-breasteds; note Common's more sloping forehead and thicker base of the bill. References: *American Birds* 44:1203-1205 and *Advanced Birding* guide.

Red-breasted Merganser — Common in summer and in migration on Lake Superior, and uncommon there most winters; uncommon migrant elsewhere, mostly E half.

- ID: See Common Merganser.

Ruddy Duck — Uncommon in summer mostly W; more common in migration W and SE.

FAMILY ACCIPITRIDAE: OSPREYS, KITES, EAGLES, AND HAWKS

Osprey — Uncommon NE and more locally so SE in summer in wooded lake country; an estimated 500 nesting pairs statewide. Migrants seen almost daily at Hawk Ridge in September; valid winter records virtually nonexistent.

> • ID: Under wing pattern is unlike misleading field guide illustrations which stress a Rough-legged Hawk-like black wrist patch; wing linings and wing tips are also black, forming a "W"-pattern. Osprey's brown tail may appear reddish in some light conditions. Also see Bald Eagle (sub-adults with dark stripe through eyes often mistaken for Ospreys).

Swallow-tailed Kite — Accidental; at least a dozen 20th century records, only one of these recently; formerly nested in central Minnesota in the 19th century.

White-tailed Kite — Accidental; one May 2000 record from the Twin Cities.

Mississippi Kite — Currently considered Casual, but nearly Regular in recent years, mostly in the S half, but there are four or five recent September records from Hawk Ridge in Duluth. Has the dubious distinction of being the only species on the Casual list without a specimen or identifiable photo record.

Bald Eagle — Uncommon in summer NE (especially in the Chippewa and Superior national forests), northern SE, along the Mississippi River in the southern SE, plus a few pairs now locally elsewhere throughout, with a statewide total of about 700 nesting pairs. Possible in winter near open water throughout, especially along the Mississippi River in southern SE where hundreds can be counted on peak days from Wabasha to Houston counties in early or late winter. Easily seen most days at Hawk Ridge October-November.

> • ID: Juveniles have whitish wing linings contrasting with darker flight feathers, and many have dark throat/chest contrasting with whiter belly; this combination results in erroneous Swainson's Hawk reports, especially in winter. Also in winter, beware of sub-adult Balds with a brownish stripe through the eyes, which often are mistaken for Ospreys; and note Bald Eagles often glide with an Osprey-like wing profile. Many juvenile Bald Eagles have a black band at the tip of their whitish tail, and these are confused with juvenile Golden Eagles. Reference: *American Birds* 37:822-826.

Northern Harrier — Uncommon in summer throughout, more common in migration, and a few overwinter S in milder years.

> • ID: juveniles/females have a blackish area on the under wing coverts, and a distant harrier with wings set, gliding into the wind, can bear an uncanny resemblance to a Prairie Falcon (and migrating harriers often fly at unexpectedly high altitudes). Also see Swainson's, Rough-legged, and Red-tailed hawks.

Sharp-shinned Hawk — Uncommon in summer NE; common throughout in migration, with hundreds per day frequently counted at Hawk Ridge in fall. A few overwinter S half, and then more likely than Cooper's.

> • ID: All three accipiters frequently soar, fan their tails, and are easily mistaken for buteos. Or, they can appear more pointed-winged and falcon-like when flying into a headwind. Compared to Cooper's, a Sharp-shinned flaps more rapidly, has a smaller head/neck projecting little beyond curved fore edge of wings; Cooper's flaps more deliberately, has "flying cross" shape with longer head/neck projection in front of straighter fore edge of wings, and often soars in a shallow dihedral. Perched Sharp-shinned has a rounder head shape, its nape and crown the same color; Cooper's shows a flatter crown which looks darker than the nape. Tail shape and amount of white on tip of tail are both variable and often unreliable to distinguish Sharp-shinned from Cooper's. juvenile Sharp-shinned has thicker under-parts streaking extending to the under tail coverts; juvenile Cooper's has thinner breast streaking with a whiter lower belly and under tail coverts. Paler underparts on juvenile Cooper's may make its head appear darker, resulting in a "hooded" appearance in flight. Also see Merlin. References: *Birding* 16:251-263 and 32:428-433, *American Birds* 33:236-240, and *Advanced Birding* guide.

Cooper's Hawk — Uncommon in summer W, SE, and western NE. Always outnumbered in migration by Sharp-shinneds (at Hawk Ridge the ratio is around 100 to 1); a few sometimes overwinter SE.

> • ID: See Sharp-shinned Hawk and Northern Goshawk.

Northern Goshawk — Rare, local, secretive, and seldom reported in summer in denser NE woodlands. More widespread but uncommon in migration and winter mostly N half, with wintering birds ranging widely and difficult to find. Generally absent in migration and winter S half except in peak years of its 10-year cycle. Most easily found at Hawk Ridge in Duluth, when migrants occur most days from mid-October to mid-November, with sometimes dozens seen per day (or even hundreds in peak years!).

> • ID: Like other accipiters, goshawks often soar and appear buteo-like; also note that back-lit accipiters can show buteo-like wing "windows." A goshawk typically appears to have more tapered, falcon-like wing tips; it can then be misidentified as a Gyrfalcon, or an adult with its dark ear coverts is mistaken for a Peregrine. In flight, goshawks are similar to Cooper's with their round tail shape and more obvious white tail tip; at close range on perched goshawks, look for "zigzag" tail banding, the dark bands narrowly edged with white. Contrary to information in field guides, accipiter tail bands are not of equal width: the dark bands are actually narrower. Like Sharp-shinneds, goshawks lack flatter crown and paler nape of Cooper's, and juveniles lack Cooper's pattern of finer breast streaking contrasting with whiter lower belly. White supercilium on juvenile goshawks often obscure and unreliable as a field

mark. Goshawks of all ages have paler upper wing coverts contrasting with darker flight feathers. References: see Sharp-shinned Hawk.

Red-shouldered Hawk — Uncommon and quite local in summer SE (especially along the Minnesota River and at Whitewater Wildlife Management Area), southern NE, and in wooded areas of the southern NW; a few sometimes winter SE. Distribution is poorly known, and it is apparently more common in the northern half of its range.

• ID: Beware of some Red-shouldereds with dark and light tail bands appearing of equal width. juveniles similar in plumage to juvenile Broad-wingeds; perched Red-shouldereds best told by banded pattern on folded secondaries (all dark on Broad-wingeds). Flying birds of all ages have narrow, crescent-shaped "windows" just inside the wing tips (Broad-wingeds' windows differ in shape). Also see accipiters and Red-tailed Hawk.

Broad-winged Hawk — Common in summer E half, uncommon NW. Migrates throughout, with one-day counts in the thousands in mid-September at Hawk Ridge in Duluth; 10,000-plus days are not unusual, and the one-day record is nearly 48,000. Despite frequent reports November to March, there are virtually no valid records then.

• ID: Many birders are unaware that juveniles have translucent wing "windows" and are thus mistaken for Red-shouldereds; a Broad-winged's windows are wider and more rectangular than a Red-shouldered's narrower, crescent-shaped windows. Also note juvenile's dark and broad malar area (somewhat suggestive of a Peregrine) from which the underparts streaks emanate. Many adults have a Swainson's Hawk-like bib. Relatively and uniformly pale under wings with clean-cut black edge to wing tips and trailing edge distinctive on both juveniles and adults. Contrary to many field guide illustrations, adult Broad-winged's tail typically only shows two black bands and one white band; the white band usually a bit narrower, not the same width as the black bands. In flight, often shows more tapered, pointed wings; when circling, fore edge of wing often relatively straight; when gliding or "streaming" out of thermals, trailing edge of wing relatively straight. Also see accipiters and Red-shouldered Hawk (all far more likely in winter and all sometimes misidentified as Broad-wingeds).

Swainson's Hawk — Uncommon in summer mostly SW, rarer and more local NW and southern SE. Arrives in mid-April and mostly gone by October. Despite occasional winter reports, there are no valid records then.

• ID: See Bald Eagle, Broad-winged, Red-tailed, and light-morph adult Rough-legged hawks, which all can show a dark Swainson's-like throat/chest. Under wing pattern is usually the best field mark. Light-morph immatures also show the same, but not as contrasting, under wing pattern; immatures usually appear more spotted, less streaked below than other buteos, with dark smudges on sides of chest and a whitish head. On perched Swainson's, note wing tips extending beyond

tail tip, unlike almost all other Minnesota raptors. Also note the white, harrier-like patch at the base of the tail on light-morph birds. Many immatures and dark-morph birds of all ages can be quite variable and confounding: an under-appreciated ID problem.

Red-tailed Hawk — Common in summer throughout; uncommon most winters mostly S half. This and the kestrel are the most widespread migrant raptors along roadsides in open country throughout. Can be seen on some days by the hundreds at Hawk Ridge in October-early November.

• ID: As some field guides fail to portray, Red-tailed show varying amount of white at base of tail and are frequently mistaken for harriers, Rough-leggeds, and Ferruginous Hawks. Also, juveniles have translucent "windows" and are then confused with Red-shouldered and Ferruginous hawks. The Red-tailed's windows are similar to the juvenile Broad-winged's: wider, more rectangular, extending on the upper wing coverts, and aligned parallel to the body. The Red-shouldered's narrow crescent-shaped windows lie near the tips of the outer primaries; the Ferruginous' windows are oriented perpendicular to body along base of flight feathers. Many prairie Red-tailed lack the characteristic "belly band," are extensively white on head, wings and tail, and are misidentified frequently as Ferruginous. Field guides generally fail to show many Red-tailed have dark sides of the neck which often appear to meet as a single band; such individuals are frequently mistaken for Swainson's Hawks. On most perched birds, note dark-light-dark pattern on underparts (formed by dark neck/throat, white chest, and dark belly band); most also have pale spotting on upper wing coverts that form a whitish "V" on back. Dark-morph juveniles uniformly dark and nondescript except for wing windows. Also see Rough-legged Hawk. References: *American Birds* 39:127-133 and 40:197-202.

Ferruginous Hawk — Rare and barely Regular W, with most records (only one or two most years) in spring SW and southern NW. One of the most difficult Regular species to find in Minnesota.

• ID: See Red-tailed Hawk (paler individuals frequently misidentified as Ferruginous).

Rough-legged Hawk — Common N half and uncommon S half in migration; uncommon in winter throughout in milder years, rare or absent in snowier winters. Most easily seen mid-October through November at Hawk Ridge, the Sax-Zim Bog (St. Louis County), in northern Aitkin County, and in the NW.

• ID: For decades, light-morph adult male Rough-leggeds had never been shown in any field guide! These lack "normal" pattern of buffy head/chest contrasting with blackish belly; instead, their upper chest is heavily streaked and dark (suggesting Swainson's), the lower chest whitish, and the belly heavily streaked (suggesting Red-tailed). Also, their tails are multi-banded, unlike the illustrations in most guides. Tails of dark-morph birds either all dark above or with narrow white bands.

Note longer wing shape compared with Red-tailed and its often harrier-like flight style: quicker upstroke of wings with slight pause at top of stroke. Many Rough-leggeds are hard to classify by morph, age, or sex. Also see Osprey.

Golden Eagle — Rare migrant throughout, mostly in fall, and best looked for at Hawk Ridge mid-October to mid-November, with 50-100 counted in an average year. In spring best looked for along the Minnesota River in the SW; also a few winter annually at Whitewater Wildlife Management Area (Winona/Wabasha counties).

• ID: See Bald Eagle, which is far more common in Minnesota; dark immatures are frequently assumed to be Goldens by beginners. Golden color on nape usually hard to see. Typically glides with obvious dihedral, more so than most Bald Eagles. Cadence of wing beats often distinctive and like a Rough-legged Hawk. Somewhat dihedral wing profile, two-toned under wing, and smaller head (projects in front of wings less than half of tail length, unlike Bald Eagle) all suggest Turkey Vulture. Reference: *American Birds* 37:822-826.

FAMILY FALCONIDAE: CARACARAS AND FALCONS

Crested Caracara — Accidental; one July 1994 sight record from Scott County of an individual possibly escaped/released from captivity.

American Kestrel — Common in summer throughout; a few winter S half most years.

• ID: Paler underparts than most Merlins; in flight, back-lit males have translucent row of white spots along trailing edge of wing. Wings typically appear narrower, with more rounded tips than on Merlin. A kestrel tends to have a more aimless flight with looser wing beats; Merlin's flight is usually more direct and deliberate.

Merlin — Uncommon in summer N half; more common throughout in migration (with a few pale "Richardson's" Merlins W), and a few winter locally some years. Most easily seen September-October in Duluth at Hawk Ridge and in the harbor area, and along the North Shore. For reasons unknown, it has been more widespread and common throughout in all seasons in recent years.

• ID: Perched Merlins similar to juvenile Sharp-shinneds; look for narrower white tail bands on Merlin (on Sharp-shinned dark bands are a bit narrower) and Merlin's dark eye (yellow on young Sharp-shinned). Prairie subspecies (richardsoni) is paler overall than typical Merlin, with malar mark faint or lacking, and resembles Prairie Falcon. Also see American Kestrel and Peregrine Falcon.

Gyrfalcon — Rare and barely Regular N half in fall-winter; most records are from Duluth, either in late fall at Hawk Ridge or in winter in the harbor, but not seen every year there. Probably most often occurs NW, especially where there are grouse or prairie-chickens to prey on, but there are too few observers there to find (or correctly iden-tify) them. One of Minnesota's most difficult Regular species to find.

• ID: Some individuals have bold "sideburns" and resemble Peregrines; others have narrower sideburns and pale superciliums and thus resemble Prairie Falcons. Two-toned under wing pattern with wing linings darker than the flight feathers also suggests Prairie Falcon. Most Gyrfalcons in Minnesota are gray-morph juveniles which are grayish-brown overall. Soaring Gyrs show relatively rounded wing tips, more like an accipiter or buteo than a falcon. Also see Northern Goshawk (often misidentified as a Gyr). References: *Birding* 32:22-29 and *Birding World* 6:67-74.

Peregrine Falcon — Rare migrant throughout, with most records in fall, especially at Hawk Ridge in September where about 50 are seen most years. In recent years, reintroduced birds are seen near nest sites any time of year, though generally absent in winter. First nesting of hacked birds occurred in the late 1980s, with most nests now on buildings, cliffs, bridges, and smokestacks on the North Shore of Lake Superior, along the lower Mississippi River valley, and in various cities (e.g., Duluth, St. Cloud, the Twin Cities, and Rochester).

• ID: Most migrants here are of the tundrius subspecies; the juveniles are quite pale-headed with narrow "sideburns" and whitish supercilium, similar to Merlins, Prairie Falcons, and most Gyrfalcons. Juvenile tundrius Peregrines are also paler brown on back/wings and thus similar to Prairie Falcons. Because of publicity and mystique surrounding this species, beginners and non-birders frequently mistake several other raptors for Peregrines. Also see Northern Goshawk.

Prairie Falcon — Rare and local but Regular in migration W, mostly in fall; also possible in summer or winter. Probably best looked for at Rothsay Wildlife Management Area (Wilkin County) in October, and there have been sightings at the Twin Cities airport in recent winters.

• ID: Blackish under wing linings more extensive than shown in some field guides. See Northern Harrier, Merlin, Peregrine Falcon, and Gyrfalcon.

FAMILY PHASIANIDAE: GALLINACEOUS BIRDS

Gray Partridge — Uncommon and elusive but widespread permanent resident W and southern SE. Prefers cultivated fields rather than native grasslands, best looked for along roadsides at dawn or dusk, but usually spotted by chance when not being looked for. Hardest to find when paired up and nesting May-June, and easiest to see in winter against a snowy background. Numbers may be declining in recent years.

Ring-necked Pheasant — Common permanent resident mostly S half, and uncommon southern NW.

• ID: See Sharp-tailed Grouse.

Ruffed Grouse — Uncommon permanent resident N half and eastern SE in mixed or deciduous woods, and overlaps ranges and habitats of both Spruce and Sharp-tailed grouse. Can be tracked down when drumming in April-May, but most easily seen in fall/winter at dawn and dusk when they come into feeders or when feeding on catkins in aspens, birch, and alders. Often as tame as any Spruce Grouse, especially in summer when family groups are seen along roadsides.

> • ID: See Spruce and Sharp-tailed grouse.

Spruce Grouse — Rare and local permanent resident northern NE and in Roseau County in predominantly coniferous forests, especially where there are jack pines. Best looked for in the morning along roadsides in winter when grouse come out to pick at salt and grit, with the northern third of Lake County Road 2 the place where birders have the most success: note the flock of 27 in this road in February 1999! Also found along other roads in Lake (Highway 1) and Cook (Gunflint Trail) counties, on the Echo Trail (St. Louis County), around Scenic State Park (Itasca County), in Beltrami Island State Forest (Lake of the Woods County), and on Highway 310 (Roseau County). Besides winter (with late winter perhaps best), a good time to look is spring (when males sometimes come in to tape recordings) or July-September (when family groups are roaming around); the hardest time is June when birds are paired up and nesting. Several birders with 700+ life lists have yet to see this most elusive species.

> • ID: Females/juveniles have darker, more densely and uniformly barred underparts than Ruffed Grouse, which show thick vertical stripes on sides. Crown seldom appears crested; Ruffed Grouse almost always show an obvious crest. Ruffed Grouse are always more common and widespread, and they often act every bit as "tame" as Spruce Grouse, which results in many misidentifications.

Willow Ptarmigan — Accidental; besides a large and difficult-to-explain invasion in the N in the winter of 1933-34, there have been two late winter/early spring Lake of the Woods County records, in 1914 and 1964.

Rock Ptarmigan — Accidental; one surprising record from Grand Marais in May 1996.

Sharp-tailed Grouse — Uncommon and local permanent resident in hayfields and open brushlands in the northern half of NW and the NE, mostly in Aitkin, Carlton, and St. Louis counties. Most often seen when displaying at dawn on leks March-May, especially southeast of Crookston (Polk County), south of Palisade (Aitkin County), and in the Sax-Zim Bog (St. Louis County). Difficult to find at other times of day or year, but often perches up in tamaracks and alders at dawn or dusk. Overlaps prairie-chicken range and habitat in northern NW, and also occurs with Ruffed Grouse in brushier and more wooded areas. Numbers greatly reduced in recent decades, probably due to habitat loss.

> • ID: Underparts are lightly spotted with brown and paler than a Ruffed Grouse or prairie-chicken; the latter species is more heavily and uniformly barred below. Upperparts heavily spotted with white which gives flying birds an overall "frosty" appearance. Beware shorter-tailed juvenile pheasants which have been mistaken for Sharp-tailed Grouse.

Greater Prairie-Chicken — Uncommon and quite local permanent resident NW, from western Pennington County south to eastern Wilkin County; also a few in parts of Hubbard, Wadena, and Cass counties. A total of about 150 individuals recently introduced in the vicinity of Marsh and Lac Qui Parle lakes, with at least four leks now active. Most easily seen when displaying at dawn on leks March-May, especially southeast of Crookston (Polk County), at Felton Prairie (Clay County), and Rothsay Wildlife Management Area (Wilkin County). Usually difficult to see at other times of day or year, but perhaps easiest then at Rothsay. Prefers native grasslands but also frequently seen in adjacent cultivated fields.

> • ID: See Sharp-tailed Grouse.

Wild Turkey — Uncommon, local, and now a well-established introduced resident of the southern SE, generally south and southeast of the Twin Cities. Most releases began in the 1980s and continue today, with some birders considering turkeys to be established and "countable" throughout most of the S half. However, "non-countable" turkeys recently escaped or released from farms are possible anywhere in the state and often hard to distinguish from truly wild birds. Most often seen in deciduous woodlands or adjacent fields.

FAMILY ODONTOPHORIDAE: QUAIL

Northern Bobwhite — Rare and very local permanent resident only in Houston County, especially in the southwestern part of the county near Wilmington. Recent evidence, however, suggests that most (perhaps all?) Houston County birds are recent releases from game farms. Best looked for when calling in May-June, but almost always difficult to find. Also possible in Fillmore, Olmsted, and Winona counties, but birds there probably escapes or releases; such "non-countable" bobwhites, like turkeys, are possible throughout the state.

FAMILY RALLIDAE: RAILS, GALLINULES, AND COOTS

Yellow Rail — Uncommon and local in summer in shallow, sedge-type marshes in NW and western half of NE. Relatively easy to hear late May-early July; ventriloquial and farther away than it sounds, and most vocal at night but can also call by day. However, these rails can often be unpredictably and frustratingly silent on some days/nights. Can be seen with patience, a spotlight, and careful stalking: either stand still near a calling bird, imitate the call with tape recorder or tapping stones, and try luring one into view; or try surrounding the rail with a group of birders and slowly close the circle. Yellow Rails call less and less as you approach, often falling silent for long periods; they will either freeze in place, walk away from nearest person, or flush. By noting where a flying rail lands and heading there immediately you can often relocate the bird, which typically resumes calling. Most birders look for it at McGregor Marsh (Aitkin County), but it is also found in western Roseau County, Agassiz National Wildlife Refuge, southeast of Crookston (Polk County), and in Cass County (Swamp Lake and Boy River); may also regularly nest south to Wilkin, Todd, Morrison, and Pine counties. Almost never seen during migration.

- ID: Juvenile Sora is also brownish-yellow, but white streaks on back/wings run lengthwise (white feather edges on Yellow Rail form cross-barring pattern). Juvenile Sora in flight may show white along trailing edge of secondaries and thus be easily mistaken for a Yellow Rail.

Black Rail — Accidental, but possibly Casual in spring/summer since no one surveys Minnesota's marshes at night when the species is most vocal; about seven S records.

- ID: Chicks of coots and other rails are blackish overall and sometimes mistaken for Black Rails.

King Rail — Casual, but might possibly prove to be Regular in spring-summer in marshes in the S half if there were more observer coverage in this habitat. Formerly nested and was more common and widespread.

Virginia Rail — Common in summer W and SE, uncommon western NE. Like other rails, sometimes ventures into the open at dusk and will come into view in response to tape recordings.

- ID: Besides the oft-heard "kiddick" and descending grunting or quacking call, Virginias also give a rattling "tic tic trrrr" (similar to King Rail but not as loud) and a single loud note (similar to Sora but not as sharp). Wood Frog also has a "kiddick" call similar to Virginia Rail.

Sora — Common in summer throughout except eastern NE. Generally more vocal and widespread than Virginia Rail and more often seen out in the open.

- ID: See Yellow Rail.

Purple Gallinule — Accidental; three records, one of these was of a bird found dead in the Sax-Zim Bog in November!

Common Moorhen — Uncommon and very local in SE marshes in summer; found most often in Mississippi River backwaters from Goodhue County south, especially at La Crescent and Mound Prairie marshes (Houston County). Can be as secretive as any rail, is often rare and quite difficult to find some years, and seldom seen in migration.

American Coot — Common in summer throughout except eastern NE; migrants more widespread throughout, with concentrations in the thousands on some lakes in fall.

FAMILY GRUIDAE: CRANES

Sandhill Crane — Uncommon and local in meadows, fields, and brushlands in summer in the NW, western NE, and northern SE. Migrants are locally common NW in April and October at staging areas along the glacial Lake Agassiz beachline, especially southeast of Crookston (Polk County) and at Rothsay Wildlife Management Area (Wilkin County).

- ID: Some abnormally pale individuals are off-white or pale buff overall and strongly suggest Whooping Cranes. Sandhill Crane's outer primaries are somewhat darker than rest of wing; in some light conditions wings appear whitish with contrasting dark primaries, and this can result in erroneous Whooping Crane reports.

Whooping Crane — Accidental; formerly nested until the 1870s. Since 1900 only five acceptable records, only one recently (October 1990), plus numerous rumors and several undocumented sight records. Sightings may increase as a result of recent Wisconsin introductions.

- ID: See Sandhill Crane. Like the Peregrine Falcon, there is mystique and publicity associated with this endangered species; as a result, optimistic and overeager beginners have mistaken the likes of pelicans and other large white birds for Whooping Cranes.

FAMILY CHARADRIIDAE: PLOVERS

Black-bellied Plover — Uncommon migrant throughout, more often in fall and most consistently in Duluth September-October.

- ID: Some Black-bellieds may appear more brownish than gray and look very similar to golden-plovers. With direct comparison, Black-bellied has shorter primary extension with wing tips barely beyond tail tip (golden-plover's extend noticeably beyond), it is larger overall with a larger bill, the contrast between white supercilium and darker cap usually not as strong, and its underparts more two-toned with a whiter lower belly. Flying birds much easier to separate, both by plumage and call: Black-bellied has mellower, lower-pitched, usually three-syllabled whistle, unlike golden-plover's higher, screechier, one- or two-syllabled call. Also see Red Knot.

American Golden-Plover — Uncommon migrant throughout; also more often in fall and most easily seen in Duluth September-October.

- ID: See Black-bellied Plover.

Snowy Plover — Accidental; eight spring or summer records, mostly in the W.

Wilson's Plover — Accidental; two records in consecutive years (1981-82) in Duluth, possibly of the same individual.

Semipalmated Plover — Common migrant throughout.

Piping Plover — Still on the Regular list, but only marginally so, with a few pairs at most now nesting only on Pine-Curry Island on Lake of the Woods. Only occurs casually in migration, mostly in spring and mostly in the W or in Duluth. Formerly bred at Duluth until the mid-1980s.

Killdeer — Common in summer throughout.

FAMILY RECURVIROSTRIDAE: STILTS AND AVOCETS

Black-necked Stilt — Accidental; four spring/summer records.

American Avocet — Uncommon and local spring migrant mostly W and in May; often seen at Salt Lake (Lac Qui Parle County) and larger sewage ponds. Rarely seen E half; also rare in summer and fall throughout.

FAMILY SCOLOPACIDAE: TYPICAL SHOREBIRDS

Greater Yellowlegs — Common migrant throughout; tends to migrate earlier in spring and later in fall than Lesser Yellowlegs.

- ID: Bill is longer and thicker than Lesser's, usually appears slightly upturned, and in good light is two-toned with black tip and gray base; Lesser's bill straighter, shorter, and usually all-black. Greater's call a more strident, higher-pitched "dear dear dear" (Lesser's call a mellower, softer "too too too"); number of notes not as reliable as their quality. Reference: *Birding* 14:172-178.

Lesser Yellowlegs — Common migrant throughout, usually outnumbering Greater.

- ID: See Greater Yellowlegs.

Solitary Sandpiper — Common migrant throughout; a few may breed in northern NE bogs.

- ID: Juvenile Spotted also has eye ring and white spots on upperparts and can be mistaken for a Solitary. Conversely, Solitary often has "teetering" behavior and is

thus mistaken for a Spotted; note Solitary's unique tail pattern, often visible on a standing bird.

Willet — Uncommon and local spring migrant mostly W; rare E half (but nearly annual at Duluth) and also rare in summer and fall throughout.

Spotted Sandpiper — Common in summer throughout.

- ID: See Solitary Sandpiper.

Upland Sandpiper — Locally common W and uncommon SE and western NE in grasslands in summer. Only rarely seen in fall with most birds having migrated south by August. Formerly more common.

Eskimo Curlew — Extirpated and probably extinct. No records here since the 19th century when the species was considered a Regular spring migrant in the W, but most of the reports were anecdotal and ambiguous.

Whimbrel — Rare and local but Regular in mid- and late May in Duluth and the North Shore of Lake Superior. Most often found at Park Point in Duluth and on rocky points, breakwaters, and islands farther up the North Shore, with only a few sightings most springs. Casually occurs there in fall and elsewhere in the state in spring or fall.

Long-billed Curlew — Accidental now in migration, mostly in spring, and possible statewide; formerly bred in the W in the 19th century.

Hudsonian Godwit — Uncommon in spring (late April-early June) mostly W; rare in spring E half and in fall throughout.

- ID: Some spring birds are brownish overall with no rusty coloration below and quite difficult to tell from Marbleds; when in doubt, wait for birds to fly or call.

Marbled Godwit — Uncommon and local in summer in grasslands NW and northern SW; rare in spring E half and in fall throughout, with most birds migrating south out of the state during July.

- ID: See Hudsonian Godwit.

Ruddy Turnstone — Uncommon and local migrant throughout, usually along the shores of larger lakes, especially Lake Superior.

Red Knot — Rare and barely Regular migrant in Duluth at Park Point or elsewhere in the harbor area, with most records (normally only a couple per year) in late May or late August-early September. Casually found elsewhere in the state in spring or fall.

- ID: Fall birds are nondescript and suggest dowitchers or Black-bellied Plovers; note bill length, and in flight look for plain grayish-white rump/tail pattern.

Sanderling — Uncommon migrant throughout, especially along the shores of larger lakes, and most consistently seen at Park Point in Duluth.

- ID: Very pale overall in fall and strongly resembles Western Sandpiper in basic (winter) plumage; often shows diagnostic black patch at bend of wing. Reddish-brown spring migrants in alternate (breeding) plumage are unfamiliar and confusing to even some experienced birders.

Semipalmated Sandpiper — Common migrant throughout.

- ID: Compared with Least Sandpiper, note Semipalmated's grayer upperparts, whiter underparts, larger size with direct comparison, thicker and straighter bill, and shorter and lower-pitched "chut" call note. Least is browner or extensively reddish-brown on upperparts, has darker wash across breast, a thinner and slightly but noticeably decurved bill, and a longer, higher-pitched "crreeep" call note. Leg color often difficult to determine in poor light or when Least has mud on legs/feet. Not mentioned in most field guides is that Semipalmateds can have rusty feather edges on head, back, scapulars, and wings; these have a long history of being misidentified as Westerns. Note Semi's rusty color duller but more extensive; on fall Westerns, rusty coloration limited to scapulars and contrasts more with grayish color on rest of upperparts. If present, Semipalmated's rusty color limited to feather edges; some juvenile Westerns similar, but rust on adult Westerns is on bases or centers of feathers. Also note some female Semis have bills as long as male Westerns. A plain, grayish Western in basic (winter) plumage is quite similar to a Sanderling. References: see Western Sandpiper.

Western Sandpiper — Formerly and erroneously thought to be Regular, with other shorebirds often mistaken for Westerns over the years. Now only considered Accidental, since there have been only three documented and accepted sight records, no photographic records, and one specimen from 1960. Are Minnesota birders overlooking Westerns, are birders in nearby states (where the species is reported annually) making ID errors, or do Westerns actually stop elsewhere in the Midwest and somehow bypass Minnesota during migration?

- ID: See Semipalmated, Least and White-rumped sandpipers, Sanderling, and Dunlin, which all have been misidentified as Westerns: an under-appreciated ID problem for decades. Unless it's an adult in alternate plumage, none of the field guides alone is helpful: do not attempt to identify this species in Minnesota without consulting *American Birds* 38:853-876 (reprinted 41:212-236); also see *The Loon* 68:121-124 and *Advanced Birding* guide.

Least Sandpiper — Common migrant throughout.

- ID: See Semipalmated Sandpiper. Since field guides fail to mention Least's decurved bill, reddish-brown upperparts coloration (especially on juveniles), and sometimes apparently dark legs (when muddy), this species is frequently misidentified as Western Sandpiper. Note Least's reddish-brown upperparts are more extensive and uniform. References: see Western Sandpiper.

White-rumped Sandpiper — Uncommon E half and common W in spring; most often seen NW in late May. Only rare in fall throughout, with many records in October in Duluth or the North Shore of Lake Superior.

- ID: Has decurved bill like Western Sandpiper and strongly resembles Western in both alternate plumage (rows of spots on breast and sides, rusty coloration on crown, ear coverts, and upperparts) and juvenile plumage (rusty scapulars). Call note is also similar to Western: soft and thin "jeet," higher-pitched than Semipalmated and not as long or trilled as Least. Besides rump, note pale base of bill, larger size, and elongated shape with folded wing tips extending beyond tail (same as Baird's Sandpiper). Reference: *Birding* 19 (2):10-13.

Baird's Sandpiper — Uncommon migrant throughout; more often seen in fall.

- ID: Juveniles are rich buffy brown on head, neck, and breast; except for leg color, they can strongly resemble Buff-breasted Sandpipers. Also see White-rumped Sandpiper.

Pectoral Sandpiper — Common migrant throughout.

- ID: See Ruff.

Purple Sandpiper — Accidental; four late fall records, three of these from Lake Superior.

Dunlin — Uncommon migrant throughout; most consistently seen in Duluth.

- ID: Fall birds are solid dull gray overall (darker and more uniform than almost all other shorebirds), some with contrasting rusty feather edges on scapulars; thus, the potential for mistaking one for a Western Sandpiper. Reference: *American Birds* 44:189-192.

Curlew Sandpiper — Accidental; one May 1994 record from Goodhue County.

- ID: See Dunlin.

Stilt Sandpiper — Uncommon in spring throughout; more common in fall.

- ID: Long bill and vertical feeding motion suggest a dowitcher; note Stilt's shorter, decurved bill, and it tends to probe more slowly and walk around more than a dowitcher while feeding.

Buff-breasted Sandpiper — Rare to locally uncommon in August-September at Duluth and the North Shore of Lake Superior, but in recent years most consistently seen at sod farms, especially in the Twin Cities and vicinity. Can also be found statewide on pastures, along mown edges of airport runways, and on berms of sewage ponds. Hardly ever seen in spring.

- ID: See Baird's Sandpiper.

Ruff — Casual in migration, with most records of juveniles/females in May or August in the W and SE; not as many records in recent years.

- ID: Fall birds and spring females brownish and resemble Pectoral Sandpipers. Ruff's brownish wash on breast not as sharply cut off and extends lower on belly. Overall proportions more like yellowlegs, but note distinctive "pot-bellied" and "hump-backed" shape. Has two white ovals along sides of tail, similar to Pectoral and other shorebirds, but ovals are larger, nearly meet, and may appear as a single, U-shaped patch.

Short-billed Dowitcher — Common migrant throughout; mostly migrates in May and July-early September.

- ID: Hendersoni subspecies migrates through Minnesota. In alternate (breeding) plumage is brightly marked on upperparts and only lightly marked on sides of breast; Long-billed Dowitcher darker on upperparts and more heavily spotted/barred on sides of breast. Juveniles brighter above and more reddish below than grayer juvenile Long-billeds; juvenile's tertials patterned with rusty and black markings (Long-billed's tertials unmarked). Tail barring variable and difficult to see. Best separated by calls: Short-billed gives lower-pitched, louder, mellower, Lesser Yellowlegs-like "tu tu" or "tu tu tu;" Long-billed's call higher-pitched, softer, thinner "keek" or "keek keek keek." Note Long-billed migrates earlier in spring and later in fall than Short-billed. Also see Red Knot and Stilt Sandpiper. References: *Birding* 15:151-166, *Birding World* 8:221-228, and *Advanced Birding* guide.

Long-billed Dowitcher — Uncommon migrant throughout and usually outnumbered by Short-billeds; mostly migrates in early May and late August-October.

- ID: See Short-billed Dowitcher.

Common Snipe — Common in summer throughout, especially N half. Most easily seen when winnowing overhead or perched on snags and fence posts in spring-summer.

- ID: See Boreal Owl.

American Woodcock — Common and widespread in spring N half and SE, more local and uncommon SW. Most easily found when displaying overhead and "peenting" on the ground at dusk and before dawn in clearings and brushy edges of woodlands, mid-March to late May. Still present but difficult to find in summer and fall.

- ID: Male's buzzy "peenting" resembles Common Nighthawk's call and sometimes results in erroneous nighthawk reports in early spring.

Wilson's Phalarope — Uncommon and local in shallow wetlands in summer, mostly NW; more widespread W and SE in migration, often at sewage ponds.

- ID: Adults in fall uniform pale grayish-white overall, paler than any other Minnesota shorebird. When walking on shore, phalropes can be confusing to even experienced birders.

Red-necked Phalarope — Uncommon migrant mostly W, especially in May and August and most often at sewage ponds.

- ID: See Red Phalarope.

Red Phalarope — Casual; about a dozen records, mostly in fall, and possible statewide.

- ID: Paler base of bill often hard to see; thicker bill than Red-necked difficult to determine without direct comparison. Back pattern on fall birds easier to see: Red Phalarope solid grayon back/wings, sometimes with dark stripes; Red-necked with two pale stripes on sides of back/wings.

FAMILY LARIDAE: JAEGERS, GULLS, AND TERNS

Pomarine Jaeger — Now considered Accidental, but more likely Casual; about a dozen records, all but two from Duluth, and all but one in fall.

- ID: See Parasitic Jaeger.

Parasitic Jaeger — Rare but Regular in fall (late August to mid-October) on Lake Superior at Duluth, and only casually there in spring. Most often seen from Park Point in September on days with east or northeast winds, with a few sightings each year. Most jaegers seen are too far from shore to identify but are probably Parasitics in most cases. Hardly ever seen elsewhere in Minnesota, even on the North Shore of Lake Superior.

- ID: At a distance, which they usually are, jaegers either appear uniformly dark (darker than first-year Herring Gull) or dark above and white below (more contrasting than gulls). Watch for jaegers' falcon-like, aggressive, and close pursuit of gulls; note that gulls also chase other gulls but flight not as maneuverable or aggressive. Never identify jaegers solely by shape, size, or flight without direct comparison with another bird of known identity, or unless you are a skilled veteran of pelagic trips. Parasitics can appear large, slow-flying, and Pomarine-like when not in pursuit. Also beware the size variation within each species (females larger than males): e.g., both Pomarines and Parasitics can seem Ring-billed Gull-size, and some Pomarines appear as large as Herring Gulls. ID of jaegers without fully grown tails is beyond the scope of this book; best to consult *Skuas and Jaegers* guide. Other references: *Birding* 28:129-131 and 29:372-385, and *Advanced Birding* guide.

Long-tailed Jaeger — Accidental; about eight records, all but one of these in fall, and most likely in Duluth.

- ID: See Parasitic Jaeger.

Laughing Gull — Casual during migration, with records scattered statewide; fewer reports in recent years.

- ID: Even experienced birders are unaware one- and two-year-old Franklin's Gulls typically lack white bar adjacent to black wing tips and may appear to have complete black hoods; these have often been misidentified as adult Laughing Gulls. Note adult Laughing's larger size overall (with direct comparison), longer and slightly decurved bill, and more extensive black on under wings. Laughings in basic (winter) plumage have less black on head than Franklin's; immatures have complete tail band out to sides of tail (Franklin's have white outer rectrices). References: *Birding* 26:126-127 and *Advanced Birding* guide.

Franklin's Gull — Locally common in summer W, mostly non-breeding birds, with nesting colonies even more local; the largest and most consistent colony at Agassiz National Wildlife Refuge (Marshall County). More common W and SE in migration, and rare NE.

- ID: See Laughing Gull. Molting adult Franklin's in

spring or fall are highly variable; some show little or no black on wing tips, and resulting upper wing pattern suggests adult Little Gull.

Little Gull — Rare and barely Regular migrant throughout, mostly in Duluth; usually only one or two sightings per year, with most records in May of lone adults within a flock of Bonaparte's Gulls. Unsuccessfully nested in 1986 at Heron Lake (Jackson County).

• ID: Juveniles, not shown in most field guides, have a blackish nape and "M"-pattern on wing, similar to immature kittiwakes. Little Gulls in some plumages quite similar to Ross's Gulls; note Ross's tail and wing shape and paler head. Also see Franklin's Gull.

Black-headed Gull — Considered Accidental, but possibly Casual or even Regular, at least in Jackson County where all seven or eight records occurred, mostly on the north side of Spirit Lake.

• ID reference: *American Birds* 47:1156-1159.

Bonaparte's Gull — Uncommon migrant throughout, but locally common in Duluth in May and at Mille Lacs and Lake Winnibigoshish in fall, often in the hundreds; non-breeding summering birds possible throughout.

• ID: Juveniles, also not shown in most field guides, have extensive brownish markings on head, neck, back, and wings, and a distinct dusky smudge on nape suggesting immature Black-legged Kittiwakes (and Little or Ross's gulls).

Mew Gull — Accidental; three fall records, on Lake Winnibigoshish and twice on Lake Superior.

• ID: First-winter bird (West Coast brachyrhynchus subspecies) has darker gray back, paler brownish primaries, browner tail, and browner wash on belly and under wing than larger first-winter Ring-billed; second-winter bird best told by smaller body and bill size and darker gray mantle. Larger males may approach smaller female Ring-billeds in overall size, bill, and crown shapes. References: *American Birds* 34:111-117 and *Birding* 25:386-401.

Ring-billed Gull — Common in summer throughout, though actual nesting colonies only local; largest colonies at Lake of the Woods, Mille Lacs, and Duluth. Uncommon in early winter SE but does not overwinter most years.

• ID: Third-year gulls of other species (e.g., Herrings) typically have "ringed" bills; inexperienced birders often misidentify these as Ring-billeds. Also beware some juveniles and first-winter birds with all-black tail, like California Gulls. Second-year Ring-billeds may have no white "mirrors" in primaries; beginners have mistaken these for adult kittiwakes. Contrary to the field guides, second-winter birds often have dark eyes and pinkish or grayish legs. Molting adults in summer/fall show less black in wing tips, sometimes apparently none at some angles; such individuals are frequently miscalled Thayer's or Icelands. Also see California and Mew gulls.

California Gull — Casual; possible at any season statewide, but best looked for in the W in spring.

• ID: First-year birds difficult to separate from first-year Herrings: some Herrings have two-toned bills like California, and larger male Californias may approach smaller female Herrings in size. Best told in flight by California's darker primaries (Herring's inner primaries paler than secondaries and outer primaries). Second-year birds more similar to first-year Ring-billeds: male Ring-billeds may approach size of female Californias; best told by California's darker mantle. Fourth-winter Herring Gull may have apparently dark eye, often has both red and black spots on lower mandible, and thus easily mistaken for adult California. Also see Lesser Black-backed Gull.

Herring Gull — Locally common in summer NE, especially on Lake Superior; uncommon W and SE in summer and migration on larger lakes and outnumbered by Ring-billeds. Overwinters on Lake Superior, in the Twin Cities, and on the Mississippi River in southern SE.

• ID: Like Ring-billeds, adult Herring Gulls in molt in summer-fall show less black in wing tips, and birders mistake these for Thayer's, Iceland, or Glaucous gulls. Faded or worn Herrings also frequently mistaken for Thayer's, especially in spring, even by experienced birders. Also see Ring-billed, California, and Lesser Black-backed gulls.

Thayer's Gull — Rare to locally uncommon late October to April, with most records from Lake Superior and the Twin Cities in fall-early winter, and absent some years by mid-winter. Occurs casually elsewhere in the state. Undoubtedly conspecific with Iceland Gull.

• ID: Paler Thayer's and darker Icelands appear similar, if not identical, at all ages; their differences not analyzed here since they are undoubtedly conspecific. Thayer's/Iceland gulls average smaller overall than Herrings, with smaller bills, rounder crowns, and thinner necks; however, many males appear identical to Herrings in size/shape. Juvenile and first-winter birds have upper surface of outer primaries brownish or grayish, similar in color to rest of wing, with broader white feather edges; same-aged Herrings have contrasting blackish-brown primaries with white edges inconspicuous or lacking. Tail band and underside of primaries usually paler than first-winter Herrings. Beware of worn or faded immature Herrings in spring/summer; these strongly resemble Thayer's and are often misidentified by even experienced birders. Second-winter Thayer's paler gray on flight feathers and tail than Herring Gull. Adults usually dark-eyed, some have pale eyes, a few have one eye dark and one pale (!); also beware of fourth-winter Herrings with dark eyes. Upper surface of primaries sometimes same as adult Herrings, sometimes grayer or with reduced black and larger white "mirrors." Underside of outer primaries typically white with only narrow black trailing edge, but some show more black like Herring. Contrary to some references, there is no consistent difference between adult Thayer's and Herring in mantle or leg colors. Also see Ring-billed and Herring gulls (molting adults in summer/fall often mistaken for Thayer's/Iceland), and Glaucous-winged Gull. References: *Birding* 12:198-210 and 23:254-269, *Birders Journal* 7:305-309 and 9:25-33, and *Advanced Birding* guide.

Iceland Gull — Rare and barely Regular in fall-winter, with most records from Lake Superior and the Twin Cities. Formerly considered Casual.

• ID: See Thayer's and Glaucous gulls (darker Icelands of all ages identical to paler Thayer's; paler birds resemble Glaucous).

Lesser Black-backed Gull — Now considered rare but Regular, mostly in fall and winter in the Twin Cities; curiously and relatively scarce on Lake Superior.

• ID: Averages smaller overall than Herring Gull, but larger males may approach size of smaller female Herrings. Juveniles and first-year birds difficult to separate from first-year Herrings: best told by darker centers on back/wing feathers and darker inner primaries (Herrings have paler "windows" on inner primaries). Overall size and wing pattern of first-winter birds suggest California Gull, but bill all-dark (first-year California has two-toned bill). Second-year birds unlike Herrings or Californias, with solid areas of blackish-gray on back/wings and yellow legs.

Glaucous-winged Gull — Accidental; three (possibly four) recent late fall records: in Grand Marais, Duluth, and the Twin Cities.

• ID: Variable in appearance and can be tricky to ID. Similar to Thayer's at all ages, but larger overall and plumage generally paler and more uniform. Hybridizes with Herring, Glaucous, and Western gulls, resulting in even more complex ID problems. References: *The Loon* 68:3-13 and *Birders Journal* 9:25-33.

Glaucous Gull — Locally uncommon November to April on Lake Superior, especially in Duluth and Grand Marais, and in the Twin Cities. Rare or absent some years by mid-winter; only seen casually elsewhere in the state.

• ID: Paler Icelands of all ages similar, even identical, to Glaucous in plumage; larger male Icelands may approach smaller female Glaucous in overall size, and best separated by bill size and head/neck shape. Also note length of primaries on folded wings: Glaucous' usually extend beyond tail a distance less than bill length; Iceland's extension usually greater than bill length. First-winter Glaucous with clearly bicolored bill; Iceland's bill all-dark or mostly so with indistinct pale base (bill patterns of second-winter Glaucous and Icelands usually identical). Some adult Icelands are darker-eyed and darker-mantled than Glaucous, with gray or blackish markings in outer primaries. Also see Herring Gull (molting adults in summer/fall easily mistaken for Glaucous).

Great Black-backed Gull — Now considered Regular but rare, mostly in fall-winter, with most of the records from Lake Superior and the Twin Cities. Casually seen elsewhere in the state.

• ID: Some apparent adults (fourth-year birds?) have dark eyes and might suggest a potential first-state-record Western Gull.

Sabine's Gull — Now considered Casual, with most records of juveniles in fall, but records have been nearly annual recently. Possible statewide, but it is best watched for at Park Point in Duluth in September.

• ID: See Black-legged Kittiwake.

Black-legged Kittiwake — Also Casual, but seen nearly annually in recent years, mostly in late fall on Lake Superior. Almost all records have been of juvenile/first-winter birds.

• ID: See Bonaparte's, Little, Ross's, and Ring-billed gulls. Immature's wing pattern with black triangle on outer primaries and white triangle along trailing edge of wing suggests Sabine's Gull; note differences in nape and upper wing coverts.

Ross's Gull — Accidental; two records, both in the NW in April: 1984 at Agassiz National Wildlife Refuge and 1992 in Pennington County.

• ID: Juvenile/first-winter Ross's have a kittiwake-like "M"-pattern on the wings. Also see Little Gull.

Ivory Gull — Accidental; about 10 late fall/winter

records, all but one from Lake Superior.

- ID: Albinistic gulls can easily be mistaken for this species.

Caspian Tern — Uncommon migrant throughout, most consistently in Duluth; a few non-breeding summering birds seen some years and possible statewide.

- ID: Upper wing surface whiter than shown in most field guides and contrasts with dark area on under wings.

Sandwich Tern — Accidental; one amazing record from Duluth in June 1986.

Common Tern — Locally common in summer only near nesting colonies at Lake of the Woods, Mille Lacs Lake, Leech Lake (Cass County), and Duluth. Migrants are generally not seen except near nesting areas, and always outnumbered by Forster's except at Duluth.

- ID: See Arctic and Forster's terns.

Arctic Tern — Accidental; about 10 records, all in Duluth, and all but two of these in May or June.

- ID: Alternate-plumaged (breeding) Commons often show little or no black on bill tip, in some light conditions may appear grayish below with whiter area below cap, can look shorter-legged when belly feathers fluffed up, and often have narrow black edge on primaries on under wings. Since all these are oft-mentioned field marks of Arctics, misidentifications easily occur. Better marks on adult Arctics: folded wing tips shorter than tail tip (equal in length on Commons), uniform gray on upper surface of wings (Commons have dark wedge on middle primaries), pale underside of outer primary (blackish on Commons), and translucent under wing on all flight feathers (translucence on Commons limited to inner primaries). With direct comparison, also note Arctic's shorter bill, rounder crown shape, and shorter neck. References: *American Birds* 41:184-187, *Birding* 25:94-108, and *Advanced Birding* guide.

Forster's Tern — Common but local in summer W and northern SE; throughout except eastern NE in migration and more common than Common Tern.

- ID: Immatures and adults in basic (winter) plumage are darker on primaries, have black bills, and sometimes show black on nape like Commons. Most easily separated then by Forster's pale leading edge of upper wing coverts; Commons have a blackish carpal bar, visible both at rest and in flight. References: see Arctic Tern.

Least Tern — Casual, with most recent records in the SW (especially Lyon County!) in fall.

Black Tern — Common in summer in marshes throughout except eastern NE.

FAMILY ALCIDAE: ALCIDS

Dovekie — Accidental; two November specimen records: 1931 in Lake of the Woods County and 1962 in Itasca County.

Ancient Murrelet — Accidental; seven records, mostly NE specimens: six in fall and the other a road-kill found in Crow Wing County in late February!

FAMILY COLUMBIDAE: DOVES AND PIGEONS

Rock Dove — Permanent resident throughout.

- ID: The plain old pigeon has actually been involved in misidentifications: slate-gray birds with white wing patches have been mistaken for magpies or White-winged Doves.

Band-tailed Pigeon — Accidental; eight or nine records, four of these in fall at Hawk Ridge in Duluth.

Eurasian Collared-Dove — Currently defined as Accidental, but in reality is now Regular in the S, with over a dozen records since the first record in 1998. Almost all the records so far in towns along or south of the Minnesota River, with at least one confirmed nesting record.

- ID: Escaped/released Ringed Turtle-Doves also turn up on occasion. Two most reliable collared-dove field marks are its call (a plain three-note "coo coooo coo," accented on second syllable; turtle-dove's call a two-syllabled, rolling "cook krrroooo,"), and its exact under tail pattern (black on outer web of outer rectrices, with black extending farther towards tail tip than on rest of under tail; turtle-dove lacks black on outer web of outer rectrices). Other secondary marks include collared-dove's larger size, darker overall plumage, especially on primaries and under tail coverts, and warier behavior. References: *American Birds* 41:1371-1379, *North American Birds* 53:348-353, and *The Loon* 72:107-110.

White-winged Dove — Accidental; two fall sight records from Duluth, in 1985 and 1994.

- ID: See Rock Dove.

Mourning Dove — Common in summer throughout; uncommon and local in winter, mostly at feeders S half.

Passenger Pigeon — Extinct; formerly nested throughout much of Minnesota.

Common Ground-Dove — Accidental; one October 1993 Duluth record.

FAMILY CUCULIDAE: CUCKOOS AND ANIS

Black-billed Cuckoo — Uncommon in summer throughout most years, but can be more common and widespread in years with tent caterpillar outbreaks. Most often found in thickets and edges of more open habitats, but is usually difficult to see, only sings sporadically, and often unresponsive to tape recordings.

- ID: Can show some reddish on flight feathers, though not as much as on Yellow-billed. Also beware of juvenile with yellowish orbital ring around eye like Yellow-billed. Confusion also results when Black-billed gives series of "kowp" notes similar to end of Yellow-billed's song; such a call only identifiable as Yellow-billed when these notes are preceded by rapid "ka ka ka ka" introductory series. Also note Eastern Chipmunk has a hollow, cuckoo-like "kuk" call.

Yellow-billed Cuckoo — Uncommon in summer mostly S half most years; numbers and range often fluctuate like Black-billed. Generally less common than Black-billed, but more likely in denser woodlands.

- ID: See Black-billed Cuckoo.

Groove-billed Ani — Accidental; about 10 scattered records, most of these in October.

FAMILY TYTONIDAE: BARN OWLS

Barn Owl — Now considered only Accidental, but it was probably a Regular permanent resident decades ago, with most records from the S half.

- ID: Solid buff-and-gray coloration on back/wings unique and diagnostic; also note relatively white and unmarked underparts, though any owl in flashlight or headlight beams can appear white. In flight, note buff patches on primaries similar to Long-eared and Short-eared owls. Raspy, screeching calls associated with this species also given by Long-eared Owls and juveniles of several species. Also see Snowy and Barred owls.

FAMILY STRIGIDAE: TYPICAL OWLS

Eastern Screech-Owl — Uncommon and local permanent resident in deciduous woods in the S half and adjacent NW and NE counties. Vocalizes year around and will respond to tapes by eventually flying into view; ventriloquial and usually closer than it sounds.

- ID: Can appear "earless" when feather tufts depressed; this in combination with its black facial frames has resulted in erroneous Boreal Owl reports. Call of American Toad (and other toads?) similar to screech-owl's trill.

Great Horned Owl — Common permanent resident throughout, except uncommon eastern NE. Often seen hunting at dusk, especially in more open country, and vocalizes year around.

- ID: Low-pitched hooting often mistaken for Great Gray or Long-eared owls' calls; whitish throat patch might also be confused with Great Gray's "bow tie." Grayish-white sub-arctic birds sometimes seen here in winter and appear as pale as some Snowy Owls.

Snowy Owl — Rare to locally uncommon N half and casually seen S half in winter, with the most consistent sightings in the Duluth-Superior harbor November-March, where a few are typically present. Also seen some winters in open bog country such as the Sax-Zim Bog (St. Louis County), northern Aitkin County, and the "Big Bog" of Lake of the Woods and northern Beltrami counties. Most actively hunts late afternoon or at dawn from conspicuous perches but often hard to find when roosting on the ground during midday; in Duluth look for it then on the harbor ice. Most individuals are immatures which appear darker, not lighter, than their whiter surroundings; most of those in Duluth have been marked by researchers with green wing tags and black head dye. Numbers fairly consistent each winter, but a few significant invasions have occurred: e.g., a record 351 in 1993-94, 153 in 1996-97, and 111 in 2000-01.

- ID: Dark immature females are whitest on face and under wings. Any owl in flashlight or headlights can appear whitish overall. Also see Great Horned Owl.

Northern Hawk Owl — Rare but Regular November to March in open country, mostly in the northern NE. Can be hard to find some years, but most winters one or more "stake-outs" typically hunt by day in the same place for weeks at a time, are relatively easy to see on their usually conspicuous perches, and these are regularly reported on the internet and Minnesota's three telephone hotlines. Most consistent locations are in the Sax-Zim Bog area (St. Louis County), northern Aitkin County, and in the "Big Bog" country of Lake of the Woods, Koochiching, and northern Beltrami counties. Numbers relatively consistent each winter with only a few significant invasions on record: e.g., 159 individuals in 1991-92, 100 in 1996-97, and a record 190 in 2000-01. Casual in summer with a few nesting records in NE bogs.

Burrowing Owl — Now only Casual in spring/summer in W grasslands; formerly local and Regular in the W, but has declined drastically in the state in recent years. Best looked for in pastures with colonies of Richardson's Ground Squirrels.

Barred Owl — Uncommon but widespread permanent resident in deciduous woods E half, and locally W in wooded areas from the Minnesota River north. More often heard than seen but usually responds to "squeaking" or tape recordings of its call, even by day, and vocalizes mostly late winter through summer. Often appears in higher numbers during Great Gray Owl invasion winters.

> • ID: Often appears to have heart-shaped face, similar to Barn Owl; some vocalizations, especially of juveniles, highly varied, difficult to describe, and also may suggest Barn Owl.

Great Gray Owl — Rare to locally uncommon permanent resident NE and in northern Roseau County. Most often seen during invasion winters which have occurred four times in the past ten years: 218 in 1991-92, 342 in 1995-96, 168 in 1996-97, and a record 394 in 2000-01. Concentrations are most frequent in the Duluth area, the Sax-Zim Bog, and northern Aitkin, Koochiching, and Roseau counties. Also regularly seen March-June on its breeding grounds, typically in or near tamarack bogs, especially in Sax-Zim, northern Aitkin County, and on Highway 310 (Roseau County). Hardest to find July through October. Seldom vocalizes, even in spring, and not very responsive to tapes. Most often spotted at dawn or dusk, sometimes in midday when overcast, hunting from low or mid-level perches along roadsides and the edges of fields and clearings, usually in more coniferous areas. Like other northern owls, Great Grays are regularly included on internet reports and hotlines.

> • ID: Most evident mark, even at a distance or in poor light, is white "bow tie" with black "knot" between the white. Also see Great Horned Owl.

Long-eared Owl — Rare in summer, mostly in N half in mixed or dense deciduous woods. Best looked for November to April when migrants and overwintering birds roost in dense conifer groves throughout, mostly S half. Some 20-50 are banded most years in October-November at Hawk Ridge in Duluth. Strictly nocturnal, only infrequently vocalizes, mostly unresponsive to tapes (but will sometimes fly in to squeaking/pishing), and arguably the most difficult of all the owls (including the Boreal) to find. Tends to perch next to the trunk in the top half of its roosting tree and to flush several yards ahead of you.

> • ID: When hunting, has same bouyant, erratic flight style as Short-eared; also shows similar buff patch on primaries and black carpal (wrist) mark. Short-eared has pale trailing edge of wings; Long-eared dark on trailing edge. Also see Barn and Great Horned owls.

Short-eared Owl — Rare to locally uncommon in summer mostly NW; also possible in open bogs and clearings in the NE. Uncommon W and rare E half in migration, and a few may winter locally in milder years. Most often seen hunting at dawn/dusk in NW grasslands and meadows during migration, especially southeast of Crookston (Polk County) and at Rothsay Wildlife Management Area (Wilkin County).

> • ID: See Barn and Long-eared owls.

Boreal Owl — Rare and local but Regular permanent resident in coniferous and mixed forests in northern NE. Nests in cavities, usually in older, upland aspens in predominantly spruce woods, and roosts by day and hunts by night mostly in lowland spruce bogs. Most often found when calling on territory, mid-March to early-April most years, especially in northern Cook, northern and central Lake, northern St. Louis, and northern Roseau counties. See the Lake County chapter for hints on finding this species on its breeding grounds. A few are typically reported in winter in the NE, usually found roosting in someone's yard (often by scolding chickadees) or hunting a roadside at dusk; unfortunately, these individuals hardly ever are still there the next day. One has a reasonable chance of seeing this species during invasion winters, which have occurred four times in recent years (but with most of these individuals dying of starvation): 194 individuals in 1988-89, 214 in 1995-96, 263 in 1996-97, and 259 in 2000-01. Hardly ever seen June-September, but at least one is banded most falls (late October-November) at Hawk Ridge in Duluth.

> • ID: Contrary to some field guide descriptions, this species never has and never will sound like dripping water or a high-pitched bell: that is the saw-whet owl's call! Boreal's call a rapid rising series of hoots, very similar to winnowing of snipe, usually given at regular intervals from one spot for long periods of time; snipe winnows at less regular intervals from moving locations as it flies around. Best separated visually from Northern Saw-whet Owl by black facial frames and darker markings on face; Boreal is also larger, has spotted forehead (streaked on saw-whet) and paler bill. Also see Eastern Screech-Owl.

Northern Saw-whet Owl — Uncommon but widespread in summer in mixed woods N half. Most easily found when calling on territory early April to mid-May, and most will respond by flying in to taped or whistled imitations of their call. Roosting fall migrants can also be seen at Duluth/the North Shore, especially late September to mid-October, by carefully searching coniferous trees; they are also attracted then to tapes/whistles. Hundreds are banded at Hawk Ridge in Duluth in fall, especially on colder nights with light winds (the one-night record is 292!). Widespread but rare in migration elsewhere and locally possible throughout in winter, especially SE. Unlike Long-eareds, saw-whets tend to roost in the lower branches of conifers and to freeze rather than flush as you approach; like other owls, they can often be found by following scolding chickadees.

> • ID: See Boreal Owl.

FAMILY CAPRIMULGIDAE: NIGHTJARS

Common Nighthawk — Common in summer throughout; most easily seen/heard at dusk over cities. Thousands of late afternoon-early evening migrants pass through Duluth in mid- to late August, with a record 43,000-plus (!) on a single August evening in 1990; numbers seem to be declining in recent years.

> • ID: See Common Goldeneye and American Woodcock (their buzzing vocalizations are often confused with this species).

Common Poorwill — Accidental; one found dead in April 1963 in Swift County.

Chuck-will's-widow — Accidental; an individual sang from the same Sherburne County location for four consecutive summers, 1981-84; one other June 1984 heard-only record from Nicollet County.

Whip-poor-will — Uncommon and local but widespread in summer in most of N half and eastern SE; most easily found northern NW and in the Mississippi River valley southern SE. Its range and habitat preference are poorly understood, but most often found on wooded hillsides with clearings (NE and southern SE), in aspen parklands (NW), or in drier, sandier areas of oak and pine (northern SE). Not difficult to hear and often responds to tape recorders by flying overhead and resuming calling nearby.

FAMILY APODIDAE: SWIFTS

Chimney Swift — Common in summer throughout.

White-throated Swift — Accidental; a specimen record from the Twin Cities in May 2000.

FAMILY TROCHILIDAE: HUMMINGBIRDS

Magnificent Hummingbird — Accidental; three summer records.

Ruby-throated Hummingbird — Common in summer throughout, mostly in more wooded counties.

> • ID: Some juveniles show a bronzy tint on back and might be confused with Rufous Hummingbirds. Large sphinx moths also feed on flower nectar, and are quite hummingbird-like.

Anna's Hummingbird — Accidental; three late fall records at feeders: 1991 in Grand Marais, 1993 in Chisago County, and 2001 in the Twin Cities.

Calliope Hummingbird — Accidental; one late fall record at a Twin Cities feeder in 1994.

Rufous Hummingbird — Accidental, but possibly Casual; about 10 records, mostly in late summer and fall in the E half. All but one have been adult males, the one exception a specimen, so we have yet to be confronted with the Allen's Hummingbird ID problem.

> • ID: See Ruby-throated Hummingbird. References: *Birding* 29:18-29 and *Advanced Birding* guide.

FAMILY ALCEDINIDAE: KINGFISHERS

Belted Kingfisher — Common in summer throughout; a few winter locally in milder years, mostly SE.

FAMILY PICIDAE: WOODPECKERS

Lewis's Woodpecker — Accidental; three records.

Red-headed Woodpecker — Uncommon in summer throughout except NE, and more local NW; a few sometimes winter locally SE. Generally prefers oaks and woodlots in farmlands; formerly more common.

Red-bellied Woodpecker — Common permanent resident S half, especially SE.

Williamson's Sapsucker — Accidental; three records.

Yellow-bellied Sapsucker — Common in summer throughout except southern SW.

> • ID: A common mistake is to confuse a juvenile with a Three-toed Woodpecker because of its barred back. Yellow-bellied Sapsucker occasionally has red spot on nape and could easily be misidentified as Red-naped. On female Yellow-bellied note all-white throat (red and white on female Red-naped); on male note complete black malar line (this line broken on male Red-naped). References: *American Birds* 42:348-350, *Birding* 23:20-26, and *Advanced Birding* guide.

Downy Woodpecker — Common permanent resident throughout.

Hairy Woodpecker — Common permanent resident throughout; usually outnumbered by Downys.

Three-toed Woodpecker — Rare permanent resident in northern NE coniferous forests, with most records from mid-winter into early summer when drumming on territory and responsive to taped imitations of its drumming. Only a handful of confirmed breeding records exist. Always outnumbered by Black-backeds and one of the most difficult Regular species to find, but possible in conifers wherever Black-backeds occur, and tends to prefer smaller trees in black spruce bogs. Most sightings in recent years are along the Spruce Road (Lake County).

> • ID: See Black-backed Woodpecker and Yellow-bellied Sapsucker.

Black-backed Woodpecker — Rare to locally uncommon permanent resident in northern NE coniferous forests, especially in burned areas and in cut-over areas where snags have been left standing. Most often seen in Lake and Cook counties, especially along Lake County Road 2 and the Gunflint Trail, and best looked for February-June when on nesting territory and when responsive to taped imitations of its drumming. When young are still in nest cavities in June, listen for their loud, kingfisher-like, food-begging chatter. Otherwise quieter, more inconspicuous and harder to find than other woodpeckers. Like the Three-toed, forages by flaking bark off coniferous tree trunks, often near the ground or on fallen logs; in winter their presence often indicated by chips of bark lying on the snow. Like the Three-toed, never known to appear at feeders and seldom seen in deciduous woods. Migrant Black-backeds are frequently seen along the North Shore of Lake Superior, mostly late September-early November, and some often stop in the pines along the Pinewoods Trail at Hawk Ridge in Duluth.

- ID: Larger size overall than Three-toed; male's yellow cap appears larger with more clean-cut edges than Three-toed's. Barred backs of many Three-toeds obscure and often difficult to see, resulting in these being miscalled Black-backeds. Black-backed's call note a unique, somewhat metallic or squeaky "krik," unlike Three-toed's call which is a simple Downy-like "pic;" both species also have a raspy, rattling "growl" call. Territorial drummings usually differ: Black-backed's is long, slow, often gradually trailing off at end, and similar to Pileated's; Three-toed's drumming also slow but usually shorter and two-parted, with a few abrupt lower-pitched taps added at the end.

Northern Flicker — Common in summer throughout; a few might winter locally S half.

- ID: Call series normally lower-pitched and longer than Pileated's.

Pileated Woodpecker — Uncommon but widespread permanent resident in mature deciduous and mixed woodlands throughout except southern SW.

- ID: See Black-backed Woodpecker and Northern Flicker.

FAMILY TYRANNIDAE: FLYCATCHERS

Olive-sided Flycatcher — Uncommon and local in summer in coniferous forests NE. Almost always perches on high and conspicuous dead branches. More easily found in migration, and one of the earliest fall migrants, often appearing in the S half by late July.

- ID: See Eastern Wood-Pewee.

Western Wood-Pewee — Now considered Accidental, but formerly Casual, with seven records, all involving singing males; a pair nested in 1977 and 1978 in Roseau County.

- ID: See Eastern Wood-Pewee.

Eastern Wood-Pewee — Common in summer in deciduous woods throughout.

- ID: Eastern and Western wood-pewees safely separable only by songs and calls: "pee yer" call of Eastern clearly two-syllabled, not as burry or nasal as one-syllabled "peer" call of Western (but beware hoarse food-begging call of juvenile Eastern). Wood-pewees easily mistaken for Alder and Willow flycatchers (which also typically lack eye rings); they can also appear "vested" and resemble Olive-sided Flycatcher (which has solid, darker sides contrasting more with center of underparts). Also see Eastern Phoebe (often misidentified as wood-pewee). Reference: *Advanced Birding* guide.

Yellow-bellied Flycatcher — Uncommon but widespread in summer in coniferous forests NE; arrives in late May and sings until early July (and difficult to find when not singing). Most often seen in northern Aitkin, St. Louis (e.g., the Sax-Zim Bog), central Lake, and Cook (e.g., the Gunflint Trail) counties. Migrants are not hard to find during peak migration E half.

- ID: Song a liquid or metallic "killik" or "chebunk," accented on first syllable, phrases separated by long pauses; Least's "chebek" snappier, accented on second syllable, phrases rapidly repeated. Yellow-bellied's call note a musical, whistled "chu wee." Uniformly yellowish below from throat to under tail coverts with olive wash across breast; upperparts often look greener than on other Empidonax. Eye ring bold, often "tear"- or "almond"-shaped, and sometimes yellow. References: *Birding* 17:151-158, 17:277-287, 18:153-159 and 18:315-327, and *Advanced Birding* guide.

Acadian Flycatcher — Rare or uncommon and quite local in summer in southern SE deciduous woods. Sings mid-May through July, and has long been consistently found at Beaver Creek Valley State Park (Houston County). Also regularly present in the Twin Cities (at Elm Creek and Murphy-Hanrehan park reserves) and in heavily wooded tracts along the Minnesota, Cannon, Zumbro, and other SE rivers. Has either increased in numbers in recent years or has been discovered in areas previously overlooked.

- ID: Song a loud, abrupt "peet seet," accented on second syllable (song often described as "pizza," but that is accented on first syllable); call note a loud "peet." Eye ring often indistinct. Long primary extension beyond tertials; bill relatively long and wide. References: see Yellow-bellied Flycatcher.

Alder Flycatcher — Common and widespread in summer N half and northern SE. Easily heard late May to early July, mostly in alder swamps, but also locally in aspen groves in the NW. Late spring migrants in June frequently occur in the S half.

- ID: Alders and Willows not separable in the field except by breeding range or vocalizations. Alders never have and never will say "fee-bee-o," as described in field guides; song better described as a two-syllabled, burry "free beer," accented on second syllable. Call notes include a diagnostic, musical "peep," unlike Willow or Least, and a burry, siskin-like "zhreer." Willow's song a sneezy "fitz bew," with syllables equally accented; commonly gives two call notes: a burry "sprrit" or "fitz," and a "wit" or "wheat" (unlike Alder and more similar to Least). Eye rings on both Alders and Willows typically faint or lacking. Both have long primary extension and large bills, like Acadian. Also see Eastern Wood-Pewee. References: see Yellow-bellied Flycatcher.

Willow Flycatcher — Uncommon and local in summer S half and southern NW; most often found late May to early July when singing from willow and other thickets. Willows and Alders overlap in the NW and northern SE, with Alders preferring the edges of groves with larger trees and Willows usually in wetter thickets in more open areas.

- ID: See Alder Flycatcher.

Least Flycatcher — Common and widespread in summer in deciduous and mixed woods throughout. The Empidonax most often seen in migration.

• ID: Song a snappy, oft-repeated "chebek;" call note a flat "wit." Eye ring typically bold, often "tear"-shaped like Yellow-bellied. Has noticeably small bill which results in large-headed appearance; also has shorter primary extension than other *Empidonax*. References: see Yellow-bellied Flycatcher.

Black Phoebe — Accidental; one somewhat vague but accepted September 1952 sight record from Lac Qui Parle County (which may be reconsidered).

Eastern Phoebe — Common in summer throughout; the only flycatcher likely to be seen before late April or after early October.

• ID: Contrary to field guide illustrations, phoebes often show obvious wing bars and are then frequently mistaken for wood-pewees, especially in early spring. Besides tail-wagging behavior, note phoebe's head is darkest part of plumage.

Say's Phoebe — Casual; about 20 records, mostly in spring in the W.

Vermilion Flycatcher — Accidental; three late fall records.

Ash-throated Flycatcher — Accidental; two November records: 1990 in Morrison County and 2000 in Lake County.

• ID references: *The Loon* 63:4-11 and *American Birds* 36:241-247.

Great Crested Flycatcher — Common in summer in deciduous woods throughout except northern NE. Late fall migrants sometimes appear along the North Shore of Lake Superior (where there is one Ash-throated record).

Western Kingbird — Uncommon and local most years in summer W and northern SE, most often in towns and farm groves. Formerly more common.

Eastern Kingbird — Common in summer throughout.

Scissor-tailed Flycatcher — Considered Casual, but probably Regular with records almost annually in recent years. Possible statewide from May to October, with several Duluth/North Shore records in fall.

Fork-tailed Flycatcher — Accidental; two records, one from Duluth in September 1991 and the other from Grand Marais the following May.

FAMILY LANIIDAE: SHRIKES

Loggerhead Shrike — Mostly rare, quite local, and declining in summer and migration W and SE. Mostly prefers thickets near unplowed grasslands and pastures along the Minnesota River valley, especially in the vicinities of Mankato and Appleton, and at the Felton Prairie (Clay County). Generally arrives in April and departs in October; sometimes reported in winter but hardly ever adequately documented then.

• ID: See Northern Shrike.

Northern Shrike — Uncommon but widespread most winters throughout in open areas, mostly N half. Generally present late October-early April, hunts over a wide area from conspicuous perches, seldom stays on one perch for long, and an individual is usually difficult to relocate on subsequent days.

• ID: Field guides often stress black extending over top of Loggerhead's bill and Northern's pale base of bill and underparts barring; these marks difficult to see, even at close range, which leads to Northerns mistaken for Loggerheads in winter. Shrikes best separated by bill shapes: longer and more strongly hooked on Northern; stubbier and more finch-like on Loggerhead, with hooked tip less obvious. Masks also useful and typically diagnostic: wider, blacker, and more solid on Loggerhead; Northern's mask thinner (more an eye line than a mask) and usually broken in front of eye. Beware, however, juvenile Loggerheads with narrower mask not meeting over top of bill. Even without comparison, Northern may appear larger, paler gray overall, with whiter rump and more white above mask. A shrike in Minnesota May through September is "always" a Loggerhead; a shrike November through February almost always a Northern.

FAMILY VIREONIDAE: VIREOS

White-eyed Vireo — Now considered Casual in spring/summer, with most records from the SE, but approaching Regular status with records almost annually in recent years.

Bell's Vireo — Rare and local in summer mostly in southern SE thickets, with the most consistent location for years at McCarthy Lake Wildlife Management Area (Wabasha County). Also reported in recent years in Winona County and the Twin Cities (at Black Dog Lake and Fort Snelling State Park), and often reported elsewhere in the S half now with better observer coverage. Much more easily heard than seen.

Yellow-throated Vireo — Common in summer in deciduous woods throughout except northern NE and southern SW.

Blue-headed Vireo — Common in summer NE in mixed or coniferous woods.

Warbling Vireo — Common in summer throughout except eastern NE.

- ID: See Philadelphia Vireo.

Philadelphia Vireo — Quite local but probably uncommon in summer in eastern NE, but generally hard to find and thought of as rare since their song is so similar to the common and widespread Red-eyed Vireo's (both species will respond to the tape of the other's song). Definitely overlooked, therefore, its distribution probably less understood than any other Minnesota species. In summer most often seen along the North Shore of Lake Superior in Cook and southeastern Lake counties, especially in the vicinity of Grand Marais and along Lake County Roads 4 and 7. Sometimes found in summer farther north away from the lake. Seems to prefer mature birch trees over aspens, especially those at the edge of a cut-over area or in an alder swamp. More easily found in migration, especially fall, when uncommon throughout.

- ID: Warbling Vireo often yellowish on flanks and under tail and thus confused with Philadelphia; note Philadelphia's yellowish breast (white on Warbling) and distinctive black lores (Warbling is whitish on lores and around "beadier" black eye). Philadelphia similar to fall Tennessee Warbler, but bill thicker and crown higher and rounder than on the flatter-headed Tennessee. Philadelphia's song often sounds identical to Red-eyed's, but is typically thinner, higher-pitched, and sometimes slower. Call notes clearly differ: Philadelphia's call multi-syllabled, raspy, and scolding (Yellow-throated's and Blue-headed's calls similar); Warbling's call one-syllabled, catbird-like, pitch and volume increasing at end; Red-eyed's call also one-syllabled, but shorter, sharper, and dropping in pitch. Reference: *Advanced Birding* guide.

Red-eyed Vireo — Common and widespread and easily heard (but harder to see) in deciduous and mixed forests in summer throughout.

- ID: See Philadelphia Vireo and Purple Finch (which often gives Red-eyed Vireo-like calls).

FAMILY CORVIDAE: CORVIDS

Gray Jay — Uncommon but widespread permanent resident NE in coniferous and mixed forests; generally quiet and easily overlooked. October migrants also occur most years in Duluth and along the North Shore of Lake Superior.

Blue Jay — Common permanent resident throughout the state, but less common and more local in winter N half, mostly at feeders. Thousands migrate through Duluth, mostly in fall.

Clark's Nutcracker — Accidental in fall; three invasion years, most recently in 1972, have been documented with multiple scattered records.

Black-billed Magpie — Uncommon permanent resident in aspen parklands and farm groves in the northern NW and adjacent NE counties. A few also are present locally in northern Aitkin County and the Sax-Zim Bog (St. Louis Co.).

- ID: See Rock Dove and American Crow.

American Crow — Common permanent resident throughout, though uncommon and local in winter N half. Thousands migrate in late fall through Duluth.

- ID: Smaller size, smaller bill/head/neck profile, different flight style, and shorter, rounder tail often difficult to tell from Common Raven without direct comparison. Some crows often give more guttural call, unlike normal "cawing," and can be mistaken for ravens. Beware especially of crows in molt, especially in fall, when tail shapes sometimes irregular, wedge-shaped, and quite raven-like. Also note partial albinistic crows with white wing patches occur; these can be mistaken for magpies.

Common Raven — Common permanent resident NE and locally uncommon in winter northern SE. Commonly seen in fall migration at Hawk Ridge in Duluth.

- ID: See American Crow.

FAMILY ALAUDIDAE: LARKS

Horned Lark — Common in summer and migration W and SE; also common in fall NE. Uncommon some winters, mostly SW, with northbound migrants starting to return in the S half by late January.

- ID: Juveniles, not adequately shown in most field guides, lack black head and throat markings, have white outer tail feathers and thin bills, and run on ground; these are frequently misidentified as Sprague's Pipits. Adults typically show rusty area on wing coverts; this in combination with black on head and breast could result in erroneous McCown's Longspur reports.

FAMILY HIRUNDINIDAE: SWALLOWS

Purple Martin — Common in summer throughout, but only local or absent in eastern NE.

- ID: Females are grayish-brown with dusky throats and sometimes mistaken for rough-winged swallows.

Martin's flight usually distinctive with longer glides and slower wingbeats than other swallows.

Tree Swallow — Common in summer throughout.

> • ID: Brownish juveniles often have a dusky breast band and are mistaken for Bank Swallows; Tree Swallow's band incomplete, more diffuse, lacks Bank's V-shape on lower edge. Note white underparts extend higher on sides of rump, suggesting Violet-green's pattern. Reference: *Birding* 17:209-211.

Violet-green Swallow — Accidental; two accepted sight-only records: October 1942 in Rochester and July 1990 in Dodge County.

> • ID: See Tree Swallow.

Northern Rough-winged Swallow — Uncommon in summer throughout.

> • ID: See Purple Martin. Flight often noticeably slower with deeper wingbeats than Bank Swallow. Also note Bank's paler rump and higher-pitched, more chattering call (rough-winged's call lower-pitched and only one- or two-syllabled). References: *Birding* 17: 209-211 and 28:111-116.

Bank Swallow — Locally common in summer throughout, especially near gravel pits.

> • ID: See Tree and Northern Rough-winged swallows.

Cliff Swallow — Common in summer throughout, especially N half.

Barn Swallow — Common in summer throughout.

FAMILY PARIDAE: CHICKADEES AND TITMICE

Black-capped Chickadee — Common permanent resident throughout.

Boreal Chickadee — Uncommon permanent resident NE in coniferous forests, though mostly absent from pines; seldom seen in deciduous woods or at bird feeders (except those with suet). Usually difficult to find, quiet, relatively shy, forages in the interior branches of denser conifers, and always outnumbered by Black-cappeds. Best located by its calls, and will usually (but not always) respond to tape recordings at all times of year. Most often seen in northern Aitkin County, the Sax-Zim Bog (St. Louis County), in central Lake County (County Road 2 and Spruce Road), and along the Gunflint Trail (Cook County). Also uncommon in fall migration most years (mostly October) in Duluth and along the North Shore of Lake Superior.

> • ID: Sooty grayish-brown overall and lacks Black-capped's more clean-cut overall appearance; colors of Boreal's cap, back, cheeks, and sides blend in with each other. Brown cap often difficult to see, but cheeks noticeably grayer than Black-capped's whiter, more contrasting cheeks. Best field mark is buzzier, more nasal and slower "chick a dee" or "zhick zhee" call. Song is a slow, musical, one-pitched trill preceded by introductory note.

Tufted Titmouse — Rare and local permanent resident southern SE in extensive deciduous woods; most often reported over the years at Beaver Creek Valley State Park (Houston County) and at feeders in Rochester and Houston County. Unless "staked-out" at a feeder, one of the most difficult Regular species to find in Minnesota. Formerly more common.

FAMILY SITTIDAE: NUTHATCHES

Red-breasted Nuthatch — Common permanent resident in NE and northern SE in mixed or coniferous woods. Also uncommon most winters throughout, especially at feeders, and more common and widespread during invasion years.

> • ID: Some juvenile females are quite whitish on underparts with little rusty coloration and might be misidentified.

White-breasted Nuthatch — Common permanent resident throughout, though uncommon and local eastern NE.

Pygmy Nuthatch — Accidental; one October 1996 record from Clay County.

FAMILY CERTHIIDAE: CREEPERS

Brown Creeper — Uncommon in summer NE and locally so eastern SE; a few winter throughout, mostly S half.

FAMILY TROGLODYTIDAE: WRENS

Rock Wren — Casual during migration and summer; about 15 records, and possible statewide.

Carolina Wren — Currently listed as Regular, but rare and local and possibly still only Casual. Most records are in migration and winter at SE feeders.

Bewick's Wren — Now considered Accidental, with most records in the SE in spring; formerly more frequent with a few nesting records.

House Wren — Common in summer throughout.

> • ID: See Winter Wren.

Winter Wren — Common in summer in predominantly coniferous forests NE; also uncommon and local eastern SE along the St. Croix and Mississippi rivers. More often heard than seen, often singing from the higher branches of a tall spruce. Migrates throughout, earlier in spring and later in fall than House Wren, in areas with dense undergrowth; consistently found each October in the Hawk Ridge pine plantation in Duluth.

> • ID: House Wrens are also barred under tail and can appear short-tailed like Winter Wrens; note Winter's paler supercilium contrasting more with darker overall plumage. Winter's call note distinctive, usually two-syllabled, a somewhat blackbird-like "chimp chimp" or "chak chak."

Sedge Wren — Common and widespread in summer throughout, though more local eastern NE. Often highly-sought by visiting birders, this species is easily heard (often at night) and seen May through July in sedge marshes, hayfields, and alder swamps.

> • ID: Juvenile Marsh Wren, with its less distinct supercilium and back streaks, resembles Sedge Wren; best separated by solid dark crown (streaked on Sedge Wren). Also see Common Yellowthroat.

Marsh Wren — Common in summer in cattail-type marshes throughout except eastern NE; more often heard than seen, and often unresponsive to tapes. Eastern and western populations may be separate species, separable by song types, but which one occurs in Minnesota has yet to be determined.

> • ID: See Sedge Wren.

FAMILY CINCLIDAE: DIPPERS

American Dipper — Accidental; one record (of more than one individual?) from four North Shore rivers in Lake and Cook counties, January-April 1970; since then there have been other reports from NE rivers in summer, only one of these accepted by MOURC — marginally. Either vagrants occur on occasion, or see below.

> • ID: Other dark birds like catbirds and blackbirds might stand on rocks in rivers and appear short-tailed as juveniles; some recently fledged grackles also have dipper-like whitish legs/feet.

FAMILY REGULIDAE: KINGLETS

Golden-crowned Kinglet — Common but hard to see in summer in coniferous woods NE. Uncommon mostly SE most winters, and throughout some years.

> • ID: Often sings partial song without the descending ending; notes usually rise in pitch, but otherwise song is very similar to Cape May Warbler's.

Ruby-crowned Kinglet — Common in summer NE and in migration throughout.

FAMILY SYLVIIDAE: GNATCATCHERS

Blue-gray Gnatcatcher — Common in summer in deciduous woods mostly SE, but a few also now occur annually in summer and migration southern NW, southern NE, and in wooded SW areas. Much more common and widespread in recent years.

FAMILY TURDIDAE: THRUSHES

Northern Wheatear — Accidental; two September records: 1982 in the Twin Cities and 1995 in Duluth.

Eastern Bluebird — Common in summer throughout, though only local or absent in heavily wooded parts of NE and in more open country of the SW.

> • ID: See Mountain Bluebird.

Mountain Bluebird — Rare but Regular throughout, with most records W in grasslands in early spring, and in Duluth and the North Shore of Lake Superior in fall. Also possible in summer NW (where there are a few nesting records) and in winter in junipers in the SE (a bluebird in winter is just as likely a Mountain as an Eastern).

> • ID: Females may have a rusty wash on underparts and be misidentified as Easterns. Note Mountain's slimmer shape, grayer upperparts, less extensive and paler shade of blue, and all-black bill (Eastern's bill bicolored). Reference: *American Birds* 46:159-162.

Townsend's Solitaire — Rare but Regular in fall-winter throughout, with a few sightings most years. Most often found at Duluth and the North Shore in fall and early winter (October-December), usually in mountain ash trees.

Veery — Common and easily heard in summer in deciduous woods N half and SE.

> • ID: Cheeks are typically grayish, and orange-brownish plumage difficult to see in poor light, and thus Veery can be mistaken for Gray-cheeked Thrush. Note Veery's "veeur" or "vuree" call notes (also given at night by migrants). Reference: *Birding* 32:242-254.

Gray-cheeked Thrush — Uncommon migrant throughout, always outnumbered by Swainson's, and often hard to see. Not present here in summer.

> • ID: See Veery and Hermit Thrush. Call note "veer," raspier, sharper, and higher-pitched than Veery; similar call given by nocturnal migrants. Reference: *Birding* 32:318-331.

Swainson's Thrush — Uncommon in summer in coniferous forests northern NE; common throughout during migration.

> • ID: See Hermit Thrush. Call note a sharp "wick;" nocturnal migrants give a high-pitched "peep" (similar to Spring Peeper). Reference: *Birding* 32:242-254.

Hermit Thrush — Common in summer NE in predominantly coniferous woods, often in jack pines. The only Catharus thrush likely to be seen after October or before late April, and the only one possible in winter.

> • ID: Cheeks often grayish, eye ring often buffy, and in dim light reddish tail difficult to see; Hermits thus often misidentified as Gray-cheekeds or Swainson's, especially in early spring or late fall. Call note a soft "chuck;" nocturnal migrants have call note similar to Swainson's "peep" note, but thinner and higher-pitched. Song often confused with Wood Thrush but includes introductory "key" note not given by Wood Thrush. Reference: *Birding* 32:120-135.

Wood Thrush — Uncommon and local in summer in mature deciduous woods SE, southern NE, and along the Minnesota River in the SW; not often seen during migration. Formerly more common.

> • ID: Call note of nocturnal migrants short, burry, and low-pitched. Also see Hermit Thrush.

Fieldfare — Accidental; one record near Grand Marais in November 1991.

American Robin — Common in summer throughout; locally possible throughout in milder winters, mostly SE. Thousands migrate in October through Duluth.

Varied Thrush — Rare but Regular in fall-winter throughout, with almost all records at feeders, mostly E half, especially in Duluth and the Twin Cities. Sometimes also seen in mountain ash trees, but generally secretive and prefers yards with coniferous trees.

FAMILY MIMIDAE: MIMIC THRUSHES

Gray Catbird — Common in summer throughout.

Northern Mockingbird — Rare but Regular, usually in migration throughout. Seen only a few times most years, with many of the records at Duluth and the North Shore of Lake Superior. Prefers feeders, junipers, and mountain ash trees. Also possible almost anywhere in the state in summer and winter.

Sage Thrasher — Accidental; eight scattered records.

Brown Thrasher — Common in summer throughout, except uncommon and more local NE in heavily wooded areas.

Curve-billed Thrasher — Accidental; three records.

FAMILY STURNIDAE: STARLINGS

European Starling — Common permanent resident throughout, except uncommon and more local in winter northern NE.

> • ID: Since starlings mimic many other birds, make sure no starlings are nearby before reporting a heard-only species out-of-season or out-of-range.

FAMILY MOTACILLIDAE: PIPITS

American Pipit — Uncommon in spring, mostly W, and common in fall throughout, usually along the shores of lakes and sewage ponds. Most easily found at Duluth and the North Shore of Lake Superior in September-October.

> • ID: A confusing bird for beginners since it is quite variable in plumage and not illustrated well in some field guides. Besides white outer tail feathers, note walking and tail-wagging behavior, usually buffy underparts with "necklace" of streaks on breast, elongated shape, and thinner bill and longer tail than larks, sparrows, and longspurs.

Sprague's Pipit — Now only Casual, but may be overlooked and possibly still rare-Regular in NW grasslands and lightly grazed pastures during migration/summer. Probably best looked for in the Felton Prairie area (Clay County). Formerly considered a locally Regular summer resident NW (especially at Felton), but there is only one recent breeding record (1988 in Polk County).

> • ID: See Horned Lark (juveniles often mistaken for Sprague's Pipits). Species has a long history of inadequate field guide illustrations. In life, it is grayish-buff overall, underparts paler with thin "necklace" of streaks on breast, "beady" black eye on relatively unmarked face, ear coverts and lores often with yellow wash, bill thicker than American Pipit's and bicolored (culmen darker), and crown thinly streaked. Shape often distinctive with small head, thin neck, and "pot belly." Never has and never will wag its tail. Breezy aerial flight song suggests Veery's and easily confused with second song of Grasshopper Sparrow (which is unfamiliar to most birders). Call note a sharp "squeet," sometimes two- or three-syllabled.

FAMILY BOMBYCILLIDAE: WAXWINGS

Bohemian Waxwing — Usually common, but also local and unpredictable (and often frustrating) in fall-winter, mostly N half and northern SE. Almost all records are in cities and towns where they feed on mountain ash, buckthorn berries, crab apples, etc. Most reliable at Duluth and the North Shore of Lake Superior late October-February, but sometimes harder to find in mid- to late winter after food supplies have been depleted. Typically occurs in flocks of a few dozen to a few hundred birds which can be conspicuous and vocal in a neighborhood one day and then literally disappear overnight.

> • ID: Beware juvenile Cedar Waxwings which have grayish underparts; also note Cedar's white edge of tertials, visible on perched birds, which could be confused with white markings on Bohemian's wing. Buzzier, lower-pitched call is often slightly trilled. Has starling-like appearance in flight.

Cedar Waxwing — Common in summer throughout; locally uncommon most winters S half, but possible throughout. Thousands migrate in fall through Duluth.

> • ID: See Bohemian Waxwing.

FAMILY PARULIDAE: WOOD-WARBLERS

Blue-winged Warbler — Uncommon in summer southern SE, in semi-open areas and clearings within deciduous forests north to the Twin Cities. Not often seen during migration.

- ID: Do not rely on song alone to identify out-of-range Blue-winged or Golden-winged, since one species (not to mention the hybrids) can sing the other's song.

Golden-winged Warbler — Uncommon in summer in most of NE (absent or local northeast of Duluth) and northern SE north of the Twin Cities. Widespread but hard to find unless singing, preferring edge habitats, alder swamps mixed with trees, and semi-open woods with birch snags or black ash trees. Stop and listen frequently and you will eventually find one singing at some random location. Only infrequently seen during migration.

- ID: See Blue-winged Warbler.

Tennessee Warbler — Uncommon in summer some years northern NE, rare or absent other years; prefers taller aspens in predominantly coniferous forests. Common in migration throughout, and quite vocal in May.

- ID: See Philadelphia Vireo and Orange-crowned Warbler.

Orange-crowned Warbler — Uncommon migrant throughout, mostly late April-early May and late September-October. Not present here in summer.

- ID: Tennessees are sometimes yellowish under tail like Orange-crowneds; Orange-crowned's underparts duller, faintly streaked, and contrast little with upperparts (fall Tennessee brighter yellow below with more contrast with greenish upperparts). Some Yellows in fall are quite dull, may be vaguely streaked below, and also strongly resemble Orange-crowneds, which are often erroneously reported in August and early September; most Orange-crowneds first arrive in late September after most Yellows are gone. Typical song a distinctive two-part trill with second half lower-pitched, but song often one-pitched and difficult to tell from Wilson's. References: *American Birds* 45:167-170 and *Advanced Birding* guide.

Nashville Warbler — Common, widespread, and vocal in mixed and coniferous forests in summer NE and adjacent counties SE.

- ID: Overly optimistic beginners often mistake Nashvilles for Connecticut Warblers, especially since some females have grayish throats; note Nashville's smaller size and more active foraging in the higher branches (Connecticuts are larger, slower, lower, secretive, and walk more than hop). Also see Yellow-rumped Warbler.

Northern Parula — Uncommon in summer NE in mixed and coniferous forests; locally common where the Spanish moss-like lichen Usnea is found.

- ID: Typically looks smaller and chunkier than other warblers; parula's wing bars also distinctive, appearing shorter and thicker than other warblers'. One song very similar to Cerulean Warbler's but usually with diagnostic note dropping in pitch at end; this song at a distance also difficult to tell from faster Black-throated Blue song.

Yellow Warbler — Common in summer throughout; most fall migrants depart during August.

- ID: "Beady" black eye surrounded by yellow typically diagnostic, unlike female/juvenile Wilson's Warbler; Wilson's also darker than Yellow on cap. Yellow's song extremely variable, often nondescript, and hard to distinguish from the Chestnut-sided's, Magnolia's, American Redstart's, or Wilson's. Also see Orange-crowned Warbler. Reference: *American Birds* 45:167-170.

Chestnut-sided Warbler — Common in summer NE and adjacent counties NW and SE. Prefers edges and more open woodlands.

- ID: Fall birds more distinctive than many birders expect, with white eye ring, thick yellow wing bars, pale lime-green upperparts, and uniform off-white underparts. Alternate song nondescript, lacks distinctive drop-off at end, and resembles Yellow's and Magnolia's songs.

Magnolia Warbler — Common in summer NE in mixed and coniferous forests.

- ID: See Yellow, Chestnut-sided and Canada warblers, and American Redstart. Call note unique and un-warbler-like: hollow and "false"-sounding, suggesting a thrush, goldfinch, or Bobolink.

Cape May Warbler — Uncommon and local in summer northern NE in predominantly coniferous forests. Usually sings inconspicuous song from the tops of spruce trees and easy to miss. Often found along the Gunflint Trail (Cook County) and at the Rabey tree farm (Aitkin County). Also uncommon in spring; most easily seen as a fall migrant (August-September) at Duluth and the North Shore of Lake Superior, again mostly in spruce trees.

- ID: Some fall birds brightly, distinctively marked, but others quite dull and resemble Yellow-rumpeds: note Cape May's dull yellowish rump, pale mark on side of neck, color and streaks on underparts more uniformly distributed (Yellow-rumped's rump brighter, tinge of yellow and streaks on underparts more limited to sides of breast). Alternate song two-syllabled and virtually identical to Bay-breasted's; also see Golden-crowned Kinglet and Blackburnian Warbler.

Black-throated Blue Warbler — Rare to locally uncommon in summer only in Lake and Cook counties, mostly along or near the Superior Hiking Trail. Prefers mature and shady deciduous trees, especially maples with a few birch or balsam fir mixed in, a shrubby understory, and hillsides. Most consistently found on the west side of Tettegouche State Park (Lake County) and at Oberg Mountain (Cook County). Only rarely seen E half in migration (May and September).

- **ID:** See Northern Parula and Black-throated Green Warbler.

Yellow-rumped Warbler — Common in summer NE; widespread in migration and seen by the thousands in fall in Duluth. The most likely warbler to occasionally appear in the state November-March. Audubon's-type Yellow-rumpeds are casually seen in migration.

- **ID:** Some migrating juveniles in early fall still in molt and appear distinctively drab, quite "ragged," and unlike other warblers. Variable song nondescript: sometimes confusingly buzzy, other times almost identical to Nashville's. Also see Cape May and Palm warblers.

Black-throated Gray Warbler — Accidental; five records.

Black-throated Green Warbler — Common, vocal, and widespread in summer NE in mixed and deciduous forests.

- **ID:** Alternate "zee zee zoo zoo zee" song is relatively slow and can be confused with Black-throated Blue's.

Townsend's Warbler — Accidental; two Twin Cities records and two records the same day (30 April 1994) at opposite ends of Lac Qui Parle County!

Hermit Warbler — Accidental; two May records: 1931 in Isanti County and 1983 in Lac Qui Parle County.

Blackburnian Warbler — Common in summer NE in mixed and coniferous forests. Usually sings near the tops of spruce trees.

- **ID:** Has several songs, with variation most often heard in Minnesota suggesting Cape May or Bay-breasted: "tsss-ssah tsss-ssah tsss-ssah," usually three high, thin phrases with diagnostic lisping quality, but without thinner, higher-pitched ending characteristic of its other songs.

Yellow-throated Warbler — Currently listed as Casual, but in recent years has been essentially Regular in spring/summer, mostly in the SE, with one breeding record. Seen annually, 1994-2000, at Sibley State Park (Kandiyohi County) and probably bred there.

Pine Warbler — Uncommon in summer NE and adjacent SE counties, though more local or absent eastern NE where pines are fewer. As its name suggests, almost always found in pines, usually singing from higher branches. Relatively rare during migration.

- **ID:** Some fall birds quite nondescript and colorless; unlike Blackpoll and Bay-breasted, lacks back-streaking but this often difficult to see. More distinctive is Pine's relatively plain face pattern with dark wash on ear coverts (vaguely suggesting Peregrine Falcon!). Song similar to those of Palm Warbler, Chipping Sparrow, Dark-eyed Junco, et al., but is typically slower, shorter, with increasing volume at end. References: see Bay-breasted Warbler.

Kirtland's Warbler — Accidental; two old May records: 1892 in the Twin Cities and 1944 in Stearns County.

Prairie Warbler — Casual; perhaps a dozen records,

mostly in May or June in the SE, with the number of records increasing in recent years.

Palm Warbler — Uncommon and local in summer NE, especially in more extensive and open tamarack bogs (e.g., the Sax-Zim Bog and Beltrami Island State Forest). Much more widespread in migration throughout.

- **ID:** Has greenish-yellow rump and is thus sometimes mistaken for Yellow-rumped in fall. Trilled song often nearly identical to Chipping Sparrow's, junco's, et al., but typically is distinctively buzzier with "rolling" pattern of notes rising and falling in pitch.

Bay-breasted Warbler — Relatively rare in summer northern NE; most often found in mature aspens in predominantly coniferous forests, especially along the Gunflint Trail (Cook County). Uncommon migrant, more often seen in fall than spring.

- **ID:** Fall birds often difficult to separate from Blackpolls. Streaked underparts = Blackpoll; unstreaked underparts = Bay-breasted; short, faint smudges on underparts = either species. Pale legs/feet = Blackpoll; dark legs/feet = either species. Buff flanks = Bay-breasted; yellowish breast = Blackpoll; no color on underparts = either species. Also see Pine Warbler. Song usually weaker and shorter than similar Black-and-white's song, but often difficult to tell from American Redstart's; also see Cape May and Blackburnian warblers. References: *Birding* 15:219-222 and 28:284-291, and *Advanced Birding* guide.

Blackpoll Warbler — Uncommon migrant throughout in spring, more common in fall. Not present in Minnesota in summer.

- **ID:** See Pine and Bay-breasted warblers.

Cerulean Warbler — Uncommon, local and declining in summer mostly SE, with a few as far north as the southern NW. Most often seen in extensive deciduous forests; consistently seen for decades at Beaver Creek Valley State Park (Houston County) and St. John's University (Stearns County). Difficult to see as it sings from the higher branches of taller trees. Spring migrants are relatively rare; fall migrants seldom reported.

- **ID:** See Northern Parula.

Black-and-white Warbler — Common in deciduous and mixed woods in summer NE and adjacent counties SE.

- **ID:** See Bay-breasted Warbler.

American Redstart — Common in summer throughout except southern SW.

- **ID:** Songs variable, nondescript, and sometimes hard to distinguish from Yellow's, Magnolia's, and Bay-breasted's.

Prothonotary Warbler — Uncommon and local (but vocal) in summer southern SE, especially where there are snags for nesting in heavily wooded backwaters along the Mississippi River. Most consistently seen in recent decades at La Crescent and Millstone Landing (Houston County). Relatively rare in spring migration, and seldom seen in fall.

Worm-eating Warbler — Rare and barely Regular in spring mostly southern SE; hardly ever reported in summer. Only one or two records most years, mostly in early May and in the Twin Cities (where observer coverage is the highest).

Ovenbird — Common and easily heard in summer E half, mostly in deciduous woods. Typically sings from mid-level branches several feet above the ground and difficult to spot.

Northern Waterthrush — Uncommon in summer NE along rivers and in bogs in mostly coniferous areas. Like Ovenbird, easier to hear than see and typically sings from perches several feet up.

> • ID: See Louisiana Waterthrush. Loud, choppy song can be difficult to tell from Connecticut's song at a distance.

Louisiana Waterthrush — Rare to uncommon and local in spring-summer, mostly eastern SE in Chisago and Washington counties (along the St. Croix River), and in Winona (Whitewater State Park) and Houston (Beaver Creek Valley State Park) counties. Also found west to the Mankato area in the Minnesota River valley (Minneopa State Park) and in southern Pine County (along the Kettle and St. Croix rivers). Prefers heavily wooded creeks with limestone ledges along their banks, and difficult to find unless singing.

> • ID: Besides song, best told from Northern Waterthrush by bolder, whiter supercilium that widens behind eye; Northern's supercilium either white or buff but narrower behind eye. Louisiana usually shows pale buff patch on flanks that contrasts with rest of white underparts; Northerns lack flank patch, are more uniform white or buffy below. Louisiana has brighter pink legs, and tends to have less streaking on throat. Reference: *Advanced Birding* guide.

Kentucky Warbler — Currently listed as Regular but possibly only Casual in spring-summer with only one or two sightings most years, mostly southern SE. Probably best looked for in the Mankato area of the Minnesota River valley (e.g., Minneopa State Park and vicinity) where most recent records have occurred.

> • ID: See Common Yellowthroat.

Connecticut Warbler — Locally common and widespread in summer in the NE and Roseau County in the NW. Prefers wet tamarack bogs or drier jack pines; sometimes in stands of mature aspens mixed with jack pines. Most easily found when singing late May to early July, with many reports over the years in the Sax-Zim Bog (St. Louis County), in northern Aitkin County, and Beltrami Island State Forest (Lake of the Woods/eastern Roseau counties). Usually quite vocal, but sings from higher branches of taller trees, where it stays relatively motionless or walks slowly along its perch, and is thus difficult to spot. Will respond to a tape of its song, usually by flying into a low thicket nearby or flying overhead across the road to a new and concealed perch. Migrants are secretive (on the ground in dense cover) and only rarely seen in the E half, mostly late May and late August-early September).

> • ID: Many adult males have blackish smudge on lower edge of gray hood, similar to Mourning. Some Mournings in spring have thin or broken eye rings; Connecticut's eye ring always thicker and more complete. Fall Mournings often show nearly complete eye rings; note Connecticut's brownish hood and buffy throat (Mourning's hood grayer and throat yellower). Connecticut slower-moving and walks more than Mourning, often noticeably larger or plumper than Mourning; longer under tail coverts difficult to determine in field. Connecticut's seldom-heard call note a rich, somewhat liquid "pwit," unlike Mourning or MacGillivray's. Also see Nashville Warbler, Northern Waterthrush, and Common Yellowthroat. Reference: *Birding* 22:222-229.

Mourning Warbler — Common and widespread in summer NE and adjacent counties in the NW and northern SE. Prefers deciduous woods with dense undergrowth, edge habitats, or brushy logged-over areas of mixed forests. Easily heard late May to early July in many places, and usually sings at mid-tree level several feet above ground. Responds to tapes by flying to a low thicket nearby and giving its distinctive hollow chip note; non-singing Mournings, like Connecticuts, will also respond to pishing.

> • ID: See Connecticut and MacGillivray's warblers. Call note distinctive, loud, and hollow, unlike Connecticut or MacGillivray's; somewhat reminiscent of Wilson's or Common Yellowthroat's.

MacGillivray's Warbler — Accidental; one specimen record in May 1958 in Lac Qui Parle County, plus a few possibly correct sight records.

> • ID: Probably not safely separable from Mourning in fall in Minnesota. In spring some adult Mournings have thin, broken, hard-to-see eye rings, but these never as bold as MacGillivray's well-defined, wider eye "arcs." "Check" call note similar to Yellow-rumped's, unlike Connecticut's or Mourning's. References: see Connecticut Warbler.

Common Yellowthroat — Common and easily heard in summer throughout.

> • ID: Combination of plain brownish upperparts and yellowish underparts usually distinctive, but these combined with secretive behavior might suggest a fall Connecticut. Younger males with limited black on malar area have been mistaken for Kentuckys. Alternate chattering song is similar to Sedge Wren's.

Hooded Warbler — Rare and quite local but Regular in spring-summer in dense deciduous woodlands in southern SE, with a few pairs consistently nesting for years at Murphy-Hanrehan Regional Park (Scott/Dakota counties). Only occasionally reported elsewhere.

Wilson's Warbler — Common migrant throughout; also local in summer in alders along streams in northern NE coniferous woods.

> • ID: See Yellow and Orange-crowned warblers.

Canada Warbler — Uncommon in summer NE in mature and predominantly deciduous woodlands with dense undergrowth, and usually difficult to see.

> • ID: Song similar to Magnolia's but longer, faster, more complicated, often with diagnostic introductory chip note.

Painted Redstart — Accidental; a sight record in September 1992 along the shore of Mille Lacs Lake.

Yellow-breasted Chat — Currently listed as Regular but possibly still only Casual in spring-summer, mostly southern SE, with only one or two reports most years.

FAMILY THRAUPIDAE: TANAGERS

Summer Tanager — Rare and barely Regular migrant throughout, mostly SE and at Duluth and the North Shore of Lake Superior (usually at feeders or mountain ash trees). Only a couple of sightings in an average year.

> • ID: See Scarlet Tanager.

Scarlet Tanager — Uncommon E half and along the Minnesota River in the SW in summer. Prefers deciduous woods but also found in jack pines.

> • ID: Some juveniles/females have thin wing bars and thus can be confused with Western Tanager; note female Western's thicker wing bars and grayer back contrasting with nape and rump. Compared with Summer Tanager, female Scarlet is "colder" greenish-yellow overall with yellowish lores and a smaller bill; Summer is "warmer" orangish- or brownish-yellow overall, with gray smudge on lores and a larger bill. Reference: *American Birds* 42:3-5.

Western Tanager — Formerly Casual, now rare but Regular, with most records in May at feeders.

> • ID: See Scarlet Tanager.

FAMILY EMBERIZIDAE: TOWHEES, SPARROWS, AND LONGSPURS

Green-tailed Towhee — Accidental; four records, all at bird feeders.

Spotted Towhee — Uncommon to rare migrant mostly SW, more often seen in fall (late September-October) than in spring (late April-early May). Rare but possible elsewhere in migration; also seen casually in summer and winter.

Eastern Towhee — Common but local in open deciduous woodlands in summer, mostly in the eastern SE and western NE, generally in the Mississippi River valley. The Minnesota breeding distribution of this species is only vaguely known. Possible in migration throughout and rarely overwinters at feeders.

American Tree Sparrow — Common migrant throughout and uncommon in winter S half; present October through April.

> • ID: Breast spot difficult to see when breast feathers fluffed up, resulting in Chipping Sparrow reports in winter; note tree sparrow's bicolored bill (upper mandible darker) and rusty tinge on sides of breast.

Chipping Sparrow — Common in summer throughout. Often and erroneously reported in winter when there are few documented records.

> • ID: Trilled song often sounds identical to Pine and Palm warblers, Dark-eyed Junco, et al. Both Chippings and Clay-coloreds have occasionally been heard singing each other's song. Also see American Tree and Clay-colored sparrows.

Clay-colored Sparrow — Common in summer throughout, except more local northern NE and absent in southern tier of counties bordering Iowa. Most widespread W in thickets and edge habitats in open areas.

> • ID: Note absence of black on lores; Chipping's eye line continues on to lores. Clay-colored's ear coverts patch with more outline on lower edge; Chipping's ear coverts not as delineated. If visible, note brownish rump; Chipping's rump gray. Juveniles of both Clay-colored and Chipping streaked below and difficult to ID; Clay-colored may have pinker bill and lighter underparts streaking. References: *Birding* 28:374-387 and *Advanced Birding* guide.

Brewer's Sparrow — Accidental; one or two accepted sight records in fall from the SW in 1974 and 1975.

> • ID references: See Clay-colored Sparrow.

Field Sparrow — Common S half and uncommon southern NW in summer in open woodlands.

> • ID: See Clay-colored and White-crowned sparrows (immature White-crowned often misidentified as Field Sparrow).

Vesper Sparrow — Common W and SE and locally uncommon western NE in summer.

> • ID: See Song Sparrow.

Lark Sparrow — Uncommon and quite local in the NW and along the Minnesota and Mississippi rivers in the SE. This species' disjointed Minnesota range poorly understood, but it prefers dry oak savannah habitats NW and sandy oak and juniper areas in the SE. Most often seen in and near Agassiz Dunes (Polk County), along the Minnesota River between Granite Falls and New Ulm, in Sherburne County, and in the Kellogg-Weaver area (Wabasha County). Spring migrants are only seldom seen; hardly ever seen in fall.

Black-throated Sparrow — Accidental; five fall records, three on the North Shore of Lake Superior.

Lark Bunting — Now only Casual, with fewer records in recent years, with strays possible statewide, mostly SW. Formerly rare but Regular in SW and southern NW grasslands in spring-summer.

Savannah Sparrow — Common in summer throughout.

> • ID: Though not mentioned in field guides, Savannah has noticeable white outer edges on tail. Also see Song Sparrow.

Grasshopper Sparrow — Locally common W and uncommon SE in summer in drier grasslands and pastures. Easily seen when singing from exposed perches.

- ID: Has typical large-billed, flat-headed, short-tailed Ammodramus proportions. Like Savannah and Baird's, adult has white edges on outer tail; also has smudge on ear coverts but, unlike Baird's, lacks malar marks. Lores are yellowish, eye appears "beady" on plainer face, median crown stripe white. Juvenile less distinctive, confusing, and strongly resembles juvenile Le Conte's. Alternate song, unfamiliar to most birders, adds descending, Veery-like phrases to normal song and suggests Sprague's Pipit: "tic zzzzzzzz zeeur zeeur zeeur zeer zeer zrr."

Baird's Sparrow — Now only Casual, with almost all records of singing males from the Felton Prairie area (Clay County) May-July, but also possible in other NW grasslands. Formerly considered locally Regular in spring-summer in the NW, especially at Felton.

- ID: Best identified by song: one or more "zip" introductory notes followed by rich, musical, low-pitched trill; trill suggests end of House Wren's song. (When there are three introductory notes, song actually sounds like opening of Beethoven's Fifth!) Median crown stripe usually yellowish or pale orange, appears wider and easier to see from back; color often washes down on nape and ear coverts. Contrary to field guide illustrations, has obvious white outer edges on notched tail, generally lacks Canada Warbler-like or Henslow's Sparrow-like "necklace" (breast usually lightly and more randomly streaked), and has more "normal" proportions (not as large-billed, flat-headed, or short-tailed as other Ammodramus sparrows). Face pattern (but not the color) similar to Henslow's Sparrow, with obvious smudge on ear coverts, two malar lines or "whiskers," top whisker connected to ear coverts' smudge by vague, curved, broken line (this line may suggest a second smudge).

Henslow's Sparrow — Has long been listed as Regular only because of its consistent presence May-July at Great River Bluffs (formerly O. L. Kipp) State Park in Winona County. Still found there most years (but not all), and there are now annual reports of singing males at scattered locations elsewhere, mostly S half, but also at several southern NW places. Can occur in both old fields and native grasslands, in both drier hayfields and wetter meadows, especially those with brome grass, dense ground litter, and weed stalks for singing perches.

- ID: See Baird's and Grasshopper sparrows; has facial markings similar to Baird's but proportions like Grasshopper. Note adult's combination of olive wash on face, rusty wings, and "necklace" of streaks on breast (bolder than on Baird's Sparrow). Juvenile similar but tends to have only one malar streak and streaking limited to sides of breast. Cricket-like "tslick" song distinctive but weak and easily overlooked.

Le Conte's Sparrow — Uncommon to locally common and widespread N half, except absent eastern NE. Easily heard May-July at many sedge marshes, meadows, and hayfields in the NW; also found consistently in the NE, es-

pecially in northern Aitkin County and the Sax-Zim Bog (St. Louis County). Widespread but secretive in migration and possible statewide. Can sing (or remain silent) unpredictably at any time of day or night, sometimes visibly from a shrub or weed stalk, but often from concealed perches lower in the grass. Hard to find unless singing, and often slow to respond to tapes.

- ID: Has extensive buff on face around distinctive gray triangle and smudge on ear coverts; also note adult's white median crown stripe, pink and gray streaks on nape, buffy underparts with streaks mostly limited to sides, and bluish-gray bill. Sometimes appears more orange than buff and then easily confused with Nelson's Sharp-tailed; note sharp-tailed's gray median crown stripe and nape, bolder white stripes on back, and usually heavier breast streaking. Juvenile Le Conte's similar to adult but streaked on breast and resembles juvenile Grasshopper. Song two-syllabled, a hissing "zzzz zzt." Reference: *Birding* 24:70-76.

Nelson's Sharp-tailed Sparrow — Rare or uncommon and local in sedge marshes mid-May to July in the NW and western NE, and closely associated in range and habitat with Yellow Rails. Most often reported at McGregor Marsh (Aitkin County), but probably more common in Roseau, Marshall, and Polk counties. Sings only sporadically and unpredictably (and sometimes not at all) at any time of day or night, and seldom found unless singing. Like Le Conte's, often ignores tapes of its song, or it suddenly and silently appears nearby after a delay. Seldom seen in migration, but generally overlooked and possible statewide.

- ID: See Le Conte's Sparrow. Breezy, two-syllabled song sounds like water dripping on a hot stove: "tshhh shrrr."

Fox Sparrow — Uncommon migrant throughout, mostly during April and October. Not present in summer. All Minnesota birds are "Red" Fox Sparrows.

- ID: See Song Sparrow.

Song Sparrow — Common in summer throughout; a few sometimes overwinter, mostly SE.

- ID: Field guides tend to imply streaked sparrows with central breast spots must be Songs; however, Vesper, Savannah, Fox, Lincoln's, and streaked juveniles of other species (e.g., White-throated) also have central spots. Song's tail can look notched like Savannah's; Savannah has shorter tail, paler overall plumage, less heavily streaked underparts, brighter pink legs. Juvenile Song has thinner streaks below, buffy wash on underparts, and is thus easily mistaken for Lincoln's Sparrow.

Lincoln's Sparrow — Uncommon in summer NE; prefers open tamarack bogs (e.g., in the Sax-Zim Bog and Beltrami Island State Forest).

- ID: See Song and Swamp sparrows.

Swamp Sparrow — Common and easily heard in summer in marshes throughout.

- ID: Immature is streaked below, has somewhat buffy underparts, a grayish face, and strongly resembles Lincoln's Sparrow.

White-throated Sparrow — Common, widespread, and easily heard in summer NE and adjacent counties SE. Common in migration, with a few often overwintering at feeders, mostly SE.

Harris's Sparrow — Uncommon migrant throughout, mostly late April-early May and late September-October. Most common and widespread W, especially in fall, with a few present some winters at SW feeders.

White-crowned Sparrow — Common migrant throughout, but outnumbered by White-throateds. Like Harris's, not present in summer.

- ID: Immature poorly illustrated in most field guides and thus confusing to many birders. Note distinctive small-headed and flat-crowned profile, reddish-brown crown stripes, median crown stripe often washed with yellow (suggesting immature Golden-crowned, which has bicolored bill with dark upper mandible). Often mistaken for Field Sparrow because of pink bill and rusty color on crown.

Golden-crowned Sparrow — Accidental; two feeder records: April 1987 in Chippewa County and winter 1989-90 in Duluth.

- ID: See White-crowned Sparrow.

Dark-eyed Junco — Uncommon and local in summer NE, mostly in upland pines and lowland bogs; common and widespread throughout in migration; uncommon in winter, mostly S half.

- ID: Trilled song can sound identical to Pine and Palm warblers, Chipping Sparrow, et al., but normally distinctly more musical and ringing than others. Confusing, atypical songs may be two-parted or include

buzzy notes.

McCown's Longspur — Accidental; three records since 1900, two in Duluth and one in Grand Marais; also a few nesting records before 1900.

- ID: Besides distinctive tail pattern, note female/immature's overall paleness, unstreaked underparts, broad buffy wing bars, grayish nape, pale eye ring, distinctive shorter-tailed, longer-winged profile, and thicker base of bill. Call notes include a unique, metallic, springy "woink." Also see Horned Lark. Reference: *Birders Journal* 7:68-93.

Lapland Longspur — Common early spring migrant, mostly W in March-April, and fall migrant (September-October) in fields throughout, often in flocks of hundreds of individuals; flocks sometimes winter SW. Except at Rothsay in October or at Felton in summer (see below), any longspur in Minnesota is almost always a Lapland. Usually shy and hard to see on the ground except for those curiously cooperative and visible fall migrants along the North Shore of Lake Superior.

- ID: Females/immatures best identified by rusty patch between wing bars; also note buffy-olive tone on face with "C"-shaped line bordering ear coverts, dark smudges on breast, and usually a trace of rust on nape. Call notes include a rattling phrase and Snow Bunting-like "tew." Reference: *Birders Journal* 7:68-93.

Smith's Longspur — Rare migrant W, especially in fall, and most often reported from Rothsay Wildlife Management Area (Wilkin County) and the Jeffers Petroglyphs / Red Rock Prairie area in October. Prefers pastures, mown hayfields, and other short grass habitats; not generally found in stubble and dirt fields (these preferred by Laplands). Fall migrants are typically a week earlier than the Lapland peak, when flocks by the dozens or even hundreds have been recorded. Also rarely but annually reported at Duluth and the North Shore of Lake Superior in September. Best looked for in spring in the W in late April.

- ID: Compared with Lapland, female/immature has buffier underparts with less streaking, white eye ring, more white on outer tail feathers, often a white spot on shoulders like Chestnut-collared, and ear coverts border appears more circular and centered behind (rather than below) eye. Rattling call slower, drier, and longer than Lapland's. Reference: *Birders Journal* 7:68-93.

Chestnut-collared Longspur — Highly local and consistent in summer only in the Felton Prairie area (Clay County), where a few dozen pairs have nested for decades in lightly grazed pastures May-August. Also possible in summer elsewhere in the W, with records in Traverse, Big Stone, and western Yellow Medicine counties not long ago. Seldom seen in migration.

- ID: Besides tail pattern, note female/immature's combination of relatively plain face pattern and unstreaked underparts; often has trace of rust on nape like Lapland and white spot on shoulders like Smith's. Call notes include a metallic "quiddle." Reference: *Birders Journal* 7:68-93.

Snow Bunting — Common fall migrant in open areas throughout, especially N half and SW, and most easily seen October-November in Duluth and along the North Shore of Lake Superior. Relatively uncommon in spring migration (March-April). Uncommon in farmlands most winters in the W, western NE, and SE, with the largest wintering flocks often in the NW.

FAMILY CARDINALIDAE: CARDINALS, GROS-BEAKS, AND BUNTINGS

Northern Cardinal — Common permanent resident S half, but more local SW; a few also regularly occur farther north, especially at Duluth feeders.

Rose-breasted Grosbeak — Common in summer throughout.

- ID: See Black-headed Grosbeak.

Black-headed Grosbeak — Casual; at least a dozen accepted records, mostly at bird feeders in spring, but possible statewide any time of year.

- ID: Many birders (and field guide authors) are unaware juvenile male Rose-breasteds have extensively buffy underparts with little streaking and have long been mistaken for female Black-headeds. Note under wing linings are pink on juvenile male Rose-breasted, yellowish on Black-headed and on female Rose-breasted. Females of both species variable in amount of color and streaking on underparts; patterns often overlapping and sometimes indistinguishable. Black-headed's bill normally dark or bicolored; Rose-breasted's normally pale. Rose-breasted's primary call note a distinctive, sharp "squeak;" corresponding Black-headed note is lower-pitched, not as squeaky (both grosbeaks also give other nondescript calls). Reference: *Birding* 23:220-223.

Blue Grosbeak — Uncommon, local, but Regular in summer only in Rock, southern Pipestone, southwestern Murray, and western Nobles counties. Possible along any roadside where there are thickets and farm groves from late May through August. Most often found at Blue Mounds State Park, especially near the interpretive center.

- ID: See Indigo Bunting.

Lazuli Bunting — Casual; about 20 records, mostly in spring at bird feeders in the W, but possible statewide.

- ID: See Indigo Bunting.

Indigo Bunting — Common in summer throughout, except local or absent northern NE in heavily wooded areas.

- ID: Some sub-adult males have broad, brownish wing bars and can be mistaken for Blue Grosbeaks. Female Lazuli Bunting usually with bolder wing bars and buffier breast contrasting with whiter belly; Indigo usually streaked below (but beware confusing intermediates/hybrids). Reference: *Birding* 8:135-139.

Painted Bunting — Considered Accidental, but possibly Casual; about 10 scattered spring/summer records, mostly at feeders, and mostly in recent years.

Dickcissel — Fairly common in summer most years S half; typically easy to find late May-early August along roadsides in farmlands, especially in the SW. Less common and more local or absent some years SE, sometimes not arriving until June. In other years more widespread, spreading into adjacent NE counties and the southern NW. Generally gone from the state by late August, but a few fall migrants are sometimes found in Duluth and vicinity.

FAMILY ICTERIDAE: BLACKBIRDS AND ORIOLES

Bobolink — Common in spring-summer in meadows and grasslands throughout except northern NE. Relatively rare in fall with most birds having migrated south by August.

- ID: "Ink" flight note not entirely as distinctive as some birders think: Rose-breasted Grosbeak, Northern Oriole, and especially American Goldfinch all have somewhat similar call notes.

Red-winged Blackbird — Common in summer throughout; some locally overwinter, mostly SE.

- ID: Beware some males in spring which barely show any red in wings, even in flight; these could easily be misidentified as other blackbirds.

Eastern Meadowlark — Uncommon in summer E half, though more local or absent eastern NE. Prefers smaller and brushier fields and generally outnumbered by Westerns.

- ID: Generally with whiter malar area (yellow on Western) and darker brown plumage overall than Western, but often impossible to separate, except by voice, especially in fall-winter. Eastern's call note a high, rasping "dzert," Western's note a lower-pitched "chuck;" both also have similar rattling flight calls. Reference: *Birding* 8:349-352.

Western Meadowlark — Common in summer W and SE and adjacent NE counties; prefers larger fields in more open farmlands than Easterns.

- ID: See Eastern Meadowlark.

Yellow-headed Blackbird — Common in summer in marshes throughout except eastern NE; most widespread in the W.

Rusty Blackbird — Uncommon in spring (March-April) and common in fall throughout, with migrant flocks most easily seen late September-October at Duluth/North Shore of Lake Superior. Also rarely breeds in a few alder swamps in northern Lake and Cook counties. Rare but possible in winter S half and much more likely then than cowbirds or Brewer's Blackbirds.

- ID: In poor light, spring male difficult to separate from Brewer's; note Brewer's longer-tailed profile and more grackle-like gait. Beware of occasional female Brewer's with dull yellowish eyes and of juvenile Rustys with dark eyes. Also note some adult male Rustys in winter can appear all-black and Brewer's-like. Rustys often mistaken for cowbirds by beginners in fall/winter because of their brownish heads. Songs of both Rusty and Brewer's include final high-pitched "rusty-hinge" note: Rusty precedes this with chattering notes; Brewer's has single, raspy "kshh" introductory note. Brewer's call note a distinctively short, dry "chk." Reference: *Birders Journal* 4:97-101.

Brewer's Blackbird — Common N half and uncommon northern SE and northern SW in summer. Not as often seen in migration as other blackbirds; very few documented winter records.

- ID: See Rusty Blackbird and Common Grackle.

Common Grackle — Common in summer throughout; a few sometimes overwinter, mostly SE.

- ID: Females and winter birds duller overall and often confused with Brewer's Blackbird.

Great-tailed Grackle — Currently considered Accidental, but probably Regular, at least in Jackson County where there are several records since 1998, one of these a confirmed breeding; most often reported in the vicinity of Grover's Lake. There are also records from four or five other counties S half.

Brown-headed Cowbird — Common in spring-summer throughout. Fall migrants curiously absent NE and uncommon elsewhere; a few sometimes winter S half.

- ID: See Rusty Blackbird (frequently misidentified as cowbird).

Orchard Oriole — Uncommon in summer W and locally so southern SE; widespread and most easily seen SW when singing May-July. Can be found in isolated trees in open country as well as in towns and farm groves. Migrants seldom seen in spring or fall.

Baltimore Oriole — Common in summer throughout, except more local eastern NE.

Bullock's Oriole — Accidental; one fall 1968 record at a Duluth feeder.

- ID references: *Birding* 30:282-295 and 33:61-68.

Scott's Oriole — Accidental; one feeder record from Duluth in May 1974.

FAMILY FRINGILLIDAE: FINCHES

Brambling — Accidental; five fall/winter records, four of these at feeders.

Gray-crowned Rosy-Finch — Accidental; about 10 records, mostly at NE feeders, especially in winter.

Pine Grosbeak — Uncommon but widespread in fall-winter N half most years, but some winters more common and present in northern SE. Generally prefers mixed or coniferous forests, frequently visits feeders, and feeds on mountain ash berries. Arrives by late October and departs during March; not present in summer.

- ID: See Purple Finch.

Purple Finch — Common in summer NE and adjacent counties SE; uncommon at feeders in winter, mostly SE but throughout some years.

- ID: Metallic "tink" call note unique; calls also include two- or three-syllabled whistles practically identical to Pine Grosbeak's, and vireo-like phrases which have resulted in erroneous Red-eyed Vireo reports in winter. Juvenile may have indistinct face pattern, clearly delineated dark and light back streaking, narrower breast streaking, and streaked under tail coverts similar to female/juvenile Cassin's Finch. Most reliable field marks on Cassin's are partial white ring below and behind eye (Purple has no eye ring) and longer, straighter top edge of upper mandible (more curved on Purple). References: *The Loon* 60:3-9, *American Birds* 40:1125-1127, *Birding* 8:231-234 and 23:157-158, and *Advanced Birding* guide.

Cassin's Finch — Accidental; one November 1987 record at a Duluth feeder.

- ID: See Purple Finch.

House Finch — Now established as a permanent resident in cities and towns throughout except northern NE; common S half and southern NW, but currently still uncommon and local farther north. Partially migratory and less common statewide in winter.

- ID: One of its call notes is similar to Red Crossbill and could lead to erroneous crossbill reports.

Red Crossbill — Local, unpredictable, and possible any time of year, mostly in the NE: uncommon some years mostly in fall-winter, rare or absent other years. Can be more widespread during infrequent invasion winters. Fall migrants move down the North Shore of Lake Superior and through Duluth most years, mostly in October-November but sometimes starting in August. Often occurs in summer, but nesting records are almost nonexistent. Unlike the White-winged, has a preference for pines over other conifers.

- ID: Reportedly on the verge of being split into several species, two or three of which occur in Minnesota; field ID mostly determined by bill shape and call notes. Reference: *Birding* 27:494-501. Also see House Finch and White-winged Crossbill.

White-winged Crossbill — Status similar to the Red Crossbill's, except it prefers spruce/tamaracks over pines. Numbers and distribution tend to fluctuate more widely than Reds from year to year, it is usually easier to find in most areas, and is more likely to invade the S half in winter. Unlike Red Crossbills, will usually respond to pishing: even a flock flying by will often make a U-turn and land. Undoubtedly has bred in the state, but there is only one confirmed nesting record (unexpectedly in Rice County!).

- ID: Red Crossbill occasionally has wing bars, the lower bar a bit wider; White-winged's wing bars bolder, the upper bar wider. Both crossbills give similar single-syllabled call notes, separable with practice: White-winged's call a "wink" with rising inflection (as if asking a question); Red's "jip" call typically louder, sharper, lower-pitched, with no rising inflection, but another call is a more liquid, higher pitched, and

White-winged-like "wit wit wit." Another White-winged call is a distinctive dry chattering not given by Red Crossbill.

Common Redpoll — Common N half and uncommon to rare S half most winters, usually arriving in late October and departing in early April. In some years can be scarce to nonexistent statewide; in other years, can be seen in both wooded and open areas by the hundreds, frequently visiting feeders.

• ID: Some Hoarys are obvious and clearly stand out in a flock of Commons: note their white and un-streaked rumps and under tail coverts, "frostier" overall plumage with upperparts more gray than brown, only lightly streaked or even unmarked sides, and stubbier bills. "Classic" male Hoarys only have slight pink tinge on breast; deeper and more extensive pink on male Commons. However, many redpolls have intermediate features and are impossible to identify with certainty. Male Commons often appear frostier than females, and redpolls in trees seen from below look whiter than those on the ground. When in doubt, just call it a redpoll and wait until a "classic" Hoary comes by, or until Commons and Hoarys are lumped — which probably won't occur: if anything, some splits are more likely. References: *Birders Journal* 5:44-47, *Birding* 27:446-457, *Birding World* 9:65-69, and *The Loon* 69:214-216.

Hoary Redpoll — Present in small numbers among Common Redpoll flocks most winters N half, generally outnumbered roughly 100 to 1 by Commons, and virtually absent in years with low redpoll numbers. Tends to prefer more open areas over woodlands.

• ID: See Common Redpoll.

Pine Siskin — Common in summer N half and northern SE; common most winters mostly SE at feeders, but some winters also present W and NE.

• ID: Quite variable in plumage: some quite dark and heavily streaked with no yellow color visible on perched birds; others paler overall, sometimes greenish, with more obvious yellow, and only lightly streaked under-parts — such individuals have been confused with Eurasian Siskins. Siskin flocks give a variety of notes which can sound like Boreal Chickadees, crossbills, redpolls, or Evening Grosbeaks.

American Goldfinch — Common in summer through-out; uncommon most winters at feeders mostly S half, but throughout some years.

Evening Grosbeak — Uncommon in summer in pre-dominantly coniferous forests NE; also uncommon most winters at NE and northern SE feeders (and usually hard to find except at feeders). Some fall migrants curiously start to pass through Duluth in late June.

FAMILY PASSERIDAE: OLD WORLD SPARROWS

House Sparrow — Common permanent resident throughout, except mostly absent eastern NE.

Eurasian Tree Sparrow — Accidental; a summer 1990 record from a Twin Cities feeder, and records from three consecutive summers, 1998-2000, at a Clay County feeder.

A Birder's Guide to Non-Minnesota Birds

Any birder interested in Minnesota's (or any state's) checklist of birds will at times wonder what the next addition to the state list might be. Accordingly, included below is a list of species which have yet to be recorded in the state but would seem the most likely to occur eventually.

This selection is, of course, somewhat arbitrary and certainly incomplete, but most of these species have been recorded in two or more adjacent states or provinces. Some of these seem especially overdue as additions to the state list, given their history of occurrence nearby: e.g., Brown Pelican, Anhinga, Wood Stork, Tufted Duck, Sharp-tailed Sandpiper, Slaty-backed Gull, Plumbeous Vireo, Virginia's Warbler, Cassin's Sparrow, and Lesser Goldfinch.

Also included are birds with little or no precedence of occurring near Minnesota, but they seem to be expanding their ranges in this direction or are possibly being overlooked due to their similarity with other species. Among these more "remote" possibilities are Arctic Loon, Pacific Golden-Plover, the four species of Eurasian stints, Rock Sandpiper, Western Gull, the five species of western Empidonax flycatchers, Cave Swallow, and Shiny Cowbird.

Several birds on this list have already been reported in Minnesota (and, in some cases, previously accepted and published), but they are not now accepted by MOURC, are currently excluded from the state list, and remain as future possibilities.

For additional information on these potential first state records, see *The Loon* 67:232-237 and 68:232-27.

- **Arctic Loon** — ID references: see Pacific Loon.
- **Northern Fulmar**
- **Northern Gannet**
- **Brown Pelican**
- **Anhinga** — Three previously published and accepted records have since been reconsidered, and the species has been deleted from the state list; see *The Loon* 61:13. ID: see Double-crested Cormorant.
- **Roseate Spoonbill**
- **Wood Stork**
- **Tufted Duck** — Two published records both involved individuals which were considered to be escapes from captivity; see *The Loon* 48:78 and 72:186-187. ID reference: *Birding* 30:370-383.
- **Common Crane**
- **Pacific Golden-Plover** — ID references: *Birding* 25:322-329 and *Birding World* 4:195-204.
- **Mountain Plover** — Two previously accepted and published records were later reconsidered by MOURC, and the species was removed from the state list; see *The Loon* 46:115, 58:154-158, and 60:146-148.
- **Spotted Redshank** — ID reference: *North American Birds* 53:124-130.
- **Wandering Tattler**
- **Red-necked/Little/Temminck's/Long-toed stints** — ID references: see Western Sandpiper..
- **Sharp-tailed Sandpiper** — ID references: *American Birds* 41:1356-1358, *Birding* 33:330-341, and *Advanced Birding* guide.
- **Rock Sandpiper**
- **Heermann's Gull**
- **Slaty-backed Gull** — ID references: *American Birds* 40:207-216 and *Birding* 26:243-249.
- **Western Gull**
- **Royal Tern**
- **Roseate Tern** — ID references: see Arctic Tern.
- **Sooty Tern**
- **White-winged Tern** — ID reference: *Birding* 32:216-230.
- **Black Skimmer**
- **Thick-billed Murre**
- **Black Guillemot**
- **Long-billed Murrelet** — ID reference: *Birding* 29:460-475.
- **Inca Dove**
- **Lesser Nighthawk**
- **Green Violet-Ear** — ID reference: *Birding* 33:114-121.
- **Broad-billed/Black-chinned/Broad-tailed/Allen's hummingbirds** — ID references: *Birding* 29:18-29, *Birders Journal* 10:26-48, and *Advanced Birding* guide.
- **Red-naped Sapsucker** — ID: see Yellow-bellied Sapsucker..
- **Hammond's/Dusky/Gray/Pacific-slope/Cordilleran flycatchers** — ID references: *Birding* 17:277-287, 18:315-327 and 19(5):7-15, *Birders Journal* 8:78-87, and *Advanced Birding* guide.
- **Tropical/Couch's/Cassin's kingbirds** — ID references: *American Birds* 46:323-326 and *North American Birds* 52:6-11.
- **Gray Kingbird**
- **Cassin's/Plumbeous vireos** — ID reference: *Birding* 28:458-471.
- **Pinyon Jay**
- **Cave Swallow** — ID: beware of juvenile Cliff Swallows which often have pale throats.
- **Carolina Chickadee** — ID reference: *Advanced Birding* guide.
- **Phainopepla**
- **Virginia's Warbler**
- **Cassin's Sparrow** — ID reference: *Advanced Birding* guide.

- **Shiny Cowbird** — ID references: *American Birds* 41:370-371, *Birding* 23:233-234 and 32:514-526.
- **"Red" crossbills** — Probable future splits in the Red Crossbill may result in more than one species occurring in Minnesota. ID reference: *Birding* 27:494-501.
- **Lesser Goldfinch** — ID reference: *American Birds* 47:159-162.

Other species previously have been seen in the state which are considered to be escaped or released from captivity. Some of these records have been published, three of the species had been included on earlier state lists, but none of them are considered legitimate vagrants which should occur naturally in Minnesota or adjacent states/provinces.

- Greater Flamingo
- Barnacle Goose
- Whooper Swan
- Common Black-Hawk — Formerly accepted on the state list on the basis of an injured bird found near Bemidji which later died. This individual was later reconsidered as most likely of captive origin; see *The Loon* 50:31-34.
- Chukar — Formerly included on the state list on the basis of a small introduced population which survived for decades in Ely until 1977. This population later was reconsidered to never have been clearly established.
- Ringed Turtle-Dove
- Monk Parakeet
- Smooth-billed Ani — A published record of a reportedly escaped Smooth-billed clearly involved a misidentified juvenile Groove-billed Ani; see *The Loon* 46:34.
- European Goldfinch — Formerly included on the state list on the basis of an individual documented at a Twin Cities feeder; see *The Loon* 39:105.

Mammals, Amphibians, Reptiles

Since birders often encounter other things besides birds in the field and are usually interested in all forms of wildlife, this "Birder's Guide to Minnesota's Non-Birds" is included. The annotated ranges are only approximate (note the use of W, SE, NE, etc., as explained earlier), and rarities and species with only a limited range in the state are not included. For more information, consult *The Mammals of Minnesota* by Evan Hazard and *Amphibians and Reptiles Native to Minnesota* by Barney Oldfield and John Moriarty.

MAMMALS
- Virginia Opossum: S half
- Masked Shrew: throughout
- Water Shrew: N half
- Arctic Shrew: N half
- Pygmy Shrew: N half
- Northern Short-tailed Shrew: throughout

- Eastern Mole: S half
- Star-nosed Mole: N half
- Little Brown Bat: throughout
- Northern Myotis: throughout
- Silver-haired Bat: throughout
- Eastern Pipistrelle: SE
- Big Brown Bat: throughout
- Eastern Red Bat: throughout
- Hoary Bat: throughout
- Eastern Cottontail: throughout
- Snowshoe Hare: N half
- White-tailed Jackrabbit: W and SE
- Eastern Chipmunk: throughout
- Least Chipmunk: NE
- Woodchuck: throughout
- Richardson's Ground Squirrel: W
- Thirteen-lined Ground Squirrel: throughout
- Franklin's Ground Squirrel: throughout
- Gray Squirrel: throughout
- Fox Squirrel: W and SE
- Red Squirrel: throughout
- Southern Flying Squirrel: S half
- Northern Flying Squirrel: N half
- Plains Pocket Gopher: W and SE
- Plains Pocket Mouse: W and SE
- Beaver: throughout
- Western Harvest Mouse: S half
- Deer Mouse: throughout
- White-footed Mouse: throughout
- Northern Grasshopper Mouse: W
- Southern Red-backed Vole: N half
- Meadow Vole: throughout
- Muskrat: throughout
- Southern Bog Lemming: N half
- Norway Rat: throughout
- House Mouse: throughout
- Meadow Jumping Mouse: throughout
- Woodland Jumping Mouse: NE
- Porcupine: N half
- Coyote: throughout
- Gray Wolf: NE
- Red Fox: throughout
- Gray Fox: W and SE
- Black Bear: N half
- Raccoon: throughout
- Marten: NE
- Fisher: NE
- Ermine (Short-tailed Weasel): throughout
- Least Weasel: throughout
- Long-tailed Weasel: throughout
- Mink: throughout
- Badger: throughout
- Eastern Spotted Skunk: S half
- Striped Skunk: throughout
- River Otter: throughout
- Bobcat: N half
- White-tailed Deer: throughout
- Moose: N half

SALAMANDERS
- Blue-spotted Salamander: E half
- Tiger Salamander: throughout
- Eastern Newt: E half
- Red-backed Salamander: NE
- Mudpuppy: NW and SE

FROGS and TOADS
- American Toad: throughout
- Great Plains Toad: W
- Canadian Toad: W
- Western Chorus Frog: throughout
- Spring Peeper: E half
- Cope's Gray Treefrog: SE
- Gray Treefrog: throughout
- Bullfrog: SE
- Green Frog: E half
- Pickerel Frog: SE
- Northern Leopard Frog: throughout
- Mink Frog: NE
- Wood Frog: N half and SE

TURTLES
- Snapping Turtle: throughout
- Wood Turtle: E half
- Blanding's Turtle: throughout
- Painted Turtle: throughout

- Common Map Turtle: SE
- Ouachita Map Turtle: SE
- False Map Turtle: SE
- Smooth Softshell: SE
- Spiny Softshell: S half

LIZARDS
- Six-lined Racerunner: SE
- Five-lined Skink: S half
- Prairie Skink: W and SE

SNAKES
- Ring-necked Snake: E half
- Western Hognose Snake: W and SE
- Eastern Hognose Snake: SE
- Smooth Green Snake: W and SE
- Racer: SE
- Fox Snake: S half
- Gopher Snake: S half
- Milk Snake: SE
- Plains Garter Snake: W and SE
- Common Garter Snake: throughout
- Brown Snake: SE
- Red-bellied Snake: throughout
- Northern Water Snake: SE
- Timber Rattlesnake: SE

PRINCIPAL BIRDING LOCATIONS BY SEASON

WINTER

a – Lost River State Forest
b – Rothsay WMA and vicinity
c – Otter Tail River
d – Lac Qui Parle WMA
e – Minnesota River valley

Notes:

Several locations are listed for more than one season, and these are indicated by more than one reference letter. The reference letters on this page do not correspond with those in the individual county chapters.

The Migration season in spring may begin as early as late February in mild years. In fall, Migration starts as early as late June for shorebirds, and it may extend into December for waterfowl in mild years. Migration can be excellent at times at almost any location, including those not cited on this page or included anywhere in this book.

The Summer/Breeding season generally includes the period from late May through early July, when most birds are singing on territory. However, some species (e.g., gallinaceous birds, woodcock, owls, and woodpeckers) are much easier to find earlier in spring when they are more vocal or displaying.

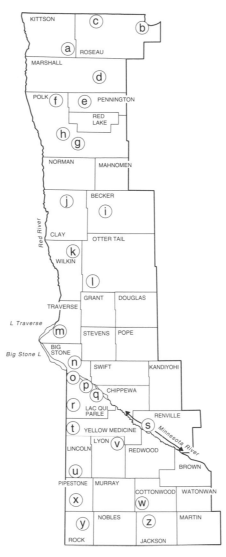

MIGRATION

a – Twin Lakes WMA
b – Lake of the Woods and vicinity
c – Roseau River WMA
d – Agassiz NWR
e – Thief River Falls sewage ponds
f – Wetlands, Pines, and Prairie Audubon Sanctuary
g – SNAs and WMAs southeast of Crookston
h – Crookston sewage ponds
i – Tamarac and Hamden Slough NWRs
j – Felton Prairie
k – Rothsay WMA and vicinity
l – Orwell WMA
m – Mud and Traverse Lakes
n – Thielke Lake and vicinity
o – Big Stone NWR
p – Marsh Lake and vicinity
q – Lac Qui Parle Lake and vicinity
r – Salt Lake
s – Minnesota River valley
t – western Yellow Medicine County
u – Lake Benton and vicinity
v – Cottonwood area
w – Talcot Lake WMA
x – Pipestone National Monument
y – Blue Mounds State Park
z – Heron Lake

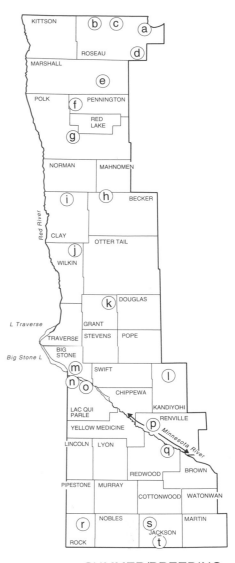

SUMMER/BREEDING

a – South Shore WMA
b – Roseau River WMA
c – Lost River State Forest
d – Beltrami Island State Forest
e – Agassiz NWR
f – Goose Lake and vicinity
g – SNAs and WMAs southeast of Crookston
h – Waubun Marsh and vicinity
i – Felton Prairie
j – Rothsay WMA and vicinity
k – Pelican Lake and vicinity
l – Sibley State Park
m – Thielke Lake and vicinity
n – Big Stone NWR
o – Marsh Lake and vicinity
p – Minnesota River valley
q – Flandrau State Park
r – Blue Mounds State Park
s – Heron Lake
t – Grover's and Spirit Lakes and vicinity

53

Kittson County

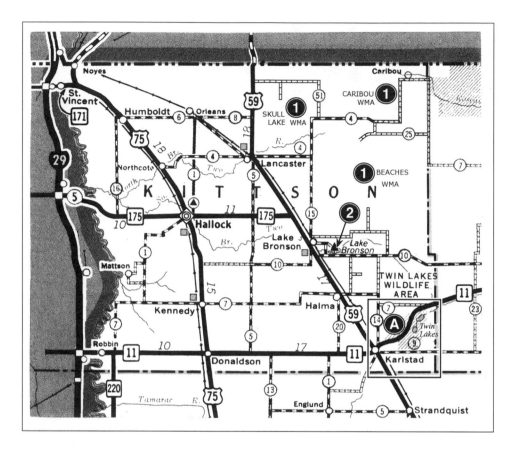

Owls, Le Conte's and Nelson's Sharp-tailed sparrows might breed, and the most accessible of these is **Twin Lakes Wildlife Management Area (inset A)**. Red-necked Grebes and Sandhill Cranes also nest here, and hundreds of cranes stage at Twin Lakes in October. Highway 11 bisects this area, with the northwest side of 11 sometimes referred to as Twistal Swamp, and inset A shows other roads to explore.

If water levels aren't right and Twin Lakes doesn't come through, those same specialties, plus Sharp-tailed Grouse, Wilson's Phalarope, and Sedge Wren, might be found at other more remote, mostly inaccessible **wildlife management areas (1)** in northeast Kittson County, which may prove harder to find than the birds themselves:

• Skull Lake — From Lancaster, go 6 miles east and 4 miles north on County Road 4 to its southeast corner; or to its northwest corner go 8 miles north on Highway 59, east 3 miles on County Road 51, then south 2 miles.

• Caribou — Its east side is along County Road 4; from the southeast corner of Skull Lake, continue 11-13 miles east and north on 4.

• Beaches — Most of it is miles from any roads: from Lake Bronson, go 0.5 mile north from Highway 59 on County Road 15, turn east and go 6.5 miles, then 1.5 miles north to the south edge of this area.

Also in northeastern Kittson County, The Nature Conservancy has recently acquired and has started to manage nearly 10,000 acres of aspen parklands, hayfields, marshes, and brushlands. For information about this extensive Wallace C. Dayton preserve, contact the Conservancy's local office, 104 S. First St., Karlstad 56732; telephone (218) 436-3455.

More civilized is **Lake Bronson State Park (2)**, just east of the town of the same name via County Road 28. In summer its lake, the only real lake in the county, may be overrun with campers and swimmers, but in migration the trees along its shore might be worth checking — a Louisiana Waterthrush even turned up here once (maybe it got

You live in the Twin Cities and want to get to Kittson County in a hurry. Do you: (a) jump in your car and start driving; or (b) fly to Winnipeg, rent a car, and head south? The answer, of course, is (b). Drive up from the Cities and it's at least a seven-hour trip; unless delayed at customs, the trip via Canada is perhaps half that long. Kittson is one of Minnesota's better counties, but it's a long way from where most birders live and fails to get the attention it deserves.

Most of the country west of Highway 59 tends to be intensely farmed, part of the Red River "valley," where one might find Gray Partridge, Franklin's Gull, Black-billed Magpie, migrant longspurs (almost all Laplands, but look and listen for Smith's), wintering Northern Shrike and Snow Bunting, and migrant passerines in the trees along the Red River itself. These same possibilities also exist in the "black deserts" of other Northwest counties along the Red River farther south.

Things get a lot more interesting east of Highway 59, where the habitat becomes a mix of aspen parklands, sedge marshes, brushlands, meadows, and pastures, so pick a side road and start exploring. Of primary interest to most birders would be those marshes where Yellow Rails, Short-eared

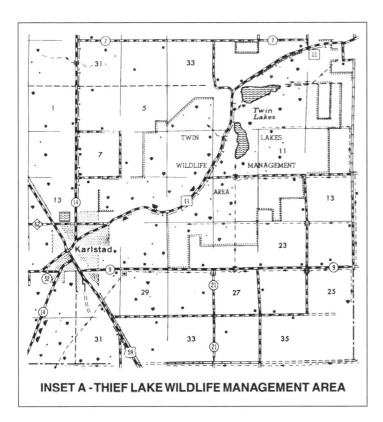

INSET A - THIEF LAKE WILDLIFE MANAGEMENT AREA

lost looking for Beaches Wildlife Management Area?).

While you're in the neighborhood, you might want to look over the oak savannahs of The Nature Conservancy's 320-acre Norway Dunes tract: from Halma, go east 0.8 mile on County Road 7, then north 1.5 miles and 0.5 mile east. Here, and in other drier areas in the vicinity, look for nesting Upland Sandpiper, Marbled Godwit, Black-billed Cuckoo, Whip-poor-will, Clay-colored and Lark sparrows.

Finally, there are five sewage ponds in the county. Though all are small, each might attract some water birds of note since natural lakes are so scarce in this corner of the state:

❑ Karlstad: located on inset A.

❑ Lake Bronson: 0.5 mile south from Highway 59 on County Road 15.

❑ Lancaster: from the junction County Roads 4 and 6 about a mile west of town, go north 0.3 miles on an unmarked road across the tracks.

❑ Hallock: 2.1 miles south from Highway 175 on Highway 75, then 0.7 mile west.

❑ Kennedy: 1 mile west on County Road 7, and 0.2 mile north.

Roseau County

As good a county as Kittson is, its neighbor to the east is even better. Though most of Roseau County is farmland interrupted here and there by aspen groves, it also has plenty of Kittson County-like marshes, meadows and pastures, plus two elements more characteristic of a Northeast Region county: Lake of the Woods and coniferous forests.

Though **Lake of the Woods** itself lies within the county of the same name, much of it can be scanned from its Roseau County shoreline **(inset A)**. The best four **vantage points (A1)** are:

• From Springsteel Island, actually a peninsula built up with cabins and trailers; limited lake views but there are marshes along the road and trees for migrants (where a lost Eurasian Collared-Dove and Lark Bunting have each turned up).

• Along County Road 74 / 4th Avenue on the north edge of Warroad.

• In Warroad at the mouth of the Warroad River (from Highway 11, turn east on Lake Street).

• From the public access off County Road 12, 2.5 miles east of Highway 11.

On the lake you might see Common Loon, Red-necked Grebe, American White Pelican (one of Minnesota's two nesting colonies is on one of this lake's remote islands), Greater Scaup, Common Goldeneye, Bonaparte's and Herring gulls, and Caspian and Common terns. All of these tend to be absent from the smaller lakes of the West Region. In migration, Lake of the Woods would also be a spot to hope for a rarity such as Red-throated or Pacific loon, Harlequin Duck, scoters, Long-tailed Duck, Whimbrel, Red Knot, Parasitic Jaeger, and Thayer's or Glaucous gull — species one typically looks for on Lake Superior.

As with any large lake, be sure to check as well for migrant passerines that might be funneled through the trees along this lake's shoreline. Also interesting would be any mudflats and migrant shorebirds you might find when lake levels are low. Watch especially for the rare Piping Plover which might wander over from Pine and Curry Island (see Lake of the Woods County).

But also be sure to check the sedge marshes and meadows of **South Shore Wildlife Management Area (A2)**, where Yellow Rails and Nelson's Sharp-tailed Sparrows have bred. Watch as well in the fields in this vicinity for Sharp-tailed Grouse, Sandhill Crane, Upland Sandpiper, Marbled Godwit, spring migrant shorebirds, Short-eared

ROSEAU

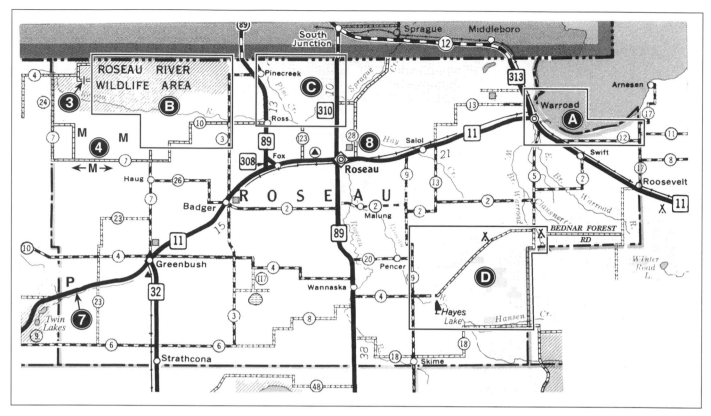

Owl, Black-billed Magpie, Sedge Wren, Grasshopper and Le Conte's sparrows.

An even better, or at least larger, place for Yellow Rails and other such birds is in the extensive marshes and fields of northwest Roseau County, especially within the vast recesses of **Roseau River Wildlife Management Area (inset B)**. This area's large pools and marshes also are home to breeding grebes, both bitterns, rails, Wilson's Phalarope, Franklin's Gull, and Forster's Tern.

Unfortunately, as the map of inset B shows, access is limited unless someone at **refuge headquarters (B3)** is willing to give you a key to the gated dike roads (which is unlikely). The headquarters are a mile north of Pool 1 just west of County Road 3, 3 miles west of Pinecreek. If you happen to be here at dusk, listen for American Woodcock, Barred Owl, and Whip-poor-will at the T-intersection west of HQ, and a good **Yellow Rail marsh** is along the gated road a mile south of the T (also marked **B3**).

Without a gate key, be content to scan **Pool 1** from the three other spots marked **B3**. Or head all the way over to the west side of the area: from the county line at the junction of Kittson County Road 4, go 2 miles east to the T; from here turn north 1 mile and then east 4 miles to the gate at the west tip of **Pool 2** (also marked **B3**), or go south to the gate a mile west of **Pool 3 (3)**. If you're energetic, you could always hike or bike for miles along the levees beyond any of the gates.

Also be sure to check the more accessible open country south of Roseau Wildlife Management Area from the roads shown on inset B or from County Road 7, especially the 4-mile stretch of **sedge marshes (4)**. Unless agricultural interests move in to drain and plow everything up, in wetter

years you'll find extensive sedge marshes (again for the likes of Yellow Rails and Nelson's Sharp-tailed Sparrows). And in wetter springs, the **Roseau River** near Duxby **(B4)** floods its banks into adjacent fields for the benefit of shorebirds.

* * *

What really makes Roseau County different, however, are its coniferous forests. Not only is such habitat virtually non-existent in the West Region, but it also provides the birder with a reason for coming here in winter. The bogs of **Lost River State Forest (inset C)**, which are most easily accessed from **Highway 310 (C5)**, are as good as anything in the Northeast for such winter/year-round specialties as: Northern Goshawk, Gyrfalcon (maybe in winter), Spruce Grouse, Northern Hawk Owl (also has nested), Great Gray Owl, Boreal Owl (rare, but has nested here), Three-toed (perhaps) and Black-backed woodpeckers, Gray Jay, Boreal Chickadee, and crossbills.

Be sure to look for Great Grays hunting at dawn/dusk, especially along 310 within the 2 miles south of the Canadian border — winter or summer, this is one of the most reliable places in the state for this owl. Additional breeding possibilities here would include American Woodcock (spring), Long-eared and Northern Saw-whet owls, Whip-poor-will, Yellow-bellied and Alder flycatchers, Cape May, Connecticut and Mourning warblers, and Le Conte's Sparrow.

If time permits, be sure to check the other roads besides Highway 310 in inset C. While the bogs along County Road 118 in the western part of the state forest aren't quite as good, in spring and summer be sure to check the north-south road between 118 and County Road 123. Here you will find some excellent **meadows** (also marked **C5**) for the likes of Yellow Rail, Sandhill Crane, migrant shorebirds,

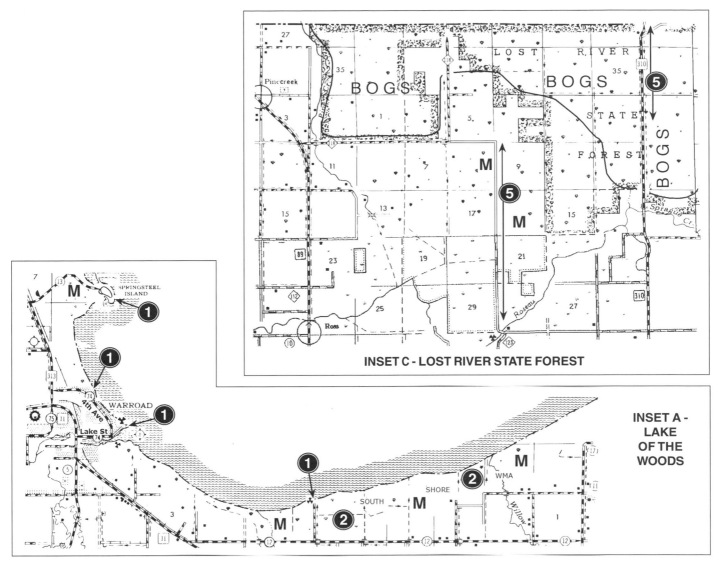

INSET C - LOST RIVER STATE FOREST

INSET A -
LAKE
OF THE
WOODS

Short-eared Owl, and Le Conte's and Nelson's Sharp-tailed sparrows.

The Roseau County portion of the **Beltrami Island State Forest (inset D)** is predominantly deciduous woods and probably not worth a winter visit. (The Lake of the Woods County portion of this forest has more pines and spruce-tamarack bogs.) However, the Roseau side is still a good place to find breeding Ruffed Grouse, American Woodcock, Black-billed Cuckoo, Barred Owl, Whip-poor-will, Alder Flycatcher, and Golden-winged and Mourning warblers.

More interesting are the extensive jack pines along much of the **Thompson Road (D6)**, which runs between the entrance road to Hayes Lake State Park and County Road 5. Though upland pine forests are generally not as interesting as spruce, tamaracks, balsam fir, or white cedars, these jack pines here are good places to look for Spruce Grouse (rare), and Pine and Connecticut warblers. In fact, Beltrami Island State Forest may have more Spruce Grouse and Connecticuts than anywhere else in the state.

Also marked **D6, Hayes Lake State Park** is often worthwhile for migrant and nesting passerines. A singing

Western Wood-Pewee was also found by the park entrance in 1992. This species might even prove to be annual in northwestern Minnesota if birders (from Winnipeg, perhaps?) came here more often.

The state's lone nesting record for this wood-pewee actually comes from the opposite side of Roseau County at **Pelan Park (7)**. This nice, heavily wooded spot is on the south side of Highway 11, 2 miles east of the Kittson County line. Also check the large Two Rivers Aspen Prairie Parkland across the highway: turn north off 11 just east of Pelan Park to best access this area. This 1,333-acre Scientific and Natural Area includes a mix of hayfields, meadows and woodlands where Sandhill Crane, Black-billed Magpie, Sedge Wren, and the highly local Lark Sparrow nest.

Elsewhere in the western half of the county (as if you didn't already have enough to do in Roseau County!), you might want to check the water impoundment at Nereson Wildlife Management Area. Since so much of this county is devoid of lakes, this seldom-birded area should attract good numbers of migrant water birds. Turn south off County Road 4, either 11 miles east of Highway 11 or 11 miles west of Highway 89, and go 2 miles on County Road 117.

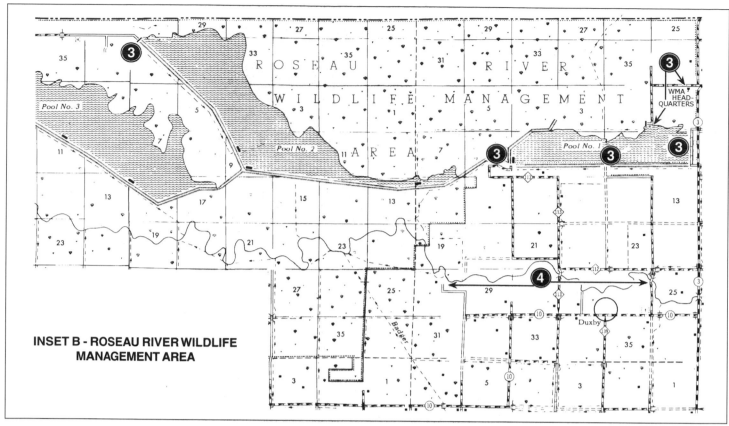

**INSET B - ROSEAU RIVER WILDLIFE
MANAGEMENT AREA**

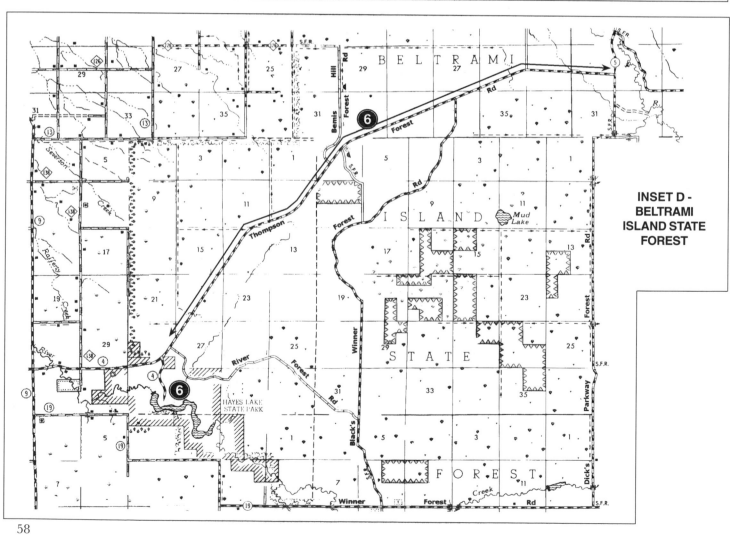

**INSET D -
BELTRAMI
ISLAND STATE
FOREST**

Finally, there are four sewage ponds in the county, with the best of these at **Roseau (8)**; in fact, most years these are among the best in all of the Northwest. Turn north off Highway 11 on County Road 28, 2 miles east of the downtown stoplight, and go 1.5 miles.

Warroad's ponds are also large and better than average:

go north on Highway 313 for 3.3 miles, turn west on County Road 137 and go 3 miles, then go south 0.5 mile and west 0.2 mile. The sewage ponds at Greenbush are also pretty good (1 mile north on County Road 7, then 0.2 mile east), while those at Badger could be skipped (0.5 mile north on Highway 11, then 0.7 mile east).

Marshall County

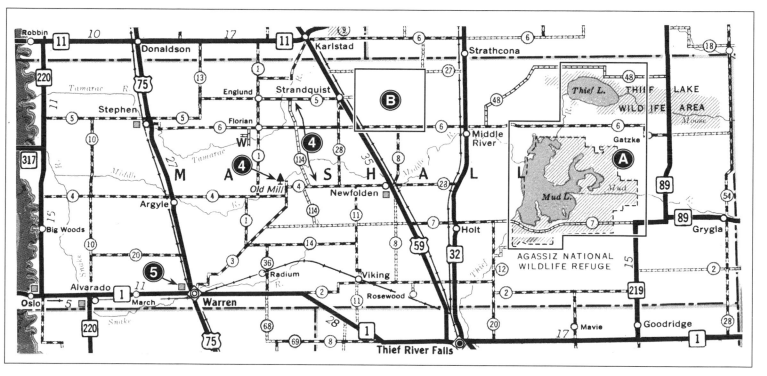

This county is not that much closer to the Twin Cities than Kittson, but it gets far more coverage, primarily because of **Agassiz National Wildlife Refuge (inset A)**, arguably Minnesota's finest refuge. Some 280 species are included on its checklist, primarily as a result of its varied habitats which range from large pools and extensive marshes to brushy grasslands and aspen woodlands.

The list of rarities documented here is long and impressive: Clark's Grebe, Snowy and Cattle egrets, Tricolored Heron, Yellow-crowned Night-Heron, White-faced Ibis, Ross's Goose, Brant, Cinnamon Teal, Mississippi Kite, Common Moorhen, Snowy Plover, Whimbrel, Western Sandpiper, California, Sabine's and Ross's (!) gulls, Least Tern, Mountain Bluebird, Sage Thrasher, Yellow-throated Warbler, and Western Tanager. In 1990, a Whooping Crane was even seen less than a mile outside the refuge boundary. None of these, of course, can be expected on your visit, but you can expect to find just about everything else that occurs regularly in the Northwest Region.

The time to come is anytime from April through October, and the place to start is at **refuge headquarters (A1)**, where maps and lists are available. When the office is open (usually Monday-Friday until 4 p.m.), be sure to inquire about recent sightings and to ask for a gate key to the dike roads. Current policy is generally to grant visitors access to these roads, but if this policy has changed, if wet weather has made the levee roads impassable, or if the office is closed (like on weekends), you'll have to be content to bird the refuge along County Road 7, from the **Lost Bay Habitat Drive (A2)**, and at Farmes Pool (see below).

If you get a key, drive as many dike roads as time permits. Just beyond headquarters, the gated Westgate Road turns left and leads to the western side of Agassiz where the water levels are often shallow enough for Yellow Rails and Nelson's Sharp-tailed Sparrows. The Northgate Road, leading to dike roads on the east side of the refuge, starts from the gate at the northeast corner of the Lost Bay road.

But often the best place to start is at **Farmes Pool** (also

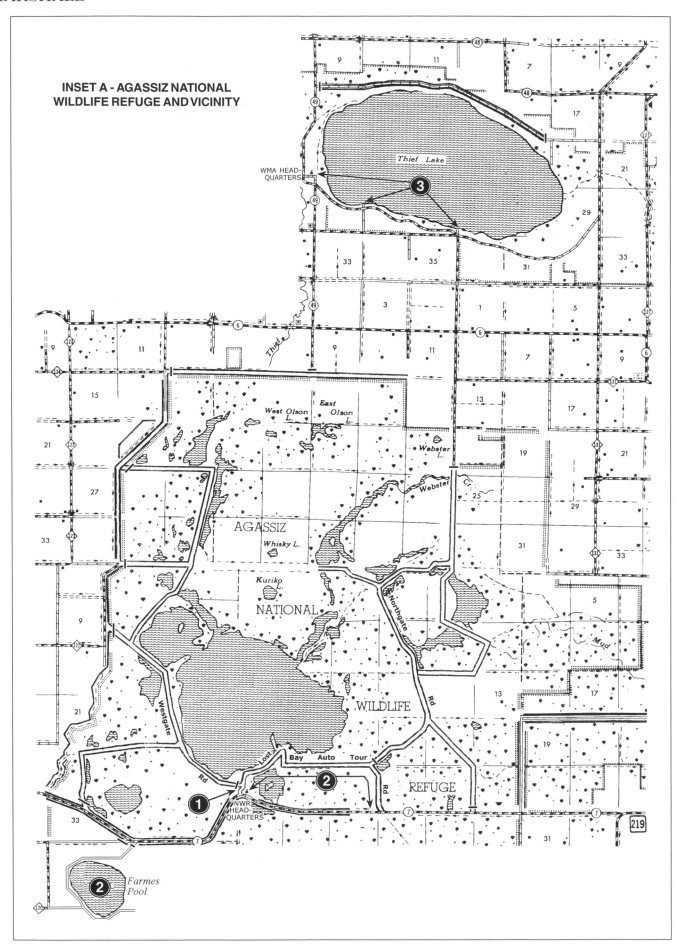

**INSET A - AGASSIZ NATIONAL
WILDLIFE REFUGE AND VICINITY**

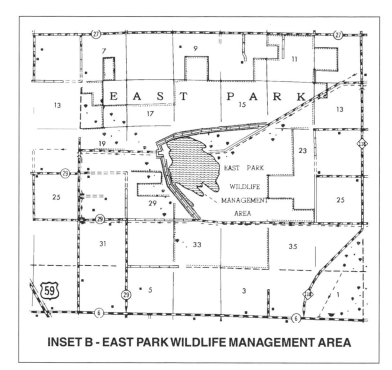

INSET B - EAST PARK WILDLIFE MANAGEMENT AREA

also want to drive west from Thief Lake along County Road 48 (turn off County Road 49, 3 miles north of headquarters). This road eventually comes out on County Road 6, 2 miles east of Middle River, and passes through oak savannah habitat where Sharp-tailed Grouse, Upland Sandpiper, and Clay-colored, Lark and Grasshopper sparrows could be seen.

Most of the western half of Marshall County is open farmland fragmented by aspen groves, part of the over-cultivated Red River valley. There are, however, a few places worth visiting here, and foremost among them is **East Park Wildlife Management Area (inset B)**. This interesting spot may be seldom birded, but its main pool (the only lake in this part of the county) and the marshes along its shore all look like they could attract something out of the ordinary. If nothing else, at least there should be some Red-necked and other grebes among the nesting water birds here.

Also of note in this part of the county, a pair of Mountain Bluebirds nested a few years ago in boxes placed along **County Road 114 (4)**. The north end of 114 turns south off County Road 5, 5.5 miles west of Strandquist (or 3 miles east of Englund), and comes to a T at County Road 4 just east of Old Mill State Park. Here, turn west on 4 towards the park, but in a mile turn south to continue on 114 until it ends 4 miles later.

County Road 114 follows the former beachline of Glacial Lake Agassiz, which comprises the unofficial eastern boundary of the agricultural lands of the Red River valley. This ridge becomes more visible and more important for birding in the counties south of here, but in Marshall County its presence is mainly evidenced by a north-south line of aspen groves, marshes, brushy hayfields, and pastures.

The woods at nearby **Old Mill State Park** (also marked **4**) might attract some migrating warblers and other passerines; the park entrance is just north of County Road 4, west of 114. Time permitting, check for migrants as well a few miles northwest of Old Mill at the county park along the Tamarac River: from Florian, it's a mile west, a mile south, and 0.2 mile west. Migrants might also funnel through the narrow corridor of trees along the Red River in Marshall and other Northwest Region counties along the North Dakota border.

Finally, with habitat for water birds so scarce in western Marshall County, you might want to check some of its sewage ponds. Certainly, the best ones in the county are at **Warren (5)**, which are almost always worth going out of your way for: go 1.5 miles west from Highway 75 on Highway 1, then 0.5 mile north. Other ponds are at:

❑ Oslo (also larger and better than most); 1 mile east, 0.5 mile north.

❑ Alvorado; 1 mile south, 0.2 mile west.

❑ Stephen; 1.8 miles west of Highway 75 on County Road 5, then 0.5 mile south.

❑ Newfolden; 1 mile south on Highway 59, then 0.5 mile west.

marked **A2**), since it is sometimes drawn down for shorebirds. As shown on inset A, turn south off County Road 7 on the gated road 2.6 miles west of headquarters. Or, without a key, go west out of the refuge on County Road 7, then south 3.3 miles on County Road 12, and turn east on County Road 120, following the signs to the pool.

Besides rails and sparrows, Agassiz is a better than average place to look for all five grebes (six, counting the rare Clark's), pelicans, flocks of migrant and nesting ducks and geese, Sandhill Crane, shorebirds (in May each year either Farmes or another pool is normally drawn down), Franklin's Gull (thousands nest most years), Short-eared Owl, Whip-poor-will, magpies, and Sedge Wren. And watch for Moose, a not uncommon mammal in most of Marshall County and elsewhere in this corner of the state. In late May, be sure to check the trees around the headquarters, which provide an oasis for migrant warblers and other passerines.

Also included on inset A is **Thief Lake Wildlife Management Area**, another place to see many of the species found at Agassiz. Without a gate key to the road on the north side of the lake, however, it is hard to bird this area. Bits of the lake can be scanned from the three spots marked **A3**, including the headquarters on the west side along County Road 49. Here there are planted spruce trees and thickets to attract migrants, and this is the place to ask for that gate key (though you'll probably be turned down).

* * *

The rest of this area, and most of the eastern third of Marshall County, is a mix of deciduous woodlands, alder thickets, and overgrown hayfields that might be worth exploring for Ruffed Grouse, American Woodcock, Alder Flycatcher, Mourning Warbler, and other species common in this habitat. While you're in the neighborhood, you might

Pennington County

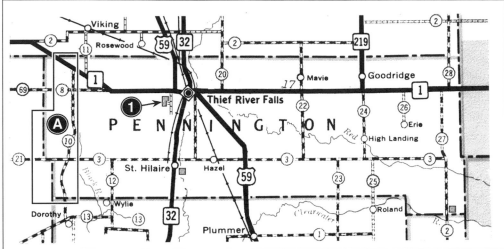

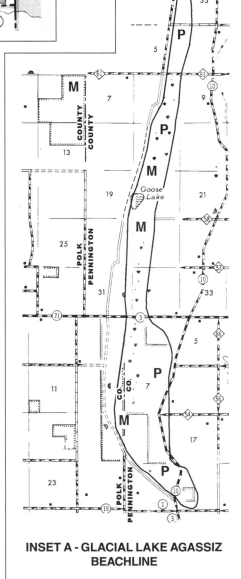

After the glaciers melted thousands of years ago, the flat agricultural lands which now extend east 20 to 30 miles from the Red River into Minnesota's Northwest Region were under water. This Glacial Lake Agassiz, which also included parts of North Dakota and Manitoba, eventually receded, leaving behind a slight but visible series of parallel ridges along the lake's eastern shoreline. Today, the primary north-south ridge is much more than an item of geological trivia. Its aspen groves, marshes, and remnant patches of virgin prairie grasslands provide the birder with some of the best birding to be found in this region.

This is particularly evident in Pennington County. If not for the **Glacial Lake Agassiz beachline (inset A)**, the only reason to visit this county would be a couple of sewage ponds. But, as shown on inset A, there is a narrow strip of wetlands and grasslands along the west edge of the county (which also includes a bit of Polk County). The grasslands may be too narrow and fragmented to attract something like a Sprague's Pipit or Baird's Sparrow, and in drier years the only sedge marshes you might find would probably be around Goose Lake.

But if you check all the roads in this area (try especially the two north-south dead-end roads approaching Goose Lake, which in former years were connected and might be again), in spring/summer you might find: Sharp-tailed Grouse, Greater Prairie-Chicken, Yellow Rail, Sandhill Crane, Upland Sandpiper, Marbled Godwit, Wilson's Phalarope, Short-eared Owl, both Alder and Willow flycatchers, Sedge Wren, and Grasshopper, Le Conte's and Nelson's Sharp-tailed sparrows.

Listen for the uncommon and local Yellow Rail and Nelson's Sharp-tailed Sparrow, especially at Goose Lake. Also note it is possible in this area to find Alder and Willow

INSET A - GLACIAL LAKE AGASSIZ BEACHLINE

flycatchers nesting literally side-by-side in the same thicket. And, while you're scanning Goose Lake, perhaps you'll spot another Ross's Gull, like the one which briefly stopped here in April 1992.

With habitat for water birds so scarce in most of this part of the state (Pennington County has but one lake), sewage ponds are always worth a look during migration and summer. The **Thief River Falls sewage ponds (1)** are among the largest and best in the state, frequently attracting grebes (especially Eareds, which have a special and curious

fondness for sewage ponds), pelicans, ducks, gulls, terns, phalaropes and other shorebirds (if water levels are low). To reach these ponds, from the junction of Highways 1 and 59 on the west side of town, continue 0.5 mile west on 1, then turn south for a mile and then west to the gate, where it is only a short hike to scan all three ponds.

If time permits, also check the small sewage pond at St. Hilaire: in the municipal park/campground in the southeast part of town, follow the left fork of the road east through the park to the gated pond.

Red Lake County

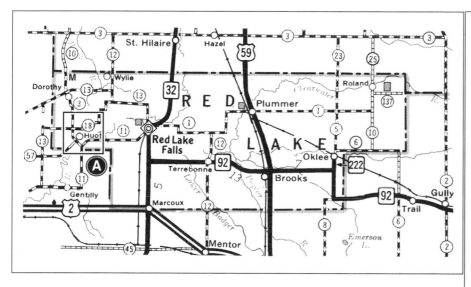

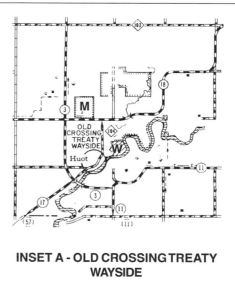

INSET A - OLD CROSSING TREATY WAYSIDE

Like its neighbor to the north, most of this county is open farmland, its woodlands are generally limited to river banks, and it is mostly devoid of wetlands. As a result, birders don't spend much time in Red Lake County, especially since evidence of Glacial Lake Agassiz's shoreline is limited to a small marsh or two, some fields, and wooded areas in and around **Old Crossing Treaty Wayside (inset A)**. If nothing else, the habitat is good for nesting Lark Sparrows, and during migration the woods along the Red Lake River should attract warblers and the like. Another spot along the river where local birders have had luck with migrants warblers and nesting Lark Sparrows is behind the cemetery on County Road 1, about a mile east of Highway 32.

In the northeastern of the county, there is a set of wild

rice paddies where you might find some good water birds in spring. From the junction of County Roads 1 and 10, go 2 miles north on 10, then east 1.5 miles on County Road 137 to the south side of the paddies. You can also access the north end of this area by backtracking a half mile west and going north 1 mile.

About the only other specific places to check during migration would be the county's two small sewage ponds. From downtown Red Lake Falls, follow Third Street S.W. west to its end at the edge of town, and then hike 0.2 mile west to the ponds. In Plummer, the sewage ponds are on Main Street on the west side of town, 0.2 mile west of the Clearwater River.

Polk County

The geography of this sprawling county divides rather neatly into three sections: the wooded lake country mixed in among the farmlands east of Highway 32; the plowed-up Red River valley, generally west of Highways 75 and 9; and the more interesting grasslands, marshes, and brushlands of the good old Glacial Lake Agassiz beachline between Highways 32 and 9.

The lakes and deciduous trees of the eastern half of Polk County would primarily be of interest to birders in search of species more characteristic of eastern Minnesota: e.g., Red-necked Grebe, Ruffed Grouse, American Woodcock, Barred Owl, Veery, Wood Thrush, and Mourning Warbler. With one exception, however, there are no spots in particular for birds such as these, so get out a county map and start exploring. One place to start would be the recently established Rydell National Wildlife Refuge: the headquarters are along County Road 210, 2.5 miles south of Highway 2 (210 turns south off 2, 3 miles east of Mentor or 3 miles west of Erskine).

Another thing to try in eastern Polk County would be to check those **wild rice paddies (8)** along County Road 2 in the northeastern corner. When flooded in April and May, such paddies often attract lots of water birds, including Tundra and Trumpeter swans and shorebirds. Several paddies are along and just west of 2, from the Pennington County line south for 2 miles. If you feel like exploring some back roads (and who doesn't?), there are probably other rice paddies to be found in this vicinity north of Highway 92.

If you're unsure of your navigating skills, of final note in eastern Polk County there is always the predictable security of sewage ponds birding:

❑ Erskine: north 1 mile on Highway 59 from Highway 2, then west 0.2 mile.

❑ McIntosh: 1 mile east on Highway 2, then north less than 1/4 mile to the corner where the road turns east, and

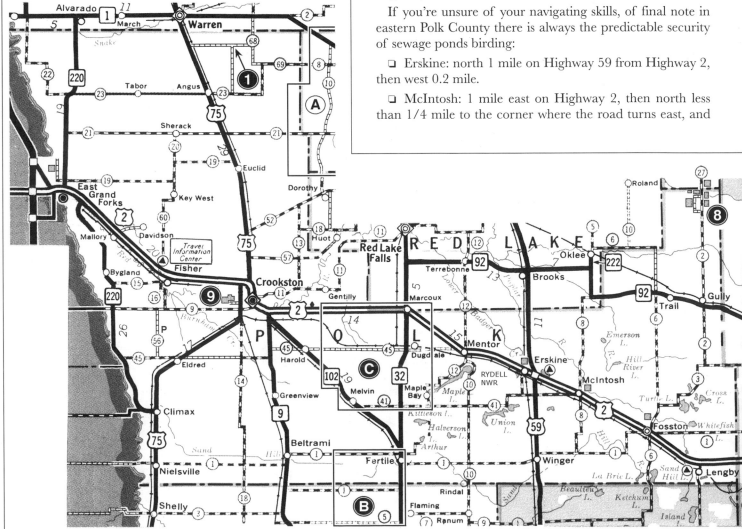

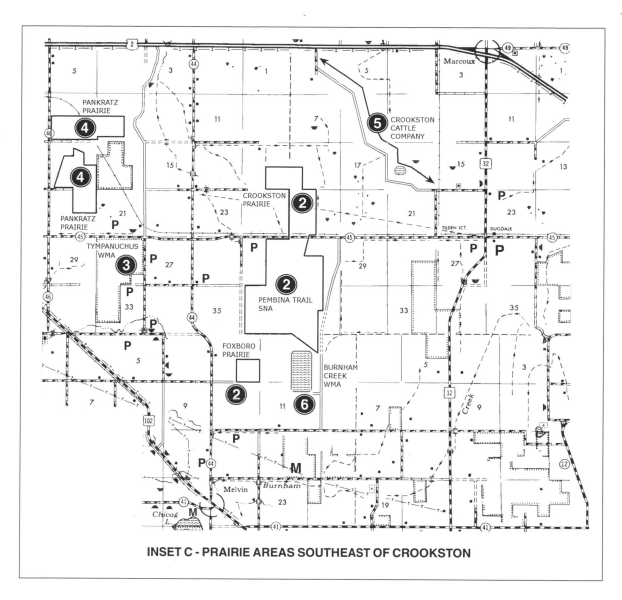

INSET C - PRAIRIE AREAS SOUTHEAST OF CROOKSTON

then continue north 0.2 mile.

❑ Fosston: turn north off Highway 2 on County Road 30, 0.4 mile west of town, then go north 0.5 mile, east 0.3 mile, and north 0.2 mile.

*   *   *

In the vast agricultural lands of western Polk County, there are three widely separated birding oases that might make a drive out here worthwhile. (In addition, don't forget the wildlife management areas in the Polk County portion of Pennington County's inset A.)

One quite isolated but pleasant spot in northwestern Polk County worth going out of your way for is the **Wetlands, Pines, and Prairie Audubon Sanctuary (1)**. From Angus, go 2.3 miles east on County Road 23, then 5 miles north and 0.5 mile east; or coming from the north, go south from Warren (Marshall County) on Highway 75 for 3 miles, then east 4.8 miles.

The grasslands, small ponds, and densely wooded shelterbelt on the former Omdahl family farm is not only a natural migrant trap for passerines, but each summer Or-

chard Orioles, near the north edge of their range, and Black-billed Magpies always seem to nest here. This would also be as good a place as any to find such widespread species as Gray Partridge, Black-billed Cuckoo, Western Kingbird, Sedge Wren, and Clay-colored and Le Conte's sparrows. There are also nesting records here for both Long-eared and Northern Saw-whet owls, two elusive species capable of nesting in any old woodlot in the Northwest Region.

Several miles to the south, and equally isolated among its intensively farmed surroundings, is The Nature Conservancy's Malmberg Prairie Scientific and Natural Area, 80 acres of grasslands somehow preserved from the plow. This site is probably too small to attract many birds or birders, but to check it out: from Crookston go west from Highway 75 on County Road 9 for 9 miles, then south 2 miles on County Road 56.

And what would birding be in the Red River valley without sewage ponds? The municipal ponds at East Grand Forks are larger than most: from Highway 2 go north 1.8 miles on Highway 220, then west 1 mile. (Even better than

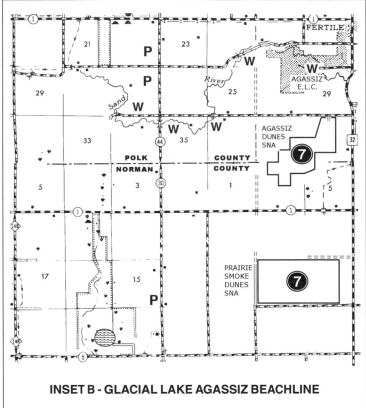

INSET B - GLACIAL LAKE AGASSIZ BEACHLINE

miles south of 45. This 2,377-acre tract, which includes the Crookston Prairie Unit on the north side of 45 and the Foxboro Prairie Unit (access off County Road 44), is one of the best places in the state to look for Short-eared Owls in migration and most summers. Watch for owls (and Moose!) anywhere along County Road 45 between Highways 102 and 32.

Other than the Pembina Trail tract, the best locations in which you'd probably want to spend most of your time are:

• The drier and more open grasslands of the **Tympanuchus Wildlife Management Area (C3)**, another good site for Greater Prairie-Chickens.

• The Nature Conservancy's **Pankratz Prairie tracts (C4)**.

• The former **Crookston Cattle Company (C5)** area, now owned by Bradshaw Gravel Supply. The 4-mile-long diagonal road bisecting this place passes mostly plowed fields, which at least are good in April and October for staging cranes and migrant longspurs, but there are also pastured grasslands and a good gravel pit pond. The land is private but it's OK to bird along the road as long as you stay out of the way of the gravel trucks.

• **Burnham Creek Wildlife Management Area** water impoundment **(C6)**, an attractive spot for migrant water birds, where a Whooping Crane even appeared in October 1990. As shown on inset C, turn north on the road along the east side of the impoundment, and hike west from the sign 3/4 mile up. (Note that entry is prohibited during the September 1 to October 31 duck hunting season.) Also watch for booming prairie-chickens along the east-west road a mile west of here.

(Note that The Nature Conservancy is beginning to acquire and manage over 24,000 acres in this area. This so-called Tilden Farms, which will probably include the old Crookston Cattle Company property, may eventually become the Glacial Ridge National Wildlife Refuge. For information and a map, see the Conservancy's website <www.nature.org>.)

*　　*　　*

The **beachline of Glacial Lake Agassiz** also emerges in another interesting form farther south along the Polk-Norman County line **(inset B)**. This drier area of oak savannah even includes some unique, grassy sand dunes (perhaps to be expected if this was once a beach?). In The Nature Conservancy's 435-acre **Agassiz Dunes Scientific and Natural Area (B7)** and along the road west of the entrance and parking area (0.5 mile west of Highway 32), you will consistently find the highly local Lark Sparrow.

The habitat also looks good for Eastern Screech-Owl (not generally known from the Northwest, but it may occur), Whip-poor-will, Mountain Bluebird (possibly — Easterns, at least, are here), Loggerhead Shrike (maybe), and Orchard Oriole. For some reason, Northern Mockingbirds have even appeared here more than once.

these are the Grand Forks sewage ponds across the state line where the "Casual" California Gull is reportedly an annual visitor.)

*　　*　　*

But most birders visiting Polk County are especially interested in the complex of prairie **grasslands and wetlands southeast of Crookston (inset C)**. Some of the wildlife management areas, The Nature Conservancy tracts, and other areas of prairie and marsh associated with the Glacial Lake Agassiz beachline are overgrown with brush or fragmented by aspen stands, but they are great places during migration and summer.

Watch for Swainson's Hawk (near the northern limit of its range), Prairie Falcon (rare but Regular migrant), Gray Partridge, Sharp-tailed Grouse, Greater Prairie-Chicken, Yellow Rail, Sandhill Crane (especially common when staging in April and October), Upland Sandpiper, Marbled Godwit, Wilson's Phalarope, Short-eared Owl, Alder and Willow flycatchers (nesting side-by-side), Black-billed Magpie, Sedge Wren, Sprague's Pipit (now only Casual), Grasshopper, Le Conte's (common) and Nelson's Sharp-tailed (rare) sparrows, and perhaps migrant Smith's Longspurs among the Laplands.

Look especially for Sharp-tailed Grouse and prairie-chickens along the road south of County Road 45 on the west side of The Nature Conservancy's huge **Pembina Trail Scientific and Natural Area (C2)**. This same road is also good for Yellow Rails; listen especially about 2

Also check the dense woodlands along the nearby Sand River for migrants. Probably the best spot along the river is at the Agassiz Environmental Learning Center: on the south side of Fertile, turn west off Highway 32 opposite where County Road 1 goes east.

On the Norman County side of inset B, there are two main attractions. One is the 1,100-acre **Prairie Smoke Dunes Scientific and Natural Area** (also marked **B7**), an area of oak savannahs and sand dunes similar to Agassiz Dunes. The other area is the large water impoundment in the Olson-Agassiz Wildlife Management Area on the north side of County Road 5: turn at the sign 0.6 mile west of County Road 30.

Finally, there are two noteworthy spots in Crookston itself. The **municipal sewage ponds (9)** are not only large, but at least one of them (usually the one farthest north) always seems to be drawn down to expose mudflats for shorebirds. Indeed, as evidenced by recent records of

Snowy Plover, Red Phalarope, and Lesser Black-backed Gull, these are certainly among the best sewage ponds in the entire state.

To reach the ponds, which are on the southwest side of town, turn west off Highway 75, 2.5 miles south of Highway 2; this access road is County Road 233, the first road south of the river. Though the sign at the entrance says the gate is only open 8:30-4:30, Monday-Friday, it is sometimes left open on evenings and weekends. (Note the American Crystal Sugar settling ponds adjacent to the municipal ponds are normally off-limits.)

And on the north side of Crookston is a nice patch of woods, for migrants at least, in the Red River Valley Natural History Area. The entrance road turns west off Highway 2, 0.2 mile south of the railroad tracks, and after 0.2 mile the road turns north to cross the tracks and then goes west again into the area.

Norman County

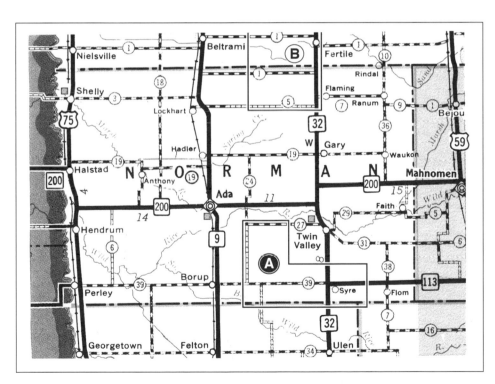

Norman County sort of falls between the cracks and is neglected on most trips as birders tend to gravitate to the more famous places in adjacent Polk and Clay counties. Indeed, there isn't much to see in the open Red River valley country west of Highway 9, though woods for migrants line

portions of the Red, Marsh, and Wild Rice rivers. And the aspen groves scattered through the farmlands in the eastern half of Norman County are nothing special for woods birds, though a stop in fall/winter at the large pine grove in the wayside rest 1 mile north of Gary on Highway 32 could result in a roosting Long-eared or Northern Saw-whet owl, some winter finches, or perhaps a stray Gray Jay, Boreal Chickadee, Townsend's Solitaire, or Bohemian Waxwing.

However, **Glacial Lake Agassiz** still makes its presence felt in northern Norman County (see Polk County's inset B), and again in the grasslands, pastures, and sedge marshes farther south in **inset A**. This latter area is a good place to look for the same specialties listed for Polk County's inset C, though I'm not aware that any Sharp-tailed Grouse have ever been reported in this county. And the only place I know of here where Yellow Rail and Nelson's Sharp-tailed Sparrow have been found is at Neal Wildlife Management Area along County Road 39, 2-4 miles west of Syre.

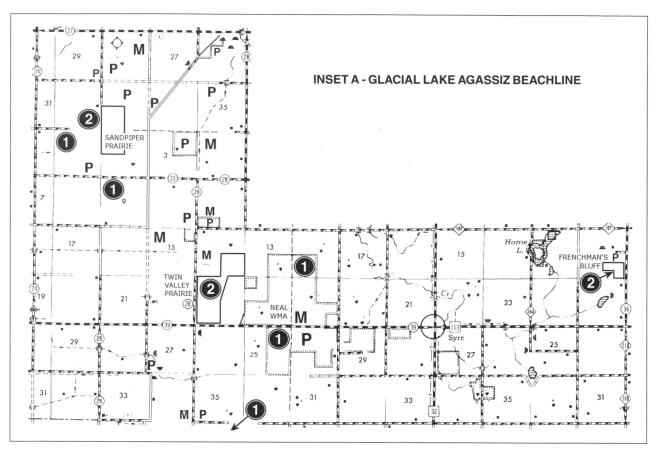

INSET A - GLACIAL LAKE AGASSIZ BEACHLINE

There also is a fair number of **Greater Prairie-Chicken leks** which were surveyed in the 1990s, and the best of these are marked **A1**. The one with the most booming males is probably on the Clay County side of the road, 4 miles west of Highway 32.

Smith's Longspurs and Gyrfalcon have both been seen in fall, the Gyr probably hunting prairie-chickens. This would also be a good area to look for the rare-Regular Prairie Falcon, and note that stray Scissor-tailed Flycatchers (twice) and a displaying male Sprague's Pipit have occurred here. Just about any of the wildlife management areas and other spots marked P and M are worth checking, with **The Nature Conservancy tracts (A2)** especially worthy of note.

These three often-wet grasslands are also classified as state Scientific and Natural Areas: the Twin Valley Prairie is easily accessed from County Roads 39 and 28; in the northwestern part of inset A, Sandpiper Prairie is accessed from the dead-end road on the north; and farther east is Frenchman's Bluff on County Road 36. This last tract may be small, but Lark Sparrows nest in this drier, sandier tract, and a Henslow's Sparrow found its way here at least once.

There are three sewage ponds worth a look in this, yet another, Northwest county practically devoid of lakes. Check especially the largest ones at Ada: from the junction of Highways 200 and 9, go west 0.4 mile, then south 1 mile on County Road 142. The ponds at Twin Valley are on County Road 27, 0.7 mile west of Highway 32. And Shelly's smaller pond is 1 mile north on Highway 75, 1 mile west, and 0.5 mile back south.

Mahnomen County

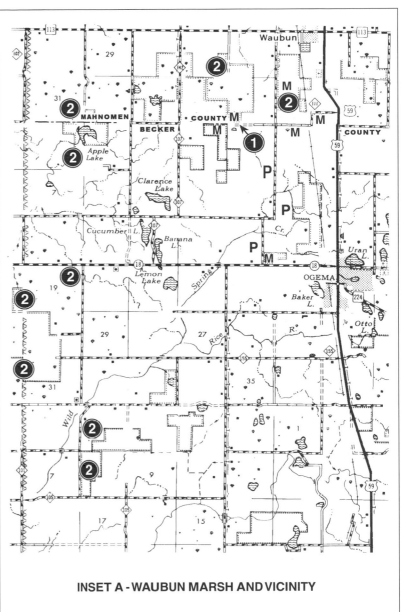

INSET A - WAUBUN MARSH AND VICINITY

This county may be small, but it has room for a wide range of habitats, as the prairie potholes and flat farmlands of the western third of the county gradually give way to more rolling terrain of oak savannahs and lakes with wooded shorelines in central Mahnomen County. This habitat, in turn, transforms into more solidly wooded country in the eastern third. Drive east from Mahnomen on Highway 200 or from Waubun on Highway 113, and within 20 minutes the countryside has magically changed from Great Plains to Great North Woods. Obviously, then, this is one of Minnesota's more remarkable counties. Yet, because there are better prairies in the West Region and better woods in the Northeast and Southeast regions, birders tend not to spend much time here.

The deciduous woods in eastern Mahnomen County may be adjacent to the Northeast Region's boreal forests, but it might be more interesting to look for species characteristic of the Southeast Region at the edge of their ranges. For example: Red-shouldered Hawk, Yellow-billed Cuckoo, Eastern Screech-Owl, Red-bellied Woodpecker, Yellow-throated Vireo, Blue-gray Gnatcatcher, Wood Thrush, Cerulean Warbler, Eastern Towhee, and Field Sparrow have all been found here, or at least nearby. One specific place to check might be the maple-basswood woodlands along County Road 3 north of Highway 113,

where Ceruleans have been found singing in years past.

In western Mahnomen County, the marshes, remnant grasslands, and pastures are good places to look for just about any of the sought-after species characteristic of the West Region. But there are so many wetlands and fields which might have something of interest, birders might want to get a county map and find their own good areas on virtually any old back road. The best place to start would be in the **Waubun Marsh and vicinity** mapped on **inset A**, which extends well into northern Becker County.

The **Waubun Marsh (A1)** itself has long been one of the state's best known birding locations, where nesting Yellow Rails and Nelson's Sharp-tailed Sparrows were discovered decades ago. These two specialties were still present in the mid-1990s, though in some years this marsh is too dry for them. If you don't have any luck, however, there are still other marsh and grasslands birds to be seen from the roads in this area. Check especially those **prairie-chicken leks (A2)** which were still active through the 1990s.

With so many wildlife management areas in **northwestern Mahnomen County,** the area included on **inset B** would also be worth exploring for the same kinds of prairie species. Be sure to check especially the large and usually wet 442-acre **Santee Prairie Scientific and Natural Area,** outlined on this map (**B3**), and the three **prairie-chicken leks** on the map just south of here (also marked **B3**).

Since water birds have so many wetlands in Mahnomen County to choose from, the county's two sewage ponds could be skipped if you're in a hurry. The ponds at Mahnomen are larger than most and might attract something: take S. Main Street to the south side of town where it becomes County Road 10, continue south 1 mile, and turn east at the cemetery to the ponds east of the tracks. There also is a small pond in Waubun: turn south off Highway 113 on 2nd Street just east of the tracks.

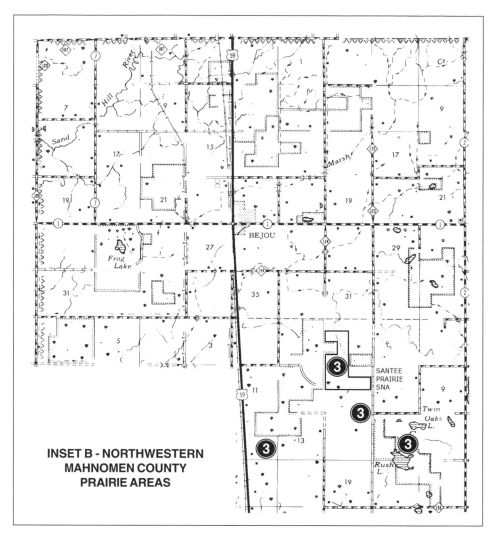

INSET B - NORTHWESTERN MAHNOMEN COUNTY PRAIRIE AREAS

Becker County

This county might be more appropriately included in the Northeast Region since most of it is wooded lake country, a better place for fishing and hunting than for birding. (A Minnesotan's Three Necessities of Life: The Weekend Cabin-In-The-Woods, The Wary Walleye, The Wily White-tailed Deer. Indeed, "W" is a most appropriate symbol to indicate woods on this book's maps. Come to think of it, given our current governor, make that four necessities:

Watching Wrestling.)

As in Mahnomen County, the woods here are predominantly deciduous, with those counties east of here in the Northeast Region are better places to look for boreal specialties. However, the likes of Common Loon, Red-necked Grebe, Trumpeter Swan, Bald Eagle, Red-shouldered Hawk, Ruffed Grouse, Barred Owl, Alder Flycatcher, Golden-winged, Pine and Mourning warblers, and

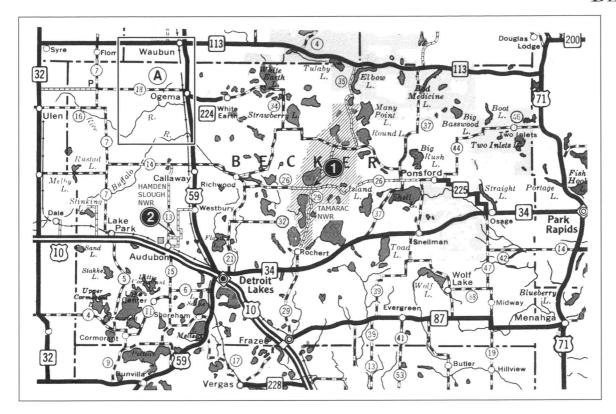

LeConte's Sparrows nest in Becker County. Several species characteristic of the bogs of the Northeast have turned up, and this county also would be good to explore for those Southeast Region-type species discussed in the Mahnomen County chapter.

All these birds can be found at **Tamarac National Wildlife Refuge**, and the place to start would be at refuge headquarters (**1**), located at the junction of County Roads 29 and 26, 10 miles north of Highway 34. Maps and other information are available in the visitors center; and there is also an information kiosk on 29, at the south entrance to the refuge. After listening to the nesting Pine Warblers by the visitors center, note the Blackbird Auto Tour on the map, which at least passes by nests of Common Loons, recently established and "countable" Trumpeter Swans, and Bald Eagles.

A better area to find on the map would probably be the gated dike road on Tamarac Lake, which turns west off County Road 29 about 3.5 miles south of headquarters. Hike beyond the gate, and for the next half mile there is habitat where both Red-necked Grebes and Least Bitterns have nested, and the wooded areas often attract migrant warblers.

Though **Hamden Slough National Wildlife Refuge** is still under development, and its "visitors center/head-quarters" (**2**) is nothing more than an old farm house, you might find the birding here more interesting than at Tamarac. The refuge lies east of County Road 13 and extends north for about 10 miles from just north of Audubon. While most of the sloughs, marshes, and mudflats currently lie within a square-mile or so at its south end (see below), more

wetlands are being restored farther north, with one good place to check there just west of the junction of County Roads 13 and 14, 3 miles west of Highway 59.

Follow the refuge signs from Audubon: from County Road 13, go east 1.3 miles on County Road 144, then north 0.7 mile on County Road 104 to the T. Wetlands are here at this corner, just to the west by the headquarters, and to the east and north for the next couple of miles along 104. The best time to visit would be during migration, especially in late summer for shorebirds.

Besides Hamden Slough, only the northwestern part of Becker County, mostly west of Highway 59 and north of Highway 10, looks like it belongs in the West Region. Several wetlands, hayfields, and pastures are scattered along these back roads, with the area included within Mahnomen County's inset A probably the best for prairie birding. Just west of inset A, another good place to check would be The Nature Conservancy's 80 acres of grasslands at Zimmerman Prairie: the location is marked P on County Road 18, 0.5 mile west of the County Road 7.

Perhaps the only lake worth a special trip for migrant water birds in western Becker County might be Stinking Lake. To see if it stinks or not, from Lake Park go west 1.7 miles from County Road 7 on Highway 10, then north 2.5 miles to the east side of the lake; continue 1 mile north and 1 mile west to scan the north side.

Finally, speaking of stinking lakes, the town of Audubon, appropriately enough, has sewage ponds! Watch for a small unmarked road on the north side of Highway 10, 0.8 mile west of County Road 13; bear left and cross the railroad tracks to the ponds.

Clay County

for breeding Swainson's Hawk, Greater Prairie-Chicken, Upland Sandpiper, Marbled Godwit, both Alder and Willow flycatchers, Western Kingbird, Loggerhead Shrike, Sedge Wren, Clay-colored, Grasshopper and Le Conte's sparrows, and Orchard Oriole. In wetter meadows, like along County Road 27 about a mile south of County Road 34, you might find Wilson's Phalarope and maybe Nelson's Sharp-tailed Sparrow in summer. And during migration, watch for staging Sandhill Cranes, Short-eared Owl, and perhaps Smith's Longspur.

The outlined areas on inset A indicate acreage that is predominantly unplowed grasslands, pastures, and meadows. It is worth checking as much of this area as possible, especially the portion between County Roads 34 and 26, the place birders generally refer to the Felton Prairie. If your time is limited, however, there are six good grassland locations to concentrate on:

• The Nature Conservancy's **Blazing Star Prairie (A1)** and the adjacent pasture to the east, where there has long been a prairie-chicken lek. The best access is from County Road 34: turn south opposite County Road 110 on 190th Street N., 4.4 miles east of Highway 9 — but beware driving this road in wet periods.

• **Bicentennial Prairie Scientific and Natural Area (A2)** and the large adjacent meadow to the south, which looks especially good for Sprague's Pipit. Along with Blazing Star Prairie, this is a good place to try for Baird's Sparrow. The easiest access is along the south side of the tract: from the east end of County Road 108, turn north and then take the first road which goes east past the south side of a large gravel pit to the tract.

• The **grasslands tract** marked **A3** west of Bicentennial Prairie, where the most recent Baird's Sparrow records occurred. As shown on inset A, you can reach this area by either turning north from the east end of County Road 108, or by turning south off County Road 34, 3.4 miles east of Highway 9.

• The grasslands, prairie-chicken lek, and Loggerhead Shrike spot along **County Road 108 (A4)**. Watch especially for prairie-chickens north of 108, 1.8 miles east of Highway 9, and the thickets and wires at the east end of

More than any other county in Minnesota, Clay County is the place to see prairie birds, the place where Glacial Lake Agassiz most left its mark and left behind an extensive complex of virgin grasslands in the so-called **Felton Prairie area (inset A)**. Nowhere else in the state can the Casual Baird's Sparrow be reasonably expected to occur from time to time (it formerly nested here). Until recently, the Casual Sprague's Pipit regularly visited this area, and it still is seen almost annually. And these prairie tracts essentially remain the state's only breeding grounds for Chestnut-collared Longspurs.

Needless to say, birders come to Felton all the time during spring and summer to search for these three specialties, and, as a result, several strays have been uncovered: Ferruginous Hawk (more than once), Gyrfalcon (fall), Prairie Falcon, Burrowing Owl, Say's Phoebe, Mountain Bluebird, Blue Grosbeak, Lark Bunting, and Henslow's Sparrow.

Rarities aside, these prairie tracts are consistently good

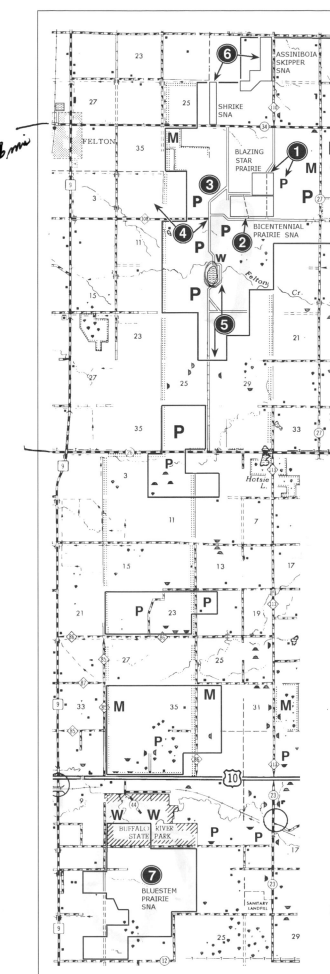

INSET A - FELTON
PRAIRIE AND
VICINITY

108 have long been one of the state's few consistent Logger-head Shrike nesting areas.

• The **Chestnut-collared Longspur pastures (A5)** along the 1.5-mile stretch of road south of the large gravel pit pond. For decades, this has been Minnesota's only consistent breeding colony for this colorful Great Plains bird. A few of these birds sometimes nest in other nearby pastures, and some recent Sprague's Pipit reports have been along the longspur road. As shown on inset A, this road can be accessed from the north: turn south off 108, continue past the large gravel pit, bear right at the fork to a nice wooded creek, and follow the road around the east side of the pond. Or from the south, take County Road 36 east 3 miles from Highway 9 (watch for Loggerhead Shrikes en route), turn north, and the first longspurs should be seen after 2 miles.

• The **Shrike** and **Assiniboia Skipper Scientific and Natural Areas (A6)** north of County Road 34. These recently acquired tracts have not yet been birded much, but, except for breeding longspurs, their potential would probably be the same as the above areas.

There are three things to keep in mind as you bird the Felton Prairie. First, neither the Baird's Sparrow nor Sprague's Pipit is Regular, so don't assume you'll see them. Overly optimistic birders misidentify other things as these rarities: e.g., a juvenile Horned Lark looks like a pipit, and the alternate Grasshopper Sparrow song sounds like one. In life, both the sparrow and the pipit fail to resemble their pictures in most field guides.

Second, be careful to respect private lands, especially those posted by the gravel companies; note, however, it is OK to ignore the no-trespassing sign posted where the road turns south from the east end of County Road 108. (And, if you have a choice, come on a weekend to avoid the roar of the gravel trucks.) Note the entire length of the longspur road may look like a private farm drive, but it has always been open to birders.

Finally, be aware these prairie tracts are continually threatened by encroaching gravel pits, overgrazing, and the farmer's plow. So don't be too surprised if last year's virgin prairie tract is next year's gravel pit.

There are also some sections outlined on the south half of inset A with hayfields, pastures, and meadows, though parts of them now are plowed or dug up. Certainly, the extensive grasslands within the 2,855-acre **Bluestem Prairie Scientific and Natural Area (A7)** comprise the most obvious and significant tract. Look especially for Greater Prairie-Chickens, you'll find Le Conte's Sparrows to be common, and singing Henslow's Sparrows have been found on occasion.

The only problem with this area is its large size, so it's hard to know where to start looking and listening. However, for more birding information or to reserve a prairie-chicken observation blind, stop in The Nature Conservancy's field office at Bluestem (go 2 miles south from Highway 10 on

Highway 9, then east 1.5 miles), or call them at 218-498-2679. For a change of pace, you also might want to look for migrant woods birds along the river in adjacent Buffalo River State Park (the entrance is marked on Highway 10).

* * *

Farther east in Clay County there are numerous wetlands, some shallow and marshy, others with wooded shorelines. Head off on just about any road east of County Roads 33/31, and you will stumble upon lots of habitat for nesting Red-necked Grebes and other water birds. (Or, if you insist on being more efficient and less serendipitous, you can always get a county map.) Wetlands are especially numerous east of Highway 32 between County Roads 26 and 10, and one consistent Red-necked Grebe site has been Flora Lake on the east side of Hitterdal.

There are a few other places in eastern Clay County which might be of interest. Possibly the nicest wooded spot in the county is the **Ulen City Park (8)** along the Wild Rice River. You can turn west into the park off Highway 32 just north of Ulen at the signs marking the campground, the city park, and the wayside rest. This would probably be most worthwhile for migrant warblers and other passerines, though there is a recent summer record of a singing Acadian Flycatcher.

Second, as you explore for wetlands, keep an eye open for grassland habitats. An especially large and intact tract is in the waterfowl production area on Highway 32, 2-4 miles south of Hitterdal (or 3-5 miles north of Highway 10).

And, if you really want to explore, head for The Nature Conservancy's 480-acre Margherita Preserve (also called Audubon Prairie). The tract is mostly wet and fragmented by brush and trees, but you might find Greater Prairie-Chicken, Upland Sandpiper, Marbled Godwit, Le Conte's Sparrow, and other prairie specialties. From Hawley, go south 5 miles on County Road 31, turn west, and go 3 miles to the end of the road.

West of Highway 9, Clay County is almost entirely plowed fields of the Red River valley, but it may be worth looking for migrants funneling through the wooded corridor along the river, and there are three areas to try in Moorhead:

• Johnson Park on the north edge of town; turn north off Highway 10 on County Road 3 / 11th Street N., go 2 miles, and turn west into the park.

• Gooseberry Park just north of Interstate 94; turn west off Highway 75 on 24th Avenue S., which curves up to 22nd Avenue S., and 22nd leads into the park.

• River Oaks Point on the south edge of town; go south from the interstate on Highway 75, in 1 mile turn west on 40th Avenue S., and turn west again on River Oaks Point Road after 40th curves south.

Over the years, several rarities have been discovered at the American Crystal Sugar sewage ponds in Moorhead: e.g., Clark's Grebe, Little Blue Heron, Cinnamon Teal, Ruff, and Red Phalarope. Unfortunately, in recent years, birders have not been permitted entry as they had in the past. If birder access is ever restored, the ponds lie on both sides of Highway 75, 1.5 miles north of Highway 10.

There also are six other Clay County sewage ponds.

❑ Glyndon (probably the best ones): 0.5 mile south on Park Avenue S., east 0.5 mile on 7th Street S.E..

❑ Felton: see inset A.

❑ Hawley: 0.5 mile south on County Road 31, 0.2 mile east.

❑ Sabin: 1 mile west on County Road 67.

❑ Comstock: 0.5 mile north on the first street east of the railroad tracks.

❑ Barnesville: take Highway 9 west 0.7 mile from the tracks, then go back east 0.2 mile on 2nd Avenue S.W.

(For more information on birding in Clay County, and adjacent Cass County, N.D., consult *Birding the Fargo-Moorhead Area* by Bob O'Connor; it is available for $15 from the Regional Science Center, Minnesota State University, Moorhead 56560.)

Wilkin County

With 90 percent or so of Wilkin County comprised of cultivated Red River valley farmlands, at least there is plenty of habitat for Swainson's Hawks, Gray Partridge, migrant Franklin's Gulls, Western Kingbirds, migrant American Tree and Harris's sparrows, wintering Snow Buntings, and migrant Lapland Longspurs. But more interesting are several tracts of prairie habitat remaining in the northeast corner of this county, thanks to Glacial Lake Agassiz. Here the beachline essentially reaches its southernmost terminus, and, with a couple of small isolated exceptions, this is the last place it has a visible ornithological impact.

Most birders refer to the area in and adjacent to **Rothsay Wildlife Management Area** (see **inset A**) as simply Rothsay, though the best birding roads lie outside the actual borders of the wildlife management area, and there are several other good tracts managed by The Nature Conservancy in the vicinity.

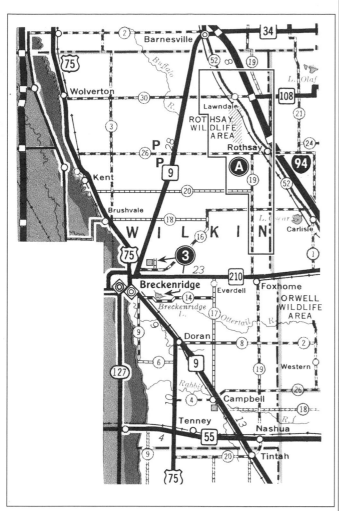

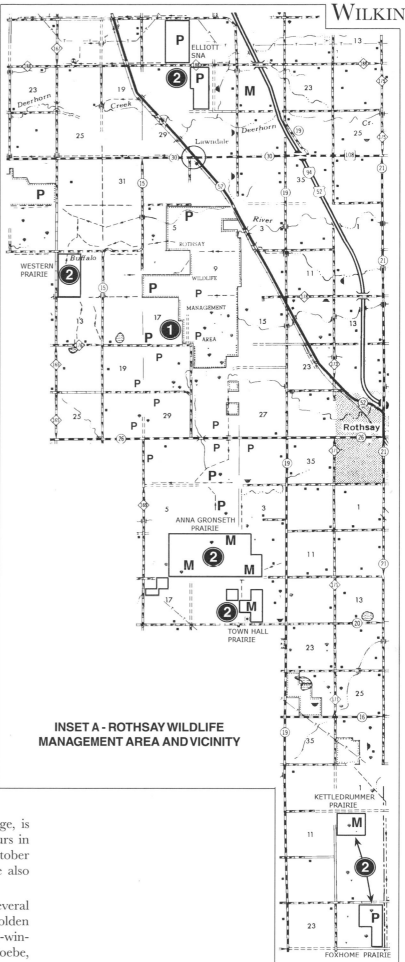

INSET A - ROTHSAY WILDLIFE MANAGEMENT AREA AND VICINITY

Rothsay is as good a place as any to see the specialties of the West Region. The Greater Prairie-Chicken is almost common here near the south edge of its range, and is perhaps easier to see here than anywhere else in Minnesota when not booming. Listen for Yellow Rail, also at the south edge of its range, especially at Anna Gronseth Prairie. Staging Sandhill Crane flocks are common in April and October. Upland Sandpiper, Marbled Godwit, and (sometimes) Wilson's Phalarope breed in the area, and Short-eared Owls occur, mostly in migration, but are possible any time of year.

Both Alder and Willow flycatchers nest practically side-by-side, the Alder in aspens at the south edge of its range, the Willow in wetter thickets. The Le Conte's Sparrow, also at the edge of its range, is common. Of special note, watch for Smith's Longspurs in migration, especially in mown hayfields in mid-October when flocks in the hundreds can occur (Laplands are also present and common, especially in late October).

Birders who frequent Rothsay have turned up several rarities over the years: e.g., Ferruginous Hawk, Golden Eagle, Gyrfalcon, Prairie Falcon (nearly annual in fall-winter), Long-billed Curlew, Burrowing Owl, Say's Phoebe,

Scissor-tailed Flycatcher, Black-billed Magpie, Mountain Bluebird, Sprague's Pipit, and Baird's, Henslow's and Nelson's Sharp-tailed sparrows. The Rothsay area is also one of the few places in the Northwest where winter birding can be productive. Those possibilities include Rough-legged Hawk, Gray Partridge, Greater Prairie-Chicken, Snowy and Short-eared owls (both rare), Northern Shrike, Snow Bunting, Common and Hoary (some years) redpolls.

The best areas to concentrate on are usually the hayfields along the roads between County Road 15 and the wildlife management area, north of County Road 26. The best single road is the east-west road along the south side of the main **Greater Prairie-Chicken lek (A1)**. As many as 100 booming males have been counted here, not only at dawn in spring, but also in fall and at dusk. This road is also a good place to find migrant Sandhill Cranes, Short-eared Owls, and Smith's Longspurs. Also, try to find the time to drive the parallel east-west road a mile to the south, and the dead-end north-south road off County Road 15, northwest of the lek.

Certainly, it would also be worthwhile to look for Rothsay's specialties at **The Nature Conservancy prairies (A2)**. From north to south on inset A:

• Elliott Scientific and Natural Area; 497 acres in two parcels.

• Western Prairie.

• Anna Gronseth Prairie; 1,300 acres of usually wet prairie, with Yellow Rails, side-by-side Alder and Willow flycatchers, lots of Le Conte's Sparrows, and perhaps Nelson's Sharp-tailed Sparrow.

• Town Hall Prairie.

• Kettledrummer Prairie.

• Foxhome Prairie.

Since natural wetlands are almost nonexistent in Wilkin County, it might be worth a drive over to Breckenridge where two spots often attract migrant water birds desperate for a place to rest and feed. (En route, you might want to stop first at Manston Wildlife Management Area, a nice grasslands area along County Road 26, 1-2 miles west of Highway 9, the site of a recent Long-billed Curlew record.)

Breckenridge's sewage ponds (3) is the better of the two "wetlands," as well as one of the largest and best set of ponds in the West Region: go north 1 mile on Highway 9 from Highway 210, then 1 mile east on County Road 16, and 0.5 mile north. **Lake Breckenridge** (also marked **3**) may look small and ordinary, but, again, the water birds around here are desperate. From downtown Breckenridge, go southeast 1.3 miles on Highway 75, then turn east on County Road 14 and go 1.5 miles.

There is also a small sewage pond 1 mile southeast of Campbell on Highway 9.

Otter Tail County

Perhaps the only thing more peculiar than this county's name — does the tail of any mammal deserve such attention? — is the name of its county seat. Or is it more odd for towns here to erect giant statues of an otter (Fergus Falls), a pelican (Pelican Rapids), a prairie-chicken (in Rothsay just across the Wilkin County line), and, the best of them all, the flying coot of Ashby (where I once lived) just across the Grant County line?

There is nothing ridiculous, however, about the birding possibilities in this county. Though more ordinary farmlands and scattered woodlots predominate in the eastern third, much of central Otter Tail County is characterized by dense deciduous woods, where several Southeast-type species occur, and hundreds of lakes, some of them quite large and attractive to migrants. And along the west edge of the county, generally west of Highway 59, is more open country dotted with numerous prairie potholes.

As is the case with counties to the east, birders seldom pay much attention to the mixed habitats of eastern Otter Tail County. However, such things as Sandhill Crane, American

Woodcock, Black-billed Cuckoo, Alder Flycatcher, Sedge Wren, Golden-winged Warbler, and Clay-colored Sparrow are around in summer.

Also, Yellow Rails have been heard in past summers at two locations marked M on the county map: 3.5 miles north of Deer Creek (or 4 miles south of Highway 10) on Highway 106; and on a back road east of Almora — turn south off County Road 40, 3.5 miles east of Highway 29, and go 1.5 miles.

Other spots which might be worth a visit in this part of the county: the marshes and bogs of Almora Wildlife Management Area (1-2 miles west of Highway 29, 3 miles south of Highway 210); and the Pine Warbler pines at Black's Grove County Park (turn south off Highway 10, 1.8 miles east of Bluffton or 2.3 miles west of the county line, and go 0.5 mile south).

The wooded lake country that predominates in much of the county also fails to attract many birders. However, these lakes and lands of fishermen and lake cabins would be worth birding during migration if one were looking for div-

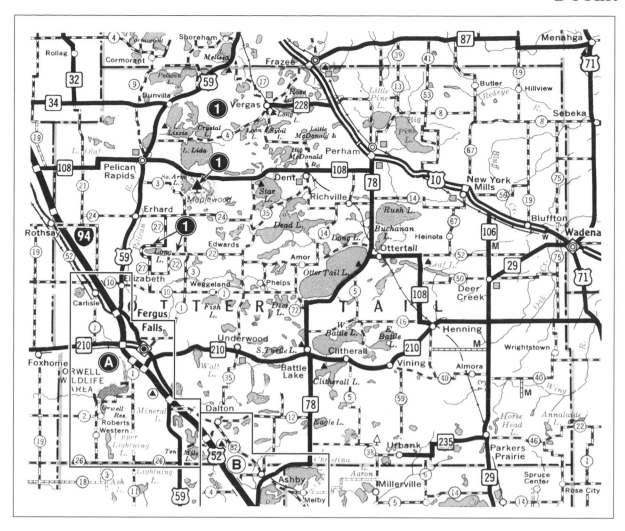

ing ducks and other waterfowl. The sheer size of some of these lakes — especially Battle, Otter Tail, Rush, Big Pine, Dead, Star, Lida, Lizzie, and Pelican — might sometimes attract a stray more characteristic of Lake Superior, like a Long-tailed Duck or scoter. In summer, Common Loons and Red-necked Grebes would also be nesting on some of these lakes.

If you're in the neighborhood in winter, check the open water in the outlet creeks below the dams on the west side of Rush Lake on Highway 78/108 and the southwest side of Otter Tail Lake on County Road 72. Among other things, Trumpeter Swans often winter here, sometimes in better numbers than in Fergus Falls.

Also of note in this heavily forested country east and north of Fergus Falls are some nesting species more characteristic of the Southeast Region. Red-shouldered Hawk, Eastern Screech-Owl, Red-bellied Woodpecker, Yellow-throated Vireo, Blue-gray Gnatcatcher, and Field Sparrow are all uncommon but widespread here. More local but regularly seen are Yellow-billed Cuckoo, and Blue-winged and Cerulean warblers.

There are undoubtedly many good but undiscovered woods where these species can be found, but you might

want to try these three **wooded areas (1)** first:

• Maplewood State Park, the easiest place to navigate without a county map: the entrance is off Highway 108, 7.5 miles east of Pelican Rapids.

• The back roads west of Vergas: try especially any of the roads going west off County Road 17; also watch here for Lark Sparrows in more open areas.

• The vicinity of Long Lake: from Elizabeth go 3 miles east on County Road 10, then north on County Road 27 for 5-7 miles to the west and north sides of the lake; and along County Road 22 a mile east of Long Lake (follow 22 where it turns east off 27, 2 miles north of County Road 10, and go 5 miles).

* * *

But, as in most other West Region counties, birders tend to be most interested in the open terrain of **wetlands and grasslands,** and most of this country is included on **inset A**. Also see the Otter Tail County portion of Grant County's inset B; there are some good roads to explore as well north of inset A, west of Highway 59. There aren't many unplowed grasslands remaining, but 320 acres of it are protected at the **Otter Tail Prairie Scientific and Natural Area (A2)**. A few Greater Prairie-Chickens still

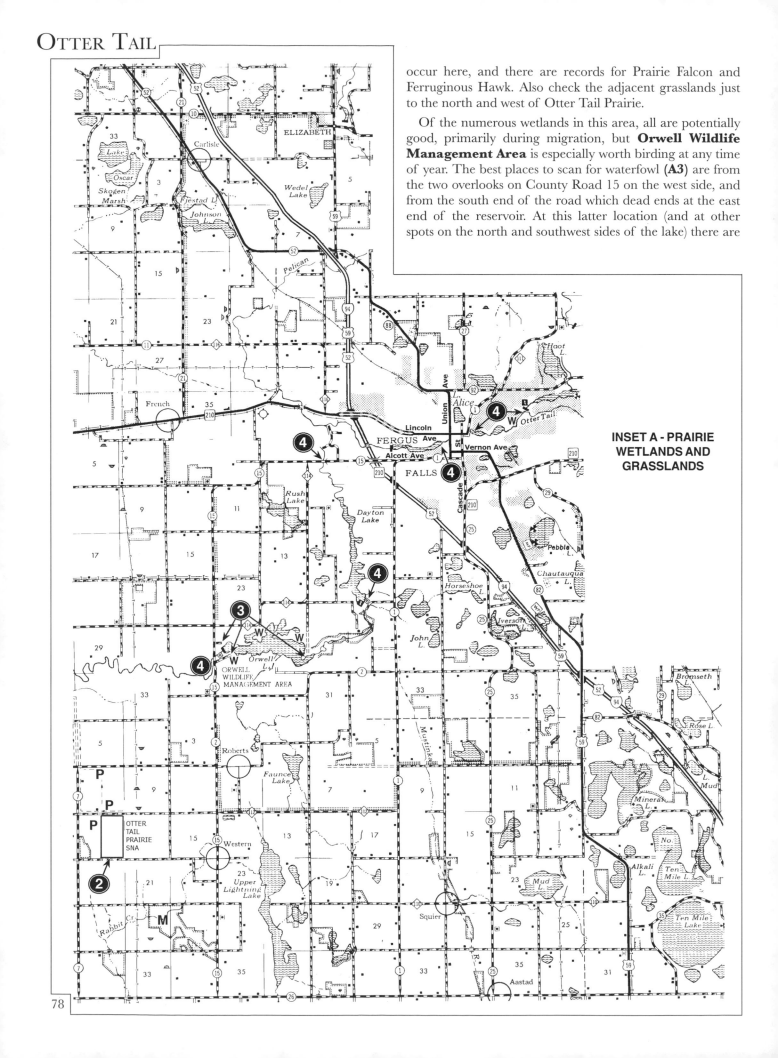

occur here, and there are records for Prairie Falcon and Ferruginous Hawk. Also check the adjacent grasslands just to the north and west of Otter Tail Prairie.

Of the numerous wetlands in this area, all are potentially good, primarily during migration, but **Orwell Wildlife Management Area** is especially worth birding at any time of year. The best places to scan for waterfowl **(A3)** are from the two overlooks on County Road 15 on the west side, and from the south end of the road which dead ends at the east end of the reservoir. At this latter location (and at other spots on the north and southwest sides of the lake) there are

INSET A - PRAIRIE WETLANDS AND GRASSLANDS

also stands of planted junipers where you might find a roosting Long-eared or Northern Saw-whet owl, a stray Townsend's Solitaire, or wintering Bohemian Waxwing.

As in any town in the Northwest with mountain ash or buckthorn berries or crab apples, the residential areas of Fergus Falls might also attract Bohemian Waxwings in winter. But more consistent then are the wintering water birds in the six open spots on the **Otter Tail River (A4)**, virtually the only such birding location in the Northwest. Canada Geese are most conspicuous, but almost any species of waterfowl is possible, and in recent years there have been overwintering Trumpeter Swans (over 300 individuals some winters) plus records of Harlequin Duck and Barrow's Goldeneye.

The extent of open water depends on the weather, with the most waterfowl usually seen from the so-called levee just east of downtown. To reach it, go east on Lincoln Avenue (downtown's east-west main street) and turn north just before you would cross the river. In two blocks turn east on Summit Avenue towards the large apartment building, and you can scan the river behind this building.

Also check below the power plant where the river is heavily wooded with cover for overwintering passerines. Just east of the levee, turn north on Concord Street, go two blocks to Mt. Faith Avenue, turn east to the river, park at the cemetery, and hike upstream.

Farther downstream, as shown on inset A, the river is also usually open and accessible at: Robert Hannah Park in Fergus Falls (from Lincoln Avenue downtown, go south on Union Avenue 4 blocks to Vernon Avenue, then west 6 blocks); County Road 15 just west of town; the dam at the south end of Dayton Lake (access from the east off County Road 1); and the dam at the west end of Orwell Lake.

Of final note in Fergus Falls is Lake Alice, where an egret/heron rookery has been active in recent summers. Though this small lake is surrounded by residential streets, strays such as Snowy Egret, Little Blue Heron, Cattle Egret, and Yellow-crowned Night-Heron have shown up among the nesting Great Egrets and Black-crowned Night-Herons. From Lincoln Avenue downtown, go north three blocks on Cascade Street to the south side of the lake.

And there are no fewer than 10 towns in the county with sewage ponds (!), with those at Frazee and Perham probably the best ones.

❏ Frazee: 0.2 mile north on County Road 10 just east of the Highway 10 wayside rest, then 0.2 mile east.

❏ Perham, which has two sets of ponds: one is 0.7 mile east of Highway 78 on 425th Street, just south of Highway 10; the other is reached by following Main Street southeast for 1 mile from downtown along the tracks, then north 0.5 mile on 450th Avenue.

❏ New York Mills: go 1 mile west from Main Avenue (County Road 67) on Nowell Street (the second street south of tracks), then 0.2 mile south.

❏ Vergas: 1 mile northeast from Highway 228 on County Road 4, then 0.8 mile west.

❏ Dent: turn south off Highway 108 on County Road 35, take the first street west, and continue west and south 0.5 mile.

❏ Deer Creek: 0.5 mile east from Highway 106 on County Road 50, then 0.5 mile south.

❏ Pelican Rapids: 0.5 mile north from Highway 108 on Highway 59, and 0.2 mile west on 8th Avenue N.W.

❏ Elizabeth: see inset A.

❏ Underwood: 0.5 mile west from County Road 35 on Highway 210, then 0.5 mile south.

❏ Dalton: see Grant County's inset B.

Douglas County

The lakes, woods, and fields of this county are not much different from Otter Tail's; therefore, its birding opportunities are essentially the same. There may not be any tamarack bogs, and there isn't as much open prairie-pothole country, but there are lots of lakes to check: some overrun with fishermen and water skiers, others with egrets, nesting loons, and Red-necked Grebes. Here as well are lots of deciduous woods for migrants and those nesting birds at or near the northwest edges of their ranges mentioned in the Otter Tail County chapter.

The densest woodlands are around the big lakes north of Alexandria, with the best place probably at Lake Carlos State Park: the entrance is off Highway 29, 8 miles north of Alex. This part of the county, however, has more people than birds on summer weekends. Another place to try for migrants might be Spruce Hill County Park: from Miltona, go 4 miles east on County Road 14, then 0.7 mile south.

This county's most interesting wetlands are mentioned elsewhere: Lake Osakis and its nesting Western Grebes are included on Todd County's inset A; Lake Christina and the

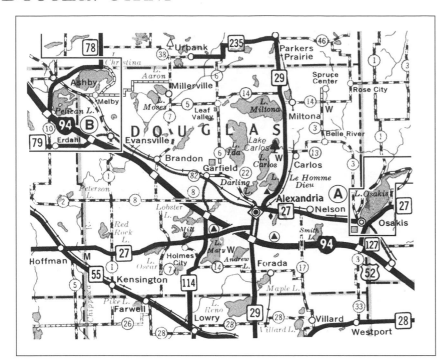

potholes in northwest Douglas County are discussed with Grant County's inset B. Otherwise, the only other lake I've seen worth a special trip during migration is Red Rock Lake: go 2.5 miles north on County Road 1 from Highway 27, then 0.5 mile west. And, as long as you're in the neighborhood, just southwest of here is The Nature Conservancy's Staffanson Prairie, a small tract of marsh and grassland: turn south off Highway 27, a mile east of the Grant County line, then go 1 mile south and 0.5 mile west.

The county's largest sewage ponds are at Osakis: from Highway 127, go west 1.2 miles on Highway 27, then 1 mile south. There are also ponds at Garfield: 0.5 mile north on County Road 12, and 0.2 mile east.

Grant County

Grant County may not have as many deciduous woodlands as Douglas County, although the three areas marked W by Pelican Lake on inset B should be good, at least during migration. But Grant County's prairie-pothole country is generally better than Douglas', and the wetlands, pastures, and hayfields scattered throughout most of the county's farmlands are as good as those in western Otter Tail County.

Many of the nesting specialties of the Northwest counties — e.g., Greater Prairie-Chicken, Sharp-tailed Grouse, Yellow Rail, Sandhill Crane, Short-eared Owl, Alder Flycatcher, Black-billed Magpie, and Le Conte's and Nelson's Sharp-tailed sparrows — are absent here in the Southwest (i.e., the south half of the West Region, from Traverse, Grant, and Douglas counties south).

However, the fields, wetlands, and woodlands of Grant and other Southwest counties are still good for migrants of all kinds, along with nesting Eared and Western grebes, Least Bittern, Swainson's Hawk, Gray Partridge (all year), Upland Sandpiper, Marbled Godwit (north of the Minnesota River), American Woodcock, Wilson's Phalarope (local), Black-billed and Yellow-billed cuckoos, Eastern Screech-Owl (all year), Willow Flycatcher, Sedge Wren, Clay-colored and Grasshopper sparrows, Dickcissel, and Orchard Oriole.

Some of the best **wetlands** to explore during migration are included on **insets A and B**, though a county map will

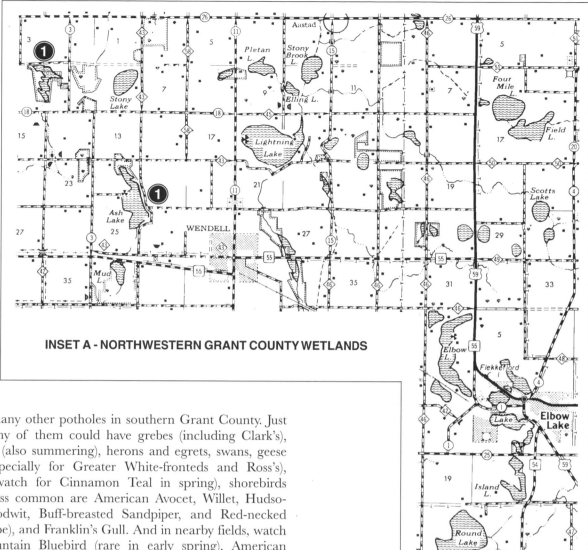

INSET A - NORTHWESTERN GRANT COUNTY WETLANDS

reveal many other potholes in southern Grant County. Just about any of them could have grebes (including Clark's), pelicans (also summering), herons and egrets, swans, geese (look especially for Greater White-fronteds and Ross's), ducks (watch for Cinnamon Teal in spring), shorebirds (those less common are American Avocet, Willet, Hudsonian Godwit, Buff-breasted Sandpiper, and Red-necked Phalarope), and Franklin's Gull. And in nearby fields, watch for Mountain Bluebird (rare in early spring), American Pipit, and Lapland Longspurs (perhaps with Smith's among them in April and October).

Check especially two wetlands **(A1)** in northwestern Grant County which have been consistently good in migration over the years: **Ash Lake** (site of the state's first Clark's Grebe record) and the **wildlife management area** a few miles northwest of Ash Lake.

Grant County, however, is best known for its nesting water birds, which frequent the area outlined in inset B (which includes parts of Otter Tail and Douglas counties). **Egret Island Scientific and Natural Area (B2)** is located on Pelican Lake and has long been one of Minnesota's largest heron rookeries. Double-crested Cormorants, Great Blue Herons, Great Egrets, and a few Black-crowned Night-Herons are the primary breeding species, a few Cattle Egrets used to (and still may) nest among them, and there have been summer sightings on the island or in the vicinity of Snowy Egret, Little Blue Heron, Tricolored Heron, and Yellow-crowned Night-Heron. The island is only distantly visible from shore, but for a closer look boats can be rented from resorts on the west and north sides of the lake.

These birds wander widely to feed in the area, so check as many wetlands as possible, but those south of Pelican Lake

as far as Highway 79 and those west of the lake within a mile of Highway 78 between Interstate 94 and Ashby are usually the most productive. One spot to check is the pasture on the south side of the lake which Cattle Egrets used to favor: turn north off County Road 54, 1 mile west of County Road 19. Another is the marshy pasture on County 19, 1.5 miles north of County 54.

Another famous lake is Christina, which lies mostly within Douglas County. Decades ago, hunters flocked to the lake for the large rafts of Canvasbacks and Redheads concentrated here. Though their numbers are diminished, Lake Christina is still good for migrant waterfowl of all kinds, and the number of coots can be overwhelming in fall. The best vantage points are from Highway 78 on the north side, and, if you're here in summer, be sure to stop at The Nature Conservancy's **Seven Sisters Prairie (B3)**, a steep hillside of native grasslands where the local Lark Sparrow regularly nests. This site is 3.5 miles east of Ashby: park at the gate at the gravel pit, and hike uphill.

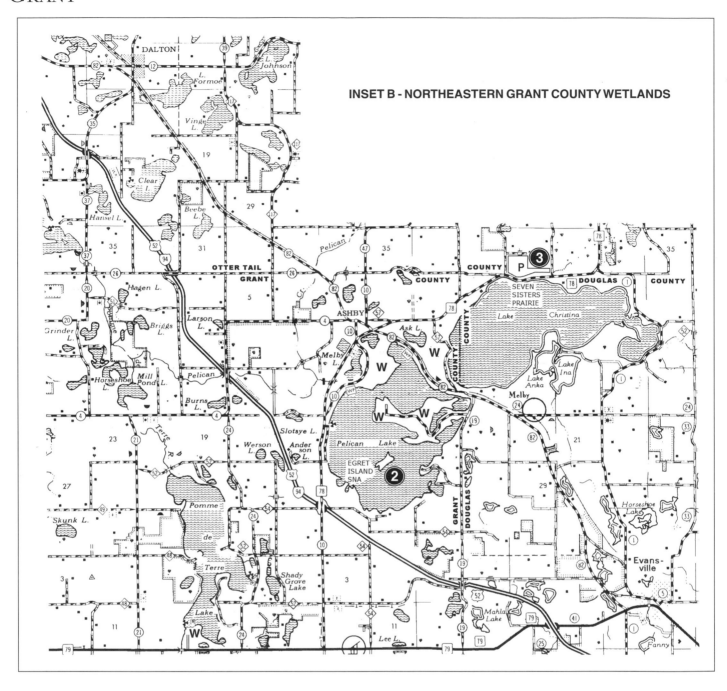

INSET B - NORTHEASTERN GRANT COUNTY WETLANDS

There are two other spots to recommend specifically in Grant County. One is the wooded area on the public access road on the south side of Pomme de Terre Lake (see inset B). More interesting is **Pine Ridge County Park (4)**: from Herman, go 4.2 miles north from Highway 27 on County Road 11, then 0.5 mile east on County Road 34. This latter location is worth going out of your way for during migration, and even in winter, since the planted conifers have attracted the likes of Northern Goshawk, Long-eared Owl, Black-billed Magpie, Boreal Chickadee, and Red Crossbill over the years. Northern Saw-whet Owl, Loggerhead Shrike, Townsend's Solitaire, Northern Mockingbird, Bohemian Waxwing, Spotted Towhee, and winter finches

would also seem possible on occasion in such a location.

More regular migrants of possible interest at this park, or anywhere in this region wherever there are trees or brush, would be both cuckoos, Philadelphia Vireo, Winter Wren, thrushes (including Gray-cheeked), warblers (such as Mourning, Canada, and Northern Waterthrush), sparrows (such as American Tree and Harris's), and Rusty Blackbird.

The best of Grant County's three sewage ponds is at Herman (1.2 miles southeast on Highway 9). There are also ponds at Ashby along Highway 78 (see inset B) and at Hoffman (0.2 mile south from Highway 27 on 3rd Street S., then 0.5 mile east on Carolina).

Traverse County

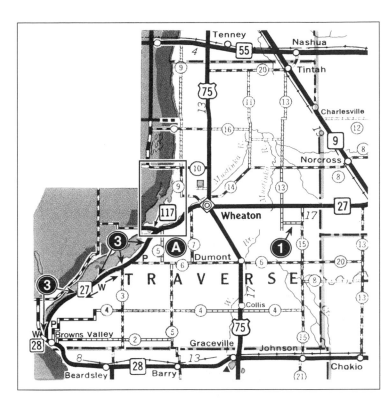

A quiz. Traverse County is ornithologically significant and unique because of: a) its former colony of Chestnut-collared Longspurs; b) a 1991 record of a family group of Clark's Grebes; c) the end (actually the beginning) here of the Red River valley and the beachline of Glacial Lake Agassiz; or d) its unusual number of sewage ponds. The answer: all of the above — well, sort of.

While there are scattered records, even in summer, of Chestnut-collared Longspurs in various West Region counties other than Clay (where the species always nests), birders haven't been able to reliably find them away from the Felton Prairie. But in summer 1980, an apparent nesting pair was discovered at The Nature Conservancy's **Miller Prairie West (1)**, and a few years later no fewer than 30 individuals and a nest were found, mostly in the adjacent pasture to the west. Significant, indeed. A reliable site, apparently not. Unfortunately, I'm unaware of any sightings in this area since 1987. It's still worth checking, though, as evidenced by some singing Henslow's Sparrows and a displaying male Lark Bunting here a few years back. To reach this site, go south on County Road 15 for 2 miles from Highway 27, then west 1 mile.

Mud Lake (inset A) is one of the best lakes in the West to bird for migrant waterfowl (especially geese — including Greater White-fronted and Ross's) and shorebirds (this shallow, marshy lake has exposed mudflats in drier years). There are two primary **access spots (A2)**: along the north-south road along its northeast shore (if passable, try the two dirt roads going west off County Road 76); and at the west end of Highway 117 at the South Dakota border (where the north end of Lake Traverse is even more visible).

At this latter site a few years ago, an adult Clark's Grebe with dependent young was discovered among the Westerns in the outlet channel on the north side of the road. Significant, yes, but there's a catch. At the time this would have been a first state breeding record, but we don't know on which side of the state line the nest was located.

The Red River starts its long flow north towards Hudson Bay from its source in Traverse County at the lake of the same name. From Browns Valley south, a new watershed begins as the waters of the Little Minnesota River flow the opposite direction into Big Stone Lake, then the Minnesota River, and eventually into the Mississippi and the Gulf of Mexico. But the ornithological significance of all this means that Traverse County is left within the grips of the Red River valley: grasslands plowed up, wetlands drained, agricultural interests prevailing.

Miller Prairie West, however, might be considered part of Glacial Lake Agassiz's beachline, and several potholes do remain near the county line between Browns Valley and Highway 75, though there is much more of the same habitat on the Big Stone County side. To explore these wetlands, turn off Highway 28 on County Road 2, just east of Browns Valley, and follow 2 east for 3 miles. From here and the next 9 miles over to County Road 5, you can turn north or south off County Road 2 on almost any road and find some potholes.

Lake Traverse is as good as Mud Lake for birding during migration, and, in addition to the spot on Highway 117 (see inset A), there are five places **(3)** along Highway 27 from which the lake is most visible. From Highway 117 southwest to Browns Valley:

• The public access 2 miles southwest of 117.

• The public access at the end of the road which goes north from the County Road 3 junction.

• The road to the lake 3 miles farther southwest, opposite the junction of County Road 60.

• The county park another 3 miles southwest.

• The levee at the south end of the lake, which runs between Highways 27 and 28.

Perhaps even more interesting than the lake's water birds would be the birding possibilities along the hillsides which run parallel to the lake on the other side of Highway 27. There remain strips of pastures too steep to plow along this stretch; the two longest pieces are marked P on the map, though they may be too narrow and fragmented to have many grassland birds.

There are also heavily wooded places where migrant warblers and the like might funnel through: try especially between County Road 3 and the county park, and at the south end of the lake. This line of hills also forms a natural ridge and flyway for migrating hawks, where there have been sightings of Ferruginous Hawk (the pair seen here once in July might have even been nesting), Prairie Falcon, and Mississippi Kite.

Back to that quiz. So, just what is significant about the number of Traverse County sewage ponds? Well, nothing any more, but up until a few years ago this had the distinction of being one of a very few counties in the entire state devoid of such "habitat". Now it has one of the better sets of ponds in the West Region at Wheaton: from Highway 27, go north 2 miles on Highway 75, then west 1 mile.

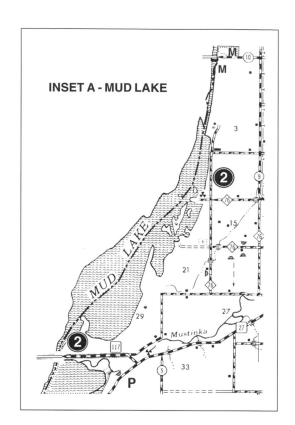

INSET A - MUD LAKE

Stevens County

Some of the general possibilities to be aware of in the Southwest have been discussed in the Grant County chapter, and, since Stevens County is adjacent and similar in habitat, this is as good a place as any to bird. A case can even be made that it is better than most, since this is where three first state records were documented years ago: Black-necked Stilt, Ruff, and Band-tailed Pigeon. Such strays as Yellow-crowned Night-Heron, Common Moorhen, Bell's Vireo, and Western Tanager have also occurred, and there have been multiple sightings of Cattle Egret, Cinnamon Teal, and Burrowing Owl over the years.

The only drawback is that there are few spots specifically better than others. Most of the lakes are in the northeastern part of the county, but their shorelines tend to be lined with trees more than marshes and mudflats. There are fewer, but more interesting, **wetlands** for migrants in western Stevens County, and the best of these are within **inset A**. At least this is where most birders go, where Western Grebes and other water birds nest, and where those three first state records occurred. My favorite wetland here is Clear Lake, where Clark's Grebes have been seen more than once.

If you have been in neighboring Traverse County and are

suffering from sewage pond withdrawal, don't despair: Stevens County has two of them! One of the largest sets of sewage ponds in the Southwest is located at Morris. Though they have to compete with natural wetlands in the vicinity for the attention of water birds, their size alone often makes them worthwhile. From the junction of Highways 9 and 59 on the southeast side of town, go 0.2 mile north on 59, then 1.2 miles east on County Road 10, and 0.5 mile south. There is also a smaller pond at Alberta: 0.5 mile north on County Road 9.

Actually, one of the most fascinating spots I've ever found in the county is the large and curious stone barn on the Big Stone County line: from Chokio, go west 3 miles on Highway 28 and south 5 miles. If you're curious, but reluctant to go out of your way to look at something without feathers, you could always pretend you're searching for Barn Owls.

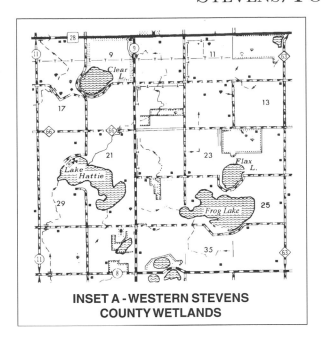

INSET A - WESTERN STEVENS COUNTY WETLANDS

Pope County

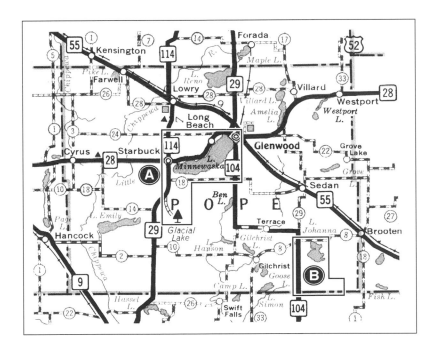

Though east of Stevens County, Pope has more of a western atmosphere because of its numerous prairie potholes throughout and its tracts of rolling grasslands in the southeastern part. These wetlands and open country are frequently wooded, but, with the aid of a county map, much of it is worth exploring for those migrants characteristic of the West. And, if its name is any indication, one lake in particular would be especially fascinating: Eckert Lake is located 4.7 miles north of Sedan on County Road 29.

One lake particularly conspicuous and interesting, by virtue of its size alone, is **Lake Minnewaska (inset A)**, one of the largest lakes in the West Region. Some migrants more characteristic of large bodies of water, which are absent or local in much of the Southwest, would most likely turn up at a lake like Minnewaska: e.g., Common Loon, Horned Grebe, Greater Scaup, Herring and Bonaparte's gulls, and Caspian and Common terns.

Such a lake would also be the place to search for a stray Red-throated or Pacific loon, Long-tailed Duck, any of the scoters, Barrow's Goldeneye, and Thayer's or Glaucous or some other unusual gull. Inset A maps the way around the lake, which is most easily scanned from the north along Highway 28 / 29. There are also a couple of interesting wetlands along this road, especially the one which often has mudflats next to the large and obvious game farm on the north side of the highway. (So use discretion before adding to your list that really unusual duck you find in this area!)

Also check the more heavily wooded spots along the shore for warblers and other passerines. One especially good

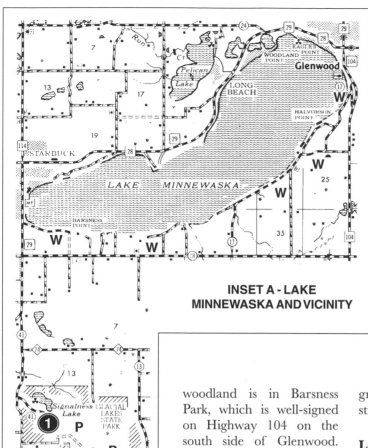

INSET A - LAKE MINNEWASKA AND VICINITY

INSET B - LAKE JOHANNA AND VICINITY

woodland is in Barsness Park, which is well-signed on Highway 104 on the south side of Glenwood. Besides migrants, look for such birds as Eastern Screech-Owl and Wood Thrush in summer.

In addition to Lake Minnewaska, Lake Emily in southwestern Pope County is also attractive to migrant water birds, though access is limited. Turn north off County Road 2, 3 miles east of the county line or 7.5 miles west of Highway 29, and go 1.5 miles to the public access.

Also located on inset A is **Glacial Lakes State Park (A1)**, a mostly open area of rolling grasslands; the entrance is on County Road 41, 2 miles south of Highway 29. A similar area is located on inset B: The Nature Conservancy's 581-acre **Ordway Prairie (B2)**. These are nice-looking tracts of geological significance, but little of particular note has ever been reported at either site, either because coverage by birders is infrequent or because the grasslands are too fragmented and too far east to attract a stray from the Great Plains.

Just as interesting as Ordway Prairie would be nearby **Lake Johanna (inset B),** where a large heron rookery is (or at least was) active on the island in the south half of the lake. Cormorants, Great Blues, and Great Egrets still nest here, Black-crowned Night-Herons at least used to occur, Snowy Egrets had occurred in years past, and this is the site of Minnesota's first breeding records for Little Blue Heron and Cattle Egret. To scan the island you would need to hike northwest from the jog on County Road 84, but you could also look for these species feeding in any of the wetlands shown in inset B.

Pope County has two sets of sewage ponds, the largest and newest and hardest ones to see at Glenwood. Turn north off Highway 28 just east of the railroad viaduct east of town, follow this road as it curves west and back north for a mile, then go 0.5 mile east to the access road (but, unless the gate is open or you have permission, the ponds are invisible). The county's other pond is at Lowry, 1 mile south on Highway 114.

Kandiyohi County

The open farmlands in the southern half of this county may look like part of the West Region, although unplowed grasslands are almost nonexistent, and there are few wetlands to recommend. You'll find most of the best birding areas in the northern half of Kandiyohi County, though the woodlands and lakes here look more like a part of the Southeast.

The best woodlands are within the area mapped on inset A, with those at **Sibley State Park (A1)** birded the most often. The park entrance is via County Road 48, 1 mile south of the junction of Highways 9 and 71. During migration, of course, this would be a good place to try for warblers and other passerines, and in the breeding season you might be able to find birds such as Red-shouldered and Broad-winged hawks, Ruffed Grouse, Red-bellied Woodpecker, both cuckoos, Barred Owl, Yellow-throated Vireo, Blue-gray Gnatcatcher, and Wood Thrush.

Probably the best place to start would be at the parking lot at the Lake Andrew boat ramp just west of the park entrance. From here, either walk east towards the picnic ground/campground or west into the woods along the bicycle path. Most notable in this area were the Yellow-throated Warblers which summered (and almost certainly bred) for seven consecutive years, 1994-2000. Though none were detected in 2001, this Casual species may well reappear here next summer.

Also interesting elsewhere in **inset A** are the scenic back roads within **northwestern Kandiyohi County**, where the terrain is a curious mix of dry hillsides, unplowed hayfields and pastures, numerous potholes, and scattered woodlands. You may not see anything different here, but grebes, bitterns, Upland Sandpiper, American Woodcock, both cuckoos, screech-owl, Willow Flycatcher, Western Kingbird, Sedge Wren, Eastern Bluebird, and Clay-colored, Field and Grasshopper sparrows should be around in summer. The habitat also looks perfect for a stray Loggerhead Shrike, Mountain Bluebird, Northern Mockingbird, Spotted Towhee, Lark Sparrow, or Orchard Oriole.

If you're birding here in May and June, be sure to drive through what may be the densest woodlands in the county on 240th Avenue N.W. Locally known as **Timber Lake Road** (also marked **A1**), this two-mile-long road looks even better than the state park for the possibility of finding a nesting Red-shouldered Hawk, Acadian Flycatcher, Blue-winged, Cerulean or Hooded warbler, or some other Southeast Region specialty.

Most of this county's wetlands don't seem to attract that many shorebirds and other specialties of the prairie pothole country, although Red-necked and Western grebes do nest

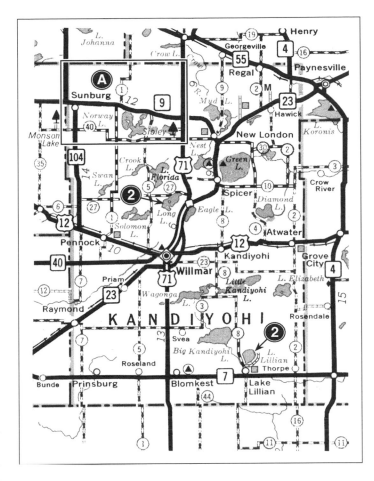

on some of its lakes (e.g., Sunburg Lake in inset A). But the county's two best lakes are probably Lillian and Long. **Lake Lillian (2)**, just north of the town of the same name, also has had nesting Western Grebes, and has been good over the years at attracting migrants, as evidenced by its fall records of Pacific Loon, Long-tailed Duck, and Sabine's Gull.

And the mostly invisible island on **Long Lake** (also marked **2**) is one of Minnesota's largest heron rookeries. During the past two decades, it has included the state's largest population of Great Blues and Great Egrets, and there have been records of Snowy Egrets and nesting Cattle Egrets. Such rookeries tend to become abandoned eventually, but, to see how it's doing, about the only place to bird the lake without a boat is on its north side along County Road 27. Turn west off Highway 71, 0.7 mile north of the Highway 23 junction.

Time permitting in summer, you might want to continue west from Long Lake on County 27 to Swan Lake to look for grebes, herons/egrets/bitterns, and rails. To scan the

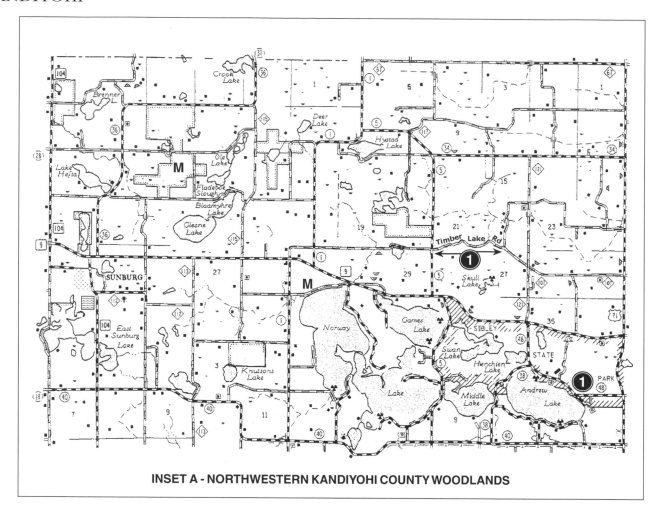

INSET A - NORTHWESTERN KANDIYOHI COUNTY WOODLANDS

west side of the lake, go west 1.5 miles from the junction of County Roads 27 and 1, then north 0.4 mile; and the marshes and backwaters on the east side are along County Road 1, 2-3 miles north of 27.

Another lake which is often good for herons/egrets or shorebirds during summer or migration is Lake Wagonga (also spelled Wagonda). Visibility is limited, however, but its west end can be scanned from Highway 71, 3 miles south of Highway 23; also try the public access on its southeast side on County Road 3.

Or, if you have the time during migration, continue north from Long Lake to the mix of fields, wetlands, and woodlands at Prairie Woods Environmental Learning Center, where there are recent records of Common Moorhen and nesting Northern Saw-whet Owl. From Long Lake, return on County Road 27 to Highway 71, go north 2.4 miles to County Road 29, then west 1.3 miles to the center's signed entrance.

Northeastern Kandiyohi County has two spots to be aware of. The fish hatchery ponds in New London might have some water birds of interest, especially when drawn down in fall exposing mudflats for shorebirds. It can also be good in spring/summer for herons and egrets, including Least Bitterns. In downtown New London, turn west off Main Street / Highway 9 on 1st Avenue N.W., go west a few blocks to the entrance gate, and hike around as many

ponds as time permits.

The other area might be worth checking in spring or summer: The Nature Conservancy's Regal Meadow, 385 acres of marshes and brushy grasslands. It's a good place to look for nesting bitterns, rails, Sandhill Crane, American Woodcock, and Sedge Wren, Yellow Rails have even been heard on occasion, and watch for Short-eared Owls during migration. The west side of it is along County Road 2, 2-3 miles north of Highway 23, or 2-3 miles south of Regal; its east side is a mile to the east along 160th Street N.E., which goes north from Hawick.

And there are five sewage ponds in the county:

❏ Lake Lillian: 1 mile east on Highway 7, 0.5 mile north.

❏ Atwater: 1 mile east on Highway 12 to the county line, 0.5 mile south, 0.2 mile west.

❏ Pennock: 0.8 mile north from Highway 12 on County Road 1, then south at the curve to the ponds.

❏ Sunburg: just south of town on Highway 104 (see inset A).

❏ The formerly excellent Green Lake District ponds, northeast of New London, which unfortunately are being abandoned (but it's possible the state may restore them and maintain the mudflats for shorebirds): turn north off Highway 23 on 115th Street N.E., 3 miles southwest of Hawick, then go 1.3 miles.

Swift County

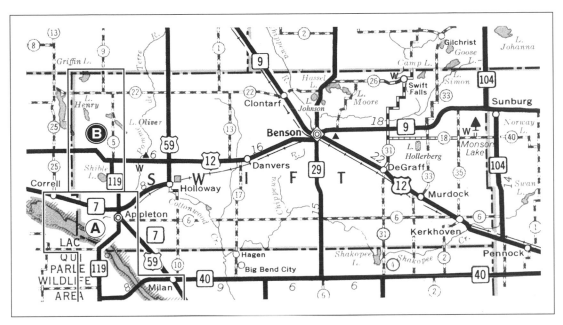

The deciduous woods of Kandiyohi County spill over a bit into this county, where the best stand of trees would be in Monson Lake State Park. From Highway 9, go south 3 miles on County Road 35, then east 1.7 miles on County Road 18, and north to the entrance. There are also two other places outside of the Minnesota River valley where migrant passerines could be concentrated (and also marked W on the map). One is at the county park in Swift Falls: from Highway 9, follow County Road 31 north for 7 miles. The other is in western Swift County at the wayside rest on the Pomme de Terre River on Highway 12, 3.5 miles west of Highway 59 or 2.5 miles east of Highway 119.

(South of this latter location, the Pomme de Terre continues into Swift County's portion of inset A in the Minnesota River valley, where the woodlands and other habitats are especially significant and are covered in the Lac Qui Parle County chapter.)

But birders will probably be more interested in this county's wetlands, many of which are concentrated in the northeastern quarter of the county, and a Swift County map will show the way to these lakes and wildlife management areas. Three of these lakes might be worth checking

first before the others.

• Lake Johnson: on Highway 29, 4 miles north of Benson.

• Lake Hassel: also along Highway 29, 6.5 miles north of Benson.

• And Lake Hollerberg: from Highway 9, go 1 mile south on County Road 33 and west 1.3 miles; or a mile south from 9 on County Road 31, and east 2.7 miles.

Usually more productive for water birds are the **western Swift County wetlands** shown on **inset B**. If you don't have time to check them all, two lakes usually prove the most worthwhile. One is **Lake Oliver (B1)**, where Western Grebes nest and where migrant shorebirds are frequently seen. The other is the southeast part of Big Stone County's **Artichoke Lake** (also marked **B1**), which can be scanned from Swift County Road 53; look especially on this large lake for migrant or summering grebes, pelicans, swans, geese, gulls, and terns.

Finally, there is a small sewage pond at Holloway: 0.5 mile north on Highway 59, then 0.6 mile east on County Road 38.

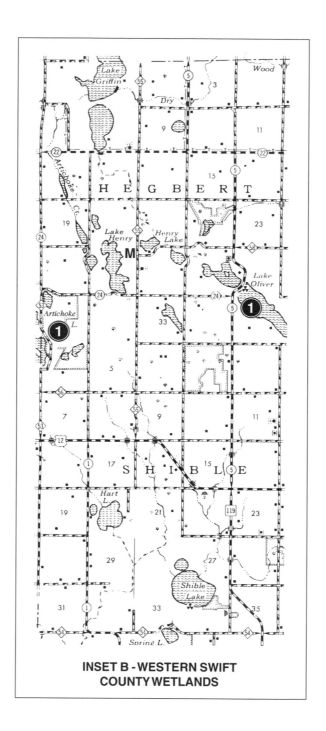

**INSET B - WESTERN SWIFT
COUNTY WETLANDS**

Big Stone County

If asked to name a county with the best birding in the West Region, which would you choose? Some might express a preference for Marshall County because of Agassiz National Wildlife Refuge, others might choose Clay County and the prairies of Felton, while many might select Lac Qui Parle County due to the popularity of Salt Lake and Big Stone National Wildlife Refuge.

For birding overall, however, it would be difficult to argue against Big Stone County. Its countryside of numerous wetlands and several intact tracts of unplowed grasslands resembles the beautiful prairie pothole country of the Dakotas; Big Stone Lake comprises the largest (or at least the longest) body of water in the West; and the fascinating habitats and possibilities of the Minnesota River valley are well

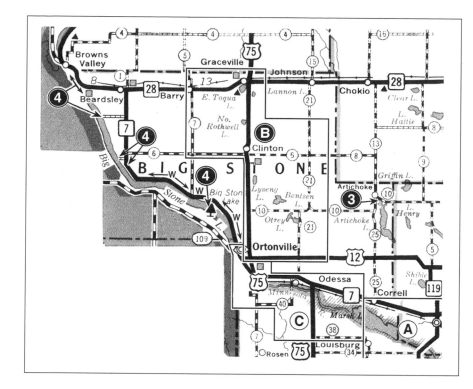

row. Chestnut-collared Longspurs have even twice shown up here not too many summers ago.

Outside of inset B there are other lakes, and two of them are especially large and usually worth checking. **Artichoke Lake (3)** is most visible along its southeast edge (see Swift County's inset B) and at its north end along County Road 10. As evidenced by records of Cinnamon Teal and Harlequin Duck, this is an attractive spot for migrants.

Vastly larger is 25-mile-long **Big Stone Lake (4)** on the other side of the county along the South Dakota border. Not only should it be checked during migration for "big lake" species that tend to be absent or local on smaller lakes in much of the West Region, but its wooded shoreline also forms a natural corridor for warblers and other migrant passerines, and there are some nice hillsides from which to scan for raptors. There are five places along the lake of special note; in addition, Ortonville's view of the lake is shown on Lac Qui Parle inset C.

• Starting at the Traverse County line, there are some nice-looking, and mostly inaccessible, pastures and meadows beyond the north end of the lake; these can at least be scanned from Highway 28.

• As you continue south on Highway 7, the first place from which to scan the lake and check for woods birds is at the public access southwest of Beardsley: turn west off Highway 7, 3 miles south of town, and go 2.7 miles.

• In another 5 miles (or 8 miles south of Beardsley) is the Bonanza Grove unit of Big Stone State Park; turn west off 7, and in a half mile go downhill.

• The next vantage point comes in another mile south at the wayside rest on Highway 7 (9 miles south of Beardsley).

• And from here on into Ortonville, Highway 7 follows the shoreline with several wooded spots and lake views; one place to stop, of course, would be at the main unit of Big Stone State Park.

All five of Big Stone County's sewage ponds are even worth checking:

❑ Southeast of Browns Valley on Highway 28, 2.2 miles southeast of the county line.

❑ Beardsley: 0.4 mile north of Highway 28 on County Road 1.

❑ Graceville: located on inset B.

❑ Clinton: also located on inset B.

❑ Ortonville: 1.5 miles east on Highway 12 from Highway 75, then 1 mile south; see Lac Qui Parle County's inset C map.

represented. All this has resulted in a long list of interesting species recorded within this county's borders.

Certainly the wetlands, prairie tracts, and wooded areas on the Big Stone County side of the Minnesota River from Ortonville to Marsh Lake are of particular importance, and these are included on Lac Qui Parle County's insets C and A. Especially significant are the Big Stone National Wildlife Refuge auto tour road, which begins in this county, and the roads on the north and west sides of Marsh Lake.

Also impressive in Big Stone County is its **prairie-pot-hole country (inset B)**, which includes numerous wetlands and several intact pieces of rocky grasslands. It's truly remarkable how many of these have never been drained or plowed. During summer and migration, one could easily spend many worthwhile hours wandering along these roads. Besides the lakes and wildlife management area tracts shown on inset B, there are many marshes and prairie pastures and other grasslands to explore — note especially the number of areas marked P south of County Road 10.

Probably the best single wetland of them all would be **Thielke Lake (B1)**, where water levels are usually low enough for shorebirds: watch especially for American Avocets, Willets, both godwits, and phalaropes. Eared and Western grebes, pelicans, and other water birds regularly summer here (there is also a record for breeding avocets), and rarities such as Clark's Grebe (several times), and California and Sabine's gulls have appeared.

And of the many grasslands, the largest is probably **Clinton Prairie Scientific and Natural Area (B2)**, a 160-acre tract 6 miles west of Clinton on County Road 6. In summer, watch for Upland Sandpiper, Marbled Godwit, Wilson's Phalarope, Sedge Wren, and Grasshopper Spar-

BIG STONE

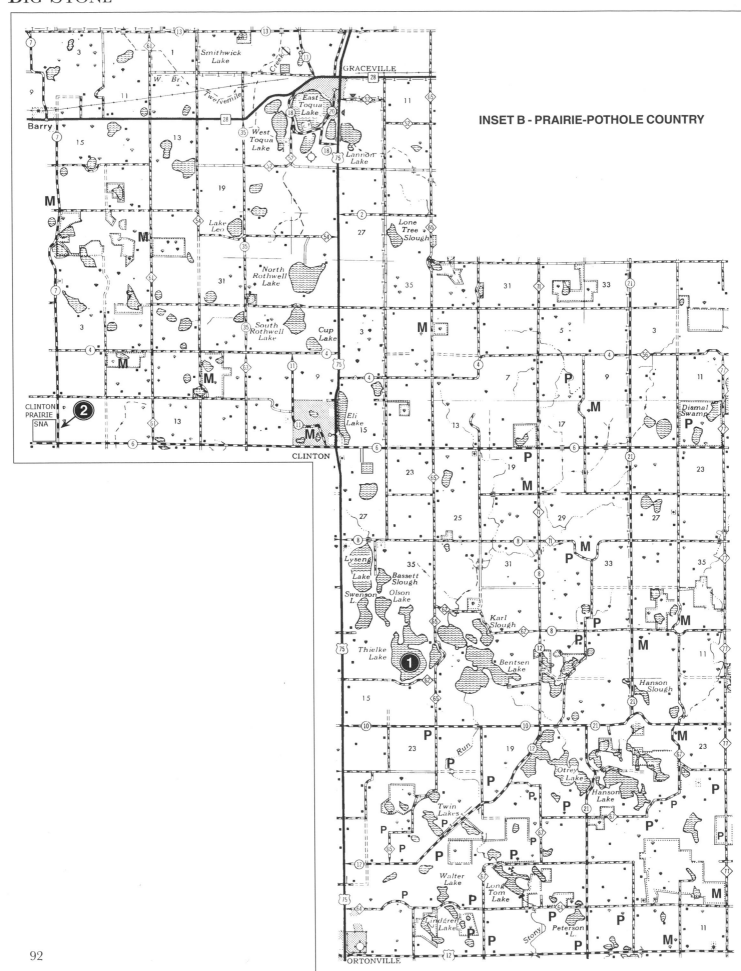

INSET B - PRAIRIE-POTHOLE COUNTRY

Smithwick Lake

GRACEVILLE

Barry

East Toqua Lake

West Toqua Lake

Lannon Lake

Lone Tree Slough

Lake Leo

North Rothwell Lake

South Rothwell Lake

Cup Lake

Dismal Swamp

CLINTON PRAIRIE SNA

Eli Lake

CLINTON

Lyseng Lake

Bassett Slough

Swenson L.

Olson Lake

Karl Slough

Thielke Lake

Bentsen Lake

Hanson Slough

Run

Otrey Lake

Hanson Lake

Twin Lakes

Walter Lake

Long Tom Lake

Lindgren Lake

Peterson L.

Stony

ORTONVILLE

Lac Qui Parle County

mer for such water birds as Western Grebes, American White Pelicans (one of the state's two nesting colonies is at Marsh Lake), Least Bittern, herons and egrets (Snowy and Cattle egrets and Little Blue Heron used to nest at Big Stone National Wildlife Refuge), flocks of migrant swans, geese and other waterfowl (especially at the southeast end of Lac Qui Parle Lake where Canada Geese congregate in fall/winter by the tens of thousands), Upland Sandpiper, and Marbled Godwit.

Other possibilities include: migrant Bald and Golden (rare) eagles, Swainson's Hawk, both cuckoos, roosting Long-eared and Northern Saw-whet owls, Willow Flycatcher, Loggerhead Shrike, Sedge Wren, a stray Mountain Bluebird or Townsend's Solitaire, Spotted Towhee, Clay-colored, Grasshopper and Le Conte's (in migration) sparrows, and Orchard Oriole.

Try to schedule enough time to drive as many roads on both sides of the river as possible within insets C and A, especially those in areas marked P and those adjacent to the river and to Marsh and Lac Qui Parle lakes. Starting in Ortonville in Big Stone County (see inset C), first scan the south end of Big Stone Lake: turn west off Highway 7 on the north edge of downtown. Then head downstream to **Big Stone National Wildlife Refuge**, certainly one of the finest areas in the valley, not to mention the entire West Region. Specifically, there are five areas to check (**C1**):

• The Auto Tour Road, which turns off Highway 7, about 2 miles southeast of Ortonville, crosses into Lac Qui Parle County, and loops for some 4 miles through heavily wooded spots, grassland tracts (dotted with rock outcrops and cactus), and flooded backwaters. The mile-long Rock Outcrop Hiking Trail along this road is always worth the time. Note the gated auto tour is sometimes open only on weekends.

• The meadows along County Road 15 which bisects the refuge. On the Odessa side of this road (Big Stone County Road 19), you'll find refuge headquarters (usually open only on weekdays), and it's worth driving the 2-mile-long Gravel Pit Road just south of headquarters if the gate is open.

• Even if the gate is closed on the Duck Banding Road, which leads east off 15 opposite the County Road 40 junction, it's always worth hiking the mile to its end at the main refuge pool. This is often the best spot for shorebirds, and

While there may be a difference of opinion as to which county in this region has the best birding, there can be little doubt that Lac Qui Parle is the most popular, the West Region county most often visited by the most birders over the years. Because of this coverage, the rarities found here are literally too numerous to mention, but the long list includes three first state records (Magnificent Hummingbird, Black Phoebe, and MacGillivray's Warbler) and two second state records (Black-throated Gray and Hermit warblers).

Certainly, then, Lac Qui Parle County has had more than its share of unusual strays and is a favorable place to look for just about all the specialties of the Southwest. Naturally, it also includes lots of good birding locations, especially within the fascinating **Minnesota River valley**, and this part of the valley — including the adjacent portions of Big Stone, Swift, and Chippewa counties across the river — has an especially impressive array of habitats. **Insets C and A** (a piece of Lac Qui Parle is also included on Chippewa County's inset B) include large lakes, island nesting colonies, smaller potholes, deep cattail marshes, extensive sedge meadows, numerous unplowed grasslands and pastures, riparian woods, patches of juniper, cactus, and rocky outcrops.

Look especially in these areas during migration or sum-

there is a decent view of the dead trees of the former heron rookery.

• The unmarked access road to the northeast end of the main pool; this road turns south off Big Stone County Road 21, 0.7 mile east of the east edge of Odessa, or 0.8 mile west of Highway 75.

• The one-way (south to north) dike road which parallels Highway 75 and overlooks the main refuge pool; it's also worth hiking beyond the gates at the south and north ends of this road.

Just south of the refuge boundary are some dense woods (marked W) to check for migrant passerines on County Road 40, 0.8 mile west of County Road 15. Also marked W southwest of here is another nice spot on the Yellow Bank River for woods birds: from County Road 15, go 4.8 miles west on County Road 40, then south 2 miles. At this latter site, there have even been records for both Hermit and Townsend's warblers!

Farther east on inset C between Highway 75 and Marsh Lake are several tracts of prairie meadows on both sides of the river that are definitely worth exploring. Check especially all 3 miles of the east-west road on the Lac Qui Parle County side which runs past The Nature Conservancy's **Plover Prairie (C2)**. And just east of here is the so-called **Louisburg Road (C3)**; be sure to drive its entire 4-mile length between County Road 38 and Highway 7 at the west end of Marsh Lake.

* * *

Continuing into inset A, the better roads tend to be those on the **south side of Marsh Lake (A4)**, especially the last 1.5 miles of County Road 34, and the two north-south dead-end roads off 34, 2 miles and 4 miles west of Highway 119. The road 2 miles west of 119 leads to some pools below Marsh Lake dam where shorebirds are often found.

But near the **east end of Marsh Lake**, check all the roads as well in Swift County on the north side of the river **(A5)**. Watch especially for Loggerhead Shrikes along Swift County Road 51 and the other roads near The Nature Conservancy's tract. And it's always worth spending time on the road which goes northwest off Highway 119, winds through some heavily wooded areas and backwaters, and dead ends at the Marsh Lake dam, a good place to scan for water birds of all kinds, including shorebirds, nesting Western Grebes, and pelicans. Next is **Highway 119** (also marked **A5**), which not only provides a good view of the northwest end of Lac Qui Parle Lake, but also goes past plenty of nice wooded backwaters, extensive marshlands, and rocky grasslands.

Lac Qui Parle Lake attracts lots of migrant waterfowl, but it mostly lacks marshes and other cover for nesting water birds. However, rocky grasslands, pastures, and meadows continue along both sides of the lake, and these three locations **(A6)** are especially worthwhile:

• Along the 3-mile-long **public access road** leading

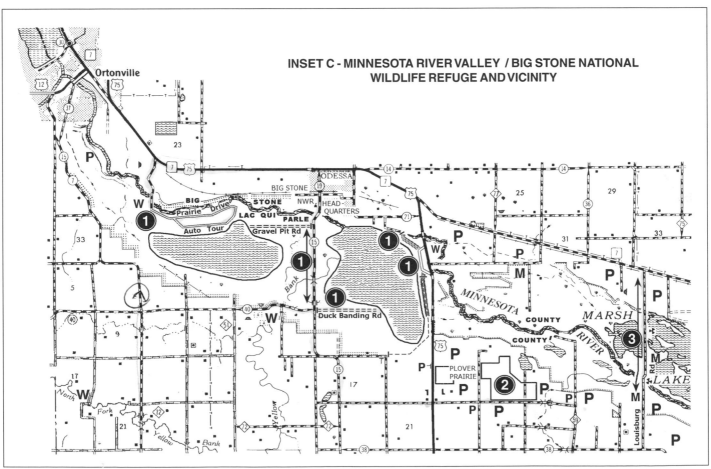

INSET C - MINNESOTA RIVER VALLEY / BIG STONE NATIONAL WILDLIFE REFUGE AND VICINITY

INSET A - MINNESOTA RIVER VALLEY / MARSH LAKE, LAC QUI PARLE, AND VICINITY

south off Highway 119 south of Appleton.

• The Nature Conservancy's large and impressive 1,143-acre **Chippewa Prairie**, which lies in both Swift and Chippewa counties (the easiest access is from the road on the county line). Don't be too surprised if you chance upon some Greater Prairie-Chickens here: some 200 have been introduced in this area recently, with at least two booming grounds becoming active.

• The sections marked P along **Lac Qui Parle County Road 66** (where an attempt was once made to introduce Burrowing Owls).

As you bird southeast toward that portion of the valley included on Chippewa County's inset B, unplowed pastures continue on both sides of the lake. Also of note on the Lac Qui Parle County side are a dense stand of planted pines by the public access on County Road 68 near the northwest end of the lake, and the junipers farther southeast around the junction of County Roads 33 and 31. Both sites are marked W, and both are possible spots for roosting owls, a lost Townsend's Solitaire, Bohemian Waxwing, or crossbills.

There are also three heavily wooded sites (**A7**) that are always worth checking during migration (and sometimes in summer):

• The **county park** southeast of the junction of County Roads 20 and 27.

• Along the Lac Qui Parle River in the **community of Lac Qui Parle**: follow River Street east from County

Road 20.

• **Lac Qui Parle State Park**: the entrance is on County Road 33 just northwest of County Road 48; recent summer records include a Kentucky Warbler and nesting Wood Thrushes.

*   *   *

Elsewhere in the county away from the Minnesota River, the best **wetlands** for birding are included in **inset D**. As excellent as the birding is in the Minnesota River valley, Lac Qui Parle County's most famous birding spot is still **Salt Lake (D8)**. This alkaline lake looks like it would be right at home in the prairie pothole country of the Dakotas, and it is easily scanned from its east side. It is a great place to find migrant water birds of all kinds, including Eared and Western grebes (both have nested), Tundra Swans, and migrating geese (especially the uncommon Greater White-fronted and Ross's).

This is often an especially good place for shorebirds since the water level is low enough most years to expose mudflats. In particular, watch for those less common migrants such as Piping Plover (now only casually seen in migration), American Avocet, Willet, Hudsonian Godwit (spring), Ruddy Turnstone, Red Knot (rare), Sanderling, White-rumped (spring) and Buff-breasted (rare in fall) sandpipers, and Wilson's and Red-necked phalaropes.

Among the other lakes, marshes and wildlife management areas within or near inset D, three areas are particularly worth checking:

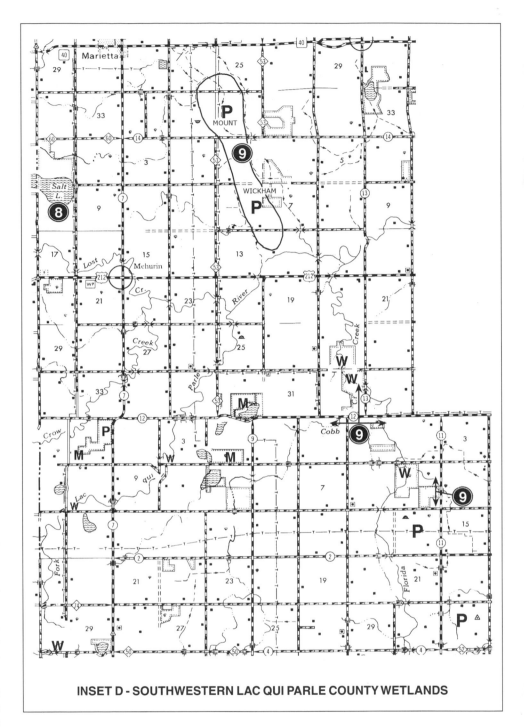

INSET D - SOUTHWESTERN LAC QUI PARLE COUNTY WETLANDS

• Those meadows and pastures along **Florida Creek (D9)** along County Roads 11, 12, and 13, which seem to flood each spring for the benefit of shorebirds; there are also some dense woodlands marked W along this creek for migrant passerines.

• The so-called **Mount Wickham** area east of Salt Lake (also marked **D9**), a similar 4-mile-long stretch of wet meadows and drier pastures.

• North of inset D is **Pegg Lake** and the adjacent **Yellow Bank Hills Scientific and Natural Area (9)**, southwest of the junction of County Roads 7 and 24. And,

if you're in the neighborhood in spring, head up County Road 7 another 5-6 miles where the low-lying fields are flooded most years for the benefit of shorebirds and other water birds.

As if there weren't already enough places to bird in this county, there are three sewage ponds:

❏ Dawson, the largest of the three; 1.6 miles east of County Road 23 on Highway 212, then 1 mile south, and 0.5 mile east.

❏ Marietta; 1 mile east and 0.5 mile south (located on inset D).

❏ Bellingham; 0.8 mile south on Highway 75.

Chippewa County

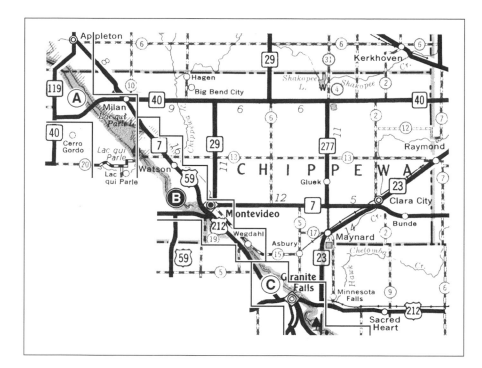

• The overlook on County Road 32, from which you can scan the southeast tip of the lake for Tundra Swans, geese (Canadas by the tens of thousands in milder winters), and other waterfowl.

• The mile of extensive deciduous woods along Chippewa County Road 32 between the overlook and County Road 13.

• The woodlands on the other side of the river just outside of Lac Qui Parle State Park along Lac Qui Parle County Road 33.

Farther downstream in inset B, there isn't usually much to see on either side of the river until Montevideo. Probably the best spot in this part of the valley is the **Wegdahl backwaters (B2)**, where water birds usually concentrate in spring, and where there are often mudflats for shorebirds in spring or fall. The wetland northwest of Wegdahl is less accessible and harder to bird; the flooded area southeast of town can either be birded by hiking down the railroad tracks along County Road 15, or take the first road north of the grain elevator which goes under the viaduct, and then take the first left onto a dead-end from which you can start hiking. The area farther downstream towards Granite Falls is mapped on Renville County's inset C.

Elsewhere in Chippewa County, almost everything is plowed up, large woodlands are almost nonexistent, there are few wetlands, and only one small sewage pond: 0.4 mile south of Maynard on Highway 23. About the only area which might be worth a visit during migration would be Shakopee Lake and vicinity. On the east side of the lake there is access from the county park off County Road 4, 2 miles north of Highway 40. The lake's outlet on the south (turn west 0.7 mile south of the county park road) often has mudflats for shorebirds in fall. Similarly, you will often find some mudflats in the wetland just south of there at the junction of Highways 40 and 277.

The trip downstream through the **Minnesota River valley** from Lac Qui Parle's inset A (which includes a portion of Chippewa County) continues into **inset B**. In turn, note that inset B includes adjacent parts of Lac Qui Parle and Yellow Medicine counties on the southwest side of the river. The birding possibilities and habitats mentioned in the Lac Qui Parle County chapter continue for the most part, although this part of the valley doesn't quite compare with the numerous fine areas in and around Big Stone National Wildlife Refuge and Marsh Lake.

Within inset B, the most productive area is around the **southeastern end of Lac Qui Parle Lake,** where there are five specific locations to check (**B1**), especially in migration. From north to south:

• The marshes and open water of Watson Sag along County Road 32. There might also be a roosting owl or some other stray in the planted pines and junipers 0.5 mile north of Watson Sag.

• Chippewa County Road 33, which passes through a variety of habitats and dead ends at the lake.

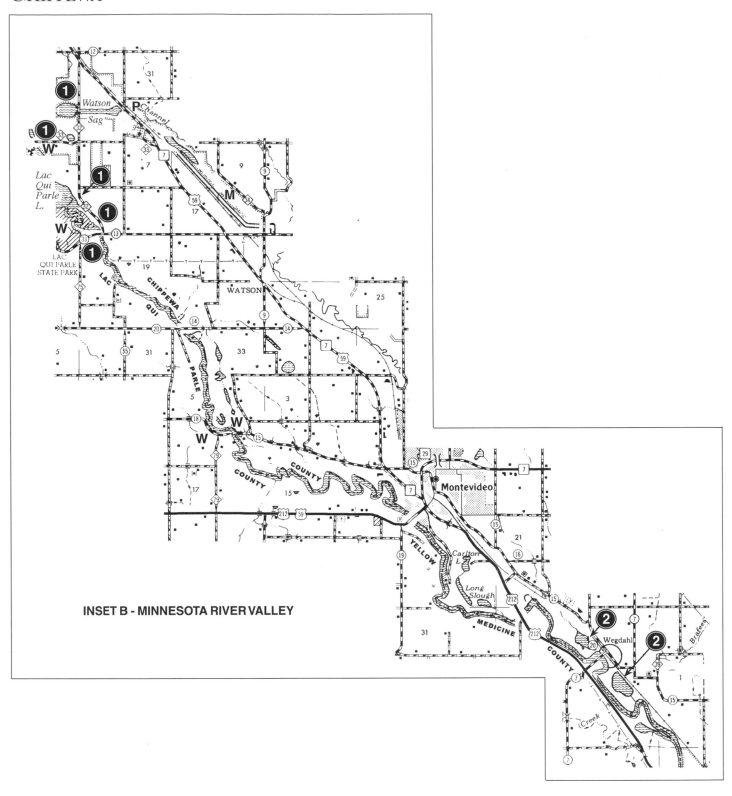

INSET B - MINNESOTA RIVER VALLEY

Renville County

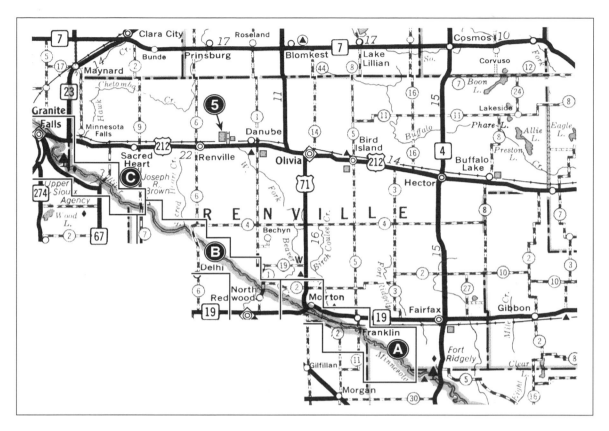

Insets C, B, and A map the way downstream along both sides of the **Minnesota River valley,** from the vicinity of Granite Falls to northwestern Brown County and the western tip of Nicollet County.

The terrain in this part of the valley differs in several ways from those areas farther northwest. There are no lakes formed by dams in the river (though after a heavy snowmelt there are flooded farmlands along the river for spring migrant water birds); marshes are less frequent; pastures and other grasslands along the river are reduced to narrower and more fragmented tracts (though there are still lots of interesting rock outcrops and some cactus in the tracts near Granite Falls); wooded areas are denser and more extensive; natural stands of junipers become common; and the hillsides are steeper and form more of an actual valley.

As might be expected, the birding possibilities also differ here somewhat, as Western Grebes, American White Pelicans, herons and egrets, migrant waterfowl, Marbled Godwits, and other wetlands and grasslands species tend to become replaced by woods birds. This part of the valley tends to be a better place to look for migrant raptors (Golden Eagles are rare but regular spring migrants in this valley), warblers and other migrant passerines, and in summer the

local Lark Sparrow is as common along these hillsides of oak and juniper as anywhere else in the state.

This fascinating portion of the valley is arguably the one area in Minnesota overlooked more than any other, as birders checking the Minnesota River valley tend to concentrate their efforts farther upstream in search of western species or in the Southeast Region portion of the valley looking for woods birds.

In summer there is much to learn about several species characteristic of the Southeast Region — we simply don't know exactly how far west their breeding ranges extend in this valley. These birds include: Turkey Vulture, Red-shouldered and Broad-winged hawks, Ruffed Grouse, Barred Owl, Whip-poor-will, Pileated Woodpecker, Yellow-throated Vireo, Blue-gray Gnatcatcher, Veery, Wood Thrush, Blue-winged, Cerulean and Prothonotary warblers, Ovenbird, Louisiana Waterthrush, Scarlet Tanager, Eastern Towhee, Lark Sparrow, and Eastern Meadowlark.

Beginning with Renville County's inset C, which also includes portions of Chippewa, Yellow Medicine, and Redwood counties, there are four areas to bird in the **vicinity of Granite Falls (C1)**:

RENVILLE

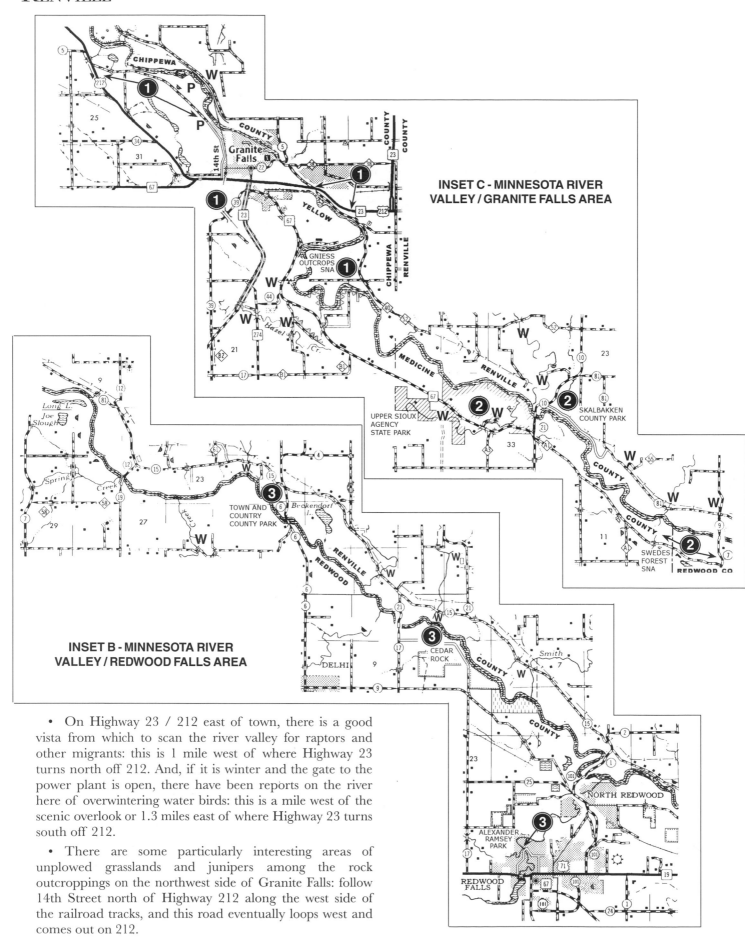

INSET C - MINNESOTA RIVER VALLEY / GRANITE FALLS AREA

INSET B - MINNESOTA RIVER VALLEY / REDWOOD FALLS AREA

• On Highway 23 / 212 east of town, there is a good vista from which to scan the river valley for raptors and other migrants: this is 1 mile west of where Highway 23 turns north off 212. And, if it is winter and the gate to the power plant is open, there have been reports on the river here of overwintering water birds: this is a mile west of the scenic overlook or 1.3 miles east of where Highway 23 turns south off 212.

• There are some particularly interesting areas of unplowed grasslands and junipers among the rock outcroppings on the northwest side of Granite Falls: follow 14th Street north of Highway 212 along the west side of the railroad tracks, and this road eventually loops west and comes out on 212.

100

• South of Granite Falls there are even more outcrops, pastures, and woods along Highways 23 and 67, but the traffic on these two roads is usually too distracting, and almost all of this intriguing habitat is fenced and posted. One small area you can hike into, though, is the Blue Devil Valley Scientific and Natural Area just west of 23 on Yellow Medicine County Road 39. The "Blue Devil," by the way, refers to a lizard: the rare Five-lined Skink.

• The larger Scientific and Natural Area, the 240-acre Gniess Outcrops, probably has more birding possibilities among its rocks and cactus. As shown on inset C, it is reached via Chippewa County Road 40, which turns south off Highway 212 just east of the power plant.

Farther downstream in inset C, there are three densely wooded areas to check. On the north side of the river is **Skalbakken County Park (C2)**: note there is access from both Renville County Roads 10 and 81. Just across the river on Highway 67 in Yellow Medicine County is **Upper Sioux Agency State Park** (also marked **C2**). But one of my favorite roads in the entire river valley goes through an especially dense stand of junipers past **Swedes Forest Scientific and Natural Area** (also **C2**), between Yellow Medicine County Road A1 and Redwood County Road 7. Look especially in this 2-mile stretch for roosting owls or a stray Townsend's Solitaire, Mountain Bluebird, Varied Thrush, Bohemian Waxwing, or crossbills.

* * *

Inset B is next and includes a portion of Redwood County on the south side of the river, where there are two especially interesting locations. Just east of Delhi is **Cedar Rock (B3)** and its excellent stands of junipers: there is access from the west off County Road 17, but it's easier to go in from the east (3.5 miles east of Delhi).

There are extensive deciduous woods in Redwood Falls at **Alexander Ramsey Park** (also marked **B3**). Either turn north off Highway 19 / 67 into the park on the first street west of the river (Grove Street); or turn north off Highway 19 / 71 on the first street east of the river (Lincoln Street), go 5 blocks to Oak Street, and then west into the park. You'll find the best woods and trails on the west, or Grove Street, side of the river.

And on the Renville County side of inset B, follow County Road 15 to **Town and Country County Park** (also **B3**), just west of County Road 6; check especially the junipers for nesting Lark Sparrows.

Farther downstream is inset A, which includes Redwood and Brown counties on the south side of the river. While the roads along this south side are worth driving (again, watch for Lark Sparrows), also be sure to check the woods at four locations on the north side (each marked **A4**):

• **Beaver Falls County Park**: the entrance is on the south side of town off County Road 2; also be sure to check those curious small ponds which dot the roads just to the east.

• **Birch Coulee Battlefield Historic Site**: the entrance on County Road 18, just south of County Road 2.

• The two apparently anonymous **Renville County Park units** shown southeast of Franklin.

INSET A - MINNESOTA RIVER VALLEY / FRANKLIN AREA

As is the case with some other counties bordering the Minnesota River, Renville County is predominantly farmland and mostly devoid of wooded areas, wetlands, or grasslands. But there are a few lakes in the northeastern corner of the county, with Boon Lake probably the best of them. There are recent records of Clark's Grebe and White-faced Ibis here, and good numbers of fall migrant shorebirds have been seen. Go east from Highway 4 along the Meeker County line for 5.6 miles on County Roads 7 and 12, and the lake is on both sides of the county line.

Time permitting, also check the unnamed wetland several miles farther south near Fairfax: from Highway 4, go 2.3 miles east on Highway 19, then north 2 miles on County Road 27, and 1 mile east. This spot is good for migrants, and both Red-necked and Eared grebes have been found nesting.

As might be expected, there are some sewage ponds in the county, and the best of these are the **Renville sugar beet ponds (5)**, owned by the Southwest Minnesota Cooperative. Turn north off Highway 212, 3 miles east of the County Road 6 junction (or 3 miles west of County Road 1), and go 0.5 mile. The water levels have always been good over the years for shorebirds, and there are ponds visible along both sides of the road. At times, overflow water and more mud collects just south of these ponds along Highway 212, and Buff-breasted Sandpipers have been found in early fall on the south side of 212.

There are also four municipal sewage ponds.

❏ Fairfax, the largest and best of the four: 1 mile south on Highway 4, then 0.5 mile east.

❏ Danube: 0.4 mile south of Highway 212 on County Road 1, then 0.2 mile east.

❏ Bird Island: turn west on Elm Avenue from County Road 5, 0.4 mile south of Highway 212, then go west to the T, and jog south and west to the ponds just beyond the cemetery.

❏ Buffalo Lake: 0.8 mile north on County Road 8 from Highway 212, then 0.8 mile east, and 0.2 mile south.

Yellow Medicine County

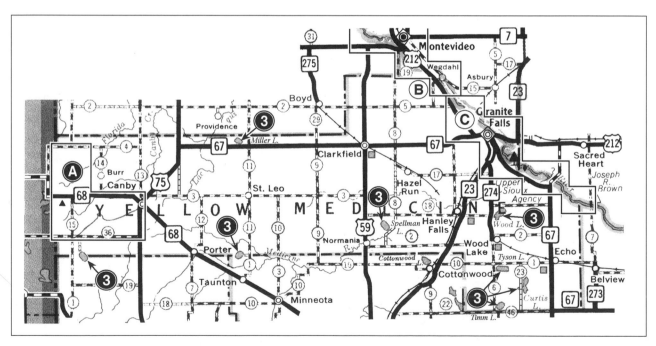

This county's territory within the Minnesota River valley has already been mapped and described within Chippewa County's inset B and Renville County's inset C (the latter including Yellow Medicine's best areas along the river). But elsewhere in the county there is certainly a lot more to see, thanks to several interesting wetlands and even some extensive prairie tracts.

One need only travel five miles or so west of the Yellow Medicine County-South Dakota border to see Chestnut-collared Longspurs nesting in the beautiful unplowed hillsides of the Coteau des Prairies. This ridge, which separates the Missouri River watershed from the Mississippi's, also passes through the southwestern corner of Minnesota, but its best grasslands and birds remain on the Dakota side of the line. However, there are several pastures and other unplowed tracts of **grasslands** still intact within this county (marked P on **inset A**), where Chestnut-collared Longspurs have been seen more than once in summer.

Although some of this acreage gets plowed up every year, it is worth driving all the roads through this area, and the two best-looking **prairie tracts** are marked **A1**. One is the 1.5-mile east-west road through the north tract between County Road 15 and the state line, which provides the nicest views of the countryside and is probably the best place to find a stray longspur. The wildlife management area farther south preserves a large area of longer grass and is best accessed from its south side.

Even if no longspurs are around, this is still a good area to find nesting species like Swainson's Hawk, Gray Partridge, Upland Sandpiper, Wilson's Phalarope (a few nest in the potholes), Willow Flycatcher, Loggerhead Shrike (maybe), Sedge Wren, Clay-colored and Grasshopper sparrows, Dickcissel, and Orchard Oriole. It also seems a better than average place during migration to encounter a rarity such as Cattle Egret, Ferruginous Hawk, Prairie Falcon, Buff-breasted Sandpiper, a Burrowing or Short-eared owl, Mountain Bluebird, Sprague's Pipit, Spotted Towhee, Lark Bunting, Smith's Longspur, or some other stray from the West. Note also the presence of several wetlands in inset A, and the wooded spots marked W along the creeks are often attractive to migrants.

Also marked on inset A is Del Clark Lake in **Stone Hill Regional Park (A2).** This relatively large reservoir often attracts a nice variety of migrant water birds, and the junipers and planted conifers here (and everywhere in the Southwest) should also be checked for roosting owls and lost migrants such as a solitaire or winter finches. The entrance to the park is off County Road 30 just southwest of Canby: from downtown at the junction of Highways 68 and 75, go 0.2 mile northwest on 68 to the sign for the park on Poplar Avenue N., then turn southwest on 30.

There are also several other **wetlands** scattered throughout Yellow Medicine County, and eight of these (all marked **3**) seem to be the most consistent in attracting migrant or nesting water birds. From west to east:

• The anonymous wetland on the Lincoln County line; from the junction of County Roads 15 and 36, go 1 mile east on 36 and 2 miles south.

• Miller Lake; on Highway 67, 1 mile west of County

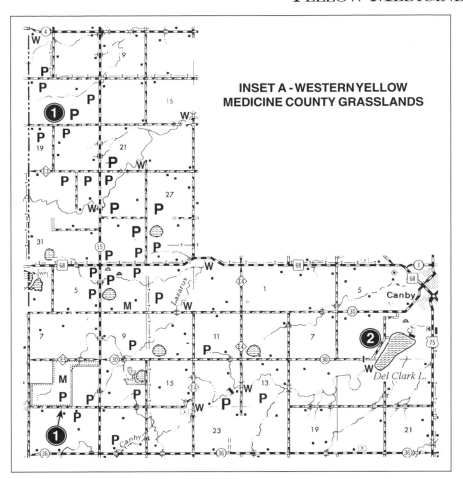

INSET A - WESTERN YELLOW MEDICINE COUNTY GRASSLANDS

Road 11.

• The unnamed lake on the Lyon County line, 0.8 mile west of County Road 11.

• Spellman Lake; from Normania, go 2 miles east on County Road 2 and 1.5 miles north on County Road 8.

• Wood Lake; most easily scanned from Highway 274 and from the county park on its north side — turn east from 274 on County Road 18, 3.5 miles north of the town of Wood Lake, then south into the park 0.7 mile east of 274.

• Tyson Lake; along the south side of County Road 1, east of County Road 6.

• Timm Lake; on the north side of County Road 46, just east of County Road 6.

• Curtis Lake; on County Road 23, 3 miles east of County Road 6: either turn south off County Road 1 and go 2-3 miles, or turn north off County Road 46, and go 2-3 miles.

Finally, the county has four sets of sewage ponds.

❑ Clarkfield: 1 mile south of town on Highway 59.

❑ Hanley Falls: 0.6 mile east of Highway 23 on County Road 18, then south.

❑ Wood Lake: on the south edge of town, at the junction of County Roads 2 and 6.

❑ Echo: 1 mile west on County Road 1.

Lincoln County

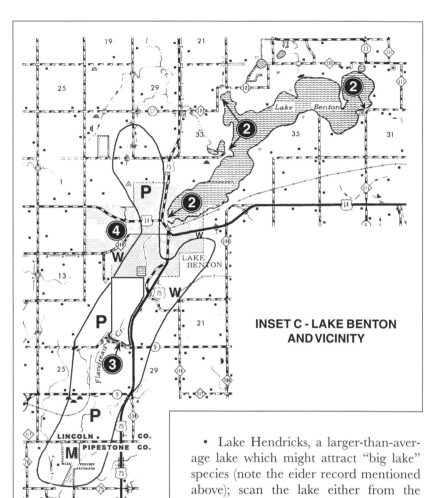

INSET C - LAKE BENTON AND VICINITY

As is the case with many of the counties in this corner of the state, Lincoln County is not covered by birders as well as it should be. Still, there are numerous wetlands attracting good numbers of migrants, a large area of unplowed grasslands, and the relatively few birding trips to this county have uncovered several vagrants over the years. These include White-faced Ibis, Eurasian Wigeon, Cinnamon Teal, Common Eider (shot by a hunter years ago at Lake Hendricks), Mississippi Kite (the state's first record was near Arco), Ferruginous Hawk, Sabine's Gull, Least Tern, and a probable MacGillivray's Warbler (at Lake Benton).

Numerous lakes and marshes are scattered through **northwestern Lincoln County (inset A)**, and seven of these **wetlands** (all marked **A1**) would probably be the best ones to check first. From north to south:

• The large wildlife management area wetland on the Yellow Medicine County line (my personal favorite); this is also accessible from the Yellow Medicine side.

• Steep Bank Lake; accessed from the north and east sides.

• Perch Lake; also accessed on the north and east.

• Lake Hendricks, a larger-than-average lake which might attract "big lake" species (note the eider record mentioned above); scan the lake either from the public access on the south side, or follow the signs off Highway 271 to the park in town on the north side of the lake.

• The large wildlife management areas on both sides of Highway 19, 2-3 miles west of Highway 75; check especially the stand of junipers 2 miles west and 0.5 mile north from 75.

• Ash Lake, especially from its north side.

• Lake Shaokatan; check both the west side from County Road 101 and Picnic Point County Park on the south side.

In the eastern part of Lincoln County are four other lakes sometimes worth visiting during migration and summer: Gislason and Dead Coon lakes are included on Lyon County's inset B; Lake Stay at Arco is visible along County Road 7 on the north and east sides of town; and Hawks Nest Lake is 0.6 mile north of Highway 19 (turn north from 19 either 1 mile west of County Road 7 or 3 miles east of Highway 75).

Even better for migrants, however, is **Lake Benton** on inset C. Like Hendricks, this relatively large lake is a good place to look for species which tend to bypass the smaller wetlands in this Region (e.g., Common Loon, Greater Scaup, Bald Eagle, Bonaparte's and Herring gulls, and Caspian and Common terns), and it should be a place where rare ducks, gulls, and other stray water birds occasionally drop in during migration. The best four places to scan the lake from are marked **C2**; from east to west:

• The small park on the east side along County Road 111.

• The bay on the north side along County Road 121.

• Norwegian County Park on the west side; turn east off Highway 75, 1.3 miles north of Highway 14.

• The public access at the southwest tip of the lake at the junction of Highways 75 and 14.

* * *

One thing you're sure to notice as you bird at Lake Benton is the collection of wind generators perched atop the ridges northwest of town. It's hard to know what to think of those big white things. On the one hand, I suppose wind power is a cleaner source of electricity than a coal or nuclear power plant, but, on the other hand, they sure clutter up the beautiful hillsides. These hillsides (and windmills) are also found southeast of here in Pipestone and Murray counties and are known as the Coteau des Prairies.

Northeast of the Coteau (the French word for "hill"), waters flow into the Minnesota River and eventually into the Mississippi. Southwest of this ridge, the creeks and rivers in this corner of the state flow the opposite way into the Missouri. As this ridge cuts across southwestern Minnesota, the birder should take note of those few places where the Coteau becomes especially visible in the form of relatively steep hillsides of unplowed pastures.

In Lincoln County, one of these larger areas of grasslands is around the junction of County Roads 1 and 15 (marked P on the map). But a much larger area of **Coteau des Prairies hillsides** is outlined on **inset C** in the vicinity of Lake

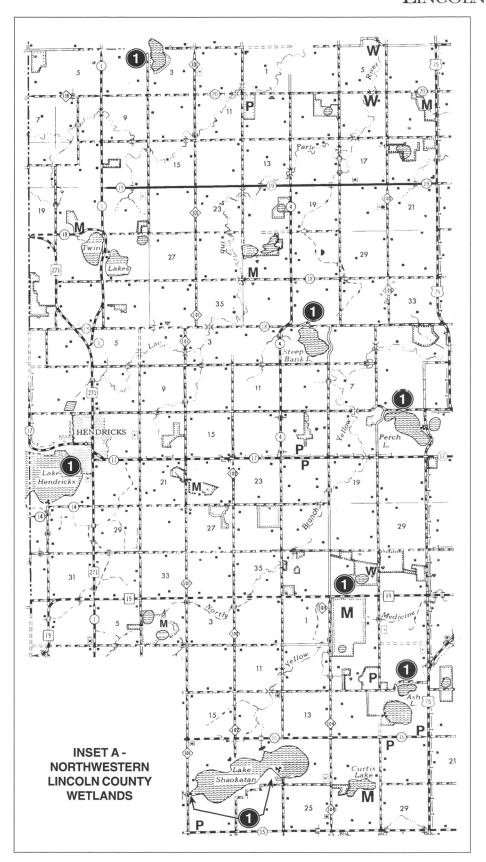

INSET A - NORTHWESTERN LINCOLN COUNTY WETLANDS

Benton, a great place to explore for those nesting and migrant species mentioned for Yellow Medicine County's inset A. The best roads to explore are the five roads shown on the map south of town leading west from Highway 75; note this inset and the hillsides extend a mile into Pipestone County. One tract particularly worth checking is The Nature Conservancy's 590-acre **Hole-in-the-Mountain Prairie (C3)**: watch for Uncas, Ottoe, and Dakota skippers — no, they're not birds, but butterflies of threatened or endangered status.

If you're in the area during warbler migration time (mid-May or September), it would be worth hiking through the extensive deciduous woods nearby at **Hole-in-the-Mountain County Park (C4)**, 0.7 mile west of Lake Benton on Highway 14. This relatively isolated woodland in this relatively treeless corner of the state is often good for migrant passerines: I once saw an adult male MacGillivray's Warbler here several Mays ago (although I can't prove it wasn't an aberrant Mourning). After turning into the park off

Highway 14, bear right past the campground to where the road ends at the picnic grounds, and follow the main trail into the trees.

There are four sewage ponds in the county, though probably none of them is worth a special trip; after all, you already have better things to do in Lincoln County than hang around sewage ponds!

❏ Hendricks: located on inset A just north of town.

❏ Lake Benton: turn west off Highway 75 at the south edge of town, 0.6 miles south of Highway 14, go 0.5 mile and turn right across the tracks (see inset C).

❏ Tyler: follow County Road 7 west from downtown for 0.5 mile, then go 0.5 mile north on County Road 113.

❏ Ivanhoe: from the junction of Highways 19 and 75, go 0.5 mile north on 75, 0.3 mile east, then north to the ponds.

Lyon County

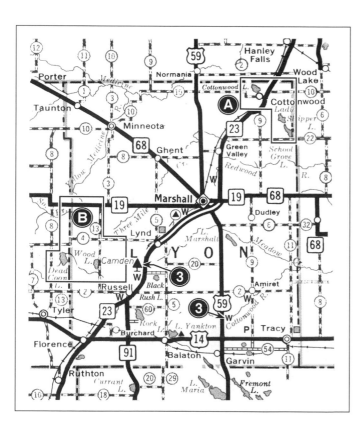

Although the habitats and associated birding possibilities are generally more interesting in Yellow Medicine and Lincoln counties, Lyon County has received more coverage over the years by both visiting and resident birders. This

was primarily due to the late, great Marshall sewage ponds, the best ponds Minnesota ever saw. But their use was discontinued in the 1970s, and they just don't make sewage ponds like they used to!

As a result, this county has had more than its share of rarities recorded within its borders, and the best evidence of this can be found in **northeastern Lyon County (inset A)** The lakes and other areas in Cottonwood and vicinity may appear ordinary, but coverage dating back to the 1950s by a single birder (Paul Egeland) has resulted in an extraordinary list of species, most of these found at Sham Lake: e.g., all three scoters, both Yellow and King rails, Long-billed Curlew, Ruff, California Gull, Least Tern (four times!), Western Wood-Pewee (Minnesota's first record), a probable Plumbeous Vireo (would also be a first state record), and Black-headed Grosbeak. Paul's yard in Cottonwood (where his mother still lives) even has the distinction of having the largest "yard list" in the state: well over 220 species.

The best five wetlands around **Cottonwood** are all marked **A1**:

• Sham Lake, on both sides of County Road 10; usually the best of the five.

• Gabriel Lake, northwest of Cottonwood (labeled Lone Tree Lake on some maps); good for Least Bittern and other marsh birds, often has shorebird mudflats, and the most recent Least Terns were here.

• Runholt Slough, just southwest of town; often has mudflats in fall for shorebirds and marshes for rails.

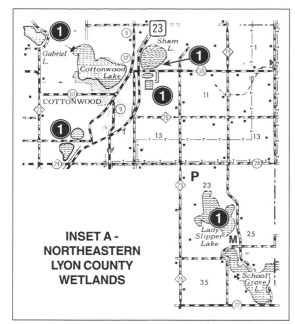

INSET A - NORTHEASTERN LYON COUNTY WETLANDS

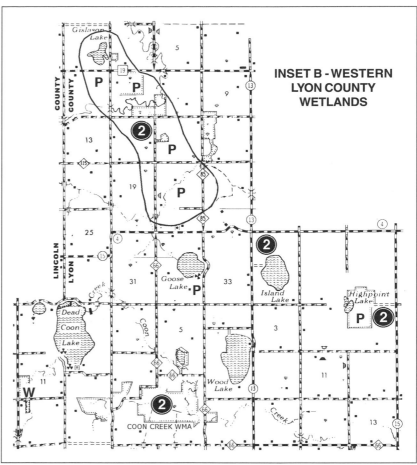

INSET B - WESTERN LYON COUNTY WETLANDS

• Lady Slipper Lake, where Western Grebes have nested; you might also find something interesting in the marshes and grasslands of Lines Wildlife Management Area, the area marked P just northwest of Lady Slipper, or at School Grove Lake.

• Even Cottonwood's sewage ponds are better than average; turn south off County Road 10, 0.4 mile east of Highway 23.

Another good area of **wetlands** is shown on **inset B**, which includes Gislason and Dead Coon lakes on the Lincoln County side of the line. While these two lakes are sometimes better than average for water birds in migration and in summer, I prefer four other areas on this map (all marked **B2**):

• **Highpoint Lake**, which is surrounded by an extensive tract of unplowed grasslands; access from County Road 15 on the east.

• **Island Lake**, best accessed from County Road 13 on the west.

• **Coon Creek Wildlife Management Area**, a sprawling area of open water, marshes, and brushy fields (look especially for Least Bitterns and other herons and egrets).

• And the extensive unplowed **pastures** outlined and marked P extending southeast from Gislason Lake for 4 miles.

There are also other scattered wetlands in southern Lyon County which might be worth a visit in summer or during migration. One of these is Rock Lake south of Russell: from Highway 23, go south 2 miles on Highway 91, then east 1 mile on County Road 60 to the north side of the lake; to scan the south side, return to 91 and go 1 mile south and 1.2 miles east.

Another is Black Rush Lake: turn east off Highway 23 a

mile south of the Camden State Park entrance, and go 1 mile on County Road 59. This restored wetland has recently been attractive to Least Bittern, rails, shorebirds (in dry periods), gulls (there is a nearby dump!), and other nesting and migrant waterbirds. Rarities such as White-faced Ibis and Great-tailed Grackle have also occurred.

Several wildlife management areas of possible interest also lie in the southeastern quarter of the county, most with wetlands and some with planted junipers or deciduous woods; a county map is recommended for those interested in exploring them.

Perhaps more significant in this part of the state, where woodlands are relatively uncommon, are the heavily wooded areas along the Redwood River southwest of Marshall and along the Cottonwood River in southeastern Lyon County. The two best locations are **Camden State Park** and **Garvin County Park** (both marked **3**), which are good not only for migrant passerines but might also have enough cover for some overwintering species. There are also some springs at Camden which keep a bit of the river open some winters. The main entrance to Camden is well-marked on Highway 23, about 2 miles southwest of Lynd.

To reach Garvin Park, which usually has better birding than Camden, go north 1.4 miles on Highway 59 from Highway 14 and turn east into the park. Unfortunately, however, you might find Garvin closed until noon from mid-April to mid-May during the park's local turkey hunting season.

Besides the sewage ponds at Cottonwood, there are ponds at Tracy (1 mile north on County Road 11, then 0.5 mile east), at Balaton (0.5 mile west from County Road 5 on Highway 14, and 0.5 mile north), and at Lynd (1 mile northeast on Highway 23, opposite the County Road 5 junction).

Redwood County

This chapter will be a short one, but only because Redwood County's excellent birding areas within the Minnesota River valley have already been discussed in the Renville County chapter and mapped on that county's insets C, B, and A. Unfortunately, the rest of Redwood County is almost entirely plowed — "black desert" farmlands essentially devoid of grasslands, with good wetlands and wooded habitats few and far between.

About the only places away from the river that might be worth going out of your way for are a couple of wetlands, both marked **1: Daubs Lake** and **Westline Wildlife Management Area**. To reach Daubs Lake, from Wabasso go 2 miles north on County Road 6, west 0.2 mile, and then north along the dirt road along the northeast side of the lake; if this road is impassable, return to County Road 6, and go 1 mile north, 1 mile west, and back south. Westline is farther west along County Road 5, 1.5 miles north of Highway 68 or 2.5 miles south of Highway 19. Eared Grebes and a variety of other water birds have nested at both locations, and both can attract migrant shorebirds when water levels are low enough to expose mudflats.

There are also sewage ponds at four towns in the county:

❑ North Redwood; where there are two sets of ponds, both located on Renville County's inset B.

❑ Belview; 1 mile east on County Road 9.

❑ Lamberton; 0.5 mile south on County Road 6, 1 mile east, and 0.2 mile south.

❑ Sanborn; 0.5 mile south from County Road 15 on Highway 71.

Brown County

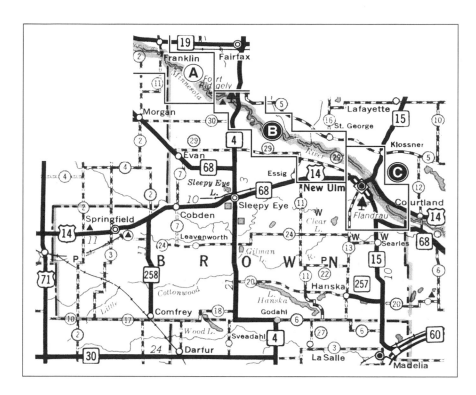

Part of Brown County's share of the **Minnesota River valley** appears on Renville County's inset A; the rest of it is shown here on **insets B and C,** which also include the Nicollet County — or north — side of the river. As mentioned in the Renville County chapter, it is worth driving as many roads as possible along both sides of the river to experience this valley's unique landscape and intriguing birding opportunities. About the only specific place to stop at within inset B would be Fort Ridgely State Park, located in Nicollet County just west of Highway 4.

But the most interesting birding along this stretch of the valley has proven to be in **Flandrau State Park** in New Ulm **(C1)**. From Highway 15 / 68 (Broadway Street), turn southwest on 10th Street S., go 6 blocks to Summit Avenue, then turn left (or southeast) to the park entrance road.

This is not just a place for migrants since several species more characteristic of Southeast Region woodlands nest here: e.g., Broad-winged Hawk, both cuckoos, Red-bellied and Pileated woodpeckers, Yellow-throated Vireo, Blue-gray Gnatcatcher (common), Wood Thrush, Cerulean Warbler (is this the western limit of its range?), Ovenbird, Scarlet Tanager, and others. Records also include White-eyed Vireo and Worm-eating Warbler, and this certainly seems a favorable place to find other Southeast specialties and strays. The best place in the park for woods birds is usually the trail loop southeast of the campground; also check the more open area along the trail north of the campground for Orchard Oriole and Sedge Wren.

Not far from Flandrau are some other excellent and dense woodlands around the **Shell Brewery** (visitors welcome; also marked **C1**). From Broadway Street, take 18th Street S. southwest to the T, and then turn left to the brewery. There are also landscaped gardens and planted conifers here, which attract a more varied assortment of birds than Flandrau.

As long as you're in town, it would also be worth checking two other wooded spots for migrants on the Minnesota River near downtown. One is Minnecon Park: from Broadway Street, take 3rd Street N. to its end at the river, where there is a trail leading north to 5th Street N. The other is a wooded oxbow just across the river where Prothonotary Warblers were once found. Just west of the junction of Highways 15 and 14 on the Nicollet County side, turn onto the dead-end road which skirts the edge of the oxbow on the south side of the highway.

The rest of Brown County has little out of the ordinary, but there are some good wooded stands along the Cottonwood River between County Road 11 and New Ulm, and along the Little Cottonwood River from County Road 13 east into Blue Earth County. There are also several lakes, none usually worth a special trip, but some birders have had luck with migrant water birds at Lake Hanska. There are few places to scan the lake, but it can be viewed from Lake Hanska County Park at the east end on County Road 11, and near the west end from the signed public access off County Road 20, 3 miles east of Highway 4.

Many of Minnesota's remnant grasslands are too small or too far east to attract many birds of interest — or to be cited in this book, even though some are preserved by The Nature Conservancy or as state Scientific and Natural Areas. But you might find something of interest in the 181 acres of hillside grasslands at the Cottonwood River Prairie Scientific and Natural Area, where Marbled Godwit, Short-eared Owl, and Blue Grosbeak (once) have been seen. Access to this tract is on County Road 2, 3.5 miles south of

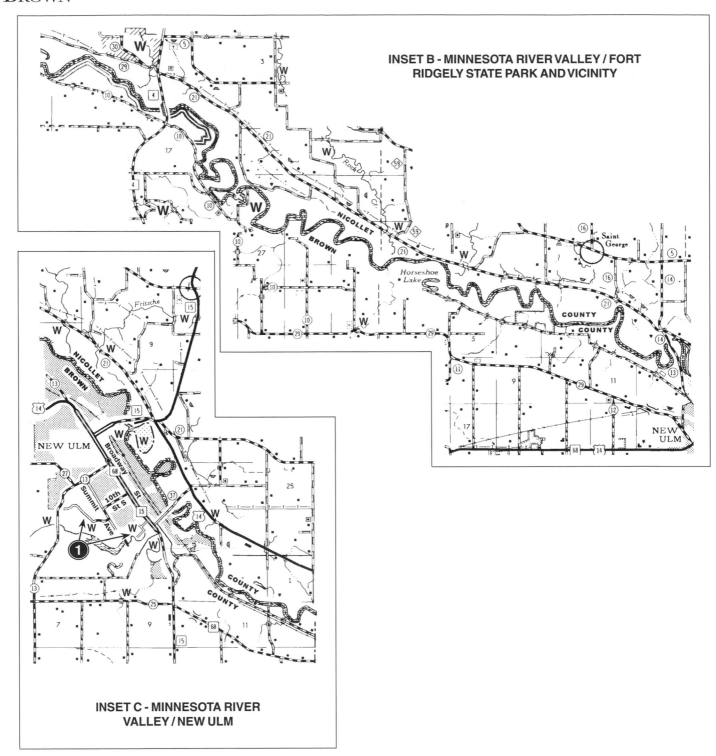

INSET B - MINNESOTA RIVER VALLEY / FORT RIDGELY STATE PARK AND VICINITY

INSET C - MINNESOTA RIVER VALLEY / NEW ULM

Highway 14.

Finally, there are two sets of sewage ponds at Sleepy Eye. One is in the southwest part of town (turn south off Highway 14 on 9th Avenue S.W., then go 0.6 mile south); the larger ponds are along Highway 4, 2.5 miles south of Highway 14.

Watonwan County

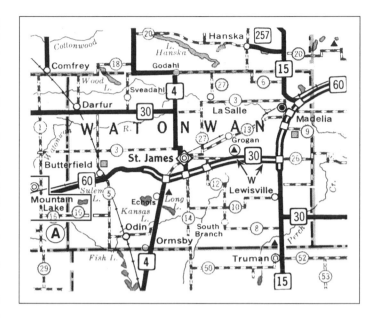

Once you leave the Minnesota River valley behind, most of the counties in south central Minnesota have relatively few areas of particular interest. Their wetlands are probably too far east and generally surrounded by too many trees to attract many water birds migrating through the prairie potholes of the Great Plains. Unplowed grasslands are scarce to nonexistent, and their woodlands tend to be fragmented and too far west to attract the specialties of southeastern Minnesota.

Watonwan County is no exception. Among its scattered lakes, about the only spot that would be considered above average is Sulem Lake, which is included on Cottonwood County's inset A. The only other "wetlands" of note might be the sewage ponds at Butterfield (0.8 mile north on County Road 5) and Madelia (turn east off Highway 15 / 60 on County Road 9, 1 mile south of downtown, and go 0.5 mile).

There are two wooded spots along Highway 30 / 60 which could be worthwhile during migration. One is the wayside rest along the Watonwan River, 4.5 miles west of the Highway 15 junction or 3.5 miles east of the first exit to St. James. The other is the Madelia Game Refuge, an area of thickets and planted pines on the south side of the highway, 2 miles west of the Highway 15 junction or 2 miles east of the wayside rest. And sometimes you might turn up

a bird or two of interest at the lake and planted conifers of Voss Park in the town of Butterfield: go north a mile from Highway 60 on County Road 5, then west to the park on County Road 105.

Cottonwood County

The birding potential of Cottonwood County is better than average, primarily due to the nice mix of habitats at Talcot Lake Wildlife Management Area, one of the best areas of unplowed grasslands south of the Minnesota River in and around Jeffers Petroglyphs, a couple of good wooded spots for migrant passerines, and lots of wetlands scattered throughout.

One place to start would be in **southeastern Cottonwood County (inset A)**, which includes a piece of Watonwan County. There are four spots to check specifically in and around **Mountain Lake** (all marked **A1**):

• Sulem Lake, on the Watonwan County side, a good

place for migrant and summering water birds.

• Regier Slough, located just west of Sulem Lake.

• The wooded hill (or "mountain" — thus the town's name) at Mountain County Park which has attracted warblers and other migrant woods birds; access from the east.

• And the town's sewage ponds; follow 10th Street north from downtown to the west side of the ponds.

More interesting, perhaps, are the nice undisturbed grasslands found in and around **Jeffers Petroglyphs (inset B)**; the entrance is marked on County Road 2, and there is an admission charge. The exposed reddish Sioux quartzite bedrock not only provided a palette for the drawings and

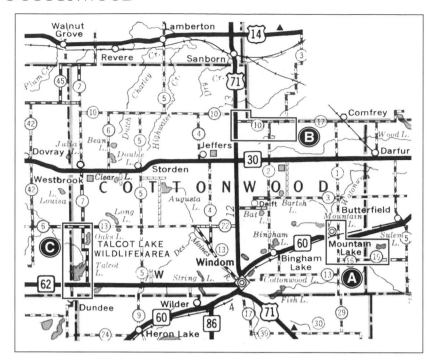

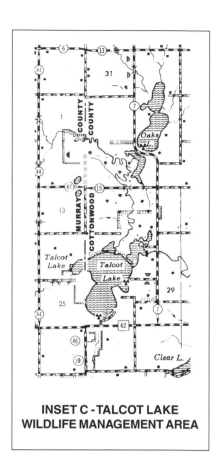

**INSET C - TALCOT LAKE
WILDLIFE MANAGEMENT AREA**

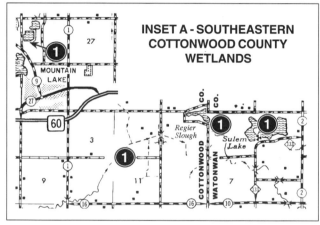

**INSET A - SOUTHEASTERN
COTTONWOOD COUNTY
WETLANDS**

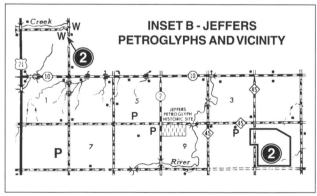

**INSET B - JEFFERS
PETROGLYPHS AND VICINITY**

others; Burrowing Owls also nested here years ago. But the main attraction in this area would be The Nature Conservancy's 611-acre **Red Rock Prairie (B2)**, a couple of miles east of the Petroglyphs, where birders have been finding migrant Smith's Longspurs in April and October in recent years. Also of interest during migration would be **Red Rock County Park** (also marked **B2**), a pretty ravine of woods and rock outcrops along Mound Creek: as shown on inset B, the entrance is 0.8 mile east of Highway 71.

A good area for just about every kind of bird found in the Southwest is shown on **inset C**: the wetlands, fields, thickets, and plantings in and around **Talcot Lake Wildlife Management Area.** From south to north, the best places to check on this map (which extends a mile into Murray County) are:

• At the south side of Oaks Lake along County Road 7.

• Along County Road 15 / Murray County Road 47, which has lots of cover, planted conifers, and two good gravel pit ponds.

• The three dead-end roads shown leading from County Road 7 to the east side of Talcot Lake.

• And the park and campground along Highway 62, where there is the widest view of the lake.

There are several other lakes scattered around the county which might be worth scanning if time permits, though I've usually not found any of them worth a special trip. Lakes shown on the county key map in western Cottonwood County are Bean (along County Road 6), Clear (just south

carvings of native Americans of pre-settlement times, but the rocks also protected this prairie from the farmer's plow. Here, at least, is a refreshing example of "progress" failing to displace native peoples and vegetation for a change — thanks to a little geological help.

The birder in summer should be able to find Upland Sandpiper, Western Kingbird, Sedge Wren, Clay-colored and Grasshopper sparrows, Dickcissel, Orchard Oriole, and

of Highway 30, 2 miles west of Storden), Augusta (1 mile south, 2 miles east, and 1 mile south of Storden), and Long (its south end on County Road 13).

And labeled on the map in the eastern part of the county are Bartsh Lake (along County Road 3), Bat Lake (sometimes called Rat Lake; a half mile south and a half mile east of Delft), and the unnamed slough on Highway 60 just west of Bingham Lake.

Also of note are some wooded spots and the pastured hillsides along the Des Moines River northwest of Windom. To check them out, take County Road 13, which starts just north of downtown Windom as 13th Street, as it follows the

river northwest out of town. Probably the best wooded spot on this river for warblers and other migrants lies west of Windom at Pat's Grove County Park, which is located 1 mile east and 1 mile north of the Highway 62-County Road 5 junction.

In addition to the sewage ponds at Mountain Lake, smaller ponds are located at Westbrook (1 mile east on Highway 30, and 0.4 mile south) and Jeffers (just east of town, 0.4 mile north of the junction of Highway 30 and County Road 4). There is also a small settling pond a half mile south of Highway 30: turn south off 30, 2 miles east of County Road 2 or 5 miles west of County Road 1.

Murray County

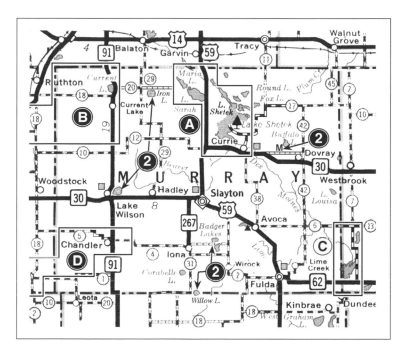

Murray seems to be one of those Minnesota counties that fails to receive as much attention as it deserves. The resident birders of nearby Lyon and Cottonwood counties already tend to have enough to see in their own back yards, and the visiting birder from the Twin Cities often bypasses this county in favor of other places in this corner of the state (e.g., Blue Mounds State Park in Rock County or Heron Lake in Jackson County). Yet, the lakes, marshes, and pastures of Murray County have lots birding potential, with one of the largest stands of deciduous woodlands in the Southwest south of the Minnesota River located here at **Lake Shetek State Park (inset A)**.

The park entrance is via County Roads 38 and 37 north of Currie, but note there are other good stands of trees and

places to scan the lake itself from other dead-end roads around the lake. The park's woodlands should be worth birding in summer as well as in migration, with the possibility of such species as Broad-winged Hawk, Yellow-bellied Sapsucker, Red-bellied and Pileated woodpeckers, Yellow-throated Vireo, Blue-gray Gnatcatcher, Northern Cardinal, and others which breed only rarely in this corner of the state. Also be sure to check nearby Lake Maria and Lake Sarah, also located on inset A, which are often more attractive to migrant water birds than Lake Shetek.

There are good **wetlands** as well shown on **inset B**, which includes a portion of northeastern Pipestone County. It is worth checking all of them, but you might have the best luck in the vicinity of the two **wildlife management areas** marked **B1**. The first area is around Hjermstad and Current Lakes, which herons and egrets seem to like especially. The other area is along the 2-mile stretch of Pipestone County Road 86 just west of the county line, where there are some good wetlands, planted junipers, and pastures.

And while you're in the neighborhood, take note of Pipestone County's pastured hillsides outlined on inset B along Highway 23 northeast of Holland, part of the Coteau des Prairies ridge. Most of these grasslands are fenced private property, some are overgrazed, and some are cluttered with wind generators. They can be scanned well enough from Highway 23 and adjacent side roads, but if you're up for some hiking away from the road, stop at the **Prairie Coteau Scientific and Natural Area** (also marked **B1**). The signed parking area is on the north side of 23, 0.4 mile northeast of the Pipestone County Road 84 junction.

A more extensive portion of **Coteau des Prairies hill-**

sides is located on **inset D**, extending from Chandler west into southeastern Pipestone County. Some of the sections within the area marked P are plowed, but it's worth exploring all the roads through here during migration. Hawks, for example, are often seen riding the thermals over the ridges, and I can think of no other place in the state where a wandering Ferruginous Hawk or Prairie Falcon would seem more at home. And don't neglect this area in summer, where such species as Swainson's Hawk, Gray Partridge, Upland Sandpiper, both cuckoos, Willow Flycatcher, Western Kingbird, Sedge Wren, Grasshopper Sparrow, Blue Grosbeak, Dickcissel, and Orchard Oriole nest.

Look and listen for the grosbeaks on fence wires near thickets and farm groves anywhere here in southwestern Murray County: this species regularly nests in this corner of Minnesota, with the Edgerton-Chandler area at the northeastern edge of its range. One spot to check for this and other woods birds would be Rock River Park on the southwest side of Edgerton on Pipestone County Road 1.

Elsewhere in Murray County, there are several other interesting **wetlands** to check for migrant and summering water birds. Usually worth a special trip are these widely separated spots (all marked **2**):

• Iron Lake is a relatively large, marshy area; turn east from Current Lake on County Road 20 and go 3-4 miles.

• Lake Wilson, on the east side of the town of the same name; easily scanned from Highways 30 and 91.

• The extensive marshes north of Highway 30 between Currie and Dovray; from Dovray, go north 1 mile on County Road 42, then west 2-3 miles on County Road 11.

• Badger Lakes; from Iona, go 0.3 mile north on Highway 267, then east 3 miles between the lakes.

• Willow Lake, south of Iona on the Nobles County line, just east of County Road 31.

Also, as shown on Cottonwood County's inset C, the west

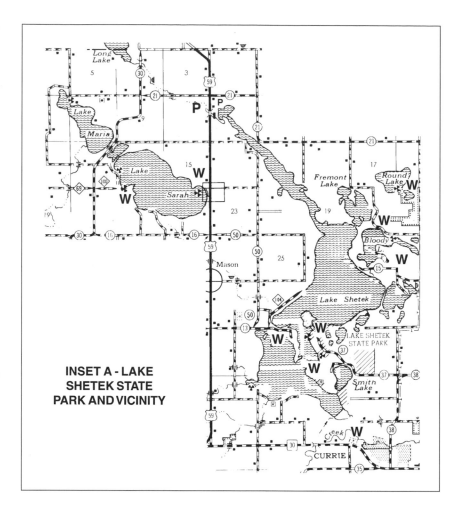

INSET A - LAKE SHETEK STATE PARK AND VICINITY

edge of Talcot Lake Wildlife Management Area lies within Murray County.

There are five sewage ponds in the county, all potentially worthwhile:

❑ Chandler; just east of town on County Road 4 (see inset D).

❑ Lake Wilson; 0.6 mile west on Highway 30, 1 mile north, and 0.3 mile east.

❑ Slayton; 1 mile north on Highway 30 / 59, 0.4 mile west, then 0.4 mile south to the access road to the tree dump and ponds.

❑ Currie; 1 mile east on Highway 30, 0.2 mile north.

❑ Fulda; 1 mile north on Highway 59.

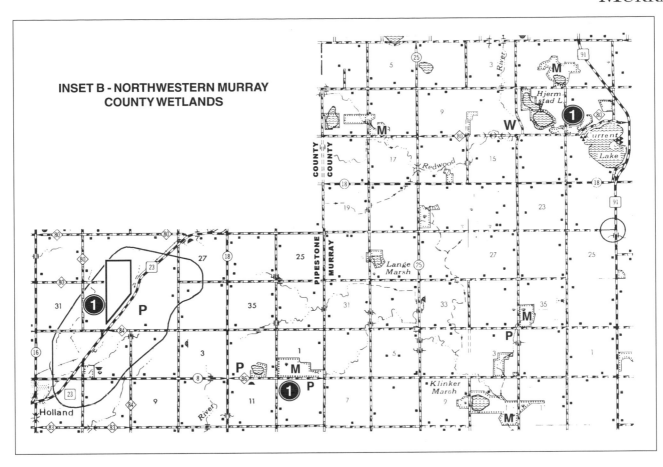

INSET B - NORTHWESTERN MURRAY COUNTY WETLANDS

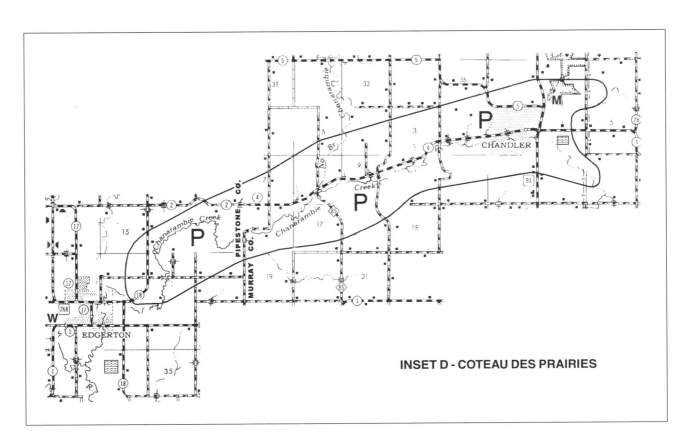

INSET D - COTEAU DES PRAIRIES

Pipestone County

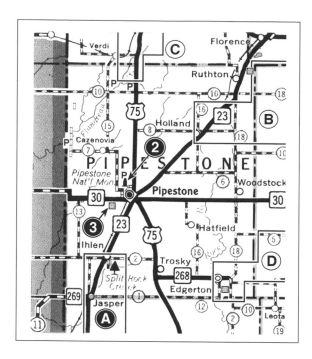

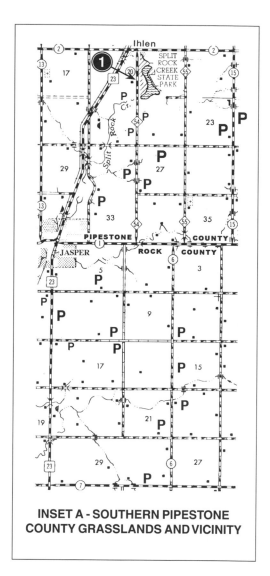

INSET A - SOUTHERN PIPESTONE COUNTY GRASSLANDS AND VICINITY

If it were possible to conduct a county-by-county census of trees in Minnesota, this county would almost certainly come in 87th place. While most of the counties of the West Region are relatively treeless, they at least have a few wooded areas along some of their rivers and lake shores. Pipestone County, however, has only one actual lake (Split Rock Lake), and its creeks are mostly lined with narrow strips of pastures rather than trees.

These tracts of pastures are probably too narrow to attract many grasslands species, but you might want to get a county map and check those along Flandreau Creek since this is an extension of sorts of the Coteau des Prairies area shown on Lincoln County's inset C, which includes a piece of Pipestone County. (Not too many years ago, there were even some summering Chestnut-collared Longspurs in pastures along this creek at the South Dakota line, 4 miles west and 1 mile north of Cazenovia.) Larger and more significant tracts of prairie in Pipestone County, part of the Coteau des Prairies, are included in Murray County's insets B and D.

There are still more **prairie grasslands** in the county shown in **inset A**, which includes a part of northwestern Rock County. These pastures may be grazed but many are still in good condition and protected from the plow by outcrops of Sioux quartzite. This rock has been used in the construction of some of the buildings in Pipestone and other nearby cities, and the softer layers of rock in the

quartzite — pipestone — have long been mined and carved by native Americans for use as tools and other utensils.

In summer, such species as Upland Sandpiper and Grasshopper Sparrow breed in this habitat, and there are records in these grassland tracts in this corner of Minnesota for Ferruginous Hawk, Prairie Falcon, Barn and Burrowing owls, Scissor-tailed Flycatcher, Rock Wren, Mountain Bluebird, Sprague's Pipit, Lark Bunting, Henslow's Sparrow, Smith's Longspur, and other rarities. Also look and listen in the thickets and farm groves here and elsewhere in southern Pipestone County for nesting Blue Grosbeaks.

Also located in inset A is **Split Rock Creek State Park (A1)** and its lake of the same name. Though modest in size, it's the only lake in the county and about the only place for miles around to harbor any water birds. Some "big lake" waterfowl such as Common Loon, Horned Grebe, Greater Scaup, and Red-breasted Merganser have dropped in here, and this was the site of the state's first California Gull record. The park entrance is on County Road 20, just south of Ihlen. The best woods and thickets to check for migrants are just south of the campground and at the south end of the park on both sides of the dam.

There may be no lake of any consequence there, but **Pipestone National Monument (2)** is certainly the most interesting birding spot in the county, and one of the nicest spots in the Southwest this side of the Minnesota River. There is a heavily wooded stream with a small but picturesque waterfall, about a half square mile of native grasslands, some beautiful outcroppings of Sioux quartzite lined with trees, a well-marked nature trail, and a visitors center with interpretive information and crafts of carved pipestone — and air-conditioning, for those hot summer afternoons on the prairie. All this makes the modest entrance fee well worthwhile.

Among other things, American Woodcock, both cuckoos, Western Kingbird, Sedge Wren, Clay-colored and Field sparrows, Dickcissel, and Orchard Oriole nest here; note the woodcock and the two sparrows are rare or local in this corner of the state. This is often a great place during war-bler migration: I once saw a male MacGillivray's Warbler here in May, but I left my camera at home and couldn't prove it. Rarities such as Bell's Vireo, Rock Wren, Spotted Towhee (probably occurs annually) and Brewer's Sparrow (well, I think that's what it was) have been found over the years, and, with birder coverage here so infrequent, certainly other strays have dropped in undetected.

To reach the monument, go north on Highway 75 and turn west at the sign on the north side of Pipestone. Time permitting, also check the pastures just north of the monument and just west of the community college: from the monument entrance road, go north 1 mile and turn west.

Finally, with so few wetlands in the county to harbor shorebirds and other water birds, be sure to check the large **Pipestone sewage ponds (3)**, arguably the best ones in this part of the state. The main gate is on Highway 30, 2.2 miles west of the Highway 23 junction, but the best way to see anything is to continue west from the gate another half mile and go south a quarter mile to the opening in the fence on the west side (and no one seems to mind that birders walk through here).

There are also smaller ponds at Edgerton (a mile south of town on County Road 18; see Murray County's inset D) and Ruthton (where both Laughing and Sabine's gulls recently appeared; 1 mile northeast of town on Highway 23).

Rock County

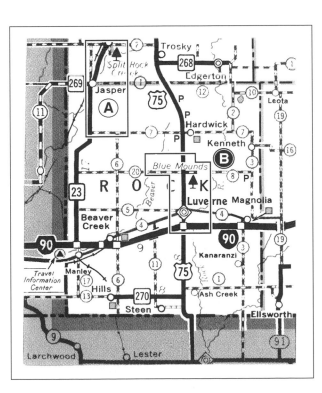

It was pages ago when I cast a vote for Big Stone as my favorite county of the West Region. That preference still stands, although if forced to select my single favorite birding location I would have to choose Rock County's **Blue Mounds State Park (inset B)**. And that's not just in the West Region, but in the entire state.

Yes, I've lived in Duluth for over 20 years, and, yes, I agree with the prevailing opinion that Duluth and the North Shore is easily the best birding area in Minnesota. There is certainly no denying the excellence of such places as Park Point, Hawk Ridge, and points along the North Shore. You don't really need to go anywhere else since, as birders have known for decades, just about any bird you'd ever want to see has been seen there, or eventually will be. But that's the problem. We keep finding all those birds in those same few great places in and around Duluth, but in the process we're not really discovering anything — any place — new.

A place like Blue Mounds was back in the mid-1970s. For four years, when I lived in this area, the park and other places in this far corner of the state were essentially home for me and relatively unfamiliar to Minnesota's birders.

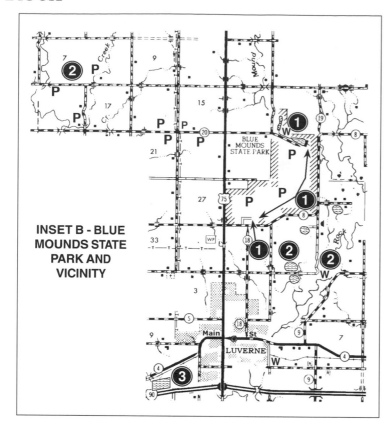

INSET B - BLUE MOUNDS STATE PARK AND VICINITY

headed Grosbeak, Lark Bunting, and Smith's Long-spur have all been seen more than once. Other records include Long-billed Curlew, Scissor-tailed Flycatcher, Rock Wren, Curve-billed Thrasher (Minnesota's first record), Sprague's Pipit, Prairie Warbler, Brewer's (also a first state record), Henslow's and Nelson's Sharp-tailed sparrows, and Chestnut-collared Longspur.

Even if you happen to be at Blue Mounds on one of those infrequent days when the birding is slow, you cannot fail to be impressed with the park's extensive and unplowed grasslands (with its resident herd of bi-son), its stands of prickly pear and brittle cactus (watch your step!) scattered among the Sioux quartzite out-crops, and the spectacular two-mile-long escarpment along the eastern side of the park which reaches up to 100 feet in height in places. In its own way, the unique view from here is perhaps my favorite in the state. The vistas in Duluth are nice enough, I suppose, but too many trees can get in the way, and my preference will always be for the endless skies and horizons of a prai-rie landscape.

As shown on inset B, the main park entrance road goes east from Highway 75, 4.5 miles north of down-town Luverne, and there are four areas the birder will especially want to be aware of (all accessible from marked hiking trails, and all marked **B1**):

• The two **lakes and creek** along the entrance road, with the heavily wooded creek between the camp-ground lake and the swimming beach lake the best place to look for warblers and other woods birds.

• That **escarpment** which runs from the end of the park entrance road south to the interpretive center (also good for migrants, including raptors).

• The **interpretive center** at the south end of the park (look and listen in this vicinity especially for Blue Gros-beaks); the driveway to the center is 0.4 mile east of the junction of County Road 8 and Highway 75.

• The broad stretch of **grasslands** which runs for no less than three miles from the main park drive southwest to Highway 75.

*   *   *

Also located on inset B are four other birding areas. Along both sides of the east-west road a mile south of the park, 1.5 miles east of Highway 75, there are relatively large **gravel pit ponds (B2)**, which are often good for shorebirds (and shorebird habitat is about the only thing Blue Mounds lacks). While most gravel pit ponds are rela-tively lifeless, when you're in a county like Rock where wet-lands are scarce they're always worth checking. Note there are a couple of more ponds shown on inset B to the north-east, and elsewhere there are other gravel pit ponds in northeastern Rock County, 0.5 mile east of the junction of County Roads 2 and 10.

Next, continue on the road east of the ponds for a half mile to the corner where the road turns north, and you'll be in some of the densest woods in the county along the **Rock**

Those years of exploration were my most eventful birding years, a period when there was still something new to dis-cover about Minnesota and its birds. That time seems to be gone now as birders have investigated practically all corners of the state in recent years. In a way, I hope this book is not too complete, that it would ever reveal everything there is to know about Minnesota's birding places. It would be sad to think if there were nothing new to find on your own — your own Blue Mounds.

More than 230 species have been recorded in the park's variety of habitats, most of these during spring and fall, of course, but in summer one can find nesting Swainson's Hawk, Gray Partridge, Upland Sandpiper, American Woodcock, both cuckoos, Eastern Screech-Owl, Willow Flycatcher, Sedge Wren, Blue Grosbeak, Grasshopper Spar-row, Dickcissel, and Orchard Oriole.

During migration this is a fine place to look for waterfowl (the park's two small lakes are all Rock County has), hawks (riding thermals above the escarpment), Alder and other flycatchers, wrens (especially Winter Wren), thrushes, American Pipit, vireos and warblers (in all, over 30 species recorded!), Spotted Towhee, sparrows (including American Tree, Clay-colored, and Harris's), Lapland Longspur, black-birds, and just about everything else that migrates.

As might be expected with so many species on its list, the park has produced a long list of rarities: e.g., Ferruginous Hawk, Peregrine and Prairie falcons, Northern Bobwhite (the few here in the early 1980s are gone now), Long-eared and Short-eared owls, Say's Phoebe (once attempted to nest), Bell's Vireo, Blue-gray Gnatcatcher, Mountain Blue-bird, Northern Mockingbird, Yellow-breasted Chat, Black-

River (also **B2**). Look and listen especially for Eastern Screech-Owl (!), Red-bellied Woodpecker, Northern Cardinal, and other nesting woods birds which are harder to find in the park. In fact, screech-owls are still consistently found at that corner, just as they have been for over 25 years — certainly, this has to be the most reliable spot in the state for this owl!

Often the woods birding is good farther south along the Rock River at the southeast corner of Luverne. Follow Main Street to the east side of town, just after crossing the river turn right into the park, and bear left immediately through the park for a half mile to the woods between the railroad tracks and the corner.

Also marked **B2** is the **rocky pasture** northwest of the park where Burrowing Owls nested up for a few consecutive years up until 10 years ago. Though the owls are gone, there are still Upland Sandpipers and Grasshopper Sparrows here in summer. There are also other pastured grasslands in the county, protected from the plow by Sioux quartzite outcrops:

• The Rock County portion of Pipestone County's inset A near Jasper.

• Along either side of Highway 75 from Hardwick north for 4 miles.

• Along Champepadan Creek at the junction of County Roads 3 and 8, between Kenneth and Magnolia.

Most of the rest of Rock County is ordinary farmland, mostly devoid of grasslands, wetlands, or woodlands, but watch for Blue Grosbeaks on fence wires along any back road wherever there are thickets and farm groves.

Of final note in inset B are the large **sewage ponds in Luverne** (**B3**), which usually have mudflats for shorebirding. From Highway 75, follow County Road 4 or Main Street west for 1.6 miles, turn south and continue past the Gold 'N Plump plant, and park by the transmitter tower on the west side. (The last couple of years it seems to be OK for birders to be here.) From here you can scan most of the ponds, but also look for a small road west of the tower which goes through the fence to the west pond.

Besides those in Luverne, Rock County has four other sets of sewage ponds.

❏ Beaver Creek: on County Road 6, just north of the Interstate 90 exit.

❏ Hills: 1 mile south on County Road 6.

❏ Magnolia: from County Road 4, go south on the east edge of town on Brooks Street, and turn east along the south side of the tracks for 0.6 mile to the ponds.

❏ Hardwick: 1.5 miles east from Highway 75 on County Road 7, then 0.2 mile south.

Nobles County

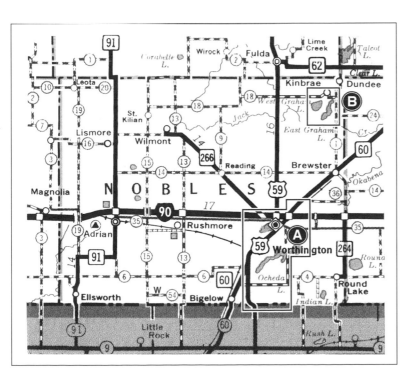

The good news is The Nature Conservancy stepped in just in time to save the last remnant of virgin prairie in Nobles County by purchasing the Compass Prairie. The bad news is this tract is a mere 20 acres in size, a sad statistic and evidence of the "black desert" agriculture which predominates here. This area is certainly too small for birding purposes, but there are two small county parks which might be worthwhile at times during migration.

One is Sunrise Prairie County Park, located 1 mile east of County Road 15 on County Road 54, a mile north of the Iowa border. The other is Midway County Park on County Road 14, 1.5 miles west of County Road 15 or 1.5 miles east of Highway 91; the small lake here once attracted a stray Least Tern. After you're done at Midway (it won't take long), you might also want to check the relatively large gravel pit pond, 0.5 mile east and 3 miles south.

Actually, there is more to see than just plowed fields in this county, as evidenced by the records

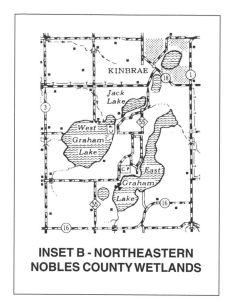

**INSET B - NORTHEASTERN
NOBLES COUNTY WETLANDS**

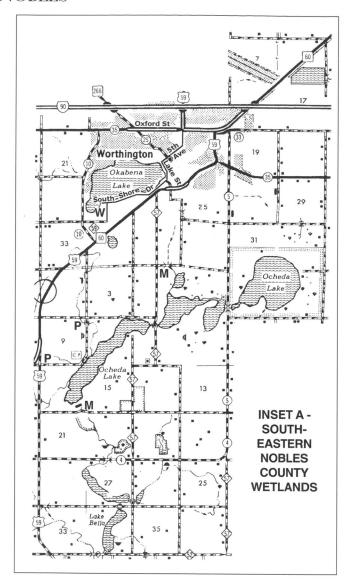

**INSET A -
SOUTH-
EASTERN
NOBLES
COUNTY
WETLANDS**

of Williamson's Sapsucker (Minnesota's first) and Painted Bunting. Much more likely to find would be the Blue Grosbeaks nesting in the farm groves and thickets in the western quarter of Nobles County. The most interesting areas are the **wetlands** in southeastern and northeastern Nobles County, as shown in **insets A and B** respectively. Migrant water birds are usually more attracted to those lakes on inset A south of Worthington, and Lake Bella is probably the best of these wetlands.

While you're in the neighborhood, a few miles to the east is Indian Lake, which can also be attractive to waterfowl. From the town of Round Lake on County Road 4, either go west 1 mile and 2 miles south, or 2 miles west and 2.5 miles

south to the county park off County Road 53.

Also within inset A is Worthington's Okabena Lake, which may harbor a wintering duck or two if the power plant on Lake Street on the east side of the lake is operating. Even if it's frozen solid in mid-winter, the lake is usually open for waterfowl earlier in spring and later in fall. The easiest way to scan the lake is to follow Lake Street south from the power plant as it becomes South Shore Drive which, of course, follows the south side of the lake. If you're looking for woods birds, when you come to Knollwood Drive, turn south and then west on County Road 59 which leads to a good wooded area along the hiking and biking trail.

The lakes within inset B around Kinbrae are also OK for water birds, and their wooded shorelines also attract migrant passerines. The best places to check first would be the two county parks: Maka-Oicu on the east side of West Graham Lake, and Fury's Island on the west side of East Graham Lake.

Be sure to check the large sewage ponds northeast of Worthington, where records of both Little and Sabine's gulls have occurred. Access is difficult, however: either turn east off Highway 60, 0.7 mile northeast of Interstate 90, or turn south off 60, 2 miles northeast of I-90. There are also fair-sized but hard-to-see ponds at Adrian: you have to hike west a half mile from the gate on Highway 91, 0.2 mile north of Interstate 90. A smaller pond is at Rushmore: turn west from County Road 13 on South Street just south of the tracks, go 1 mile and then south 0.2 mile.

Jackson County

Heron Lake is one of the few genuine historical monuments of Minnesota ornithology. White-faced Ibis used to nest here several decades ago, and in more recent times several sight records of this species have occurred. American White Pelicans formerly nested at Heron Lake not too many years ago, one of Minnesota's few documented colonies. In 1986 the state's only Little Gull nest was found here, in the same year the state's first record of Black-headed Gull occurred, and in 1991 a first-state-record Glossy Ibis appeared at this location.

Even without this history, **Heron Lake (inset A)** is still a great place to look for grebes (there are recent Clark's Grebe sightings), pelicans, Least Bit-

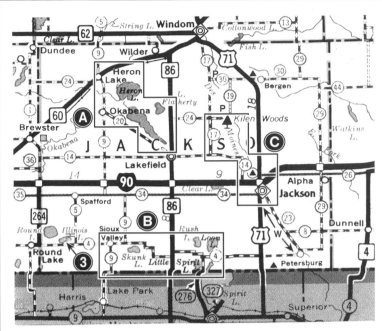

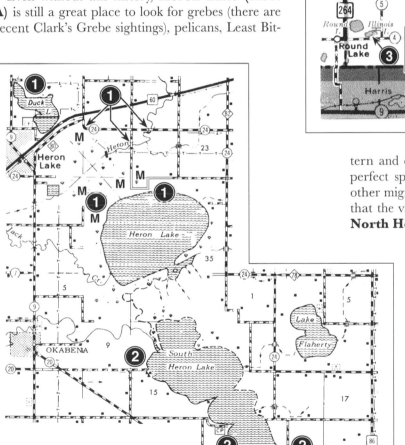

INSET A - HERON LAKE

tern and other herons and egrets, rails (this seems to be a perfect spot for a King Rail), Franklin's Gull, terns, and other migrating or nesting water birds. The only problem is that the vast marshes and private property which surround **North Heron Lake** (usually just called Heron Lake) make access difficult, but there are four places here (all marked **A1**) to try first:

• There is some open water and lots of marsh visible from the end of the road which dead ends near the northwest side.

• The Nature Conservancy's Lindgren-Trauger Bird Sanctuary on the north side of the lake is mostly marsh; it is best approached from the east, but sometimes the road coming in from the west (which might have a hand-lettered No Trespassing sign) is also passable.

• In fall, mudflats usually line the Heron Lake Outlet stream at the two spots shown; also check the marsh just to the west on County Road 24 just before it meets Highway 60.

• Duck Lake (which is actually contiguous with Heron Lake) is usually good: the best access is along County Road 9 north of the town of Heron Lake.

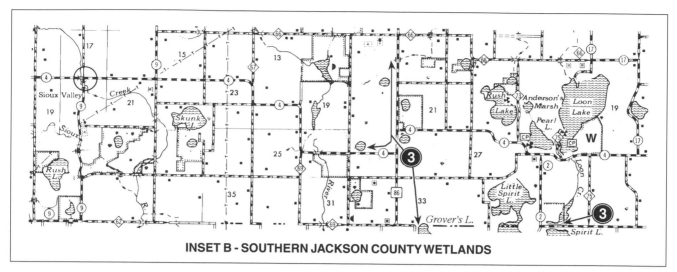

INSET B - SOUTHERN JACKSON COUNTY WETLANDS

South Heron Lake is also contiguous with North Heron Lake and, though not as interesting most years, has been excellent for shorebirds during recent dry periods. It is also more accessible than North Heron Lake, at least from the three places marked **A2**:

• The public access on its northwest side; also, check the name on the mailbox immediately to the north: if it reads Herman Becker, birders are welcome to scan the lake from his yard.

• Sandy Point County Park on the lake's west side: be sure to drive to the end of the road and walk out on the point which juts out into the lake and often attracts shorebirds and loafing gulls and terns.

• Community Point County Park on the lake's east side.

There are several other worthwhile **wetlands** in Jackson County along the Iowa border shown on **inset B**. All of them are worth exploring for water birds (as evidenced by the state's only Smew record occurring in this area), and there is a relatively large wooded area good for migrants in Robertson County Park on the south side of Loon Lake. But in recent years birders have been concentrating their efforts in two areas. One is **Grover's Lake and vicinity (B3)**, where Great-tailed Grackles are now established in small numbers and nests have been found. They were first found in 1998 at Grover's Lake, which is at the Iowa border a half mile east of Highway 86, but also check the wetlands and pastures along 86 within a few miles north of the border.

Also marked **B3** is the northern tip of **Spirit Lake**, which spills a bit over the state line just east of County Road 2. At this location there have been several recent sightings of Black-headed Gulls, mostly in fall, but there are also spring and summer records, and it seems likely the species nests somewhere nearby in Iowa. In fact, Jackson is the only Minnesota county where this species has been recorded.

While you're in the neighborhood, be sure to check another above-average lake just west of inset B. From Sioux

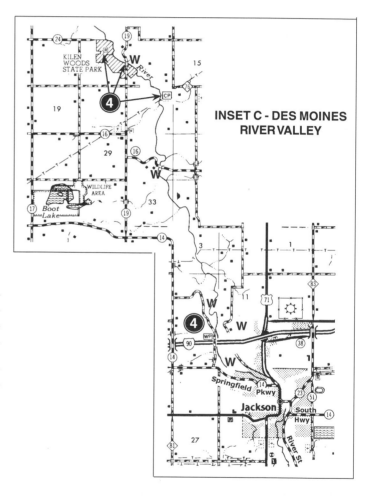

INSET C - DES MOINES RIVER VALLEY

Valley, go 5 miles west on County Road 4 to scan the south side of **Illinois Lake (3)**; to check the north side, go back east 1.5 miles to County Road 5, then north 1 mile, and west 0.5 mile.

Some of the densest deciduous woodlands in the Southwest south of the Minnesota River are found along the **Des Moines River (inset C)** as it flows through eastern Jackson County. The north-south orientation of this wooded corridor makes it a natural place to look for warblers and the like during migration, but don't overlook it in summer since this might be a good area to find some of those nesting woods birds more characteristic of the Southeast Region mentioned in the Renville County chapter. The best portion of the river to explore is between Kilen Woods and Jackson, and the three places to check first (**C4**) would be:

• The main hiking trail in **Kilen Woods State Park** (entrance via County Road 24); also be sure to check County Road 19 which crosses the river on the east side of the park.

• **Belmont County Park,** on the east side of the river a mile farther downstream. Note there are also two nearby Scientific and Natural Areas marked P just north of inset B on this side of the river: Des Moines River Prairie is accessed from County Road 30; and Holthe Prairie is west off County Road 19, 2.5 miles south of County Road 30.

• The road **northwest of Jackson** which turns north off County Road 14 / Springfield Parkway, 1.5 miles west of Highway 71; this road crosses under Interstate 90 into nice looking woodlands, and loops back west to County Road 14.

While you're in Jackson, note that its large sewage ponds (see inset C) are better than average: go east from downtown across the river on Ashley Street, turn south on the first street (River Street) to South Highway / County Road 14, then east 0.5 mile and south 0.3 mile.

Heron Lake's sewage ponds are smaller but usually better than most: turn east off County Road 9, 0.6 mile south of Highway 60. There are also small ponds at Brewster located on this side of the county line (the town is in Nobles County): go northeast 1.2 miles on Highway 60, then south 0.5 mile along the county line, and hike south from the gate on County Road 18 just east of here.

Martin County

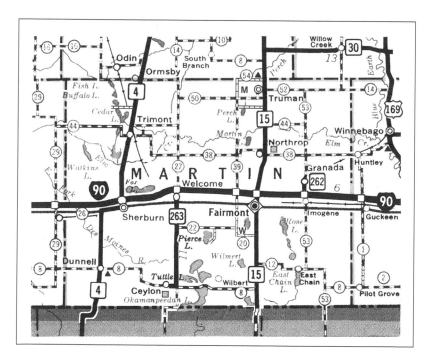

There is a cluster of wetlands in the south central part of the county, with Pierce Lake probably the best of them, if its Brant record and recent Black-necked Stilt sighting are any indication. From Highway 263, go 3.5 miles east on County Road 22, and turn south 1.3 miles to the public access; or, from the east, go 2.5 miles west on 22 from County Road 39 and then south. Also check wooded Timberlane County Park along the road between South Silver Lake and Iowa Lake: at the state line, turn northwest on County Road 41 off Highway 15, go a mile north and then west to the park.

Elsewhere in Martin County, there are three other lakes and a wooded park worth checking for migrants:

• Cedar Lake and its county park; from Trimont go 3 miles north on Highway 4, then west 1.4 miles, and south 0.5 mile to the park.

• Perch Lake and the county park on its east side; from Truman go 1.5 miles south on Highway 15, then 2 miles west, and 0.5 mile south. There are also extensive marshes in the 2-mile-long wildlife management area just north of Perch Lake: from Highway 15, go west on County Road 50 to its south side; or go west from 15 to its north side along the county line on County Road 54.

• Fox Lake might even be open by the power plant in

Martin County certainly has its share of lakes, although none of them seems to be particularly noteworthy, probably because their shorelines tend to be lined with trees more than marshes or mudflats, and they are probably too far east to attract many water birds from the prairie pothole country.

winter, or at least be open earlier in spring and later in fall than other lakes. Just north of Interstate 90, turn east off Highway 4 on to County Road 28, go 1.5 miles and then north to the plant on the south shore of the lake.

• On the south side of Fairmont, there is a nice mix of deciduous woods, thickets, junipers, and creek bottoms at Cedar Park on the west side of Amber Lake. Take Highway 15 for 5.3 miles south from Interstate 90, turn west on Lake Aires Boulevard / County Road 20, and in 1.6 miles turn north on Cedar Park Road into the park. From the parking

lot, hike on the trails west and you might turn up roosting owls, a stray Townsend's Solitaire or Mountain Bluebird, and migrant warblers and other passerines. The heavy cover in the park should be good both in winter and during migration.

There are also two small sewage ponds in the county at Northrup (go east 0.5 mile from the junction of Highway 15 and County Road 38) and Ceylon (1.2 miles south on County Roads 6 and 125).

PRINCIPAL BIRDING LOCATIONS BY SEASON

WINTER

a – Mississippi River valley
b – Whitewater WMA
c – Minnesota River valley
d – Monticello
e – Blue Lake Wastewater Treatment Plant
f – Black Dog Lake
g – St. Paul / Mississippi River
h – St. Croix River valley
i – St. Cloud / Mississippi River

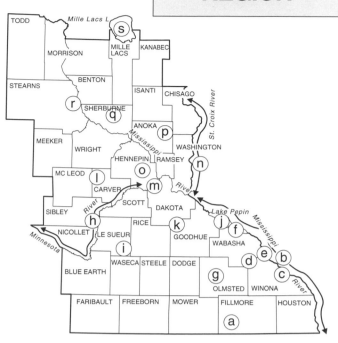

MIGRATION

a – Kappers' Ponds
b – Mississippi River valley
c – Prairie Island
d – Whitewater WMA
e – Weaver Bottoms
f – Reads Landing / Lake Pepin
g – Rochester reservoirs
h – Minnesota River valley
i – Waterville fish hatchery ponds
j – Frontenac / Hok-Si-La Park

k – Lake Byllesby
l – Crane Creek
m – Bass Ponds / Old Cedar Avenue / Black Dog Lake and vicinity
n – St. Croix River valley
o – Wood Lake Nature Center / T. S. Roberts Sanctuary / Lakes Harriet and Calhoun
p – Carlos Avery WMA
q – Sherburne NWR
r – St. Cloud and vicinity

SUMMER/BREEDING

a – Forestville State Park and vicinity
b – Beaver Creek Valley State Park
c – La Crescent and vicinity
d – Mound Prairie
e – Reno area
f – Great River Bluffs State Park
g – Whitewater WMA
h – McCarthy Lake WMA / Weaver Dunes SNAs
i – Minneopa State Park

j – Seven Mile Creek County Park
k – Swan and Middle Lakes
l – Cannon River Wilderness
m – Vasa area
n – Murphy-Hanrehan Regional Park
o – Black Dog Lake area
p – Pigs Eye Lake and vicinity
q – St. Croix River valley
r – Sand Dunes State Forest

See Notes and Abbreviations on page 53.

Faribault County

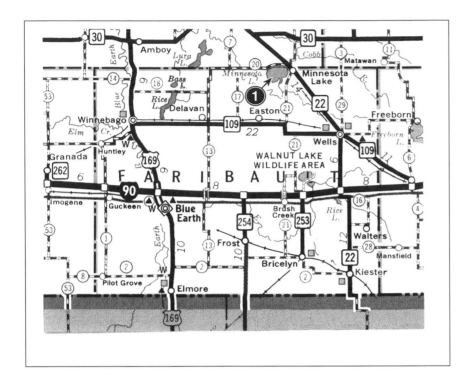

20. There is an island on the lake where some American White Pelicans have been discovered nesting in recent summers, and Clark's Grebes have been seen (and probably bred) on the lake among the Westerns.

The marshes and thickets of Walnut Lake Wildlife Management Area along Interstate 90 between Highways 253 and 22 might be good, but they are relatively inaccessible. However, you can at least scan the two halves of Walnut Lake from County Road 119 which passes between the lakes: take the Highway 253 exit off Interstate 90, and go north 1-2 miles. Part of this area's wetlands and woods lie on the south side of the interstate: take Highway 253 south 0.4 mile to County Road 16, then go east 0.4 to 1 mile through the area.

There is a decent corridor for migrant woods bird along the Blue Earth River, which runs the entire width of the county. You could turn west off Highway 169 on just about any road and you'll come to the river within a mile. But check especially the Interstate 90 wayside rests just west of Blue Earth, where nature trails pass through woods, thickets, and fields and connect the east-bound and west-bound rest stops. Dickcissels and Grasshopper Sparrows at least have been reported in summer, and such species as American Woodcock, both cuckoos, Willow Flycatcher, Sedge Wren, and Orchard Oriole probably nest here (and at Walnut Lake Wildlife Management Area) as well.

And, not to worry, there are always Faribault County's sewage ponds.

❏ Winnebago: 0.6 mile west on County Road 12, 0.2 mile north.

❏ Elmore: 0.2 mile west on County Road 9, 0.7 mile north.

❏ Bricelyn: 1 mile north on Highway 253, 0.5 mile east, and 0.5 mile south.

❏ Kiester (no jokes, please!): 0.5 mile south on Highway 22, then 0.5 mile west.

❏ Wells, where there are two sets of ponds: the largest in the county are 1 mile west on Highway 109, then 0.2 mile north; the other is 0.7 mile north on County Road 29, then 0.2 mile east.

Given its predominantly open landscape, Faribault could just as well have been considered a West Region county. As such, though, it would have been a short chapter since few wetlands or grasslands are here to attract many birds from the Dakotas. This first chapter of the Southeast Region will still be relatively brief, since its woodlands are too fragmented and too far west to host that many specialties of the Mississippi River valley.

As a result, birding activity in Faribault County has mostly ranged from infrequent to nonexistent, so that rarities have seldom turned up — and when they do, there always seems to be a catch. There was that first state record Black-bellied Whistling-Duck shot by a hunter at Rice Lake in 1984, but who can say for sure it wasn't just an escape? And for a while there was this other first state record on the books, temporarily. Some Mountain Plovers were reported near Huntley in 1986, but two years later they were reclassified as misidentified American Golden-Plovers.

By virtue of its size alone, **Minnesota Lake (1)** is worth scanning for waterfowl during migration and summer and is probably the best birding spot in the county. It is best viewed from its east side in the town of the same name and along its north shore on the Blue Earth County line from County Road

Freeborn County

This county's predominantly farmed countryside mostly resembles that of Faribault County, and thus we have another relatively brief chapter. There are, however, more resident birders in Freeborn County turning things up over the years, and there are a few more lakes as well. The best of these is probably Geneva Lake where Western Grebes, Least Bitterns, and other water birds have nested in past years: it is most easily seen from County Road 45, 1-3 miles south of Geneva. Also check the sometimes-flooded fields along County Road 26 just east of this lake: from Geneva, go 1 mile east and 1 mile south.

Albert Lea Lake might also be worth scanning in **Myre-Big Island State Park (1)**, certainly the county's best known birding spot, but also check the park's woodlands for migrating passerines, particularly the Esker Trail. The park entrance is via County Road 38 which turns south off County Road 46, 0.6 mile east of Interstate 35. The park even has its own sewage pond: go 0.2 mile on the road towards the group camp and turn right.

In Albert Lea itself there might even be something to do in winter if the channel is open for water birds between Fountain and Albert Lea lakes below the dam, just east of downtown on Main Street.

There are no fewer than eight other sewage ponds in the county, but they're mostly small and may not be worth a special trip.

❏ Alden: take the County Road 6 exit off Interstate 90, go 0.5 mile south to County Road 46, then 0.5 mile west, and 0.4 mile north.

❏ Freeborn: 1 mile southeast on County Road 29, then 0.2 mile north.

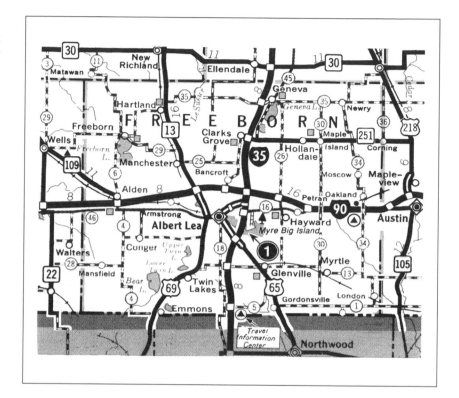

❏ Hartland: 0.8 mile west on County Road 33, then 1 mile north and 0.5 mile east.

❏ Clarks Grove: 0.4 mile south on First Avenue S.W. (the first street east of the tracks), then west across the tracks on Third Street to a 'T', and south to the ponds.

❏ Geneva: 0.7 mile north and 0.4 mile east.

❏ Hollandale: 0.7 mile east and 0.7 mile north.

❏ Hayward: 0.6 mile west from County Road 26 on County Road 46, then 0.3 mile south.

❏ Glenville: 0.2 mile south from Highway 65 on County Road 5, then west 0.2 mile.

Mower County

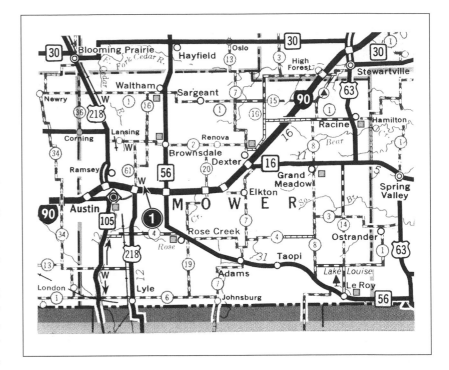

While Mower County is just as plowed up as its neighboring counties to the west, with few large wooded areas and even fewer lakes, it actually has a more impressive list of rarities to its credit as a result of coverage by its local birders. As might be expected, most of these records (and birders) are from Austin: Harlequin and Long-tailed ducks, White-eyed Vireo, Clark's Nutcracker, Carolina Wren, Townsend's Solitaire, Worm-eating Warbler (at least four records!), Western Tanager, and Black-throated Sparrow. Other county records include White-faced Ibis, Cinnamon Teal, Sabine's Gull (not bad for a county with hardly any real lakes), Mountain Bluebird, and Kentucky Warbler, plus winter sightings of Sedge Wren and Pine Warbler.

In spite of all this, the list of recommended birding places in Mower County is relatively short. Just outside of Austin, the riparian woodland trails at **J. C. Hormel Nature Center (1)** would certainly be a good place to check, since a good share of the sightings listed above came from here. It is located at the east side of town on County Road 61 / 21st Street N.E., 0.3 mile north of the Highway 218 South exit off Interstate 90.

Also in Austin is the Cedar River which flows north to south through western Mower County, and the trees along its banks form a natural corridor for migrant warblers and other woods birds. The river is most easily followed south of Austin along Highway 105, but with the aid of a county map you can also find other wooded spots along the river north of town. And, though the lake at Lake Louise State Park is too small for birding purposes, the woods in the park are extensive and worth a look; the park entrance turns west off County Road 14, 1.7 miles north of Le Roy.

Finally, Mower County has no fewer than eight sewage ponds to its credit.

❏ Austin: from Interstate 90, go south on 4th Street N.W. 2 miles to 16th Avenue S.W., then east to Main Street.

❏ Racine: 0.8 mile east of Highway 63 on County Road 1, then 0.2 mile south.

❏ Grand Meadow: 0.4 mile south from Highway 16 on County Road 8, then 0.7 mile east.

❏ Dexter: from Interstate 90, go 1.7 miles north on County Road 7.

❏ Waltham: 1 mile west from Highway 56 on County Road 1, then 0.2 mile south, and 0.2 mile east.

❏ Brownsdale: 0.5 mile north on Highway 56, then 0.2 west.

❏ Rose Creek: turn south off Highway 56, 0.5 mile west of town.

❏ Le Roy: 1 mile east on Highway 56, then 0.3 mile north.

Fillmore County

With this chapter we finally arrive at what the Southeast Region is all about: the vast deciduous woodlands of the broad valley of the Mississippi River and those many species which essentially reach the northern limits of their ranges in the Southeast. While Fillmore County may not be adjacent to the Mississippi, and birders spend a lot more time in neighboring Houston County, this county still has plenty of woods birding opportunities to explore.

And "explore" is the operative word, as surprisingly few rarities have been documented here. I've also found the county relatively difficult to bird, since it has almost too many wooded valleys to check, none of them apparently any better or worse than the next. But this is as good a place as any to test the straight vs. crooked road theory mentioned in the introduction: i.e., straight roads tend to pass through ordinary farm fields, while the more winding roads on the map pass through wooded areas and tend to be more worthwhile.

Often — perhaps too often? — the chapters of the West Region give the advice: "Look for migrants migrating during migration." However, a better time to wander around Fillmore and other counties in this corner of the state would be from mid-May to early July to look and listen for breeding woods birds. Watch especially for Red-shouldered Hawk,

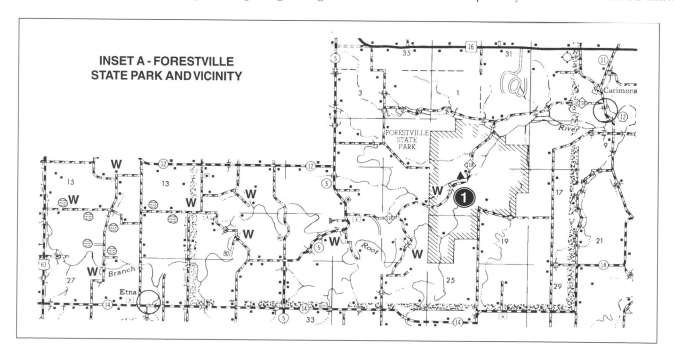

INSET A - FORESTVILLE
STATE PARK AND VICINITY

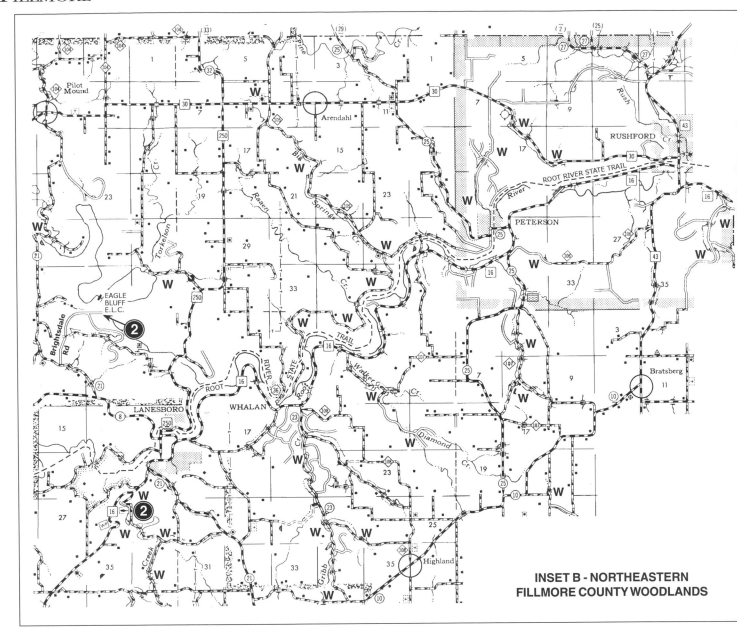

INSET B - NORTHEASTERN FILLMORE COUNTY WOODLANDS

Ruffed Grouse, Wild Turkey, both Black-billed and Yellow-billed cuckoos, Eastern Screech- and Barred owls, Whip-poor-will, Acadian (local) and Willow flycatchers, Tufted Titmouse (relatively rare), Blue-gray Gnatcatcher, Wood Thrush, Blue-winged and Cerulean warblers, Louisiana Waterthrush (local), and Orchard Oriole. Note that some of these are permanent residents and also overwinter.

Insets A, B, and C include the best **woodlands** in the county, some of which (but not all — I leave the rest for you to discover) are marked W on these maps. The best-known spot is on inset A, **Forestville State Park (A1)**, and the main park entrance on its west side is accessed on County Road 118 from County Road 5; or you can come in from the east on 118 from Carimona. The densest woodlands and best trails are in the western half of the park.

Also shown on inset A north of Etna are several small ponds (former quarries?) which, with wetlands virtually nonexistent

in this county, might be worth checking. (There aren't even any sewage ponds!) Note there is a stand of planted pines next to the westernmost pond, 0.5 mile east of Highway 63. Except for junipers, conifers are as scarce as wetlands in this part of the state, so check any you find for a roosting Long-eared or Northern Saw-whet owl, and for crossbills or other visitants from the Northeast. Other pine plantings can be found in northwestern Fillmore County (marked W on the county map, 0.5 mile north of the junction of County Roads 2 and 38), and farther east on Highway 30 in the cemetery 1 mile west of Arendahl (see inset B).

Within inset B in northeastern Fillmore County, lots of crooked roads are shown which wind through good woodlands (again, marked W) and are also well worth exploring, but there are two locations you might want to try first (both marked **B2**). **Eagle Bluff Environmental Learning Center** northwest of Lanesboro is marked by a sign on County

Road 21 at Brightsdale Road, and is probably one of the more consistent areas in the county for Tufted Titmouse, especially at the feeders. Other good woodlands are along the road past the **Lanesboro fish hatchery ponds** just southwest of town off Highway 16.

*   *   *

Also of note in this part of the county is the popular hiking/biking Root River State Trail, which starts in Fountain and runs through the width of inset B to Rushford and beyond into Houston County. There is a 5.5-mile spur which goes to Preston (the trailhead is just south of downtown), and from there another section continues south to Harmony. Trail maps are available in each town on route: e.g., just south of downtown Lanesboro (on Highway 250) and just south of downtown Rushford (a block west and a block north of the Highways 43 and 16 junction).

As nice as this trail is, mostly along a former railroad grade, the habitat and birding potential is not really any different from what you'd find along inset B's back roads along the Root River. The best part of it I've seen is the last 2 miles in Houston County, where it currently ends halfway between Rushford and Houston. The trailhead of this relatively inaccessible 6-mile section is on Ferry Street in Rushford, 3 blocks east of the downtown trailhead mentioned above.

While most of southeastern Fillmore County is open farmland, at least two heavily wooded areas along the south branch of the Root River can be good for Southeast-Region specialties. One of these is County Road 13, which heads east from Highway 43 in Choice, winds along the river to the county line, and continues towards Yucatan as Houston County Road 15. The other is the 205-acre Hvoslef (also spelled Hvoslev) Wildlife Management Area: turn east off County Road 23 in Amherst at the sign for Badgersett Farms, and go 1.2 miles to the wildlife area's sign. The best woodlands are downhill along the river east of the sign.

Besides the woodlands in and around Forestville State Park in inset A, it's also worth exploring the crooked back roads north of here shown on inset C. While these roads are not birded very often, there are at least Louisiana Waterthrush nesting records along some of these creeks. While you're in the area, be sure to check the Spring Valley fish hatchery ponds: from Highway 16, go 0.2 mile north on County Road

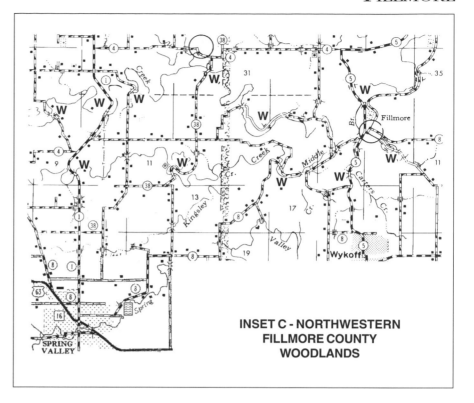

INSET C - NORTHWESTERN FILLMORE COUNTY WOODLANDS

1, then 1 mile east on County Road 8. With wetlands so scarce in the county, any water birds around have few other places to choose from; smaller fish hatchery ponds at Lanesboro and Peterson are mapped on inset B.

Of final note, and a change of pace from looking for breeding woods birds, are two locations in southwestern Fillmore County. One is the area known as **Kappers' Ponds (3)**, south of Cherry Grove, and the best access is from the road along the north side that goes east from County Road 5, 1.5 miles south of town. This spot would certainly be the best and largest place in the county to look for water birds during migration, and there are good thickets and other cover around the ponds to attract sparrows and other migrants. Note, however, this is private property, but in 2001 an arrangement was worked out to provide access to Minnesota Ornithologists' Union members; for more information, contact the author.

The other place is **Beaver Creek Wildlife Management Area (4)**, where the ephemeral Henslow's Sparrow has been found in recent summers with some consistency. Turn north from Highway 56, either 2 miles west of Highway 63 or 2 miles east of the Mower County line, go 1.5-2.2 miles north, and listen in those weedy grasslands along both sides of the road.

Houston County

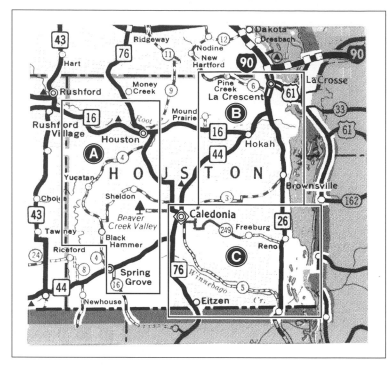

Bee, Black Hammer, Caledonia, Money Creek, Reno, Yucatan.

With such an odd and eclectic assortment of place names within its borders, you certainly know Houston County has to be a unique location. Ornithologically this is definitely true, as this has been the county of choice for decades to find southern species near the northern periphery of their ranges: e.g., Wild Turkey, Northern Bobwhite, Common Moorhen, Acadian Flycatcher, Tufted Titmouse, Blue-winged, Cerulean and Prothonotary warblers, and Louisiana Waterthrush. And, of course, Timber Rattlesnakes!

And what better place is there to hope and search for a rarity or stray such as a "southern" heron/egret/ibis (including Yellow-crowned Night-Heron), any of the kites, Black or King rail, Purple Gallinule, Chuck-will's-widow, White-eyed or Bell's vireo, Carolina or Bewick's wren, Northern Mockingbird, a Yellow-throated, Prairie, Worm-eating, Kentucky or Hooded warbler, Yellow-breasted Chat, Summer Tanager, or Painted Bunting?

As mentioned in the Fillmore County chapter, most birders are attracted to this corner of the state in late spring-early summer when things are nesting and singing. But the backwaters and wooded hillsides along the Mississippi River also provide a reason to come during migration. Watch especially for Tundra Swans, Canvasbacks, Common Mergansers, and other waterfowl which often congregate in impressive num-

bers in late fall. Look for raptors riding the updrafts above the bluffs (Bald Eagles are common and Goldens are rare but annual visitants — even in winter), and for passerines funneling through this valley's wooded corridor.

And certainly don't overlook Houston County in winter: open sections of the Mississippi and of spring-fed and fast-moving streams, heavy cover, and relatively tolerable climate all combine to induce water and woods birds alike to overwinter.

Not only is Houston County good at almost any time of year but also on virtually any road you wish to explore. This is evidenced by the amount of the county — almost all of it! — mapped on the insets, and it might appear it's hard to know where to start. But most birders are probably first attracted to **Beaver Creek Valley State Park** on **inset A**, located a few miles west of Caledonia via Highway 76 and County Road 1.

This beautiful and heavily wooded park is best known as Minnesota's first consistent breeding grounds for the Acadian Flycatcher. This species is now found locally elsewhere in the Southeast and would probably prove to be more widespread if birders weren't such creatures of habit, returning to the same reliable places to check off things on their list. Beaver Creek Valley's two best areas (both marked **A1**) would be the **main hiking trail** along the creek which leads northwest from the main parking lot just inside the park entrance, and at the end of the park road around the **campground**.

Look and listen for Acadian Flycatchers especially along the main hiking trail, but be aware that look-alike Eastern Wood-Pewees and Least Flycatchers are common here. Listen for Tufted Titmouse around the park entrance and the main parking lot, and Louisiana Waterthrush are most often found just inside the park entrance, near the north end of the campground, and about a half mile up the hiking trail where exposed limestone ledges line the creek. These three quite uncommon and local Minnesota species have long been consistently found in this park. Also keep an eye and ear open for Yellow-billed Cuckoo, Blue-gray Gnatcatcher, Wood Thrush, Blue-winged and Cerulean warblers, and other Southeast Region specialties. If you camp here, listen at night for Eastern Screech- and Barred owls and Whip-poor-will.

Besides Beaver Creek Valley, within inset A there are many other areas to explore, and it is recommended you try as many roads as you have time for — especially, of course, the crooked ones and those marked W. But also note those four miles of road marked **A2** that pass through ordinary-looking farmlands, which have proven to be the best place in the state for **North-**

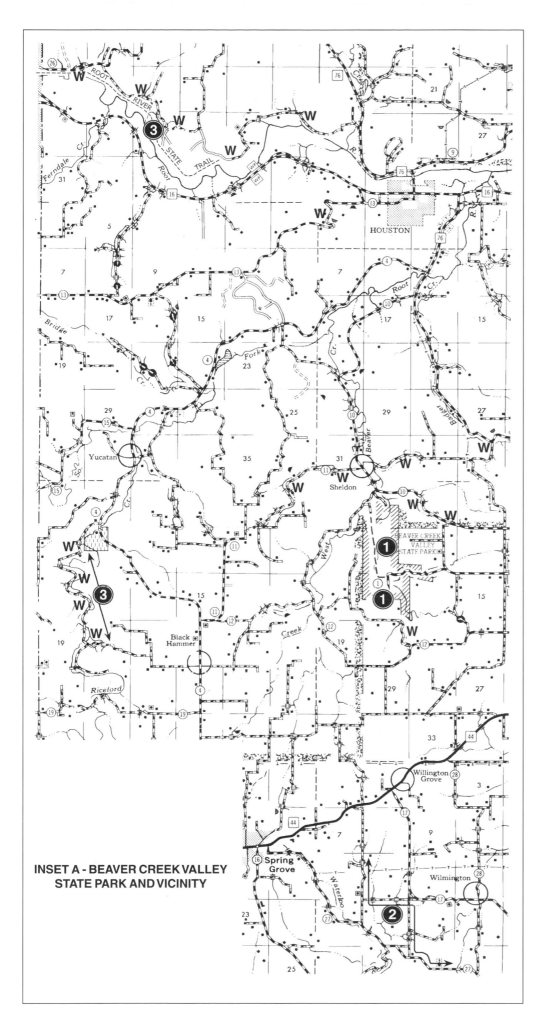

INSET A - BEAVER CREEK VALLEY STATE PARK AND VICINITY

ern Bobwhites.

This elusive species reaches the extreme edge of its range in Houston County, and it is certainly one of this state's most difficult Regular species to find. (Some are of the opinion that truly wild bobwhites are not just difficult but actually impossible to find, that all those here are recent releases from game farms, and none are really "countable.") The best time to try would be in spring or summer when they are most vocal, and, when searching these and other fields throughout the county for bobwhites, also watch for Gray Partridge, Sedge Wren, Field, Grasshopper and Henslow's (maybe) sparrows, Dickcissel, Bobolink, Eastern Meadowlark, and Orchard Oriole.

There are also two especially interesting crooked and wooded roads in inset A to visit as long as you're in the neighborhood (both marked **A3**):

• The road through the so-called **Vinegar Ridge** along the Root River passes through a large stand of pines; the entire length of this road between County Road 26 and Highway 76 is worth driving. Note that the eastern end of the Root River State Trail (see Fillmore County) also follows along the river here, and it will eventually extend at least as far as Houston.

• South of Yucatan off County Road 4, the road along **Riceford Creek** is also particularly scenic and can be good for birds at any season.

*   *   *

The northeastern part of the county in the **La Crescent area** is included on **inset B**, where there is much more than just habitat for breeding woods birds. As mentioned earlier, the Mississippi River, its backwaters, and

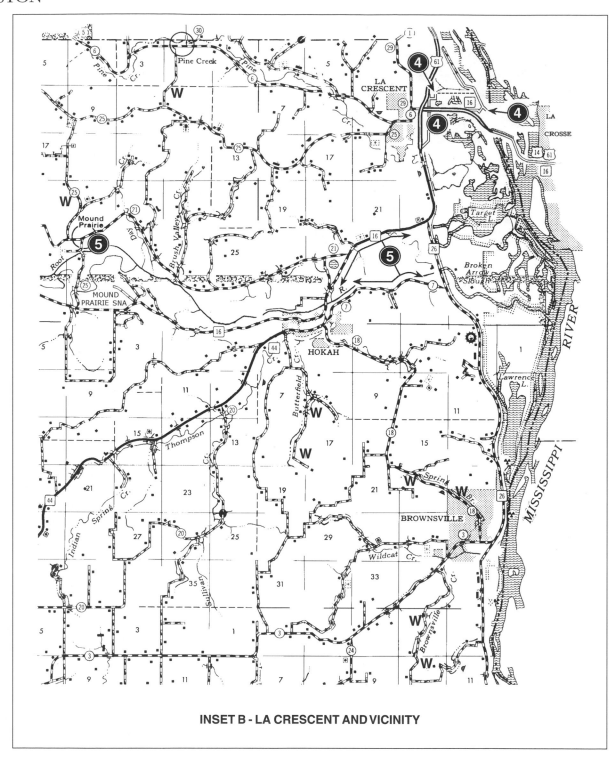

INSET B - LA CRESCENT AND VICINITY

wooded hillsides are good at all times of year, including winter. But the spring and summer nesting season remains the most popular time of year, and this area would be the best place to look for both water and woods birds.

The large and marshy **backwaters (B4)** on the south side of the Highway 61/14 causeway east of Highway 16 has been a consistent spot for Common Moorhens especially, as well as herons, egrets, and other water birds. Since the causeway is usually busy with traffic, the recommended spot from which to scan these backwaters is behind the sewage treat-

ment plant and highway department garage.

You'll see these buildings along the old highway which parallels Highway 16: as you approach La Crescent on 16 from the south, bear right on to the old highway where the four-lane section begins, and turn right across the tracks when you come to the plant and garage. (This road continues north past these buildings, goes under the causeway, passes the access to the old dump, and comes out on the main highway on the north side of La Crescent.)

Also marked **B4** is the **Shore Acres Road** area north of

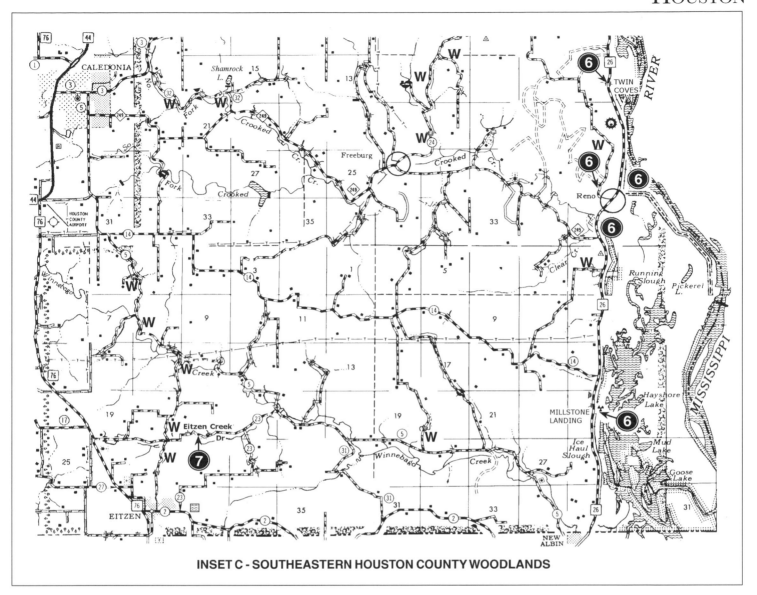

INSET C - SOUTHEASTERN HOUSTON COUNTY WOODLANDS

Highway 61/14, a heavily wooded area of backwaters where birders consistently come to find Prothonotary Warblers. This also is a good spot for other warblers (sometimes including Cerulean) and other woods birds, and there are usually lots of herons/egrets around (in former decades this was the site of Minnesota's only Yellow-crowned Night-Heron colony). Shore Acres Road turns north off the causeway 0.9 mile east of the Highway 16 stoplight, parallels the highway, and curves left to a T intersection in 0.4 mile. (Use care as you bird the first part of the road: it has narrow shoulders, few places to park, and a fair amount of traffic.)

The first place to park and bird is at the T: you can hike back along the road you drove in on and/or hike to the right from the T on the road which dead ends shortly. From the T intersection, drive the left fork which continues north past some good woodlands and eventually dead ends in 1.7 miles. But if you have time, park 0.3 mile from the T where the power line crosses the road, and hike west along an often wet and overgrown (and sometimes impassable) trail leading to the La Crescent dump area through more habitat for herons, Prothono-

taries, and Ceruleans.

Of final note in La Crescent are the backwaters and woodlands in and around the former dump (also **B4**; sometimes called **Sheperd's Marsh**) on the north side of town. From the stoplight in La Crescent, go north and bear right on Chestnut Street (the first street north of the stoplight), turn east on Main Street, cross the tracks, and go through the gate to the old dump.

Check right away in the backwaters on both sides of the road for moorhens, herons, egrets, rails, and other water birds. A consistent Willow Flycatcher thicket is on the left side of the road just before you come to the area where building materials are currently stockpiled and where trees and brush are still dumped. Park here, hike north past the lumber and brush piles up to the railroad tracks, and scan the large marsh where Least Bitterns and rails (including the occasional King Rail) have been found. Then return to where you parked, and hike east past a second gate along that trail which passes through Prothonotary and Cerulean warbler habitat and eventually comes out at Shore Acres Road (see above).

There are other good marshes elsewhere on inset B, especially the one on County Road 21 just east of **Mound Prairie (B5)**. This has been another good place to look for Common Moorhen, and it is a consistent spot for Least Bittern, rails, and Sandhill Cranes. Also marked **B5** are the wet **pastures and meadows** along Highway 16 and County Road 7 where Cattle Egrets are often spotted, and in most years there are exposed mudflats to attract a few shorebirds in the pool at the junction of Highway 16 and County Road 21.

This part of the county is as good a place as any to look for any of those deciduous forest specialties of the Southeast: again, look for those spots marked "W" on those curvy roads on the map. Of course, the birding is usually good on Highway 26 as it heads south from Highway 16 along the Mississippi through Brownsville and on into inset C. Elsewhere on inset B is the Mound Prairie Scientific and Natural Area, 257 acres of goat prairie hillsides along the north side of Highway 16 about 4 miles west of Hokah, where the local Lark Sparrow nests. Park on the state forest road a half mile east of the golf course road and hike up the hill.

*   *   *

Finally, **inset C** maps the way as you explore the roads which wind through still more extensive woodlands in **southeastern Houston County**, where there are a few areas to specifically recommend. In and around **Reno** are five spots to check (**C6**):

• The Twin Coves neighborhood is 2.8 miles north of Reno (or 3.9 miles south of Brownsville) on Highway 26, where there are bird feeders visible from the highway that often host Tufted Titmouse at any time of year (though this species seems less frequent recently). And if you're here during migration, especially in late fall, this is a good spot to scan the river for Bald Eagles, Tundra Swans (often by the hundreds), Canvasbacks, Common Mergansers, and other waterfowl.

• Turn east off the highway on the dirt road on the north edge of Reno, drive down the hill, park at the levee, start hiking east, and scan the Mississippi River for migrant waterfowl. If you're ambitious, you can walk the levee as it goes southeast about 3 miles all the way to the lock and dam.

• Follow the gravel road which leads west from "downtown" Reno, and in a half mile you will come to the Reno Recreation Area Campground where Minnesota's first White-eyed Vireo nest was found a few years back. If not vireos, there should at least be turkeys, a cuckoo or two, Yellow-throated Vireo, Wood Thrush, Blue-winged Warbler, Scarlet Tanager,

Eastern Towhee, Field Sparrow, Orchard Oriole, and other similar nesting species.

• Just south of town are some beautiful backwaters along both sides of Highway 26 for herons, egrets, and other water birds, including perhaps a moorhen at times.

• And about 5 miles south of Reno on Highway 26 is Millstone Landing, one of the most reliable places in the state for years for nesting Prothonotary Warblers: turn east from 26 at the sign, 2.7 miles north of the Iowa line.

Farther west in inset C are a couple of small reservoirs: except for marshes, these are about the only wetlands in the county away from the Mississippi. I've never seen much at the Crooked Creek impoundment southwest of Caledonia, but so-called Shamrock Lake about 3 miles east of Caledonia at least has good wet thickets where Willow Flycatchers nest and where a Yellow-breasted Chat turned up a couple of springs ago. Follow County Road 3 east from Caledonia to County Road 32, continue east on 32 a couple of miles until it turns south at a T, and you'll see a sign for an access road to the lake just east of the T.

Then, there is my favorite road in the entire county, easily the best spot in the state to find, well, Timber Rattlesnakes! I, at least, have seen them several times on **Eitzen Creek Drive (C7)**: turn west off County Road 23, 0.8 mile west of County Road 5, go about a mile, and look by the rocky ledges along the north side of the road. But even if there are no reptiles around, you could at least try your hand at, well, bird watching. The feeders at Marilynn Ford's residence just east of here have consistently hosted Tufted Titmice over the years, the Fords once had a White-eyed Vireo in their yard, turkeys are frequently seen along this road, and bobwhites have been found at times along County Roads 2 and 23 east of Eitzen. And note the sewage ponds on the map a mile east of town.

(For more information on birding in Houston County, consult *A Birder's Guide to Houston County* by Karla Kinstler and Fred Lesher; it is available for $6.50 + shipping from the Houston Nature Center, P. O. Box 667, Houston 55943.)

*   *   *

So, just where is Bee, how does one get there, and is it worth the trip? Sorry, but there are some secrets best left to the imagination, best discovered by serendipity without the benefit of guidance. Yes, Bee is worth finding — it has the unique feel of some other world, somewhere quite unlike Minnesota. Sort of like Iowa.

Winona County

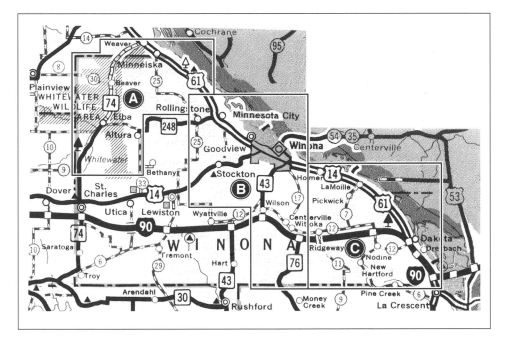

Much of this county, especially its southwestern part, is ordinary farmlands, and there are essentially no wetlands except, of course, for the Mississippi River plus a few pools at Whitewater Wildlife Management Area. Still, insets A, B, and C map a lot of roads to explore as they wind through extensive deciduous woods, and most of the Southeast specialties discussed under Fillmore and Houston counties are possible here. And "explore" is the operative word, since relatively few specific birding locations and even fewer rarities have been found in Winona County away from the Mississippi and Whitewater, even though its resident birding community has been active for decades. Perhaps they spend more time down in Houston County (which is understandable) or over in Wisconsin (which is inexcusable).

Also note, as in Houston County, there is reason to come here at all times of year since there are nesting woods birds, migrant waterfowl on the Mississippi River, and wintering birds of all sorts in the cover of the Whitewater area and in the open water below the dams on the Mississippi.

Starting in **southeastern Winona County (inset C)**, the county's primary claim to fame has been the nesting Henslow's Sparrows of **Great River Bluffs State Park (C1**; formerly, O. L. Kipp State Park). For decades, the shrubby field along the road just beyond the entrance station (follow the signs off Interstate 90 and County Road 3) has been the only consistent place in the state for this species. During the past decade, however, they have been absent in at least four

summers, and without continuation of recent habitat management efforts they could disappear for good. If there are no Henslow's singing along the park road, try the field behind the park manager's residence to the right of the entrance. Also listen in the thickets along the road between the entrance and the first parking lot for Bell's Vireo.

If Henslow's fail to return to the park some year, at least this will provide birders with a reason to explore the other scattered meadows and grasslands which line some of the ridges above the Mississippi. And if there are no Henslow's to be heard in your wanderings (listen for them from mid-May through July; one road to try might be County Road 1 south of the interstate), you might at least see Swainson's Hawk, Gray Partridge, Wild Turkey, Upland Sandpiper, Sedge Wren, Grasshopper Sparrow, Dickcissel, Bobolink, both meadowlarks, Orchard Oriole, and perhaps even a bobwhite or two — on whose origins you are free to speculate.

Elsewhere in inset C, none of the wooded back roads is known to be better than the others, so you might as well explore them all so you don't miss anything. Actually, the two best **woodlands** are probably along Highway 61 within Great River Bluffs (both marked **C1**), where at least Tufted Titmouse has been found. One is in the park's Bike Campground: look for the small sign on Highway 61, 2.6 miles northwest of the Interstate 90 junction in Dakota, or 2.9 miles southeast of County Road 3.

The other woods are along the hiking trail which starts off 61 at mile marker 13, 1.5 miles southeast of County Road 3: park at the southeast end of the frontage road in Donehower, walk southeast past the house with the large white pines, and the trail starts by the creek next to the house.

During migration and summer, the inset C portion of the river tends to provide better habitat for barges than water birds, since there are few backwaters — except around Homer (d'oh!). But if you're birding this stretch of Highway 61 in winter, be sure to check for eagles and water birds at the open water below the two lock and dams shown on the Mississippi River.

* * *

Inset B maps still more woods along back roads in **Wi-**

nona and vicinity worth wandering through, but the best areas to spend time in at most any time of year would be those in Winona itself. One good area is along the **Mud Lake Hike and Bike Trail (B2),** which begins behind the obvious Fleet Farm store at the intersection of Highways 43 and 61 and goes east a mile to the end of Shives Road near the sewage plant. Bell's Vireos have nested in these thickets, and this habitat is good for American Woodcock, both cuckoos, and Willow Flycatcher.

Another place nearby worth trying at times is Woodlawn Cemetery, which can be good for migrant warblers and the like and has a number of conifers to attract roosting owls or winter finches. From the Highways 43-61 junction, go 1.6 miles northwest on 61 to the Huff Street stoplight, turn south (left) to the frontage road (Lake Boulevard), and then go right to the cemetery.

But Winona's best-known place for both water and woods birds, especially during migration and winter, is **Prairie Island** (also marked **B2),** the site of Minnesota's only White Ibis record. These backwaters and woodlands are part of the Upper Mississippi River National Wildlife Refuge, and the best way to get there is to return to the Huff Street stoplight on Highway 61 and turn northeast toward downtown. Where Huff Street comes to the river it curves left and becomes River View Drive, which follows the river for 1.5 miles until the junction with Prairie Island Road. (If you continue straight, this road passes more backwaters and then curves away from the river to become Pelzer Street, which returns to Highway 61 at the Highway 14 junction).

Turn north (right) on Prairie Island Road which curves northwest and passes through a nice variety of habitats for the next few miles, including planted pines, thickets, and

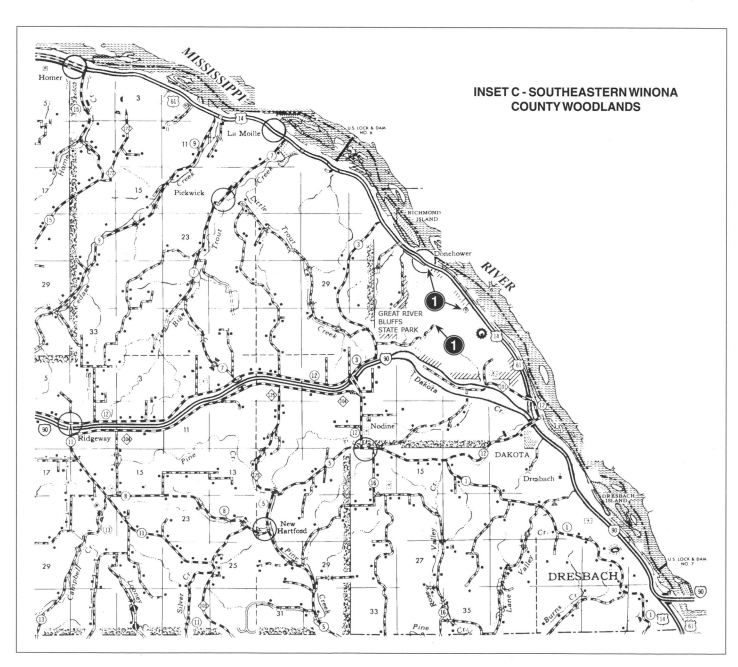

INSET C - SOUTHEASTERN WINONA COUNTY WOODLANDS

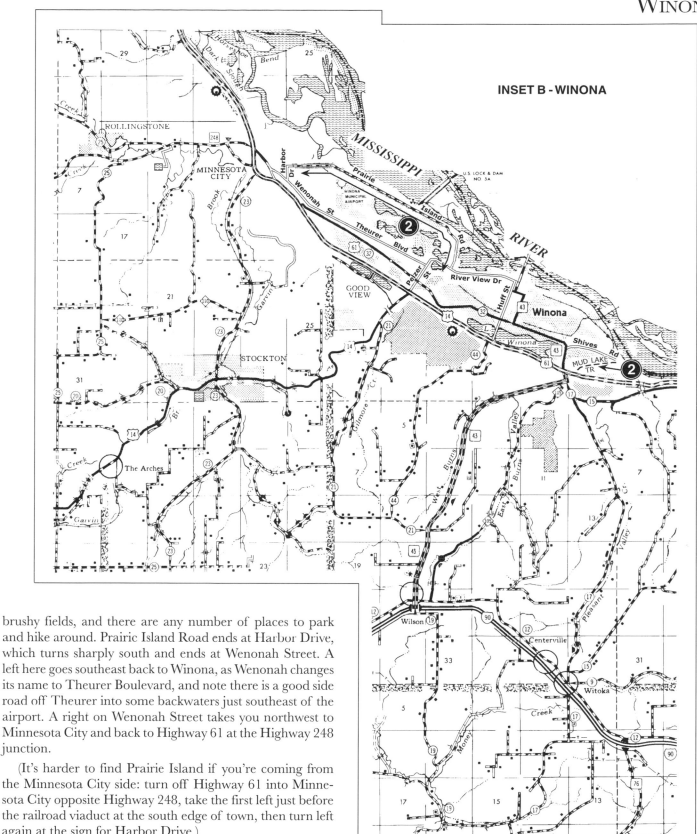

INSET B - WINONA

brushy fields, and there are any number of places to park and hike around. Prairie Island Road ends at Harbor Drive, which turns sharply south and ends at Wenonah Street. A left here goes southeast back to Winona, as Wenonah changes its name to Theurer Boulevard, and note there is a good side road off Theurer into some backwaters just southeast of the airport. A right on Wenonah Street takes you northwest to Minnesota City and back to Highway 61 at the Highway 248 junction.

(It's harder to find Prairie Island if you're coming from the Minnesota City side: turn off Highway 61 into Minnesota City opposite Highway 248, take the first left just before the railroad viaduct at the south edge of town, then turn left again at the sign for Harbor Drive.)

*   *   *

Inset A, which contains a portion of Wabasha County, includes two famous birding areas, known not just to Winona County birders but also to those throughout Minnesota: **Whitewater Wildlife Management Area** and the Tundra Swans in the Weaver Bottoms backwaters.

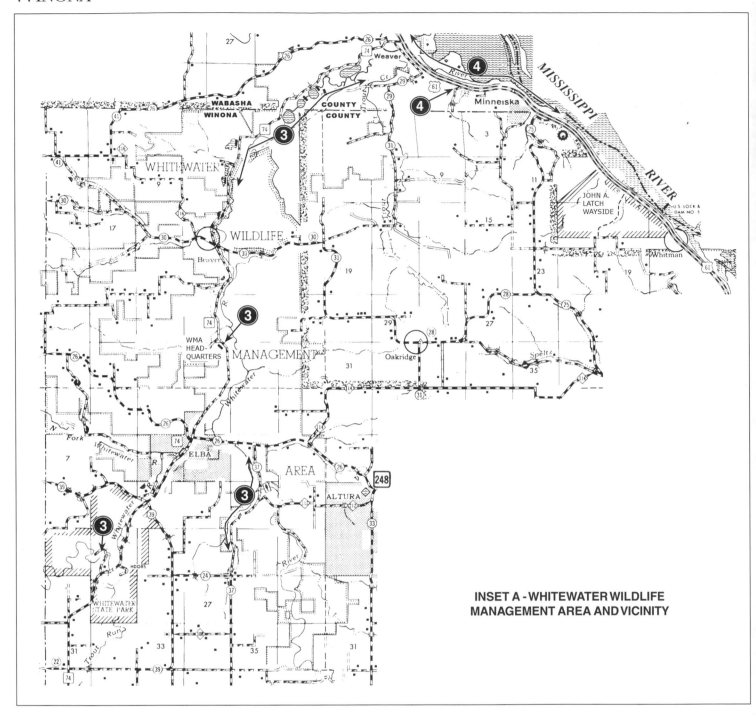

INSET A - WHITEWATER WILDLIFE MANAGEMENT AREA AND VICINITY

The Whitewater area, which includes the state park, is a broad and densely wooded valley along the Whitewater River, its limestone ridges lined in places with junipers and "goat prairie" grasslands, the river itself dotted with a series of swampy water impoundments as it flows into Wabasha County.

This area, like others in this corner of the state, is worthwhile at all times of year, and there is a wide variety of species to look for: herons and egrets, wintering ducks and other water birds in the open spring-fed creeks, Red-shouldered Hawk, Golden Eagle, Ruffed Grouse, Wild Turkey, Common Moorhen (rare), American Woodcock, cuckoos, owls (especially Barred), Whip-poor-will, Willow Flycatcher, Bell's Vireo (rare), Blue-winged Warbler, Louisiana Waterthrush (in the

state park; see below), Yellow-breasted Chat (also rare), and many other Southeast specialties.

This is one of the state's most consistent nesting and wintering areas for Red-shouldered Hawk, which is curiously absent from most of the Southeast Region south of the Twin Cities. A few Golden Eagles actually winter here annually: Whitewater is one of only two places in the entire state where birders consistently find this species. Also note this is the site of Minnesota's first successful introductions of turkeys back in the 1960s.

Most of the area can be looked over by driving along Highway 74, but all the connecting side roads are potentially good as well. Also worthwhile are the roads around the periphery of the wildlife management area since the croplands along these edges of the valley attract Wild Turkeys. If your time is limited, there are four places (each marked **A3**) that tend to be the most interesting:

• The **water impoundments**, which extend for some 5 miles along the north end of Highway 74; while these pools can be scanned from the road, it is also worth hiking around them on the levees.

• **Wildlife management area headquarters**, where there are feeders, some large pines, and some springs to keep a creek open most winters; also look for the sign to the Marnach House, and follow this road and trail into some good woodlands.

• The heavily wooded areas along **County Road 37**, in the vicinity of the fish hatchery ponds.

• The stream by the **group campground** of Whitewater State Park, where Louisiana Waterthrushes have been found in summer.

Highway 74 ends (or begins) at the junction of Highway 61 in Weaver, Wabasha County. In fall, especially November, be sure to scan the Mississippi River for Tundra Swans which annually congregate in these so-called **Weaver Bottoms (A4)**. The backwaters and swans begin just northwest of Weaver (see Wabasha County's inset B), and continue for some 4 miles to Minneiska on the Wabasha-Winona County line. In years past, the swans used to annually peak at more than 10,000 individuals counted per day (with smaller concentrations in late March-early April), and numbers of other migrant waterfowl congregate here as well. In recent Novembers, however, the counts are perhaps a tenth of what they used to be.

If you watch for traffic, you can see the swans fairly well from the shoulder of Highway 61, but the best **vantage point** (also marked **A4**) is reached by turning southwest off Highway 61 just before the cemetery, 1.7 miles southeast of Weaver, and bearing right to the top of the hill. Another good spot from which to scan is along the frontage road in "downtown" Minneiska, which is higher than Highway 61. (And, if you are one of those oddball birders who couldn't care less about a Minnesota list, good numbers of swans gather at close range across the river in Reick's — also spelled Riecks — Park, along Highway 35 just north of Alma, Wisconsin.)

If you happen to be in this area when warblers and other passerines are migrating, stop a few miles farther downstream at the John A. Latsch Wayside. If you're energetic, hike up the old road which begins a half mile southeast of the signed parking lot off Highway 61 and continues for a mile to the top of the hill. And if you're here in winter, check for water birds a mile farther downstream below the dam.

Winona County also has five sewage ponds:

❑ Rollingstone: see inset B; from the junction of County Road 25 South and Highway 248, go 1 mile east on 248, then south on a dirt road which zig-zags through a field and across a creek to the ponds.

❑ Stockton: see inset B; along Highway 14 west of town.

❑ Utica: on the north side of Highway 14 on the east side of town.

❑ Altura: see inset A; turn south off County Road 26 just west of Highway 248.

❑ Lewiston: probably the best of the five (though these are apparently on the verge of closing); 1 mile south on County Road 29, then 0.7 mile west.

Wabasha County

The habitats, possible species, seasons, and strategy of selecting crooked roads on the map all remain pretty much the same in Wabasha County as discussed in the previous three chapters (although Northern Bobwhite, Acadian Flycatcher, Prothonotary Warbler, Louisiana Waterthrush, and Henslow's Sparrow would prove harder to find in this county). And note this county's portion of Whitewater Wildlife Management Area and the Tundra Swan backwaters between Weaver and Minneiska are included on Winona County's inset A.

Curiously, the most interesting birding in this county has little to do with Mississippi River valley woodlands or backwaters. That open area generally known as the Kellogg Sand Prairie lies east of Highway 61 between Wabasha and Weaver,

is mapped on inset B, and is a unique combination of sedge marshes, sandy grasslands, wet thickets, planted pines, and junipers among the farm fields.

While there are some good woods and backwaters along the river on this map, unless one has a boat they are generally hard to reach, and the best use of your time in spring and summer would be at **McCarthy Lake Wildlife Management Area (B1)**, on the west side of County Road 84. This vast area is mostly inaccessible, but fortunately a nice part of it is adjacent to County Road 84: park by the sign for McCarthy Lake, and hike through the gate to the small thicket-lined pond. Not only has this thicket been Minnesota's most reliable spot for Bell's Vireo for decades, but it is also a good place for Willow Flycatcher and Orchard Oriole, and the surrounding grasslands host Sedge Wrens, a few Dickcissels, and Lark and Grasshopper sparrows. Look also for Sandhill Crane, which has been found here in recent summers.

Next, check the sandy grasslands, junipers, and edge habitats in the two **Weaver Dunes Scientific and Natural Areas** on the east side of County Road 84 (also marked **B1**), where there are more Lark Sparrows to be seen. Watch or listen for American Woodcock, both cuckoos, Whip-poor-will, Eastern Towhee, and Clay-colored Sparrow; these areas also seem like they could occasionally attract something like a Loggerhead Shrike, Mountain Bluebird, Townsend's Solitaire, Northern Mockingbird, Yellow-breasted Chat, or Spotted Towhee.

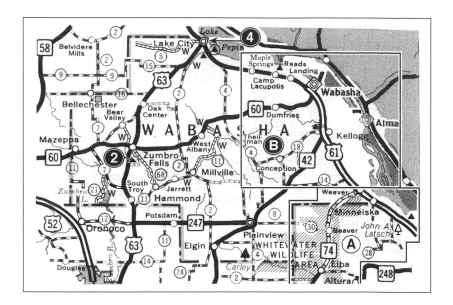

Farther south on 84, the road curves back towards Highway 61 and passes through some nice woods and wetlands, which are worth checking if you can find a place to park along this narrow road. If you're here in November, turn southeast on 61 and you'll begin seeing swans on the river just before you come to Weaver (see Winona County's inset A). In spring/summer, however, turn northwest on Highway 61 and note the vast and inaccessible marshes along the west side of McCarthy Lake Wildlife Management Area. I've driven past here for years and always wondered if King (or even Black) Rails could be found if birders would penetrate this area by canoe.

Elsewhere in **eastern Wabasha County** are lots of woods and roads to explore during the nesting season which are mapped on **inset B**. One place to start birding would be just southwest of Wabasha at Kruger County Park: it's on County Road 81 just south of its junction with Highway 60. A larger area with lots of hiking trails to explore is the so-called **Zumbro Bottoms**, with the two best trailheads and parking spots marked **B2**.

A similar area along the Zumbro River farther west in the county is the 300-acre **Zumbro Falls Woods Scientific and Natural Area (2)**. The east side of this area is along County Road 68, which turns south off Highway 63 on the south side of Zumbro Falls; to access the west side, turn east off Highway 63 on Township Road 7, 1.7 miles south of Highway 60. Both these tracts are good places to look for Red-shouldered Hawk, Acadian Flycatcher, Tufted Titmouse, Cerulean Warbler, and other local Southeast Region specialties.

Then, if you get a Wabasha County map and want to try your hand at finding other good woodlands outside of inset B using the crooked vs. straight road theory, I would recommend the following roads:

• County Road 5 west of Lake City.

• County Roads 7 and 21 south of Highway 60.

• County Road 11 between Highways 60 and 63.

• And at Carley State Park, south of Plainview on County Road 4.

Also located on inset B is **Reads Landing (B3)**, long a

favored spot for Bald Eagles wintering along this stretch of the river which is usually kept open by the current from the Chippewa River as it joins the Mississippi. Unless severe cold limits the amount of open water, daily counts of 50 eagles or more are typical in mid-winter in this vicinity: you can scan the river in "downtown" Reads Landing or from the pull-offs on Highway 61 just northwest of town. While you're in the neighborhood, you might also want to head into downtown Wabasha to the National Eagle Center, where there are interpretive displays and an observation deck overlooking the river.

Even larger single-day eagle counts of 300-400 are possible between here and nearby Lake Pepin (that widest part of the river upstream from Reads Landing) in late fall or early spring, as the river starts freezing over or opening up for the season. At the same times of year on Lake Pepin, especially during freeze-up in late November, large numbers of migrant water birds congregate, most notable among them being those peaks of Common Mergansers numbering in the thousands. Also scan the lake for other "big lake" birds such as Common Loon, Horned Grebe, Greater Scaup, and Herring and Bonaparte's gulls.

Lake Pepin would also be a likely place to occasionally attract such strays as Red-throated and Pacific (seen in 2001) loons, Harlequin Duck, any of the scoters, Long-tailed Duck, Barrow's Goldeneye, jaegers (a Pomarine was here in November 1996), or rare gulls.

The length of **Lake Pepin**, which extends into Goodhue County, can be scanned fairly well from Highway 61, but the best place to look it over is in Lake City (**4**):

• If you're driving in from the northwest, take Park Street, the first left off 61 you come to in town, and follow it to the point and marina behind the trailer park.

• Next, check the breakwaters just southeast of downtown along Highway 61 / S. Lakeshore Drive.

• Continue southeast on 61 another 5 blocks to Roschen Park, and in 2 more blocks bear left on S. Oak Street which follows the lake and dead ends at the Sportsman's Club. This

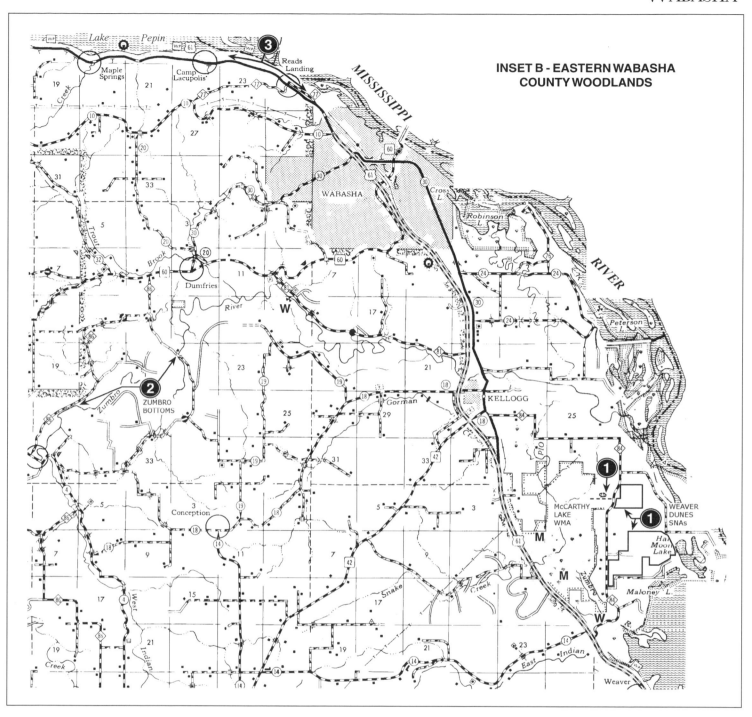

INSET B - EASTERN WABASHA
COUNTY WOODLANDS

site can also be reached by turning off Highway 61 at the Wild Wings store, a couple of miles southeast of downtown.

Finally, Wabasha County's only sewage ponds are at Bellechester, 0.2 mile east on County Road 16.

(For more information on birding in the Lake City area, consult the Lake City Birds pamphlet, published by the Lake City Tourism Bureau, 1515 N. Lakeshore Drive, Lake City 55041, website <www.lakecity.org>.)

Olmsted County

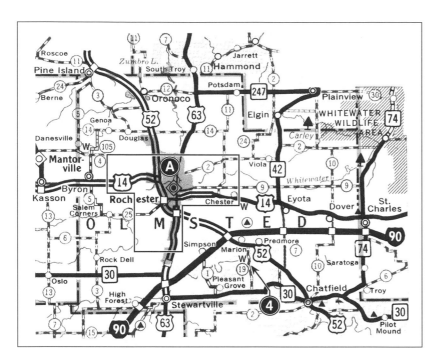

At first glance, one would guess Olmsted County to be quite ordinary: it is mostly farmed, wetlands are few and small in size, and it is devoid of the vast stands of woodlands which characterize other counties in this corner of Minnesota. However, it does have an especially active birding community represented by the Zumbro Valley Audubon Society, and they have long been turning up remarkable rarities at generally unremarkable locations.

Rochester (inset A) may be best known for its Mayo Clinic, attracting patients and visitors from all over the world — and Peregrine Falcons, which have nested atop the clinic and other downtown buildings. Rochester also owns the dubious distinction as being a haven for wintering Canada Geese. A power plant keeps **Silver Lake (A1)** open all winter, and the local residents keep them well-fed. Some 30,000 individuals (geese, that is, not people) crowd into this small lake in late fall/early winter, which is most easily scanned along its west side from West Silver Lake Drive: from Highway 63 / N. Broadway just north of downtown, take 7th Street N. E. east for 3 blocks, and turn north to the lake.

With so many geese around, there doesn't seem to be much room for anything else, and the variety of wintering waterfowl is generally limited. This may be the best spot in the Southeast Region, though, to find Greater White-fronted Goose in the fall, there are several winter Snow Goose records (plus an occasional Ross's), and in early spring the lake can be good for waterfowl if everything else is frozen.

There are three other spots in town (each marked **A2**) that would be worth a visit, especially during migration:

• In the southwest part of Rochester are some good woodlands along the Zumbro River in the **Izaak Walton area**. From Highway 14, go west on Salem Road S.W. / County Road 22, stay on Salem Road as it becomes County Road 25, and in about 2 more miles park at the sign for the property on the south side of the road. Follow the trails through the pine plantation and the mix of other habitats to the river, and look for roosting owls, warblers and other migrants.

• On the east side of Rochester are the marshes of **Eastside Wildlife Management Area**, a good spot in spring/summer for Least Bittern, rails, Marsh Wren, Yellow-headed Blackbird, and other marsh birds — even Common Moorhen and Great-tailed Grackle have each been found here. Take Highway 14 east from Highway 52 for about 3.5 miles, turn north on County Road 22 / East Circle Drive, go 0.6 mile to County Road 9 / Collegeview Road E., then east 1.4 miles to the parking lot on the south side of the road just before the railroad tracks.

• Just west of Eastside is **Quarry Hill Park**, not only a good place for migrants along any of its hiking trails, but the feeders at the nature center also attract a variety of wintering birds. From Eastside, go back west to County Road 22, turn north and cross the railroad tracks in a half mile, and take the first left (west) on Silver Creek Road N. E. to the park's main entrance. You can also access the west side of the park by going east from 11th Avenue N.E. on 9th Street N.E.

But of primary interest are the six water impoundments developed in recent years for flood control around Rochester, some of which have proven attractive to water birds. Some currently are inaccessible and can only be distantly scanned with spotting scopes, but more access roads and trails are being opened, and at present four of these reservoirs (all marked **A3**) have been worth birding.

• **East Landfill Reservoir**, on the west side of town: from the junction of 19th Street N.W. and 70th Avenue N.W., go north on 70th a half mile.

• **South Landfill Reservoir** is nearby: from the corner of 19th and 70th, go west on 19th a half mile.

Recent records at these two areas include Cattle Egret, Little Blue Heron, White-faced Ibis, White-winged Scoter, Long-tailed Duck, American Avocet, Red-necked Phalarope, and

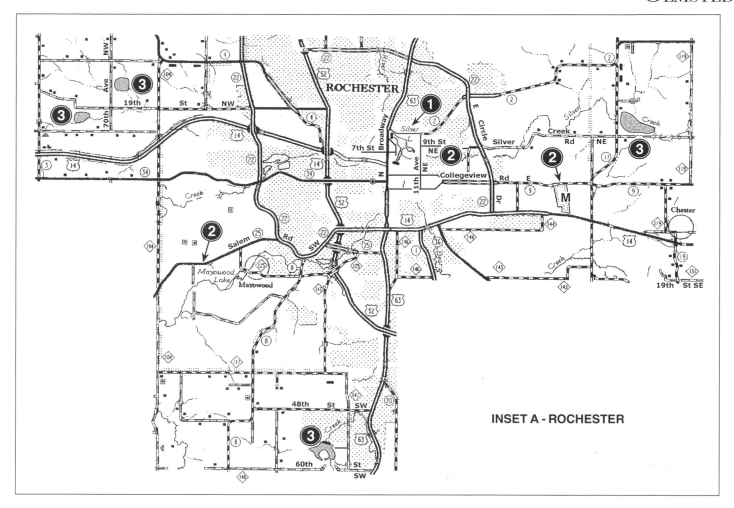

INSET A - ROCHESTER

Le Conte's and Nelson's Sharp-tailed sparrows.

• **Willow Creek Reservoir**, south of town: turn west off Highway 63 on 48th Street S.W., go 0.5 mile, then 0.8 mile south on County Road 147, and west on Lone Pine Drive to the parking lot. A lost Long-tailed Duck turned up here once in spring.

• **Silver Creek Reservoir**, east of Rochester: from Highway 14, go north 2 miles on County Road 11, then east on Silver Creek Road N.E. 0.8 mile. Past shorebird sightings include avocet, both godwits, and Piping Plover.

The best roads to bird for those woodland specialties of the Southeast Region are those in southern Olmsted County along the Root River and its tributaries between County Road 1 and Chatfield. The best of these is probably County Road 19 along **Kinney Creek (4)**, between 1 and 2.5 miles south of Highway 52. Residential feeders used to consistently host Tufted Titmice (but apparently not recently), Blue-winged and Cerulean warblers are among the nesting specialties, and there are records for Louisiana Waterthrush.

Finally, there are a couple of county parks which can be good places to find migrants. Oxbow Park is in western Olmsted County: from Highway 14 in Byron, go north 2.8 miles on County Road 5, then east on County Road 4 across the creek, and take an immediate left (north) on County Road 105 to the park. Hiking trails begin at the nature center, and if the birding is dull you could always take in the small zoo at Oxbow.

And the entrance to Chester Woods County Park is east of Rochester on Highway 14, 1.7 miles east of Chester. There is a variety of habitats (including one of those flood-control reservoirs, which usually is unproductive), and recent records include Bell's Vireo, Northern Mockingbird, and Orchard Oriole. Also check the fields on the west side of the park which have attracted both Henslow's and Lark sparrows. Go back west to Chester on 14, go 0.7 mile south on County Road 19, then east through the grasslands towards the park on County Road 131 / 19th Street S.E. (see inset A).

(For lots of additional information on birding in Olmsted County, visit Bob Ekblad's website, <home.rconnect.com/~ekblad>.)

Dodge County

A quiz. Dodge County is most famous for: a) the way some of its county roads are identified; or b) sewage ponds. While it's a close call, I'll have to go along with the sewage ponds at Claremont (1 mile south from Highway 14 on County Road 3, then 0.5 mile east, and 0.2 mile north) where there are records of both Red Phalarope and Violet-green Swallow. Before these vagrants turned up, though, I would have answered (a). I, at least, find it interesting that some of this county's roads are identified by letters, rather than numbers. (Ramsey County also does this, as does Yellow Medicine to a limited extent, and Wisconsin counties do it all the time. As if you haven't already guessed, I'm easily amused.)

If this trivia doesn't strike you as particularly fascinating, it's the best I can come up with since significant birding locations are almost nonexistent. Besides those sewage ponds, about the best place to recommend would be the wooded cemetery in Mantorville on the Zumbro River (along the east side of Highway 57 on the south side of town). Besides looking for migrant passerines, also check the planted pines in case there is a roosting owl in hiding. There are also some good wooded portions of another branch of the Zumbro between Concord and Berne, but access is limited.

Another spot to try would be the gravel pit ponds around the junction of County Roads 1 and G, 2.5 miles north of Claremont. Since there are so few lakes in and around Dodge

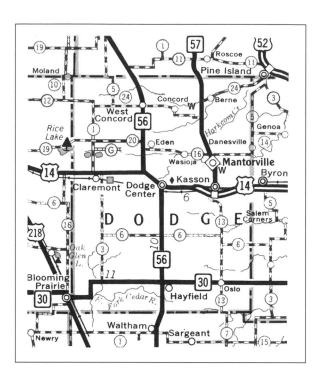

County, water birds desperate for a place to land should end up here — if not at the sewage ponds.

Steele County

While this county's roads lack the distinction of those lettered roads in Dodge County, at least there are more wetlands in Steele County. One of these is the large pond at the game farm in the northeast corner: from the junction of County Roads 10 and 12, go west on 12 for 2 miles, then 0.7 mile south. (If there are no birds here, you might at least add Elk to your mammal list.) Another is the sewage pond at Ellendale: turn north off Highway 30 on the unmarked gravel road along east side of the railroad tracks, and go 0.6 mile.

The largest lake in the county is at **Rice Lake State Park (1)**, located off County Road 19, a mile west of the Dodge County line. A stray Red-throated Loon once turned up here, but more interesting would be the park's extensive woodlands which attract migrant passerines. About the only other wetland worth birding might be marshy Oak Glen Lake, 1.5 miles southeast of Bixby on the east side of Highway 218. And note a White-eyed Vireo was found once in the wildlife management area along the west side of 218 just north of the lake.

But that would be about all Steele County specifically has to offer, although there was something appealing enough about this county to have attracted a first-state-record Brambling to Owatonna several winters ago and a Black-bellied Whistling-Duck in 1998.

Waseca County

Perhaps a better find than Steele County's whistling-duck might be that Garganey which appeared at Goose Lake a few years ago. In spite of this, Waseca County has little to distinguish it from its two neighbors to the east, though there are at least more lakes here.

Unless you want to sit at Goose Lake to see if that Garganey ever returns, probably the county's best lake to bird, by virtue of its size alone, would be Lake Elysian. It is best scanned from either County Road 3 along its east shore, or from the park and dam on its south side (go north from Janesville on County Roads 19 and 53 for 2 miles). And farther south you might want to check Mott Lake, where Red-necked Grebes have nested: from Waldorf, go 2 miles north on County Road 3, then east 1 mile on County Road 78.

The only other "wetlands" in the county possibly worth a special visit would be the sewage ponds at Janesville (turn west off County Road 3 on County Road 55 just south of the tracks, and go 1 mile) and at Waseca (go 2 miles west from Highway 13 on Highway 14, then 1 mile south on County Road 27).

My only other suggestion is to check the thickets in the wildlife management area on the west side of Highway 13, 6 miles south of Waseca, where Bell's Vireos were present three consecutive summers, 1997-99.

Blue Earth County

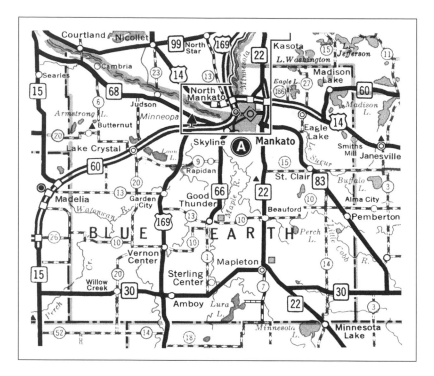

But the best portion of the **Minnesota River valley** is mapped on **inset A**, which includes pieces of Nicollet and Le Sueur counties. The most heavily wooded spots are in **Minneopa State Park**, especially in the Falls Area and at Williams Nature Center (both marked **A1**). The Falls Area, off County Road 69 and well-marked by the sign on Highway 169 west of Mankato, is especially known because of its breeding records of Louisiana Waterthrush. And a bit farther east is Williams Nature Center on Highway 68, 0.7 mile west of Highway 169, where Kentucky Warbler was found in the summer of 2000 (and possibly in earlier years).

The dense woods at both places should also be good for finding Red-shouldered Hawk, Barred Owl, Whip-poor-will, Acadian Flycatcher (maybe), Yellow-throated Vireo, Wood Thrush, Cerulean Warbler, and other breeding woods birds. Also check the more open areas near the state park campground just to the west along Highway 68 for nesting Upland Sandpiper, American Woodcock, Black-billed Cuckoo, Willow Flycatcher, Loggerhead Shrike (rare), Sedge Wren, Eastern Towhee, Clay-colored, Lark and Grasshopper sparrows, Dickcissel, and Orchard Oriole. Also listen for Bell's Vireos which have been found near the campground the last few years, and there is a good trail from the picnic area parking lot near the campground which leads to heavily wooded Minneopa Creek.

Look as well for the local Loggerhead Shrike and Lark Sparrow among the grasslands, junipers, and interesting rock outcroppings along the back roads in the Le Sueur County portion of inset A north of Mankato. The best places to start would be at and around The Nature Conservancy's **Ottawa Bluffs** tract, on County Road 23 north of Highway 99, and the **Kasota Prairie Scientific and Natural Area**, just southwest of Kasota — both marked **A2**.

Besides shrikes and sparrows, such habitat in this part of the valley has also been visited by rarities such as Mountain Bluebird, Townsend's Solitaire, Northern Mockingbird, and Spotted Towhee. Also note on inset A the large but difficult-to-access St. Peter sewage ponds just north of Highway 99, and just south of here is a good stand of conifers in the cemetery south of 99.

As far as the rest of Blue Earth County is concerned, several lakes are scattered throughout, and probably the best of these for migrants would be relatively large Lura Lake. The

Readers who glance at the map of this county and who have read those chapters on neighboring counties could probably predict what this chapter will have to say. For that matter, some could even write a better chapter. ("The countryside is mostly farmed, the river banks are wooded but too far from the Mississippi to have many Southeast Region specialties, the lakes are too far east to attract that many migrant water birds of the Great Plains. And, of course, don't forget about those sewage ponds and the good ol' Minnesota River valley. The end. PS: Look for migrants.")

The terrain and birding possibilities along Blue Earth County's portion of the Minnesota River as it reorients its flow towards the northeast remain basically the same as described in the Renville County chapter. In addition, be aware that from here downstream to the Twin Cities the river is most apt to overflow its banks and flood adjacent fields for the benefit of migrant waterfowl in early spring if there has been a heavy snowmelt.

This far east one also starts seeing at least a few of those Southeast-type woods birds, which are local or even absent farther upstream in the West Region. The part of the valley in northwestern Blue Earth County can be accessed from Highway 68, from a few roads off 68 which dead end at the Minnesota River, and from County Roads 45 and 42 which cross the river at Courtland and Judson.

best access would be from Daly County Park on its east side: from Highway 30 in Mapleton, go 3.5 miles south on County Road 7, then 2 miles west on County Road 191 to the park entrance.

Mankato birders have also had good luck a few miles east of town at Eagle Lake, finding such things as Least Bittern, Willow Flycatcher, and Bell's Vireo in the marsh and thickets along the Sakatah Singing Hills Trail. From the junction of Highways 14 and 22, go east 2 miles on 14, north 0.6 mile on County Road 186 to the trail access, and hike east.

And don't forget the north shore of Minnesota Lake can be scanned from Blue Earth County. As described in the Faribault County chapter, this is one of the best lakes in the Southeast Region.

There are also sewage ponds at Mapleton (from the junction of Highways 22 and 30, go northwest 0.2 mile on 22 to 8th Avenue N.E., then 0.5 mile north) and at Good Thunder (0.2 mile east of Highway 66 on County Road 10).

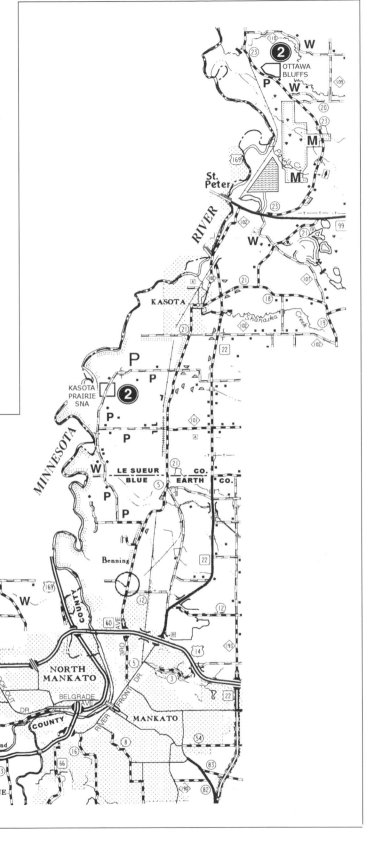

INSET A - MINNESOTA RIVER VALLEY

Nicollet County

There may be more miles of the Minnesota River valley within this county than any other, but there isn't a whole lot to say about it in this chapter. The possible birds of this wooded corridor have already been discussed under Renville County, insets B and C in Brown County map the Nicollet County side of the river from Fort Ridgely to Courtland, and Blue Earth County's inset A includes the vicinity of North Mankato. The area in between is shown on **inset D**, with the most notable thing about this stretch of the **Minnesota River valley** being the Chuck-will's-widow record in 1984 — it was a mile west of where County Road 62 turns north away from the river.

Between North Mankato and the Sibley County line, the Nicollet County side of the valley is difficult to bird, since the only road through it is busy Highway 169. But, if you find a safe place to pull off, scan for migrant hawks above the hillsides west of 169; in wet springs, when the fields east of the highway are flooded, you might see herons/egrets, waterfowl, and shorebirds.

Certainly the best place to get off the highway to bird would be at **Seven Mile Creek County Park (1)**. Here, a pair of Kentucky Warblers was found around the junction of trails 2 and 3 for at least five consecutive summers, 1992-96, and they even nested. The Kentuckys seem to be gone now, possibly

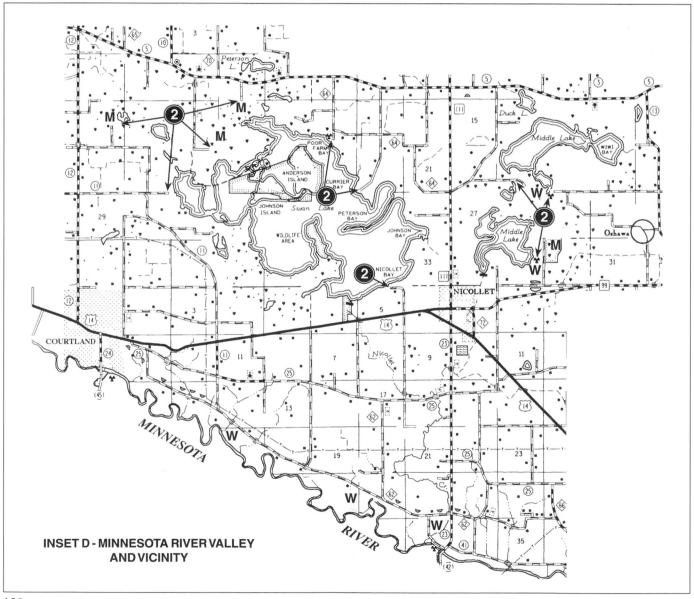

INSET D - MINNESOTA RIVER VALLEY AND VICINITY

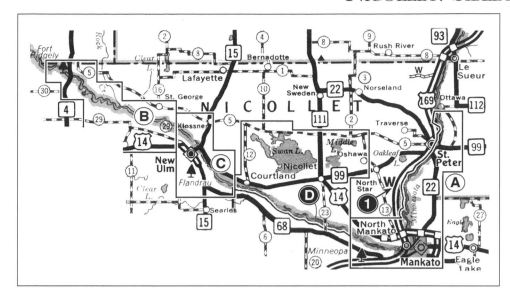

moving to the Minneopa State Park area (see Blue Earth County), but the Acadian Flycatchers and Cerulean Warblers turned up by those searching for Kentuckys might still be there. Look for the park sign on the west side of Highway 169, 4.6 miles south of the Highway 99 junction, or 4.9 miles north of Highway 14.

Farther north, you might want to also try the road along Barney Fry Creek. Turn west off Highway 169, 8 miles north of downtown St. Peter or 2 miles south of the Sibley County line: a mile of dense woodlands along the creek begins 1.5 miles west of 169.

Almost as famous as Jackson County's Heron Lake — and every bit as inaccessible — is **Swan Lake**. This large and marshy lake on inset D has a long history as a breeding site for Red-necked, Eared and Western grebes, Least Bittern, Common Moorhen (now rare), Forster's Tern, and other water birds (like an occasional King Rail?). Unless you have a boat, however, the best you can do is approach the marshes and shoreline from the seven dead-end roads on the map marked **D2**. Also marked **D2** are the three spots from which to check **Middle Lake** just to the east of Swan Lake, where the birding possibilities are similar

and where there are some heavily wooded shorelines.

There are few other wetlands in the county, but one of them is Oakleaf Lake, where Eared Grebes and other water birds nest, and where there are old records of both Eurasian Wigeon and Purple Gallinule. From St. Peter, go west 2.4 miles on Highway 99 and turn south on a dirt road which leads to the lake.

Finally, the county's only sewage ponds are at Nicollet, 0.5 mile south of Highway 14 on County Road 23 (see inset D).

Sibley County

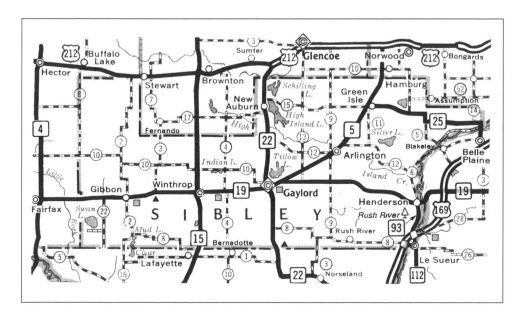

As is the case with the Nicollet County side of the Minnesota River north of Mankato, the Sibley County portion of this wooded valley is easily followed. From Nicollet County, it's simply a matter of taking Highway 93 into Henderson and County Road 6 from Henderson into Carver County. En route, as previously mentioned, the fields adjacent to the river might be flooded in early spring following a heavy snowmelt for the benefit of waterfowl. Generally, however, birders do better covering the valley between Mankato and the Twin Cities on the east side of the river in Le Sueur and Scott counties, rather

151

than on the Nicollet/Sibley/Carver side.

This county's best wooded spot in the valley would be Rush River State Wayside. From Henderson, turn west off Highway 93, 0.5 mile south of Highway 19, in 0.3 mile take a left on the first unmarked road going south, then go southwest 1.5 miles and south 1 mile.

The rest of the county is mostly farmed with several lakes and some fair-sized woodlots scattered throughout. Any of these places could attract migrants at times, but there are two spots in southwestern Sibley County that might be worth a special trip, especially if water levels are low enough for shorebirds. To check Swan Lake (where at least Red-necked Grebes nest): from Gibbon, go 2.3 miles west on Highway 19, then 3.3 miles south on County Road 22, and 1.2 miles west. And

to reach Mud Lake from Gibbon, go 4.7 miles south on County Road 2).

Finally, there are five sets of Sibley County sewage ponds:

❏ Gibbon has two of them: one is 1.7 miles east on Highway 19 from County Road 2, then 0.2 mile south and 0.5 mile west; the other is 0.6 mile south from Highway 5/19 on Highway 22, then 0.6 east on County Road 67.

❏ Winthrop: 2.2 miles east on 19 from Highway 15, then 0.2 mile south.

❏ Gaylord: 1.1 miles east of downtown on Highway 5, then south on Town Street.

❏ Le Sueur: its large and obvious ponds are on the Sibley County side of the river on the north side of Highway 169.

Le Sueur County

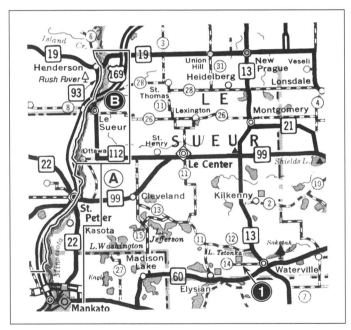

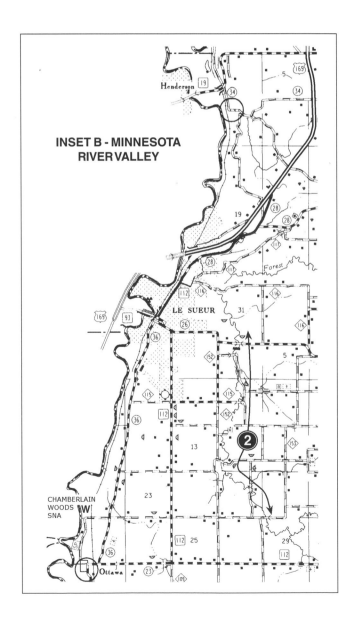

INSET B - MINNESOTA RIVER VALLEY

While Le Sueur County has more lakes than any other Southeast Region county south of the Twin Cities, none of them will usually have anything significant to see. However, there is a rookery for egrets and cormorants on Lake Jefferson: you can scan the east side of the lake from the public access on County Road 13, or follow County Road 18 between County Roads 15 and 13 on the lake's north side.

More interesting are the **Waterville fish hatchery ponds (1)** on the south side of Lake Tetonka, which are good for shorebirds when their water levels are drawn down in the fall. Also, for some reason, Sabine's Gulls like these ponds enough to have dropped in at least a couple of times — including the fall of 1993 when a group of three paid a visit.

From Highway 13 in Waterville, go west 2.2 miles on County Road 14 (the town's east-west main street), and turn north.

As might be expected, though, the best part of Le Sueur County is along the **Minnesota River**. The south half of this county's portion of the valley is included on Blue Earth County's inset A, and **inset B** maps the way from the town of Ottawa to the Scott County line. As mentioned in the Blue Earth County chapter, there is more than deciduous woods for migrants to see, as some places along this portion of the valley open up into an interesting mix of dry grasslands, wet meadows, junipers, and rock outcrops. Again, watch especially for the highly local Loggerhead Shrike and Lark Sparrow, two species with unique, disjointed, and poorly understood ranges in Minnesota.

Within inset B, the best area would be along the 4-mile stretch of the **Le Sueur Creek (B2)** where the junipers are especially thick, a good place to search for roosting owls and for such rarities as Mountain Bluebird, Townsend's Solitaire, or Bohemian Waxwing. Elsewhere on inset B, for deciduous woods birding along the river, a large undisturbed tract is the 254-acre Chamberlain Woods Scientific and Natural Area: to access these woods, go north 1 mile from Ottawa on County Road 36, then west 0.3 mile to the entrance.

There are two small sets of sewage ponds in the county: at Elysian (on the north side of town, turn west from County Road 11 on County Road 14, and go 0.7 mile) and at Kilkenny (0.2 mile north on County Road 3). Then you are confronted with the large, cosmopolitan St. Peter sewage ponds: the city is in Nicollet County, but the ponds are in Le Sueur County, and their location is mapped on Blue Earth County's inset A. (Beware, confused county listers!)

Rice County

Although Rice County falls between the Minnesota and Mississippi rivers and misses out on most of the potential those valleys have to offer, it at least has had the benefit of an active birding community for decades. Such sought-after Southeast Region specialties as Red-shouldered Hawk, Wild Turkey, Acadian Flycatcher, Tufted Titmouse, Blue-winged and Cerulean warblers apparently occur regularly, and rarities like White-faced Ibis, White-eyed Vireo, Worm-eating Warbler, and Yellow-breasted Chat have all turned up in Rice County more than once. There are even recent records for Swallow-tailed Kite, Long-billed Curlew, Great-tailed Grackle (the state's second record), and Minnesota's first and only actual White-winged Crossbill nest.

As in neighboring Le Sueur County, there are several lakes to check here, all in the western half of the county, although none is better than any other at attracting to migrant waterfowl. But any of them might be worth scanning in summer, since nesting Red-necked Grebes and colonies of cormorants and herons/egrets do occur in Rice County.

More interesting would be this county's deciduous woodlands, which are worth birding for nesting specialties as well as migrants. Probably the best habitat for all those specialties listed above is in the so-called **Cannon River Wilderness (1)** along the river of the same name between Faribault and Northfield. The best access point is reached from Dundas by turning southeast off Highway 3 on County Road 20, and going 2.7 miles to the parking area on the west side of the road. The other access is from the west: return to Dundas, go about 5 miles south on Highway 3, turn east on 151st Street E., and go 1.3 miles.

Rice County's best-known woodlands, and another good place for Southeast Region nesting specialties, is **Nerstrand Big Woods State Park** (also marked **1**); the park entrance is via County Road 40, 2 miles west of Nerstrand. While you're in the neighborhood, also check heavily wooded Carow County Park: from Nerstrand, contunue west 3.5 miles on County Road 88.

In and around Faribault there are three places to recommend for migrant woods birds:

• Teepee Tonka Park: turn south off Highway 60 on 3rd Avenue just east of the Straight River, go 1 block south, west to the T, and south to 1st Street S.E. to the park entrance; check first the Dairy Lane Trail in the south part of the park. There are several other nice looking spots along this river, many of which can be accessed from the hiking/biking trail.

• River Bend Nature Center: turn south off Highway 60 on Shumway Avenue, which is 1 block east of the turn-offs for the state academies for the deaf and blind, and follow the signs to the center.

• Falls Creek County Park: turn north from Highway 60 on Garr Avenue, 2 miles east of downtown Faribault.

And just south of town is the Faribault Wildlife Management Area, where no one could have predicted Minnesota's first confirmed breeding record of White-winged Crossbill would occur in 1996. From downtown Faribault, turn south off Highway 60 on Willow Street which leads to County Road 19, and then follow 19 for 3 miles to the area. Look for the

coniferous plantation on the west side of 19 just before the junction with County Road 21. There are also grassy openings which are certainly worth a look and listen, since several Henslow's Sparrows were found here in 1999.

In the pleasant college town of Northfield are some nice woodlands and landscaped habitats for migrants on the campus of St. Olaf College (its entrance on the west side of town on Highway 19). Even more worth birding are the mixed habitats, including some nice stands of planted conifers, in the Carleton Arboretum on the east edge of town along both sides of Highway 19. Look for the hiking trails which begin on 19 on the east side of the Carleton College campus. This large area extends for a mile into Dakota County along the west side of Canada Avenue: turn north from 19, 2 miles east of downtown Northfield.

There are sewage ponds at Lonsdale (south on Main Street / County Road 33 to the T at 80th Street W., then east 0.4 mile) and at Dennison (0.5 mile west of the Goodhue County line, and 0.2 mile south).

Goodhue County

For decades, Twin Cities bird clubs have been making annual pilgrimages each May to Goodhue County, primarily to look for warblers at Frontenac. But there is much more to see here at all times of year, and other places as worthwhile as those mentioned in the Mississippi River valley counties farther downstream. There may not be any Tundra Swan staging areas, Northern Bobwhites, or Kellogg Sand Prairie-like terrain, but just about every other specialty of the Southeast Region is possible in this county: Wild Turkey, Common Moorhen (rare), Acadian Flycatcher (now annual in occurrence), Bell's Vireo (probably), Tufted Titmouse (also rare), Blue-winged, Cerulean and Prothonotary warblers, Louisiana Waterthrush, and Henslow's Sparrow.

Because of the frequent coverage in the **Frontenac area (A1)**, a long list of spring migrants has been compiled, both regulars and rarities alike. Hike the streets in and around the historic town itself, which is as good a place as any to find lots of warblers. Worth hiking as well is

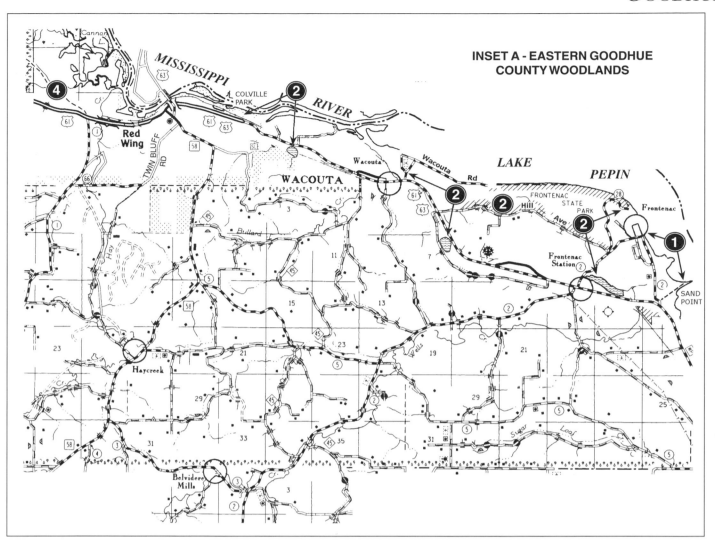

County Road 2 south of town at least as far as the grounds of the Villa Maria Academy and the cemetery on Wood Street. Henslow's Sparrows have also been heard in some of the fields in and around town.

Farther south on 2, just north of Highway 61, is a parking lot posted with maps of the Frontenac State Park trails. The trail to take is the one east to Sand Point which starts on the east side of County Road 2. In years with high water you may not get very far, but a few Prothonotary Warblers nest here, along with Blue-wingeds and Ceruleans and other Southeast specialties. If possible, continue all the way to Sand Point, a beach frequented by migrant shorebirds and loafing gulls and terns during times of lower water levels.

But don't limit your coverage to Frontenac, since there are several beautiful roads to choose from on **inset A** which wind their way along dense **woodlands** south of Highway 61. If your time is limited, however, if you're insecure about your map-reading skills, or if you prefer predictability over serendipity, there are at least seven spots you could check along or near Highway 61 on this map (all marked **A2**). Starting in Red Wing and heading downstream:

• From late fall to early spring there is usually open water

at **Colville Park** for concentrations of wintering waterfowl, Bald Eagles, and gulls. Follow the park signs off Highway 61 on the southeast edge of Red Wing, just northwest of the Training School.

• The two muddy and marshy **Highway 61 ponds** along the south side of the highway are often good for herons/egrets, rails, shorebirds, and the occasional Common Moorhen. The first pond is 1 mile southeast of the training school, and the other is 1.7 miles southeast of Wacouta.

• In Wacouta, turn north off 61 on the **Wacouta Road** which can be good at all times of year. It leads past another pond, through some dense woodlands, and on to several houses with bird feeders along the shore of Lake Pepin. See the Wabasha County chapter for the possibilities on this wide portion of Mississippi.

• About a mile after Wacouta, watch for **Hill Avenue** as it turns left off 61 and offers a nice, quiet, and scenic alternate route to Frontenac; it comes out on County Road 2 near the state park entrance.

• The main part of **Frontenac State Park** is located on a bluff high over Lake Pepin, a good place to scan for waterfowl, eagles, and migrating hawks. In summer, look and listen

INSET B - NORTHERN GOODHUE
COUNTY WOODLANDS

in the thickets and open areas along the entrance road for cuckoos, Willow Flycatcher, Loggerhead Shrike (maybe), Bell's Vireo (ditto), Eastern Towhee, Orchard Oriole, and others.

• And herons, egrets, and other water birds (like a stray Eurasian Wigeon on one occasion) frequent the **lake at Frontenac Station** along the north side of Highway 61, just southeast of the turnoff to Frontenac and the state park.

Farther downstream, just beyond inset A and just before the Wabasha County line, watch for the sign on the northeast side of Highway 61 for **Hok-Si-La Park (3)**. This is one of the best spots in all of the Southeast Region for warblers and other spring migrants — better even than Frontenac, accord-

ing to many birders. Recent records in this wooded peninsula on the shore of Lake Pepin include White-eyed Vireo and Western Tanager.

Goodhue County's **inset B** also includes several heavily **wooded back roads** worth exploring west of Red Wing, where there are four places (all marked **B4**) to specifically recommend:

• The so-called **Vasa area** is along the road which turns south off Highway 19, 1 mile west of Vasa, and is almost as famous as Frontenac for warblers in spring and summer. While this pretty spot looks no different than others in this area, it has long been visited by birders who, among other things, have found nesting Acadian Flycatchers in recent years.

• Just as scenic and with more varied birding habitats than Vasa is the length of **County Road 7** between Vasa and Welch.

• A few miles to the west along the Dakota County line is the **Miesville Ravine**, still another good spot for woods birds in summer and during migration. One way to get there is to go north from Cannon Falls on Highway 20 to 280th Street at the county line, then east about 4 miles; watch for the sign and hiking trails leading from the parking area on 280th / Orlando Trail.

• If you want some exercise, you can hike or bike the **Cannon Valley Trail** which runs on the course of the railroad grade through lots of nice countryside along the Cannon River between Cannon Falls and Red Wing. Unlike some other state hiking/biking trails, this one offers access to lots of good areas which are relatively far from any roads. From the west, this trail begins in downtown Cannon Falls on W. Main Street / Highway 19. The trail's eastern terminus is on Old West Main Street in Red Wing, just north of the junction of Highway 61 and County Road 1 (located on inset A: **A4**).

Also on inset B are the variety of habitats of the Prairie Island area, north of Highway 61. These deciduous woods,

backwaters, thickets, and open fields along County Roads 18, 19, and other back roads can be worth birding at all times of year. Some birders, however, may find it unsettling to bird in the vicinity of a nuclear power plant, and it's hard not to find the casino traffic distracting. The best and quietest area to bird is, or at least used to be, along the dead-end road leading to the lock and dam on the river. After the events of September 2001, however, this road past the power plant was closed. If reopened, the road turns south beyond the casino (you can't miss it — like other casinos, it's the ugliest building in the county) and its sewage ponds (!).

Also note the north end of County Road 18 continues beyond inset B into Dakota County's inset C as County Road 68. It was in the flooded area just east of the county line where both Eurasian Wigeon and Curlew Sandpiper (the state's first and only record) showed up a few years back.

Of final note in Goodhue County, unless you want to check the sewage ponds at Kenyon (0.5 mile east on County Road 12, and 0.2 mile north), would be Lake Byllesby. This relatively large reservoir on the Dakota County line attracts a good number of migrant water birds and is most easily birded from the Dakota County side. Read on.

Dakota County

Some of the best parts of this county, from Hastings upstream along the Mississippi River and along the Minnesota River, are included on Twin Cities' insets Aa and B. Basically, that leaves this chapter with three significant birding areas in the rest of Dakota County: the deciduous woods along the river southeast of Hastings (inset C), Murphy-Hanrehan Park (inset D), and the northern half of Lake Byllesby.

The heavy cover and pieces of open water kept open by springs along the **Vermillion River** induce a good variety of water and woods birds to overwinter within the area mapped on **inset C**. This area, therefore, is worth birding at all times of year and is most easily reached from the Hastings side: turn east on 10th Street from Highway 61, one block north of the Highway 55 junction. You can also turn east off 61 on Highway 291, which passes through some excellent woodlands around the veterans home. As shown on inset C, Highway 291 ends at 10th Street, which becomes County Road 54 / Ravenna Trail and passes by lots of backwaters and more riparian woods along the Vermillion River. This road ends at County Road 68, and a left here leads east to Goodhue County Road 18 and that county's inset B.

A more interesting area, especially in summer, would be **Murphy-Hanrehan** (sometimes misspelled Hanrahan) **Re-**

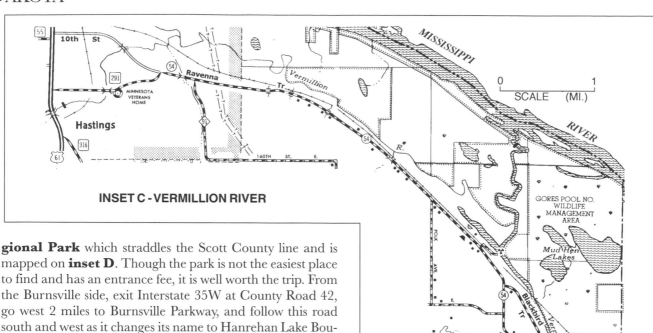

INSET C - VERMILLION RIVER

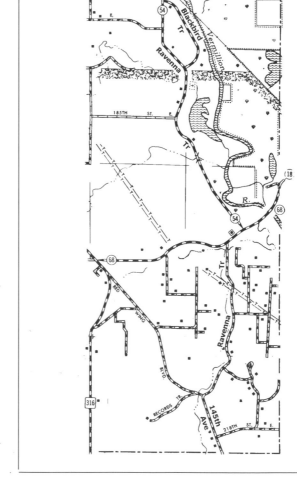

gional Park which straddles the Scott County line and is mapped on **inset D**. Though the park is not the easiest place to find and has an entrance fee, it is well worth the trip. From the Burnsville side, exit Interstate 35W at County Road 42, go west 2 miles to Burnsville Parkway, and follow this road south and west as it changes its name to Hanrehan Lake Boulevard and ends at Murphy Lake Road. From the Savage or Scott County side, turn east off Highway 13 on County Road 42, go 0.7 mile to County Road 27, then south to 154th Street / County Road 74, and east to Murphy Lake Road.

The park entrance is a short distance down Murphy Lake Road: park here, pick up a trail map, and pay the $5 entrance fee. Note that sometimes trail maps have not been available here; so, before your visit, you might want to download one from the Hennepin Parks website <www.hennepinparks.org>.

Since 1984, Hooded Warblers have consistently nested here (35 territories mapped in 2001!), and it's still the only place in Minnesota where this warbler reliably occurs. In addition, more "mundane" species such as Red-shouldered Hawk, both cuckoos, Acadian Flycatcher, Blue-gray Gnatcatcher, Wood Thrush, and Blue-winged and Cerulean warblers all nest at Murphy-Hanrehan. While you can start hiking east from the park entrance, most birders drive down Murphy Lake Road about 0.7 mile, then turn left (southeast) on Sunset Lake Road, and park in 0.2 mile at trailhead 14 on the left. (Note, however, there is now a No Parking sign here, some birders have been ticketed, so you are advised to park elsewhere and walk back to the trailhead.)

Start hiking north from the road, and the trail will shortly split: follow the right fork to **trail marker 15 (D1)** at the next trail junction. Listen in this area especially for Hooded Warblers and the rest; if you hear nothing, either go right on the trail to marker 16 or left to marker 13. In the past, you could also continue hiking north from marker 15 to marker 4 and beyond, another area favored by those Southeast Region specialties, but this trail is now posted and closed to hiking.

If you have no luck with warblers and flycatchers around 15, return to Sunset Lake Road, go 0.4 miles southeast to the trailhead at marker 17, and hike east. Listen especially along the first half mile of this trail, which eventually loops north and back west to trail marker 16.

There are four things to take special note of when birding in this park:

• Be sure to have an annual park permit for your car or to pay the daily entrance fee; cars parked at trailheads or along park roads without a permit will be ticketed. Also be careful to observe No Parking signs.

• It is very easy to get lost on these trails, even with a map, so pay close attention to trail markers and other landmarks as you wander around.

• Certain trails have been posted for use by mountain bikes only, 1 August to 31 October, and during this time hiking is prohibited on these trails; hiking seems to be condoned, though, during the other months. Trails marked for horseback riding are open to hiking at any time.

• And, since this is a unique and tenuous breeding site for Hooded Warblers, the use of recordings to attract them is discouraged.

The other place of special note is **Lake Byllesby (2)** along the Dakota-Goodhue County line. This relatively large lake is the only body of water for miles, and it has attracted several migrants of note over the years — like that Western Sandpiper in 2001. It is most easily scanned from the north along County Road 88 / 292nd Street east of Randolph and side roads off 88 leading south to the lake.

One access is just east of Highway 56 at the unmarked county park property just west of the cemetery: park at the gate and hike over the hill to the lake. And at the east end of the lake, turn south off 88 on Gerlach Way to the dam in Lake Byllesby Regional Park. (To reach the lake from the east, turn west off Highway 20 on the north side of Cannon Falls on Goodhue County Road 17, which becomes Dakota County Road 88.)

Finally, as more suburban areas continue to develop and sprawl around the Twin Cities, businesses and homeowners anxious to start mowing a lawn have prompted several sod farm operations to spring up in recent years. Whenever you find one of these farms, it's always worth stopping to scan for shorebirds, especially in August and September when Buff-breasted Sandpipers are passing through. Such sod farms are the most reliable places to find this relatively rare species in the state, although most farms don't attract shorebirds every year, and a new favorite seems to be discovered by Twin Cities birders annually.

Recently, Buff-breasteds have been attracted to two sod farms in Dakota County. One is along Blaine Avenue, just south of County Road 66 / 200th Street, 4.3 miles east of Highway 3 or 2.5 miles west of Highway 52. The other is on County Road 86 / 280th Street between Castle Rock and Highway 3.

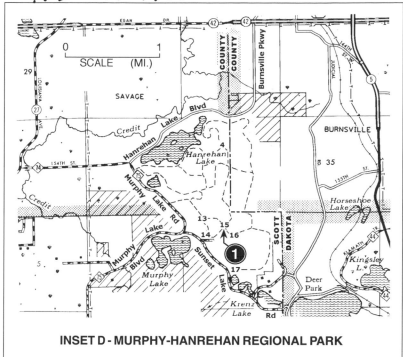

763-694-7777

INSET D - MURPHY-HANREHAN REGIONAL PARK

Scott County

This county's portion of the Minnesota River valley from Highway 41 downstream is included on the Twin Cities' inset A, and Dakota County's inset D covers the unique possibilities at Murphy-Hanrehan Regional Park. The rest of Scott County is a mix of farmlands, scattered lakes, and woodlands, with the most interesting birding, of course, along the **Minnesota River** as shown on **insets B and C**.

Besides those wooded places along the river, which should be checked for nesting birds as well as migrants, there may be flooded fields full of waterfowl in spring if the river has overflowed its banks. This part of the valley should have Upland Sandpiper, American Woodcock, Loggerhead Shrike (maybe), Sedge Wren,

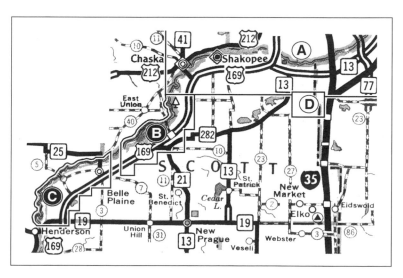

159

SCOTT

Eastern Towhee, Lark (perhaps) and Grasshopper sparrows, Dickcissel, and Orchard Oriole nesting among the junipers, thickets, rocks, pastures, and wet meadows. And, in these same habitats during migration and winter, continue to watch for a stray Mountain Bluebird, Townsend's Solitaire, Northern Mockingbird, Bohemian Waxwing, or Spotted Towhee.

In the Jordan area, there are two places (both marked **B1**) to check especially. There is a variety of habitats in the **Louisville Swamp** section of the Minnesota Valley Trail, which currently extends along the river between Shakopee and Belle Plaine. Turn west to the trailhead parking lot off Highway 169 at the sign on 145th Street, 2 miles south of the Highway 41 junction. Then check the pastures and woods southwest of Jordan along **County Road 57**, which passes through Minnesota Valley State Park (which includes another section of the Minnesota Valley Trail).

Farther southwest within inset C, the best roads to explore are County Roads 6 and 51. This latter road ends at Highway 19 in the northwestern corner of Le Sueur County (see that county's inset B).

Like Dakota County, Scott County has its share of sod farms which might attract Buff-breasted Sandpipers in August-September. A good one in 2000 was on County Road 10 / 205th Street, a mile west of Highway 13.

For waterfowl, at least, Scott County's best sewage ponds have been at Shakopee's Blue Lake Wastewater Treatment Plant — see the Twin Cities' inset A. There also are these three relatively large sets of ponds:

❑ Jordan: see inset B; access off Syndicate Street.

❑ Belle Plaine: see inset C; access off County Road 6.

❑ New Prague: 1 mile north from Highway 19 on Highway 21, then 0.6 mile east on 270th Street W.

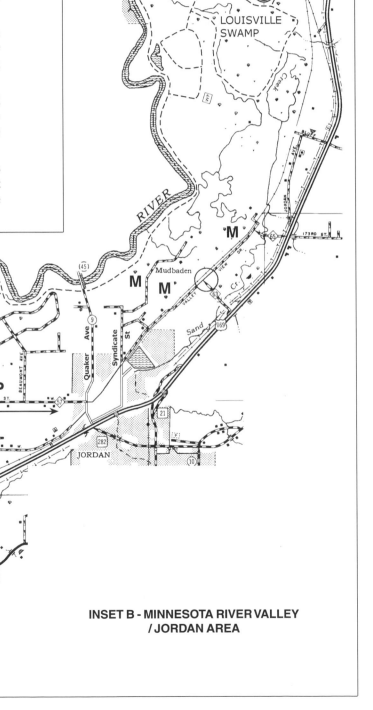

INSET B - MINNESOTA RIVER VALLEY / JORDAN AREA

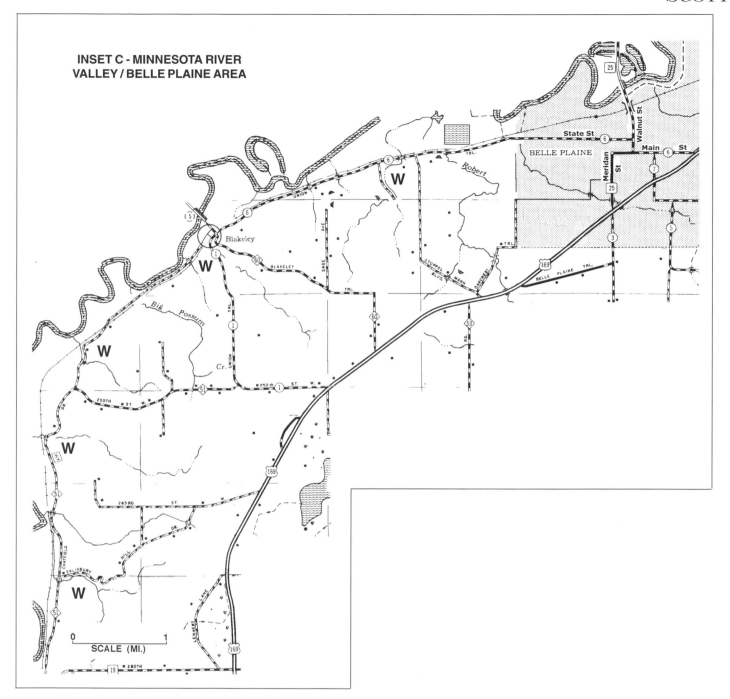

INSET C - MINNESOTA RIVER VALLEY / BELLE PLAINE AREA

Carver County

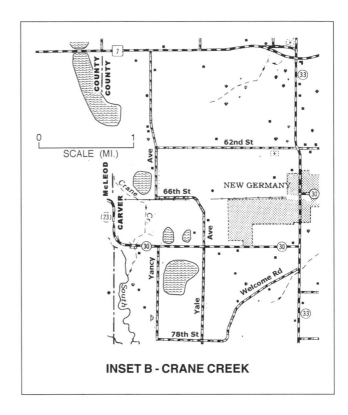

INSET B - CRANE CREEK

As in Dakota and Scott counties, there is a portion of this county included on the Twin Cities' inset A. But the best parts of Carver County lie elsewhere, including one of the most consistent shorebird areas in the state, one of the best park reserves in the Cities, several lakes, a nice spot on the Minnesota River, and no fewer than six sewage ponds — an amazing number of birding spots for such a small county.

For some reason, the waters of **Crane Creek** near New Germany (**inset B**) regularly overflow into surrounding fields and create ideal habitat for shorebirds, herons/egrets, and other water birds. Except in winter, of course, this excellent spot is worth birding at almost any time of year, as evidenced by sightings of no fewer than 30 of the 32 species of shorebirds on the Regular Minnesota list. Records include American Avocet, Willet, Whimbrel, both godwits, Red Knot, Buff-breasted Sandpiper, and Red-necked Phalarope; there was also a Ruff sighting here and even a report of a possible Curlew Sandpiper.

Just as impressive is this area's list of herons, egrets, and bitterns. Of the 10 species on the Regular list, only Yellow-crowned Night-Heron has not been reported, but it seems only a matter of time before this and White-faced Ibis are seen. Least Bittern, Snowy and Cattle egrets, and Little Blue Heron have all been found, and there is one Tricolored Heron record.

This area's acreage of flooded fields and birding potential has shrunk in recent years, and it now tends to be better in late summer and fall. As shown on the inset B map, the best roads to check are Yancy, Yale, and County Road 30; in wet years, this area also extends west about a half mile into McLeod County along both sides of Highway 7.

Elsewhere in the county, there are many other wetlands to attract migrant water birds, and some of these have had nesting Western Grebes and marsh birds. None of these lakes or marshes, though, is especially noteworthy.

Some are called park reserves, others are named regional parks, and until recently all of them were considered part of the Hennepin County Parks system — even those outside Hennepin County. (This entity has since been renamed the Three Rivers Regional Park District.) Whatever you call it, **Carver Park Reserve (1)** is one of the best in the system. The deciduous woods are at least known to have nesting Wood Thrush and Blue-winged Warbler, there is a good stand of junipers near the picnic grounds that might conceal a roosting owl (and where Townsend's Solitaire has appeared), and one of the state's three Green-tailed Towhee records was at the park's Lowry Nature Center feeders. The entrance to the park is via County Road 11 and is well-signed on both Highways 7 and 5.

Outside of inset A, there are few places to bird along the Carver County portion of the Minnesota River valley. There are some dead-end and loop roads to check between County Road 40 and the river, but the best spot might be at the southern tip of the county on County Road 40, 0.5 mile east of Highway 25. On the east side of 40, hike beyond the gate into a section of the Minnesota Valley State Park where Whip-poor-wills can be heard at dusk, there are planted pines for roosting owls, and the habitat in places looks potentially good for nesting Prothonotary Warblers.

There are six sewage ponds in the county, but all are small and none usually worth a special trip.

❑ Bongards: on County Road 51, just south of Highway 212.

❑ Cologne: turn northwest on Henry Avenue from County Road 36, just east of the Highway 212 viaduct on the west side of town.

❑ Hamburg: 0.9 mile east, 0.5 mile south.

❑ New Germany: 0.5 mile north, 1 mile east.

❑ Mayer: 1 mile west on County Road 30.

❑ Watertown: from County Road 10, go north 0.5 mile on County Road 27 / Lewis Avenue N.W. along the west side of the river.

McLeod County

It's time for another quiz. What do The Nature Conservancy and sewage ponds have in common? Answer: without them, this book would only include 86 counties — there are 87 counties in Minnesota, but there wouldn't be anything to say about McLeod.

Yes, there are lakes in this county, but none of them is par-

ticularly noteworthy. And there are tracts of deciduous woodlands, remnants of the so-called "Big Woods" which once extended between Stearns and Rice counties, but these tracts are generally too small and fragmented now to be of particular significance.

Fortunately, the 160-acre **Schaefer Prairie (1)** was preserved by The Nature Conservancy, and is an island oasis of grasslands and marsh surrounded by agriculture. As might be expected, though, this tract is too far east to attract much from the West, although in summer you might find the likes of Gray Partridge, Upland Sandpiper, Sedge Wren, Clay-colored and Grasshopper sparrows, Dickcissel, and Bobolink. Perhaps a few Short-eared Owls and Le Conte's Sparrows stop here in migration, and maybe a singing Henslow's will turn up some year. Turn south from Highway 212, 2.8 miles east of Brownton or 4.3 miles west of the Highway 22 junction, and go 0.6 mile.

Since this county's small portion of the Crane Creek area is already included with Carver County's inset B, of final note are a couple of sewage ponds. Glencoe's are larger and better than average, as evidenced by a Long-billed Curlew record, although birders have not been permitted here in recent years. But to give them a try: turn west off Highway 212, 1.2 miles southwest of the County Road 2 viaduct, then go 0.7 miles; turn north here to one set of ponds, and another pond is 0.5 mile farther west.

There is also a small pond at Winsted: on the south edge of town, go 0.5 mile east on County Road 9 from County Road 1, then south 0.5 mile and west 0.2 mile.

Meeker County

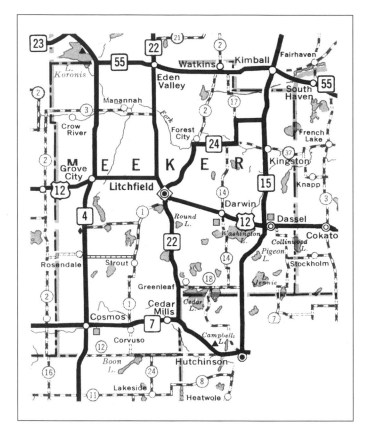

Some cynic once wrote about Meeker County in an earlier bird-finding guide, saying it was "humiliating to be a county whose only birding spot of note is a sewage pond." That is hardly the case now in this county, since there are actually three small sewage ponds to check.

❑ Cosmos: 0.7 mile east on Highway 7.

❑ Darwin: 0.7 mile south on County Road 14, then 0.2 mile west.

❑ Dassel: from Highway 12, go 0.3 mile north on Highway 15.

There are even two lakes which birders have been attracted to in recent years. One is Pigeon Lake with its summering pelicans and cormorant/heron/egret rookery: watch for the parking area on the east side of Highway 15 at mile marker 112, 3.5 miles south of Dassel or 4.5 miles north of the McLeod County line. The other is Boon Lake on the Renville County line, where there are recent sightings of Clark's Grebe, White-faced Ibis, and shorebird concentrations: turn east from Highway 4 on County Road 12, and go 5.5 miles.

The rest of Meeker County is up to you. Get yourself a county map and you'll eventually stumble upon a Gray Partridge along some back road in the farmlands, you could find Common Loons or Red-necked Grebes on some of the lakes, or check out any woodlands you come to for cuckoos.

And now, insert your own joke here about the loons and cuckoos of Meeker County: _____.

Wright County

Wright is another of those counties that geography has placed too far east to have that many grasslands and wetlands birds characteristic of the prairie pothole country, and too far west and north to attract all the specialties associated with the Southeast Region. And, although the Mississippi flows along one side of this county, the river valley here is shallow, less continuously wooded, and not conducive to funneling through many migrants.

There are, at least, more lakes in this county than any other in the Southeast Region, some of them with nesting Common Loons, Red-necked Grebes, and sometimes a pair or two of Eareds or Westerns. From north to south, four lakes to try for Red-necked Grebes would be:

• Clearwater (along Highway 24).

• Millstone (4 miles north of the town of Maple Lake on County Road 8).

• Smith (2.2 miles west of Howard Lake on Highway 12, 0.5 mile north on County Road 5).

• Shakopee (from the McLeod County line, north 1 mile on County Road 1, 0.9 mile east, 0.4 mile south).

Two other lakes of note are:

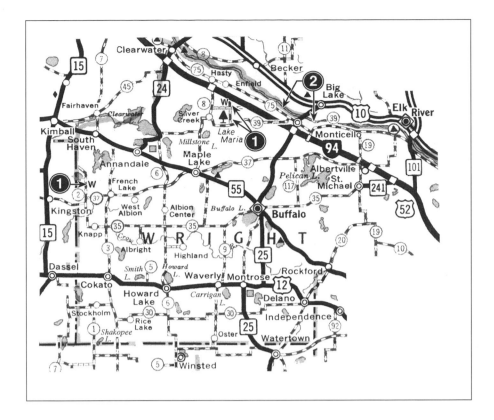

and turn east off 2 to the park's trailheads in 1 mile, 1.4 miles, and 3.2 miles. Farther east, to reach Harry Larson County Park and Lake Maria State Park, take the Hasty exit off Interstate 94, go south 2.4 miles on County Road 8, then east 2 miles on 127th Street N.W. to the junction with County Road 111 / Clementa Avenue N.W. From this corner the entrance to Harry Larson is 0.5 mile north; Lake Maria's entrance is 1 mile south.

In and near Monticello on the Mississippi River are two additional places of interest. **Montissippi County Park (2)** is located off County Road 75, 2 miles northwest of the Highway 25 junction in Monticello. Besides migrants, watch in summer in the mixed habitats here and elsewhere along this stretch of the Mississippi for things like American Woodcock, Western Kingbird, Loggerhead Shrike (rare), Sedge Wren, Clay-colored and Lark (maybe) sparrows, and Orchard Oriole (perhaps).

If you're here in winter, head to the southeast edge of Monticello on Broadway Street / County Road 75, turn left (east) on Riverview Drive / County Road 39, and in 2 blocks turn north to the river on Mississippi Drive. The river here below the power plant is usually ice-free all winter, and there are typically hundreds (some 500 or more recently) of wintering **Trumpeter Swans** (also marked **2**) among the Canada Geese and other waterfowl. Occasionally a Tundra or Mute swan joins them. Though these introduced Trumpeters are considered wild, established, and "listable," one can't help but wonder what would happen to this population if the power plant shuts down and the river freezes, or if the local residents quit feeding them.

There are two sewage ponds in Wright County:

❏ Annandale: 0.9 mile northeast on Highway 24 from Highway 55, then east 0.7 mile on 80th Street, and southwest 0.5 mile on Conservation Club Road.

❏ Montrose: 0.5 mile south on Highway 25.

• Pelican (for Western Grebes; best scanned from County Road 117 on the west side).

• Carrigan (often good for shorebirds in fall and site of a recent White-faced Ibis record; 1 mile east of Waverly on Highway 12).

There are lots of trees along Wright County's lake shores and rivers, but the most interesting spots for nesting woods birds would be **Stanley Eddy** and **Harry Larson county parks** and **Lake Maria State Park** (all marked **1**). These three parks all comprise remnants of the "Big Woods" and are good places to look for Red-shouldered Hawk, Ruffed Grouse, both cuckoos, Eastern Screech- and Barred owls, Red-bellied Woodpecker, Acadian Flycatcher (at Harry Larson), Yellow-throated Vireo, Blue-gray Gnatcatcher, Wood Thrush, and Blue-winged and Cerulean warblers.

Stanley Eddy County Park is in the western part of the county: go north from County Road 37 on County Road 2,

Hennepin, Ramsey, and Washington Counties

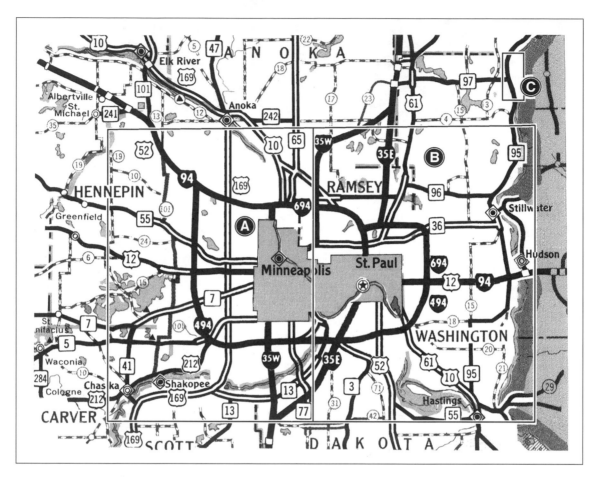

If I were condemned to live in a large metropolitan area, perhaps it wouldn't be so bad in the Twin Cities. Yes, there is too much traffic, and not just during weekday rush hours — vehicles heading north out of town Friday evenings and returning Sunday afternoons can jam up major highways for many miles. And, yes, like other major cities, there is crime: more than one birder has returned from a hike to find his or her car broken into.

But Minneapolis-St. Paul consistently ranks high in those quality-of-life surveys, and these surveys apparently include ornithological considerations. Here the birder will find three significant river valleys, extensive tracts of deciduous woods, and numerous lakes and marshes within the Cities and their suburbs. Indeed, some of the best birding spots in the entire state are found here, and, since so many Minnesota birders are Twin Citizens, someone always seems to be turning up a good bird at some local site.

As might be expected, most Twin Cities birding areas are best during migration. However, there is a lot to do in winter, since there are plenty of bird feeders and dense cover at resi-

dences and nature centers to attract overwintering species, while winter finches and other boreal species turn up at planted stands of conifers. And, except for Lake Superior, there is no better place to find waterfowl, gulls, and other wintering water birds at locations such as Black Dog Lake and open stretches along the Minnesota, Mississippi, and St. Croix rivers.

There are also birds of note in the Twin Cities in summer. Some of the breeding birds in area woodlands and thickets include Red-shouldered Hawk, American Woodcock, both cuckoos, Eastern Screech- and Barred Owls, Acadian and Willow flycatchers, Bell's and Yellow-throated vireos, Blue-gray Gnatcatcher, Wood Thrush, Blue-winged and Prothonotary warblers, Louisiana Waterthrush, and Scarlet Tanager. At some Twin Cities lakes and marshes are nesting Western Grebe, Least Bittern, rookeries full of herons and egrets, rails, and Forster's and Black terns. And there are fields and other open areas for summering grasslands species such as Upland Sandpiper, Western Kingbird, Sedge Wren, Clay-colored, Field, Lark and Grasshopper sparrows, Dickcissel, and Bobolink.

This chapter includes all of Hennepin, Ramsey, and Washington counties plus portions of Dakota, Scott, Carver, and Anoka counties, and insets A and B map almost all the areas discussed below. Note the scale of these two maps is 1 inch = 3 miles; also note that five other detailed maps are included (insets Aa, Ab, Ba, Bb, and C), and the scale of these maps is 1 inch = 1 mile.

MINNESOTA RIVER VALLEY / NORTH SIDE / AIRPORT TO CARVER COUNTY

It should be no surprise that most of the best birding spots are along the Minnesota, Mississippi, and St. Croix rivers, and those spots on or near the **Minnesota River (inset Aa)** tend to be the most popular. Beginning at the confluence of the Minnesota and Mississippi near the international airport and working your way upstream along the north side of the river, the first place to stop is **Fort Snelling State Park (Aa1)**. The park entrance is via the Post Road exit off Highway 5, and, at least in previous years, Bell's Vireos have nested in the thickets on Pike Island. Take the main park drive all the way under the Highway 55 Mendota Bridge, park in the first lot and follow the signs and trail to the island.

The next stop upstream (i.e., southwest) would be the **Minnesota Valley National Wildlife Refuge headquarters** (also **Aa1**), located at 4101 E. 80th Street. Follow Highway 5 to Interstate 494, take the 34th Avenue E. exit, go south to the stoplight at 80th, and turn east. Maps and other information are available here, and this non-contiguous refuge includes several tracts for several miles along the river. Birding is good around the building and the trail down to the river, as evidenced by recent records of stray White-eyed Vireo, Rock Wren, and Worm-eating Warbler, as well as nesting Prothonotaries in the flooded bottomlands. Trails also extend from here and Fort Snelling State Park along one side of the river or the other all the way southwest to Belle Plaine in Scott County.

Return to 34th Avenue and turn south as 34th becomes Old Shakopee Road and curves west towards the Mall of America. After dropping off your non-birding companions, follow Old Shakopee south to the two most popular spots for warbler watchers on the river: the **Bass Ponds** and the **Old Cedar Avenue Bridge** (both marked **Aa1**). The Bass Ponds area is east off Old Shakopee on 86th Street: bear left at the sign to the parking lot, and hike downhill to the wooded trails around the old fish hatchery ponds by the river. Trails also pass through more extensive deciduous woods and past the marshy backwaters of Long Meadow Lake. One of these, the Hogback Trail, leads upstream to the next stop at the Old Cedar Avenue Bridge.

If you'd rather drive than walk to the Old Cedar area, return to Old Shakopee Road and follow it southwest to the first stoplight west of the new Cedar Avenue / Highway 77 bridge. This is Old Cedar Avenue, which goes downhill and dead ends at the parking lot where there are more signs, maps, trails, and birds. One good trail follows the north side of Long Meadow Lake and leads southwest to Mound Springs Park, located at the east end of 102nd Street. Another trail here

goes back northeast to the Bass Ponds.

But be sure to hike southeast on the old road across the bridge towards the Minnesota River, where one trail leads back to the wildlife refuge headquarters and another crosses the river via a pedestrian bridge to the Black Dog Lake area. While you're on the bridge above the marsh and mud, be sure to look down for bitterns, herons, egrets, rails, and shorebirds: the better records in this vicinity include Least Bittern, Tricolored Heron, White-faced Ibis, King Rail, and Black-necked Stilt.

West of Interstate 35W, the route on the north side of the Minnesota River into Carver County is shown on the inset A map, although there are relatively few birding spots to recommend. One of these few is the Izaak Walton property on Auto Club Road: continue west on Old Shakopee Road to Normandale Boulevard, turn south to Auto Club Road, and go 1 mile west to the Izaak Walton sign at 6601 Auto Club. Hike down the driveway towards the river, and on the way check the feeders at the residence and the planted pines for roosting owls. At the west end of Auto Club Road there is access to a pedestrian bridge which crosses the river and leads through lots more woods to James Wilkie Regional Park in Scott County.

A bit farther west, Old Shakopee Road ends at Highway 169. Here, Riverview Road continues west from 169 and passes over Purgatory Creek (often open in winter), through some heavily wooded areas, past residences with productive feeding stations, and it soon dead ends in a maze of housing developments. Years ago this used to be a consistent area for Tufted Titmouse. Years ago, as well, Riverview used to continue west through a nice mixture of fields, woods, and marshes, and it came out on Highway 212, 3.2 miles east of the County Road 101 intersection. You can still drive or hike in from this west end of Riverview Road to at least some of these riparian habitats.

The junction of 212 and 101 is in Carver County. Either take 101 south across the Minnesota River into Shakopee and Scott County, or stay on the north side of the river on Highway 212 to Chaska. From Chaska, Highway 41 goes south and crosses the river into Scott County; on both sides of the river there are parking lots with signs and access for the Minnesota Valley Trail system. Return to 212 to complete the route along the north side of the river. Continue west, and in 1.2 miles turn south on Carver County Road 40 through the town of Carver: for the next 1.5 miles there are more extensive woods along Carver Creek.

MINNESOTA RIVER VALLEY / SOUTH SIDE / SHAKOPEE TO AIRPORT

The return trip back downstream (i.e., northeast) on the south side of the Minnesota River is also mapped on inset A. After checking the riparian woodlands along the river crossings on Highway 41 and County Road 101, continue east on 101 a mile from the bridge in downtown Shakopee to Dangerfield's Restaurant. In winter, the Mill Pond behind the restaurant is normally open, and, for reasons unknown, Gadwalls are especially fond of this pond.

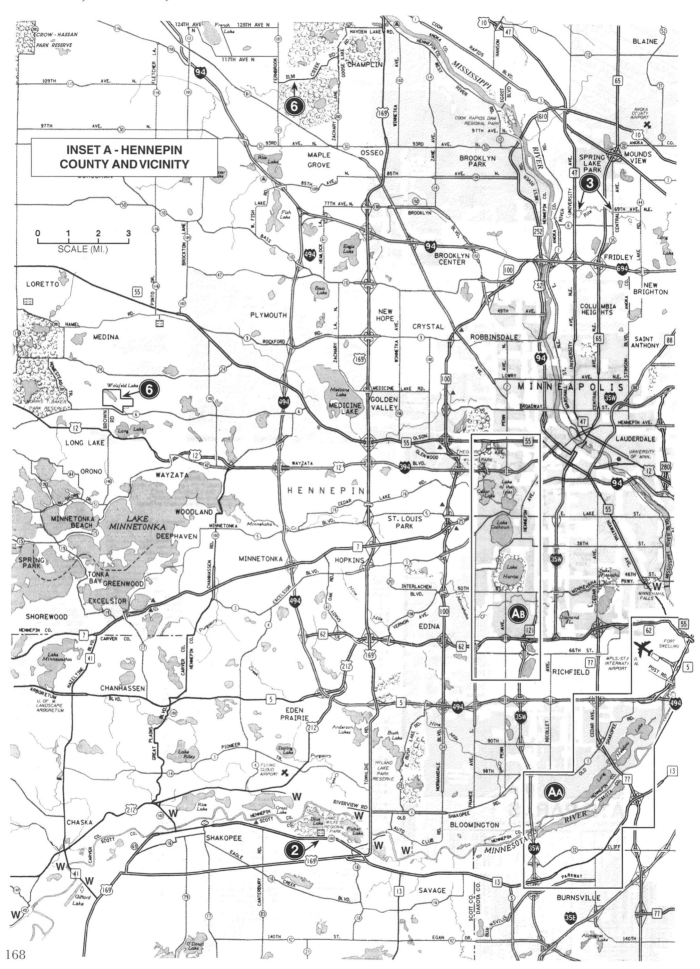

INSET A - HENNEPIN
COUNTY AND VICINITY

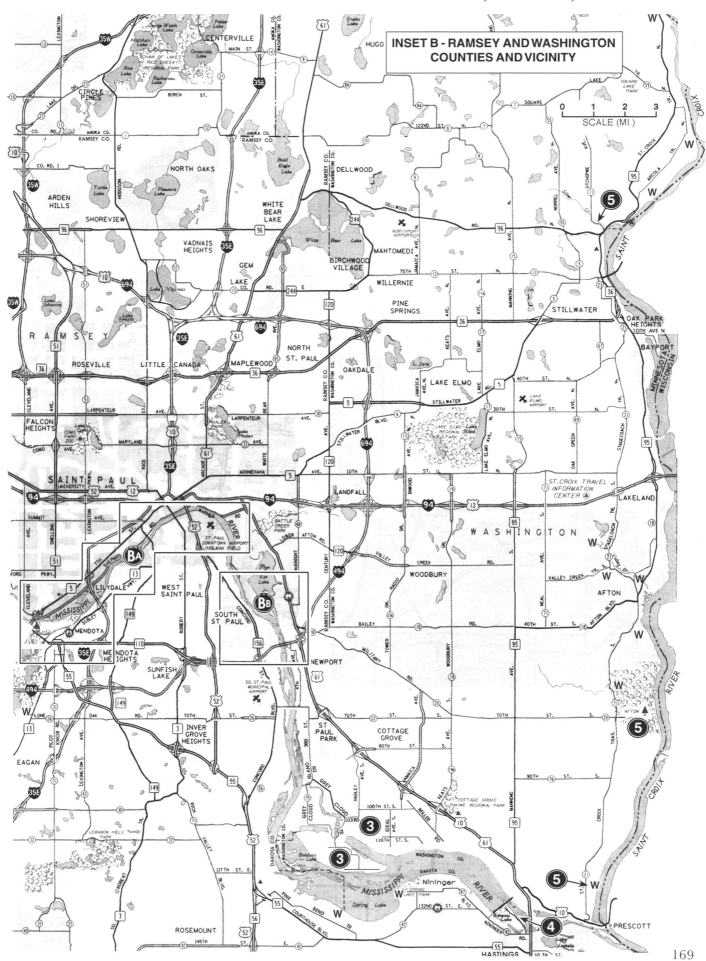

INSET B - RAMSEY AND WASHINGTON COUNTIES AND VICINITY

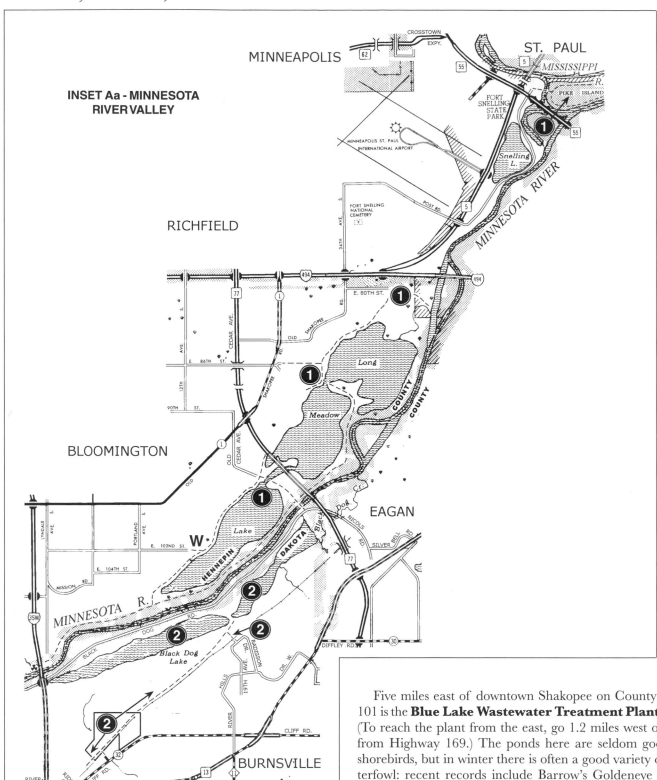

INSET Aa - MINNESOTA RIVER VALLEY

Five miles east of downtown Shakopee on County Road 101 is the **Blue Lake Wastewater Treatment Plant (A2)**. (To reach the plant from the east, go 1.2 miles west on 101 from Highway 169.) The ponds here are seldom good for shorebirds, but in winter there is often a good variety of waterfowl: recent records include Barrow's Goldeneye and a Tufted Duck — which, unfortunately, escaped from a game farm. Be sure to note a strict new access policy was recently implemented. It is open to birders 8 a.m.-4 p.m. on Saturdays and Sundays only; check in with the security guard for directions to the areas where birders are permitted.

Just east of the plant is a small pine stand at the parking lot and access for James Wilkie Regional Park and the Minnesota Valley National Wildlife Refuge. (For unknown reasons, however, entry into these pines has recently been prohibited.)

A bit farther east is the junction with County Road 18, which leads northeast to a larger stand of conifers (check for roosting owls and winter finches; Gray Jay and Boreal Chickadee records exist), under Highway 169, and through the riparian woodlands to the pedestrian bridge near Auto Club Road.

Continue east of 169 to Highway 13, continue east past the Burnsville landfill (see the end of this chapter), take I-35 north to Black Dog Road, and go east to the best place of all along the Minnesota River — arguably the most popular birding spot of any kind in the Twin Cities. **Black Dog Lake** and vicinity **(Aa2)** is worth checking at any time of year: besides a place to bird in spring and fall, it includes open water for wintering water birds plus extensive marshlands and thickets for a wide variety of nesting species.

In winter, watch especially for ducks and other waterfowl, Bald Eagle and other raptors, Thayer's and Glaucous gulls (seen almost every year), Northern Shrike, and American Tree Sparrow. Breeding birds (mostly south of the lake) include American Woodcock, Black-billed Cuckoo, Willow Flycatcher, Bell's Vireo (rare but possibly annual), Sedge Wren, Clay-colored Sparrow, and Orchard Oriole; Peregrine Falcons have nested on the power plant smokestacks. Rarities seen over the years include Ross's Goose, Long-tailed Duck, Barrow's Goldeneye, Prairie Falcon, California, Iceland, Great Black-backed and Lesser Black-backed gulls, Black-legged Kittiwake, Yellow-breasted Chat, and Great-tailed Grackle.

There are two sides of the lake itself to check. Warm water discharge from the power plant keeps part of the lake open all winter, and the west half of the lake can be scanned from Black Dog Road. The portion of the lake east of the plant is fenced off and harder to access, but from the outlet stream farther east you can hike back west to the lake. Black Dog Road ends at Nicols Road, just west of the Highway 77 bridge. From here, you can hike across the river on the pedestrian bridge back to the Old Cedar Avenue Bridge area mentioned earlier. Nicols Road leads south to Silver Bell Road which comes out on Highway 13, 0.7 mile east of Highway 77.

Those areas on the south side of Black Dog Lake are actually more varied and interesting. Take the Cliff Road exit off Interstate 35W, follow River Ridge Boulevard east across the railroad tracks and turn left (east) on Cliff Road just beyond the tracks. In a half mile, stop at the Park and Ride lot on the left, and the trail through the marshes and thickets along the railroad tracks begins at the information kiosk on the east side of the parking lot.

Part of this area is within The Nature Conservancy's Black Dog Scientific and Natural Area, and this is the habitat in which to look and listen for woodcock, cuckoos, Willow Flycatcher, Bell's Vireo, and the rest. The main trail leads northeast along the tracks to Black Dog Park and the power plant. If this seems too far to walk, take Cliff Road east 1.4 miles from the parking lot, turn north on West River Hills Drive, go to 19th Avenue S., turn north again as 19th becomes Territorial Drive, and at the bottom of the hill turn left at the park sign into a parking lot. From here you can hike to the lake by the power plant via the gated road along the tracks or via the pedestrian bridge.

Highway 13 goes northeast along the south side of the Minnesota River to Highways 101 and 55 and the Mendota Bridge (see inset B), which takes you back to the starting point near the airport. Along this stretch there are only a few places to bird. One is the trail around the Gun Club Lake portion of Fort Snelling State Park: watch for the signed access on Highway 13, a quarter mile north of Lone Oak Road. Willow Flycatcher and perhaps Bell's Vireo are possible in summer; in winter, check for waterfowl. (Also be sure to note that Acacia Park Cemetery is nearby and will be described below: see the inset Ba map.)

MISSISSIPPI RIVER VALLEY / NORTH OF AIRPORT

Though the Mississippi is a far more famous river than the Minnesota, in the Twin Cities it is not birded as often. As you head upstream (north) from the airport / Fort Snelling area along the west side of this river (see inset A), you'll find two widely separated parks that might be worthwhile for migrants. Minnehaha Falls Park is only a couple of miles or so from the airport: take Highway 55 / Hiawatha Avenue north to 46th Street, turn east to 46th Avenue S., and go back south to the wooded trails around the falls.

(If you're here in winter, by the way, don't be too anxious to leave the airport. Here, and around the grain elevators on Hiawatha Avenue, there have been occasional records of Prairie Falcon and Snowy Owl. It's now difficult to scan the airport for raptors, but try taking the 24th Avenue exit north off Interstate 494 or the 28th Avenue exit south off the Crosstown Expressway.)

Much farther north is Coon Rapids Dam Regional Park along West River Road up in Brooklyn Park, which includes open water below the dam for wintering water birds. Just north of the new Highway 610 bridge over the Mississippi, West River Road curves west and becomes 97th Avenue N.; turn north off 97th on County Road 12 / Russell Avenue N. / West River Road, and in less than a mile you'll come to the park entrance. The park can also be accessed from the east side of the river in Anoka County: turn south off Coon Rapids Boulevard on Egret Boulevard (which is 5 blocks east of Hanson Boulevard).

As you return downstream along the east side of the river, you'll want to stop at **Rice Creek West Regional Park (A3)** in Fridley, an area where local birders have had several days with 20+ warbler species. Among their finds in recent years have been Prairie, Yellow-throated, Connecticuts (more than once), and Louisiana Waterthrush. The best access to the park's trails is from the parking lot on 69th Avenue N.E., just east of University Avenue: hike south and then east at the bottom of the hill. Another good trail access is farther east on the west side of Old Central Avenue at 69th Street N.E.

MISSISSIPPI RIVER / NORTH SIDE / AIRPORT TO HASTINGS

The birding along the Mississippi is more interesting as it continues downstream from its confluence with the Minne-

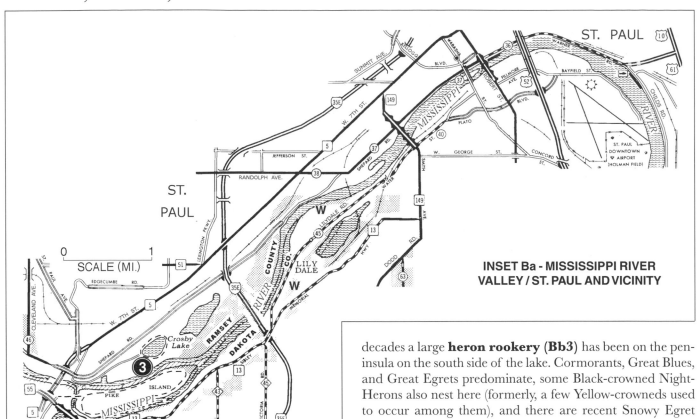

INSET Ba - MISSISSIPPI RIVER
VALLEY / ST. PAUL AND VICINITY

sota River, through **St. Paul (inset Ba)**, and down to Hastings. Along the north side of the river the first place to stop during migration would be at the **Crosby Farm Nature Area (Ba3)**. Follow Highway 5 from the airport into St. Paul, and take the Mississippi River Boulevard / Shepard Road exit off Highway 5 (the first exit north of the river). Follow the ramp which loops back to Shepard Road, and the park entrance road is on the south side of Shepard. Besides migrants, also check the flooded woodlands for the possibility of nesting Prothonotary Warblers or even the occasional Yellow-crowned Night-Heron.

Return to Shepard Road and head northeast along the Mississippi River toward downtown St. Paul. From late fall to early spring scan the river as you go for ducks, gulls, and other water birds: this is one of the best places to search for a stray Barrow's Goldeneye or rare gull. Shepard Road eventually becomes Warner Road which ends at Highway 10/61 just south of Interstate 94. You can also scan the river from Childs Road, which turns south where Warner Road turns away from the river.

The **Pigs Eye Lake area (inset Bb)** is next, and for

decades a large **heron rookery (Bb3)** has been on the peninsula on the south side of the lake. Cormorants, Great Blues, and Great Egrets predominate, some Black-crowned Night-Herons also nest here (formerly, a few Yellow-crowneds used to occur among them), and there are recent Snowy Egret records.

Without a boat, however, this lake is virtually inaccessible and can only be glimpsed from Highway 10/61 (or from the Concord Street area on the other side of the river). But there are good woods and backwaters to be explored south of the lake. Take the Maxwell Avenue exit off Interstate 494 (the only exit between Highway 10/61 and the river), go north to the T, and bear left on **Red Rock Road** (also marked **Bb3**) which passes by these backwaters and eventually dead ends.

Farther downstream along the north side of the Mississippi is **Grey Cloud Island (B3)** and vicinity in Washington County. This is another area worth birding at any time of year. Dense cover, planted pines, and open water spots attract overwintering birds, deciduous woodlands host a variety of migrant passerines, and there are records of Western Kingbirds, Loggerhead Shrikes, and Lark and Grasshopper sparrows nesting in the more open thickets and grasslands.

There are two areas to try especially. One is the island itself: follow Grey Cloud Trail south from County Road 75 or from Hadley Avenue S. The other is Gray Cloud Dunes Scientific and Natural Area: the access is southeast from the corner of Hadley Avenue and 103rd Street. Also explore any of the nearby side roads shown on inset B along Highway 10/61: e.g., Miller Road (along the tracks at the south end of Keats Avenue S. / County Road 19), and Cottage Grove Ravine Regional Park (access from County Road 19).

Continue southeast to Hastings on Highway 61.

MISSISSIPPI RIVER VALLEY / SOUTH SIDE / HASTINGS TO AIRPORT

The return trip back to the airport along the south side of

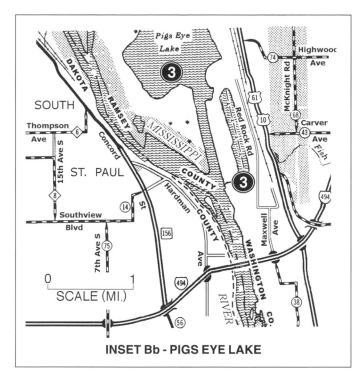

INSET Bb - PIGS EYE LAKE

look for goldeneyes and gulls.

Return to Plato Boulevard and go west to its end on Water Street, and follow Water Street southwest along the south side of the river. This street becomes Lilydale Road / County Road 45, leads through dense woodlands, and eventually comes out on Highway 13 just east of Interstate 35E.

Finally, before heading back to the airport and the starting point of this loop, take Highway 13 southwest to Highway 110, and just south of 110 take the first street (Acacia Boulevard) west to the entrance of **Acacia Park Cemetery (Ba4)**. Not only are the planted conifers and other trees here attractive to roosting owls, crossbills, and migrant passerines, but this is where an awed observer once watched a Magnificent Frigatebird drift by years ago. More recently, this was the site of Minnesota's first confirmed Yellow-throated Warbler breeding record in 2001.

ST. CROIX RIVER VALLEY

The third major river valley in the Twin Cities is the St. Croix in Washington County, which is mapped on insets B and C. This river may not be birded as often as the other two, but there is a variety of habitats worth exploring at all times of year: dense woodlands, open fields, some open water in winter, groves of planted conifers, and stands of native white pines. Beginning at its south end with its confluence with the Mississippi River, the river is paralleled by County Road 21 / St. Croix Trail from Highway 10 north to Interstate 94.

Besides checking any connecting side roads off 21 that look promising, be sure to stop at **Carpenter Nature Center** and **Afton State Park** (both marked **B5**). The private Carpenter Nature Center is located 1.2 miles north of Highway 10, and it is open to the general birding public. However, its hours are somewhat limited and it is recommended you not hike the trails along the river when the center and gate are closed.

Not far north is the entrance to Afton State Park at County Road 20 / 70th Street S. Besides the heavily wooded trails, which are extensive enough to be worth birding for breeding woods birds as well as migrants, also listen in the fields on the way in for the occasional Henslow's Sparrow. Note, as well, the state's first and only White-tailed Kite showed up in 2000 in the fields on the north side of the park.

In the town of Afton, County Road 21 bears northwest, becomes Stagecoach Trail S., and follows the heavily wooded Valley Creek. Louisiana Waterthrushes have nested in this area, so it's worth checking any of the four side roads which go west off 21 in the next 2 miles. When County 21 comes to Interstate 94, go back east towards the St. Croix River and pick up Highway 95 as it heads north all the way into Chisago County.

In winter, your next stop would be the King Power Plant in Bayport, where warm water discharge often keeps the river ice-free. Turn east off Highway 95 on 10th Avenue N. to the plant. In summer, stay on 95 through Stillwater, and turn west just north of the Highway 96 junction on County Road 11 / Fairy Falls Road N. Along this road is **Fairy Creek Falls**

the Mississippi River (see inset B) begins in downtown Hastings in Dakota County. From Highway 61, go west 2 blocks on 2nd Street to Lock and Dam Road, and turn north to the **Rebecca Lake area (B4)**. This road leads past a variety of habitats for migrants and dead ends at the dam on the river where there is open water to attract wintering birds. From the end of the road, there is a good trail along the dam going southwest to Nininger Road.

Return to 2nd Street and follow County Road 42 / Nininger Road northwest past the cemetery (check the conifers), and continue west on 42 to check one unit of Spring Lake Regional Park on the river (turn north to the park on Idell Avenue). County Road 42 goes west to Highway 55, and 0.6 mile west of this junction turn north on Pine Bend Trail which passes through more good woodlands in and around another part of Spring Lake Park (formerly Schaar's Bluff Park). Pine Bend Trail ends at Highway 52 just south of the Highway 55 junction.

Go north on Highway 52 past the turn-off to the Pine Bend Landfill (see the end of this chapter), turn northeast on Concord Boulevard / County Road 56, and continue into South St. Paul and back into inset Bb. In winter, there are places here to scan the river to look for ducks and gulls (two Ivory Gulls even appeared here in December 1991!); in summer, watch for herons and egrets coming from and going to Pigs Eye Lake. One access point is from the trail along the levee just north of Interstate 494: take the Hardman Road exit off 494, go north 1 block to Verderosa Avenue, and turn east to the levee.

Continue upstream towards downtown St. Paul on Concord Street and Highway 52. Take the Plato Boulevard exit off 52 which leads east to Holman Field via Bayfield Street (see inset Ba). In winter, follow Bayfield between the airport and the river until it dead ends: this is another good place to

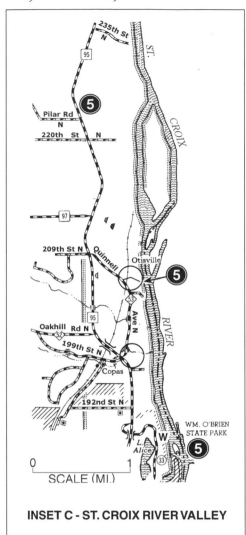

INSET C - ST. CROIX RIVER VALLEY

ing at the southern edge of their range. The native white pines in this area probably host a few nesting Pine Warblers as well — another species at the edge of its breeding range.

OTHER WOODLANDS

But there is much more to birding the Twin Cities than its three river valleys, and there are several popular **Minneapolis woodlands** for warblers and other migrants. Four of these places have proven consistently good over the years, and all are included on **inset Ab**.

• **Wood Lake Nature Center (Ab6)** is located on the north side of Wood Lake in Richfield: turn west off Lyndale Avenue on Lake Shore Drive, which is one block south of 66th Street. The wooded trails circling the lake can be excellent during migration, as evidenced by several 20+ warbler species days, and the Yellow-throated, Worm-eating, and Hooded warblers which were all seen here once on the same May day! In summer, also check the boardwalks across the middle of the lake for herons, rails, and other marsh birds; for years this has been one of the most reliable spots in the state to see Least Bitterns.

• A favorite spot for decades among Twin Cities birders has been the **T. S. Roberts Sanctuary (Ab6)** on the north side of Lake Harriet, where thorough coverage at this famous spot has turned up lots of warbler waves and rarities too numerous to mention. Unfortunately, a tornado took out several trees here years ago, and Roberts is no longer as great as it used to be — it is merely good. From Lyndale Avenue, go west 4 blocks on 42nd Street to King's Highway / Dupont Avenue S., go north 1 block to Rose Way Road, then west to the first parking lot on the right (a $1 parking fee is enforced). The trail west through the sanctuary starts here at the gate.

Many birders remember Lakewood Cemetery, adjacent to Roberts Sanctuary on the north, as equally good for warblers in fall, as evidenced by its records of both Townsend's and Black-throated Gray warblers. Unfortunately, for reasons unknown, the birding here has been disappointing in recent years and is no longer recommended by Twin Cities birders.

• Another excellent spot for migrants on inset Ab, though less well known, are the woods of **Cedar Lake Park (Ab6)** on the east and north sides of the lake. But there is more than just woods in this park: the marsh at the northeastern corner of the lake is often good in summer for rails and bitterns (including Least), and the more open areas along the tracks north of the marsh have had Short-eared Owl, White-eyed Vireo, Rock Wren, Northern Mockingbird, and Le Conte's Sparrow records. The easiest way to reach the hiking trails is to take Franklin Avenue west to its end at Penn Avenue, go south 1 block to 21st Street, then west 5 blocks across the tracks to the end of 21st. Park here and hike the trails south through the woods or north to the marsh and meadows.

• And a final spot on inset Ab, another old favorite among warbler watchers, is **Theodore Wirth Park** (also **Ab6**). Exit north off Interstate 394 at Theodore Wirth Parkway, and the best birding trails are in the vicinity of the Eloise Butler Sanctuary; look for the trail signs on the east side of the parkway, about a half mile north of 394.

(also **B5**), a nice spot to find breeding Louisiana Waterthrush. To reach the falls, go 0.2 mile up County Road 11 to Orwell Avenue, park on this side road, and from this corner follow the trail north of County 11 to the falls and limestone bluffs along the creek.

Continue north on Highway 95 off inset B and into the **inset C** portion of the river valley, which birders sometimes refer to as the **Copas area**. The next noteworthy spot is **William O'Brien State Park (C5)**, where there are deciduous woods worth birding, though you may find more people than birds on weekends from May to September. A quieter spot is reached by turning off 95 at Copas on County Road 53 / Quinnell Avenue N., in 0.8 mile cross the tracks in **Otisville** (also **C5**), and take an immediate right back across the tracks, along the creek, and towards the river. Look and listen especially for Louisiana Waterthrush, which has been found here for several summers.

One last spot for nesting waterthrushes is at **Falls Creek Scientific and Natural Area** (also marked **C5**): look for the sign on the east side of Highway 95, a mile north of the Highway 97 junction. Also of note here and elsewhere along this part of the St. Croix River valley are Winter Wrens nest-

Outside of inset Ab, on the inset A half of the Twin Cities, there are a couple of other wooded spots which have proven worthwhile for local nesting specialties:

• Acadian Flycatcher and Louisiana Waterthrush have occasionally been found singing along the trails through the 220-acre **Wolsfeld Woods Scientific and Natural Area (A6).** The main trailhead is at the Trinity Lutheran Church parking lot at the corner of Brown Road and County Road 6, just north of Long Lake.

• And Acadian Flycatchers have been found consistently up in Maple Grove at **Elm Creek Park Reserve** (also marked **A6**). Turn east on Elm Creek Road off Fernbrook Lane / County Road 121, 1 mile north of County Road 81, and the park's Eastman Nature Center is 0.5 mile east. The best place to start birding would be along the Ox Bow Trail: watch for the trail signs at the nature center.

Outside of inset Ab and beyond the three major river valleys discussed earlier, there are several other nature centers, park reserves, and city, county and regional parks scattered throughout the Twin Cities. Any of these can be as good for migrant woods birds as those locations listed above, and I will be amazed if no one criticizes this chapter for ignoring his or her favorite park. Some of these are current favorites; others seemed to be more popular in past years:

• Crow-Hassan Park Reserve in Hanover; entrance on 109th Avenue N.

• French Regional Park in Plymouth; entrance on Rockford Road.

• Hyland Lake Park Reserve in Bloomington; entrance on E. Bush Lake Road.

• Lebanon Hills Regional Park in Eagan; entrance on Cliff Road.

• Dodge Nature Center in West St. Paul, entrance on Marie Avenue W.

• Maplewood Nature Center in Maplewood; entrance on 7th Street E.

OTHER LAKES

Lakes represent another significant facet of birding in the Twin Cities. Minneapolis, after all, calls itself the City of Lakes with the same modesty that Minnesota prides itself on its 10,000-plus lakes. The potential for water birds at Long Meadow, Black Dog, Pigs Eye, Wood, and other lakes has already been discussed, and there are two other lakes which are especially worth checking: **Lakes Harriet and Calhoun** in Minneapolis (**Ab7**).

These two lakes tend to be overrun with people much of the time from April through October, but, as they start to freeze up in November or early December and reopen in late March or early April, there is plenty of elbow room for birders to scan them. Look for loons (both Red-throateds and Pacifics have occurred), grebes (including Red-necked, Eared, and Western at times), swans, ducks (rarities include Harlequin and Long-tailed ducks, all three scoters, and Barrow's Goldeneye), and roosting gulls. As shown on the inset Ab map,

INSET Ab - MINNEAPOLIS WOODLANDS AND LAKES

these lakes can be scanned from the two parkways which circumnavigate their perimeters.

Just before and after sunset, gulls come to Harriet and Calhoun to roost for the night in fall: watch especially for the rare-regular Thayer's, Lesser Black-backed, and Glaucous. Strays such as Little, California, Iceland, Great Black-backed, Black-legged Kittiwake, and even a first-state-record Glaucous-winged have all been recorded. Scoping the gulls from the west sides of the lakes will result in the best light conditions, and birders usually have better luck at Lake Calhoun.

Elsewhere in the Twin Cities, good numbers of waterfowl and stray migrants have turned up on occasion at various other lakes: e.g., Minnetonka, Medicine (in Plymouth), George Watch, Centerville, Vadnais, and White Bear (these last four north of St. Paul). And in summer there are two lakes which are often worth a special trip for breeding water birds: French Lake and nearby Diamond Lake. Look especially for Red-necked, Eared and Western grebes, both bitterns, and rails.

To reach French Lake (see inset A): in Maple Grove take the County Road 30 / 93rd Avenue N. exit off Interstate 94, go west to Brockton Lane N., then north beyond the interstate to 124th Avenue N., and then east to French Lake Road W. to the west side of the lake. Then proceed south to 117th Avenue N., then east to French Lake Road E. to check the other side of the lake. Summering grebes can also be seen at Diamond Lake just to the north of French Lake: return to Brockton Lane, go north 1.2 miles to 133rd Avenue N., and turn east 0.5 mile to the lake.

*   *   *

Three final thoughts: sod farms, sanitary landfills, and sewage ponds.

As mentioned in the Dakota and Scott County chapters, sod farms are sometimes visited by migrant Buff-breasted Sandpipers during August and September. In previous years,

at least, two of the largest and best ones were (see inset B):

• Along Washington County Road 15, just north of Interstate 94.

• On Anoka County Road 12 / 109th Street west of Lexington Avenue, just north of Interstate 35W.

There are two dumps which attract numbers of gulls in some years. One is the Pine Bend Landfill in Inver Grove Heights, just west of Highway 52/55 on 117th Street E. (see inset B). Although visibility is limited to what you can scope from 117th, gulls such as California, Iceland, and Lesser Black-backed have been spotted here.

The other landfill is in Burnsville: go west 1.5 miles on Highway 13 from Interstate 35, turn north at the Washburn Avenue stoplight by the Menard's store, and go across the tracks to the gated entrance. If the gate is closed, visibility is adequate from there; if the gate is open, it has been OK for birders to drive in and park along the fence to the right out of the way of truck traffic.

Finally, there are even a few small sewage ponds in western Hennepin County:

❏ Rogers: go west on Diamond Lake Road off Highway 101 just north of Interstate 94, then 1 block to Northdale, north 1 block to 137th Avenue N., and west to the ponds.

❏ Hamel: from the junction of Highway 55 and Pinto Drive, go 0.2 mile south, 0.2 mile east, and 0.2 mile south.

❏ Loretto: on the south side of the tracks, 0.2 mile east of town.

(For additional information on birding in the Twin Cities, consult Paul Budde's and Mark Ochs' Minneapolis-St.Paul chapter of *A Birder's Guide to Metropolitan Areas of North America*, edited by Paul Lehman, published by the ABA Sales, telephone 800-634-7736.)

Anoka County

The southern part of this suburban county, from Highway 242 / County Road 14 south, is included on the Twin Cities insets A and B. North of here, relentless suburban sprawl continues with lots of housing developments, but there are still three general areas (see insets C, D, and E) where more natural acreage remains intact. There are even a few breeding and wintering birds more characteristic of the Northeast Region in Anoka County's tamarack bogs, alder thickets, and sedge marshes.

The largest and best known of these places is the sprawling 23,000-acre **Carlos Avery Wildlife Management Area (inset C)**, which extends into Chisago County. Its diversity of wetlands, woods, thickets, and fields can be worth birding at all times of year, and some 250 species have been reported. However, this area can be dull and difficult to cover at times, since birds tend not to be concentrated in any particular locations.

There are almost too many back roads to explore (and get

lost on), but in the wetlands look for nesting herons/egrets and Sandhill Cranes; there are also recent records of wandering White-faced Ibis and Common Moorhen. Red-shouldered Hawk, Ruffed Grouse, Willow and Alder flycatchers, Golden-winged and Pine warblers, and other passerines nest in the wooded areas. In winter, you might find raptors, Northern Shrikes, and the occasional Common Raven in the more open areas.

There are three specific spots to be aware of (all marked **C1**):

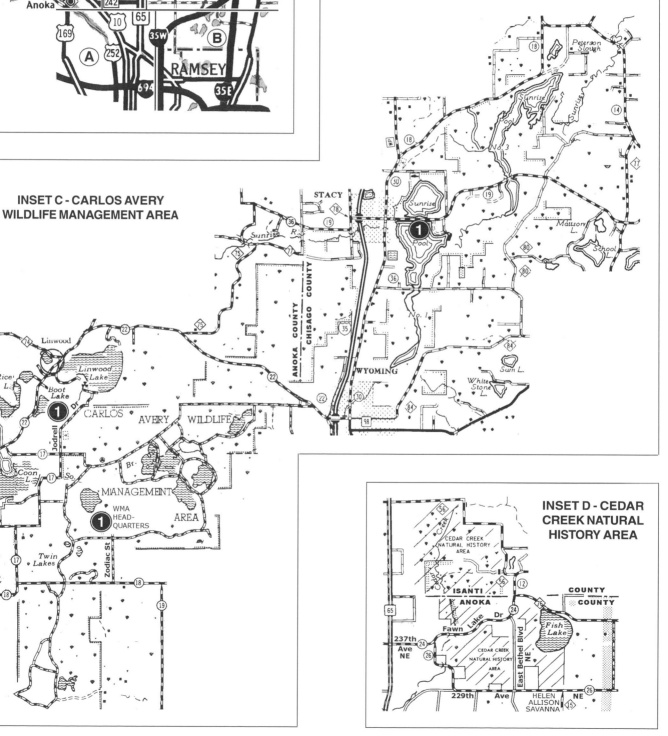

INSET C - CARLOS AVERY WILDLIFE MANAGEMENT AREA

INSET D - CEDAR CREEK NATURAL HISTORY AREA

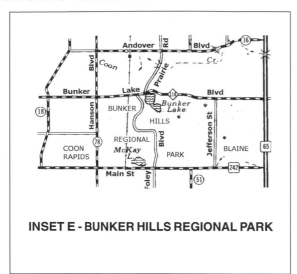

INSET E - BUNKER HILLS REGIONAL PARK

• The place to begin is at **Carlos Avery headquarters**, located at the north end of Zodiac Street, a mile north of County Road 18: check the planted pines (for crossbills, perhaps) and bird feeders, and be sure to pick up a map of the back roads.

• **Boot Lake Scientific and Natural Area**: watch for the sign on the west side of Jodrell Drive, 0.6 mile north of County Road 17; the tamarack bog and other wooded areas along this road would probably be the best spots for nesting passerines.

• **Sunrise Pool**, just east of Stacy on Chisago County Road 19: this is often the best area for water birds, including migrant shorebirds at times.

Just northwest of Carlos Avery is the **Cedar Creek Natural History Area (inset D)**, a similar blend of habitats with similar birds extending into Isanti County. Breeding records include Red-breasted Nuthatch, Black-and-white, Nashville, Chestnut-sided and other warblers, Northern Waterthrush, and White-throated Sparrow, all at the extreme edge of their range. Area headquarters are on Fawn Lake Drive / County Road 24, 0.8 mile east of County Road 26; the best-looking bogs are along this same road and along the west side of Isanti County Road 56, a half to one mile north of the county line.

There are also nesting Lark Sparrows in the area's oak savannahs and other open areas. One place to look is along East Bethel Lake Boulevard (where some Prairie Warblers summered not too many years ago); another is at The Nature Conservancy's Helen Allison Savanna Scientific and Natural Area at the junction of County Roads 15 and 26.

Another traditional place for Lark Sparrow is **Bunker Hills Regional Park (inset E)**. Though this park is surrounded by more houses every year, the habitat is still good along the railroad tracks and both sides of Foley Boulevard / County Parkway A, between Highway 242 / Main Street and Bunker Lake Boulevard. Other species to watch for in summer here — and at Carlos Avery and Cedar Creek — include Wild (well, sort of) Turkey, American Woodcock, both cuckoos, Eastern Screech-Owl, Whip-poor-will, Western Kingbird, Sedge Wren, Eastern Towhee, Clay-colored, Field and Grasshopper sparrows, and Dickcissel. Also look for rarities such as Loggerhead Shrike, Northern Mockingbird, Blue-winged Warbler, or Orchard Oriole.

There may not be any sewage ponds in Anoka County, but there are sod farms to check for fall migrant Buff-breasted Sandpipers. Besides the one on County Road 12 included in the Twin Cities chapter, there are (or at least used to be) sod farms on:

• County Road 14 / 125th Avenue / Main Street, between County Roads 17 and 23.

• County Road 17 / Lexington Avenue, between County Roads 14 and 18.

• County Road 18 / Crosstown Boulevard, between Highway 65 and County Road 17.

• Highway 65, just north of County Road 22.

Chisago County

Besides the Chisago County portion of Carlos Avery Wildlife Management Area (see Anoka County's inset C), birding in this county is most worthwhile in the deciduous woods and scattered stands of white pines along the **St. Croix River (inset A)**. This scenic river lined with limestone bluffs is also popular with canoeists and other boaters; you will want to avoid the Taylors Falls area on weekends from May to September. But there are three places where there is room to roam and look for woods birds.

One traditional site for Louisiana Waterthrush in summer is the community of **Franconia (A1)**: turn east off Highway 95 on Franconia Trail, 0.6 mile south of Highway 8, and listen along the creek at the bottom of the hill. Veteran Minnesota birders used to looking for warblers in spring at Frontenac in Goodhue County will find the atmosphere and birding in Franconia oddly familiar. Search any of the residential streets between the creek and the St. Croix River for migrants during May and September.

North of Taylors Falls, follow County Roads 16 and 71 to County Road 12 and the entrance to **St. Croix Wild River State Park** (also marked **A1**); the park can also be reached by taking Highway 95 to Almelund and turning northeast on 12. Here, and farther upstream at the **Sunrise Cemetery** (also **A1**), are extensive deciduous woods and stands of white pines which for both migrant and breeding woods birds. Besides waterthrushes along the river (both Louisianas and Northerns are actually possible), look especially in summer for Red-shouldered Hawk, Ruffed Grouse, both cuckoos,

Barred Owl, Whip-poor-will, Winter Wren, Blue-gray Gnatcatcher, Wood Thrush, and Pine, Cerulean (maybe) and other warblers.

Just west of Sunrise, the river valley curves north and the riparian woods get harder to access without a canoe, but County Road 3 does lead east to the river from Highway 361, 2.2 miles north of Rush City.

Elsewhere in the county, you might want to check the island heron rookery in the southwestern part of Rush Lake; from the town of Rush Point, go 1 mile north on County

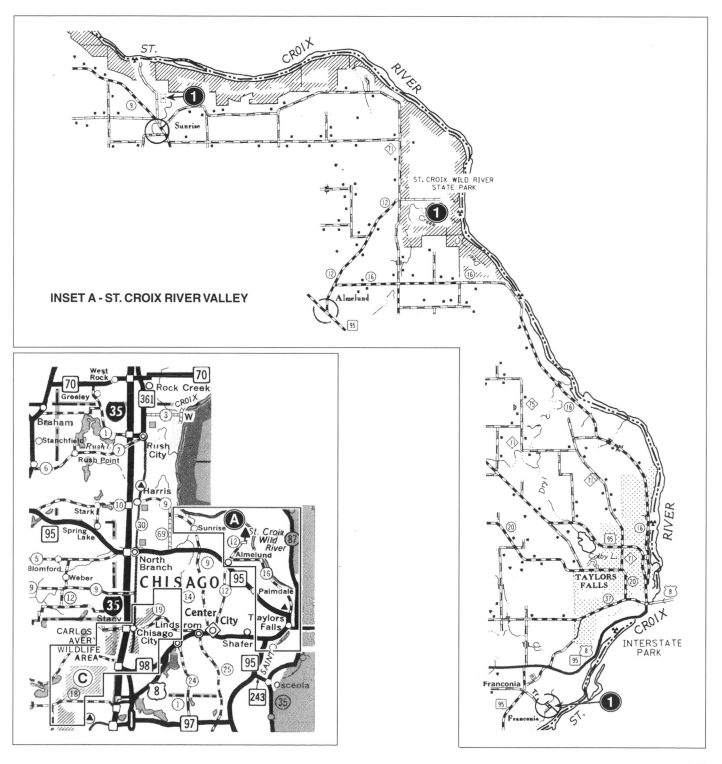

INSET A - ST. CROIX RIVER VALLEY

Road 4. Also note the extensive set of sod farms east of Harris and North Branch. To find them, take almost any road into the area north of Highway 95, west of County Road 69, south of County Road 9, and east of County Road 30. As noted in previous chapters, such habitat often attracts the rare Buff-breasted Sandpiper in August-September. Also watch for shorebirds such as American Golden-Plover and Baird's Sandpiper; later in the fall, you might find Horned Lark, American Pipit, Lapland Longspur, Snow Bunting, and other migrant field birds.

Finally, there are four sewage ponds in Chisago County:

❑ Stacy: 0.7 mile south on County Road 30 (see Anoka County's inset C).

❑ North Branch: 0.6 mile north to Ash Street, 0.5 mile east, then south to the ponds.

❑ Harris: 1 block east to Gladstone Avenue, then south 5 blocks.

❑ Rush City: 1.7 miles north on Highway 361, then 0.5 mile east.

Isanti County

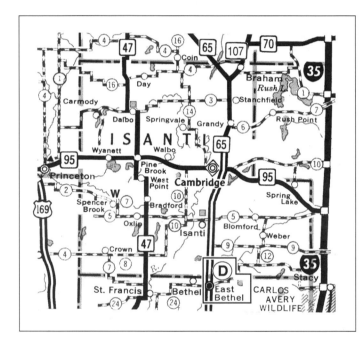

It's time for a quiz. What is the Homemade Pie Capital of Minnesota?

As you ponder this profound mystery, consider this even deeper enigma: where does one go birding in Isanti County? Yes, there are lakes and woods and fields here, but, no, except for this county's small slice of Cedar Creek Natural History Area (see Anoka County's inset D), none of them seems to be of particular interest. This is one of those counties located too far south for boreal species of the Northeast Region, too far north for most Southeast Region specialties, and its wetlands and grasslands lie too far east to attract many prairie birds. Too bad.

Still, like everywhere else, migrants do pass through Isanti County (duh!), and there are some impressive planted stands of conifers along Highway 65 between Grandy and Stanchfield, as well as some dense woods along the Rum River just north of Spencer Brook on County Road 7. If nothing else, you can at least search for lost Hermit Warblers — after all, one found its way to Cambridge only 70 years ago. Or look for shorebirds at the small sewage ponds in Dalbo (0.2 mile west) or the larger ones in Isanti (from Highway 65, go 0.6 mile west on County Road 5 to 3rd Avenue, north 0.5 mile to 293rd Avenue N.E., and east to the ponds).

On second thought, forget the warblers and sewage ponds. Instead, head up to Braham for a slice of pie.

Sherburne County

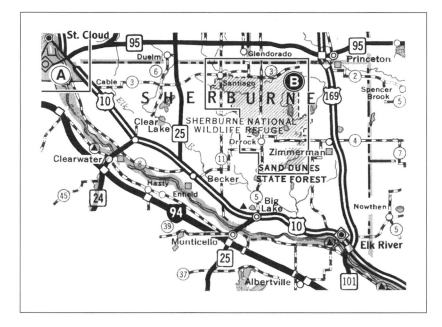

boundaries for maps and other information; another kiosk is at the junction of 9 and 5. If it's open (usually on weekdays only), stop at **refuge headquarters (B1)** on County Road 9, 2.5 miles east of County Road 5. If your time is limited, you might at least want to take the 7-mile **Prairie's Edge Wildlife Drive** (also **B1**) which starts a mile north of Orrock: it loops east of County Road 5 past water impoundments and a variety of other habitats.

And, as the name Sand Dunes suggests, the state forest includes drier areas of sandy fields, oaks, and planted pines. Explore any of the forest roads shown on inset B, with probably the best place to hike in the **Uncas Dunes Scientific and Natural Area (B2)**, which is best accessed by hiking south from the campground on the west side of Lake Ann, or by driving to the end of the road which turns west off County Road 15, 2 miles south of County Road 10.

Look and listen in summer in both the refuge and the state forest especially for Whip-poor-wills, Golden-winged Warblers, Eastern Towhees, and the highly local Lark Sparrows — the Sand Dunes area is one of its few consistent breeding locations in the state. Trumpeter Swans, Bald Eagles, and Sandhill Cranes have also nested at the refuge. Other rare possibilities in summer might include Northern Mockingbird, Loggerhead Shrike, and Orchard Oriole. Over the years, the area in this vicinity has attracted a long list of interesting vagrants, including first-state-records Chuck-will's-widow and Lewis's Woodpecker.

There are also four sewage ponds to check:

❏ Clear Lake: from the junction of Highway 24 and County Road 8, go straight south 0.6 mile on the dead-end road.

❏ Becker: go 2 miles southeast on Highway 10, then west on 137th Street S.E. for 2 miles.

❏ Zimmerman: south 1 mile from County Road 4 on 2nd Street E, just west of Highway 169.

❏ Princeton: 0.5 mile east of Highway 169 on County Road 2, then north 0.3 mile.

Though the Mississippi River flows along the entire length of Sherburne County, this portion of the river doesn't funnel through as many migrants as it does farther downstream. There isn't any actual valley to speak of north of the Twin Cities, and the woodlands along the river here (and on the Wright County side) are smaller and more fragmented by housing developments limiting access to the trees and river.

But pastures and other open areas dotted with junipers line the river in places, and this habitat should at least have nesting Gray Partridge, Upland Sandpiper, Western Kingbird, Clay-colored and Field sparrows, and meadowlarks (possibly both species). To explore these fields, try any side roads you find between Highway 10 and the river, especially County Road 8 between Becker and St. Cloud. And note the St. Cloud portion of Sherbune County is included on Stearns County's inset A.

The best birding in the county is actually away from the river, in and around **Sherburne National Wildlife Refuge** and **Sand Dunes State Forest (inset B)**. If you're entering the refuge from the east on County Road 9 or from the south on County Road 5, stop at the kiosks at the refuge

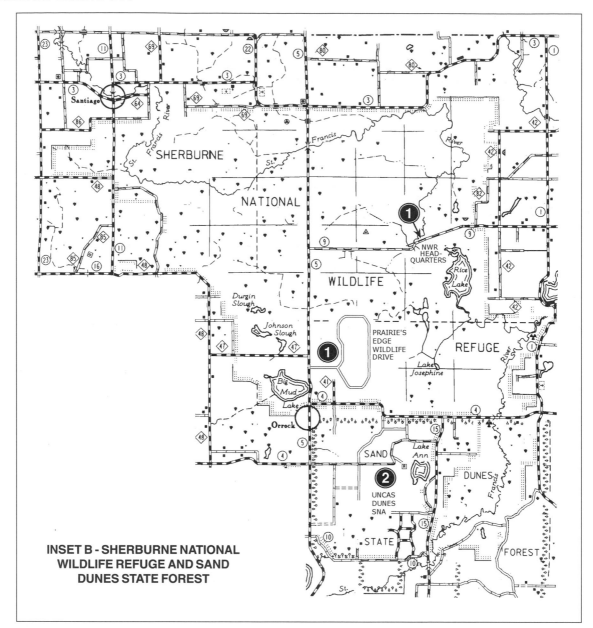

INSET B - SHERBURNE NATIONAL
WILDLIFE REFUGE AND SAND
DUNES STATE FOREST

Benton County

With almost all of this county consisting of farmlands interspersed with small marshes and woodlots, a glance at the map would correctly suggest the only places of particular interest might be the Mississippi River and Little Rock Lake. Aside from the Sauk Rapids side of the Mississippi, which can be good in winter as well as in migration (see Stearns County's inset A), the only heavily wooded area is in the northwestern corner of Benton County. And, as is the case farther downstream in Sherburne County, there are some pastures and junipers that can be checked from any of the side roads between Highway 10 and the river.

Sometimes Little Rock Lake is also worth a look for migrant water birds, since it is the only lake of any size for miles around. Western Grebes and American White Pelicans, at least, have been noted here; these two species are relatively rare this side of the Mississippi. The best places to scan the lake are from the county park on its west side on West Lake Road, and from the north side on County Road 2 at Benton Beach County Park.

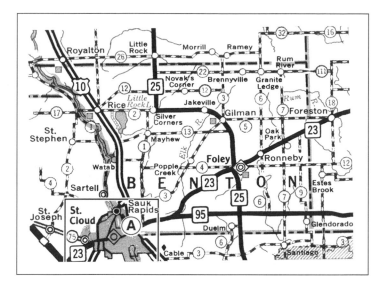

colored Sparrow, and other birds nesting in the grasslands and brushy edges. Perhaps an occasional Short-eared Owl or Le Conte's Sparrow migrates through as well. One place to check would be the wildlife management area northeast of Rice: follow County Road 12 for 1.2 miles northeast from town, and turn north.

With so few lakes around, the county's five sewage ponds might also be worth a scan:

❑ Foley has two sets of ponds: one is 0.6 mile south from Highway 23 on Highway 25, left on Norman Avenue, and an immediate right on Birch Drive for 2 blocks; be sure to walk the trail to the left which leads to a pond often drawn down to expose mudflats. The other pond is 0.5 mile farther south on Highway 25, then east 1 mile on County Road 51, and north 0.2 mile.

❑ Gilman: 0.5 mile southwest on County Road 3.

❑ Rice: 0.5 mile west on County Road 2, then 0.5 mile south.

❑ Royalton: 0.6 mile south from Morrison County Road 26 on the first street west of the tracks.

About the only other interesting area in the county is just north of this lake where, up until a few decades ago, a few prairie-chickens still existed. Today, one still could at least look for Sandhill Crane, American Woodcock, Sedge Wren, Clay-

Stearns County

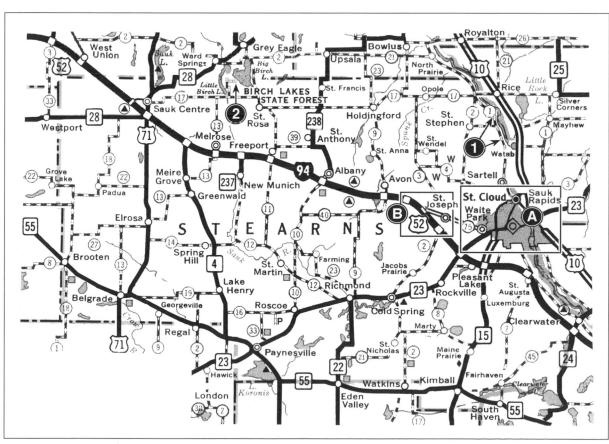

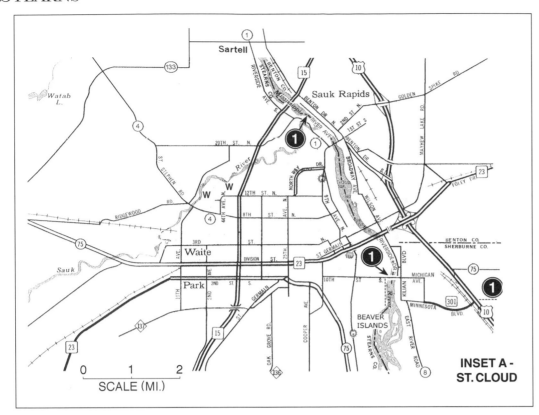

INSET A - ST. CLOUD

SCALE (MI.)

side. Take either the Highway 15 or 1st Street S. bridge into Sauk Rapids, take Benton Drive to the **Municipal Park (A1)** sign at 10th Street N., cross the tracks toward the river, and follow River Avenue in either direction to look for woods birds and wintering ducks (a Harlequin Duck showed up here once).

On the south side of St. Cloud, similar birding possibilities are in the **Beaver Islands / Munsinger Gardens / Riverside Park area** (also **A1**). The 2-mile-long trail to the Beaver Islands is along the west side of the river below the 10th Street bridge/dam — en route, watch for Peregrine Falcons which have nested under the bridge in recent years. If you're less energetic, the woodlands and planted conifers in the Munsinger Gardens north of the dam on the east bank are reached by taking Kilian Boulevard north from the bridge for 3 blocks to 13th Street S.E., then west a block to the river. And just south of the dam and bridge along Kilian Boulevard is Riverside Park.

For a change of pace, try some summer birding at the nearby **Sand Prairie Wildlife Management Area** (also marked **A1**). The parking lot is signed on the east side of Highway 10 across from the Highway 301 intersection. A trail leads east for a mile to an observation deck past a nice mix of woods, restored grasslands, and marshes. Some of the nesting possibilities in these 700 acres include rails, Sandhill Crane, American Woodcock, Black Tern, and Bobolink.

Elsewhere in St. Cloud, you might find something of interest wintering in the spruce trees or along the sometimes-open Sauk River by the veteran's hospital: from Highway 15, turn west on 8th Street North / County Road 4.

Neither side of the river is all that interesting south of St. Cloud, so head north. Follow County Road 1 north from the Sartell bridge for 4 miles, and turn east on **Pine Point Road (1)**. This road passes through dense cover and lots of impressive stands of conifers and dead ends at the river after a mile. You pretty much have to bird from the road, since it's mostly private property on both sides, but roosting owls, Bohemian Waxwings, and winter finches would be possible in fall-winter. This also looks like a perfect spot to host a stray Northern Goshawk, Black-backed Woodpecker, Gray Jay, Boreal Chickadee, Townsend's Solitaire, or Varied Thrush.

Some planted pines are also found at **Mississippi River County Park** (also marked **1**), but probably more interest-

Stearns hardly rates as one of Minnesota's best counties for birding. Yet, it will always be one of my favorites. It was here as a student at St. John's University in the 1960s that I was first introduced to the endless and fascinating birding possibilities in Minnesota. Coming from the Chicago area, where suburb after birdless suburb seemed to continue forever, I found it an amazing revelation to live where trees and lakes and fields — rather than relentless subdivisions — extended to the horizon and beyond.

I know now, over 30 years later, I was not the expert I thought I was then. (Come to think of it, my expertise is still overrated, but don't tell anyone.) I never did find much out of the ordinary in Stearns County. I seldom visit St. John's any more and no longer know anyone there, but they keep track of me and still make those irritating calls for donations. Perhaps I should send some money some year. After all, ornithologically and otherwise, those four years remain the most meaningful time I've ever spent.

Working your way through the county from east to west, the natural place to start is along the Mississippi River in **St. Cloud (inset A)**, which includes Benton and Sherburne counties on the east side of the river. The woods along the river, of course, would be good for migrants, but this area is also worth checking in winter since the river is open in places below the dams in Sartell and at 10th Street S. / Michigan Avenue in St. Cloud.

On the Stearns County side of the river north of St. Cloud, you can follow the river well enough from County Road 1 up to the dam in Sartell (it's just north of the 2nd Street S. bridge), but there is better access in Sauk Rapids on the Benton County

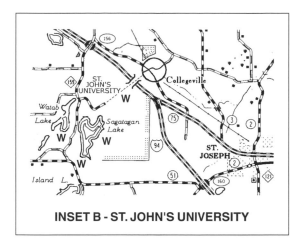

INSET B - ST. JOHN'S UNIVERSITY

ing here would be the fields, junipers, and deciduous woods along the river. Turn east off County Road 1, 3.5 miles north of Pine Point Road, or 2.3 miles southeast of the County Road 17 junction.

*   *   *

Of course, the best spot in the county — if not the state — has to be **St. John's University (inset B)**, an area worth birding at all times of year. The university property, synonymous with the Collegeville Game Refuge, includes lakes, stands of tall spruce trees on the campus, a large stand of planted pines, and, especially, a large remnant of the so-called Big Woods. Except for the campus itself, this natural area has remained mostly intact for some 150 years under the care of the Benedictine monks.

As you enter the campus from the north off Interstate 94, it is recommended you first stop at the information desk in the Great Hall next to the church (you can't miss it!) and get a trail map. There are four areas at St. John's of particular note:

• The large conifers in the center of campus, especially behind the church, which are good in winter and during migration; there is often an active bird feeder here.

• The trail which circles Lake Watab (misidentified as Stump Lake on many maps) on the west side of campus; the part of the trail towards the south end of the lake is usually best for warblers and other migrants.

• The large stand of planted pines along the former entrance road: look for owls and winter finches. Follow the road which bears left (east) around the football field and ends just beyond the Prep School; from here, hike northeast to the pines on the old road.

• The dense deciduous woods on the east side of Lake Sagatagan, which are most worthwhile in summer. The system of trails through these woods begins as a dirt road which goes south along the east side of the athletic fields just east of the Prep School and radio tower. Look especially for Red-shouldered and Broad-winged hawks, Ruffed Grouse, Barred Owl, woodpeckers, Yellow-throated Vireo, Blue-gray Gnatcatcher, Veery, Wood Thrush, Cerulean Warbler (relatively common and reliable in these woods for decades), and Scarlet Tanager. Over the years there have also been records of Yellow-crowned Night-Heron, Tufted Titmouse, Blue-winged and

Prothonotary warblers, and Louisiana Waterthrush. Be sure to bring your trail map with you and watch where you're going; even with a map, it's quite easy to get lost.

Elsewhere in the county, there are few specific places to recommend, as wooded areas mostly give way to more open farmlands. But just north of St. John's is the extensive, mostly inaccessible, and so-called St. Wendel bog, an area of alders and tamaracks with Alder Flycatcher, Golden-winged and Mourning warblers, and other nesting species. From St. Joseph, follow County Road 3 northwest for 3.5-5.5 miles to the bog's west side; then turn east on the first road north of the bog to County Road 4, which goes back southeast through the tamaracks.

There are plenty of lakes scattered around, some of them with heavily wooded shorelines, others with nesting Common Loons and Red-necked Grebes, and a few which attract numbers of migrant waterfowl. One small lake in western Stearns County which seems consistently attractive to swans and other migrants is on Highway 71, 4 miles south of Interstate 94.

Farther south, The Nature Conservancy has preserved a small grassland which is still large enough to host a nesting pair or two of Upland Sandpiper and Marbled Godwit, and the thickets here look good for Willow Flycatcher and Sedge Wren. To reach the Roscoe Prairie Scientific and Natural Area, go 2.2 miles west from Roscoe on County Road 16, then 0.6 mile south on 273rd Avenue.

But the most interesting place in the western half of Stearns County might be in and around **Birch Lakes State Forest (2)**. The actual forest boundary may include an area only a single square mile in size, but the deciduous woodlands along the road to the campground are dense and impressive. They are known to have at least nesting Blue-gray Gnatcatcher, Wood Thrush, and Scarlet Tanager, and there are probably Red-shouldered Hawks and Cerulean Warblers here as well. To reach the area, go north from Melrose on County Road 13 for 5 miles, east on County Road 17 for 2 miles, and north 2 miles to the sign for the campground.

There are no fewer than eight sewage ponds in the county, and two of them are better than average:

❏ Paynesville, the best and largest of the eight; 2 miles east from Highway 55 on Highway 23 to County Road 33, and 0.6 mile north.

❏ Albany; from the Interstate 94 exit, 0.5 mile south on County Road 41, and 0.2 mile west.

The six smaller ponds are at:

❏ Watkins; 1.5 miles north from the Meeker County line on County Road 2, 0.5 mile east, and 1 mile north.

❏ Eden Valley; 0.5 mile north from the Meeker County line, and 0.2 mile east.

❏ St. Martin; 1.2 miles south on County Road 195, and 0.5 mile east on County Road 32.

❏ Belgrade; 0.8 mile south on County Road 197, and 0.5 mile east.

❏ Brooten; 0.8 mile southeast on Highway 55, and 0.5 mile south.

❑ Freeport; 1.2 miles east on County Road 157 (or old Highway 52).

There's also this area we used to call Padua. I now know the small wetlands and scattered pastures and other grasslands in western Stearns County around the community of Padua are nothing unique. But back in May of 1965 this was the first I had ever seen of prairie-pothole country, and it was indeed something special. It still is. I have been fascinated by and attracted to such country ever since, and there is still no place I would rather bird.

Todd County

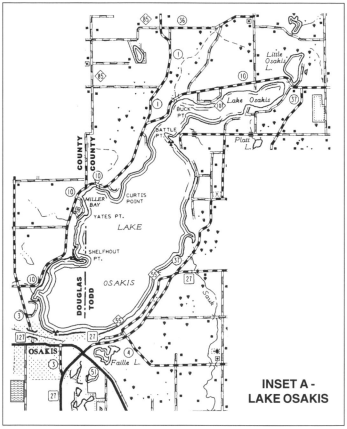

INSET A - LAKE OSAKIS

Take a poll among Minnesota's experienced birders, ask which counties are among the least known ornithologically, and I'll bet Todd County would be on most lists. This is another of those counties in the middle which mostly falls between the cracks: too far east for West Region specialties, too far northwest for Southeast birds, but not far enough north for Northeast Region species.

But at least there are lakes with nesting Common Loons and Red-necked Grebes, meadows and sedge marshes for Sandhill Cranes and Le Conte's Sparrows (and maybe even a Yellow Rail, Short-eared Owl, or Nelson's Sharp-tailed Sparrow), and woodlands with perhaps Red-shouldered Hawk, Blue-gray Gnatcatcher, or Cerulean Warbler near the periphery of their breeding ranges.

Actually, Todd County is hardly a vague ornithological entity, thanks to **Lake Osakis** (see **inset A**, which includes a part of Douglas County). This is one of Minnesota's most famous birding lakes, primarily because of its large number of nesting Western Grebes. A few Clark's Grebes have been documented among them, along with apparently intermediate Western/Clark's types. Red-necked Grebes nest on Osakis as well, and one of Minnesota's largest Forster's Tern colonies was once documented here. A pair of Common Moorhens with young was found several summers ago, and this should be a good lake to scan for migrant waterfowl — a King Eider turned up in a hunter's bag several Novembers ago.

This lake also attracts lots of fishermen, water skiers, and jet skis (it is amazing the grebes put up with all that nonsense), so avoid weekends from May to September. The best places to scan the lake are from the town of Osakis in Douglas County, along Todd County Road 55, at the Battle Point and

Miller Bay public accesses in Todd County, and near the southwest end of Douglas County Road 10.

Besides the Osakis sewage ponds in Douglas County (located on inset A), there are smaller ponds at:

❑ Eagle Bend: 1 mile southeast on Highway 71.

❑ Browerville: from the junction of Highway 71 and County Road 14, go 0.2 mile east and 0.2 mile south.

❑ Grey Eagle: 0.8 mile west on Highway 287, 0.2 mile south.

Morrison County

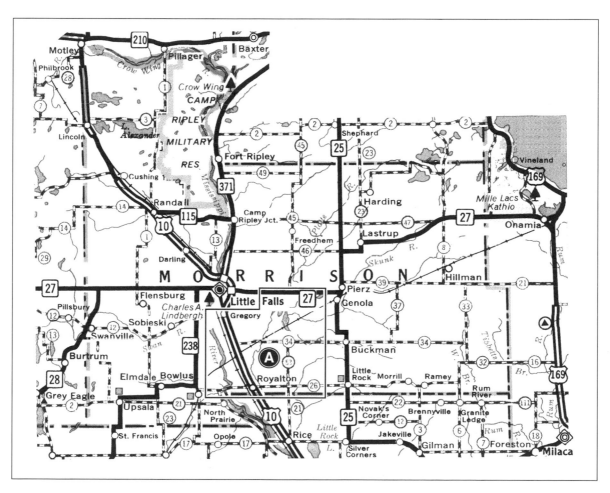

This far north, the Mississippi looks much the same as other rivers, and many visitors have been more than a little surprised by its modest width in Morrison County and farther upstream. Similarly, the birding possibilities along this portion of the river are nothing out of the ordinary, primarily because there is no longer much of a valley to funnel through migrant woods birds.

In winter, though, you might find some open water for waterfowl in the river below the dam located just south of the

Highway 27 bridge in Little Falls, and at the railroad bridge/dam shown on inset A, 2 miles north of County Road 26. In summer, stop at the wayside rest on the river on County Road 26 (also on inset A) for the possibility of Red-shouldered Hawk, Yellow-billed Cuckoo, Eastern Screech-Owl, Red-bellied Woodpecker, Blue-gray Gnatcatcher, Cerulean Warbler, and Northern Cardinal — all approaching the north edge of their ranges.

You might also find some migrants of note anywhere along

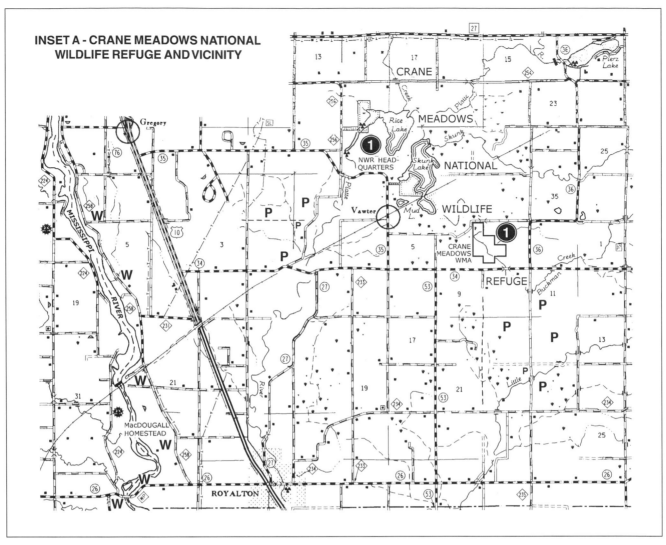

INSET A - CRANE MEADOWS NATIONAL WILDLIFE REFUGE AND VICINITY

County Road 258 on the east side of the river (again, see inset A). Try especially The Nature Conservancy's MacDougall Homestead tract on 258, 1 mile north of County Road 26, where the property includes white pines that may have nesting Pine Warblers.

In **Crane Meadows National Wildlife Refuge** and vicinity (**inset A**) are several tracts of marshes, pastures, and grasslands where a few prairie-chickens survived until about 40 years ago. Today, these areas with former leks (marked P on inset A) are still worth exploring in summer for Sandhill Crane, Upland Sandpiper, Short-eared Owl (rare), Sedge Wren, and Le Conte's Sparrow; in fall/winter, look for hawks, Northern Shrike, Snow Bunting, and redpolls. Researchers have also found both Yellow Rails and Nelson's Sharp-tailed Sparrows at undisclosed sites in Morrison County, and I wager they were summering somewhere within this area.

The refuge is still under development, which is why there are no outlined boundaries shown on the inset A map, but you can at least stop for further information at **refuge headquarters (A1)**, located on County Road 35. One specific tract within the refuge which has long been good for birding is outlined a few miles southeast at **Crane Meadows Wildlife Management Area** (also **A1**). I'd also be tempted to

investigate a large and inviting area shown on the county map farther east. It's a mostly roadless rectangle with few farmhouses south of Hillman, bounded by County Roads 39, 33, 34, and 37.

One large but inaccessible area with lots of birding potential is Camp Ripley, a National Guard training area west of the Mississippi. Like other military reservations, there is lots of relatively undisturbed natural habitat here (bomb craters aside), off-limits to the general public. A few years ago, researchers surveyed its spring-summer birdlife, and they found such things as Eared Grebes with young, several Red-shouldered Hawks, a few Yellow Rails, calling Northern Saw-whet Owls, Blue-gray Gnatcatchers, a singing Connecticut Warbler, and vagrant Hooded Warbler and Lark Bunting.

There were indications then that birders might be able to arrange access, though I don't know anyone who has done this. But for more information, write the Training Site Environmental Office, P. O. Box 150, Little Falls 56345.

Morrison County has three sewage ponds:

❏ Little Rock; 0.2 mile north.

❏ Bowlus; from the bend of Highway 238, go 1 mile south on County Road 24, 0.2 mile west, and 0.2 mile south.

❑ Upsala (home of the mythical Upsala Uffdas, frequent opponent of the Lake Wobegon Whippets); I don't know where the ballfield is, but the ponds are 0.5 mile north on Highway 238.

Mille Lacs County

If you glance at the map of Mille Lacs County and assume the best places to bird would be in the vast Mille Lacs Wildlife Management Area and along the shores of huge Mille Lacs Lake, you'd be half right. Unfortunately, the wildlife management area is little more than a mix of aspens and alders (start humming) where the deer and the woodpeckers play. But one could at least find Ruffed Grouse, American Woodcock, Alder Flycatcher, Golden-winged and Mourning warblers nesting here. (Also, as you listen for singing passerines, you'll find this is an area where seldom is heard a discouraging word. And the skies are not cloudy all day!)

The southern half of **Mille Lacs Lake (inset A)** lies within this county of the same name, and the lake is most interesting during fall for loons, ducks, gulls, and other water birds. Its many possibilities are discussed in the chapters on Aitkin and Crow Wing counties which include the northern half of the lake, where birders generally have the best luck. Starting on the west side of the lake and going counter-clockwise to the Aitkin County line, the best **access points** in Mille Lacs County are all marked **A1**; if pressed for time, at least check these first three areas:

• Wigwam Bay, 2 miles south of the Crow Wing County line, one of the best spots on the entire lake; easily viewed from Highway 169 and from the northern end of County Road 35.

• Continue southeast on 35 which rejoins Highway169, go 0.4 mile south on 169, and turn back on 35 to the historical monument and cemetery, where there is a trail from which to scan Vinland Bay (also spelled Vineland on some maps).

• Return to 169, and pick up County Road 35 again as it continues southeast to its end just west of the junction of Highways 169 and 27; there are continuous views of the lake along this stretch.

Where Highway 169 turns south, follow Highway 27 east to Isle and then Highway 47 north; accesses from these two roads are:

• Mazomannie Point, west of Bayview.

• Izaty's Resort, at the north end of County Road 152.

• The north end of County Road 142.

• Wahkon Bay, in the town of the same name.

• Father Hennepin State Park.

• Malone Island; watch for the sign off Highway 47.

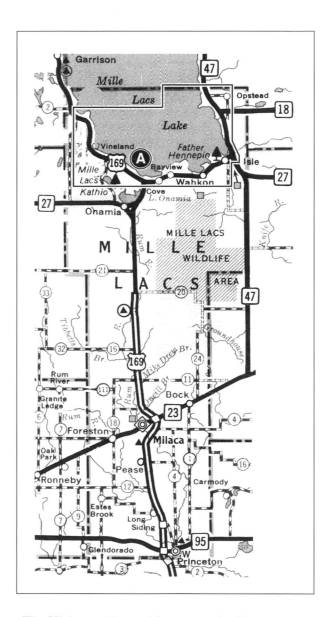

• The Highway 47 wayside rest north of Isle.

• Along County Road 127.

• The public access on Highway 47.

• West of the junction of Highways 18 and 47.

• And the west end of County Road 28, a mile south of the Aitkin County line.

While you're birding Mille Lacs, be sure to stop at the fish

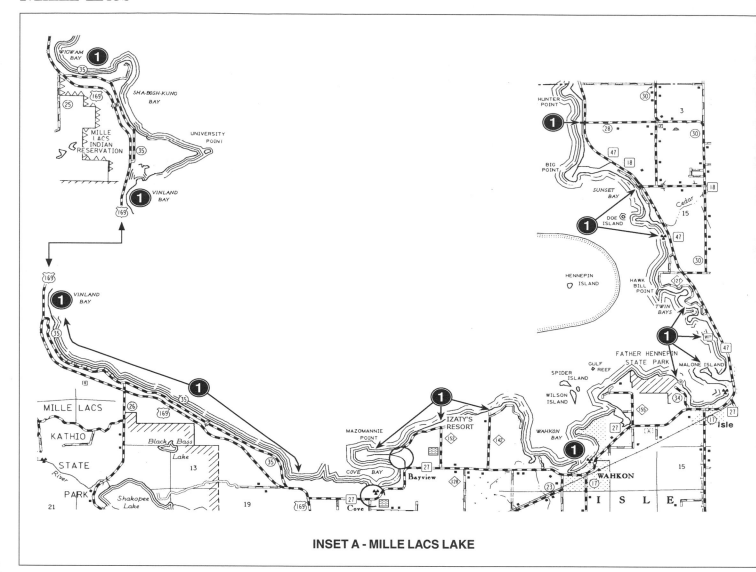

INSET A - MILLE LACS LAKE

hatchery pond behind the levee across the road from the public access parking lot in Cove (see inset A); it's sometimes good for shorebirds after drawn down in fall. There are also these sewage ponds in Mille Lacs County:

❏ Bayview; also located on inset A.

❏ Wahkon; 1.4 miles south on County Road 17.

❏ Isle; 0.7 mile southeast on Highway 27/47, 0.2 mile west on Oak Street, and 0.2 mile south.

❏ Milaca, the largest ones in the county; go west 0.5 mile on Highway 23 to River Drive, then north 0.8 mile to the ponds on the northwest side of the cemetery.

Kanabec County

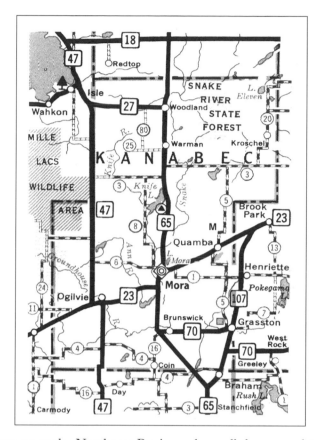

This last of the counties of the Southeast Region is so over-looked by birders more interested in nearby Mille Lacs Lake, and Pine and Aitkin counties, that even the proper pronun-ciation of "Kanabec" remains a mystery. Puzzling as well is why no one ever sees much at the county's only sewage ponds in Grasston, 1 mile north on County Road 5.

There are, however, a few places recommended by local birders, which can be covered in a clockwise loop starting in the northeast corner of the county:

• There are feeders and coniferous trees along the south side of Lake Eleven; check these in fall/winter for roosting owls, winter finches, and other boreal species.

• Watch for Sharp-tailed Grouse leks and Sandhill Cranes along and east of County Road 20, between Lake Eleven and County Road 3.

• A good marsh for cranes and rails is just north of Quamba: go 1.5 miles north on County Road 5, then 0.5 mile west, and 0.5 mile north.

• Lake Mora, along both sides of Highway 65 on the north side of Mora, is sometimes good for fall shorebirds.

• Knife Lake, 7 miles farther north on 65, is probably the best lake for migrant waterfowl.

• There is an extensive coniferous bog north of Knife Lake to look for Northeast Region specialties: turn west from High-way 65 on County Road 25 just south of Warman, go 2.5 miles to County Road 80, and north 2 miles.

One last recommendation. Instead of searching for North-east Region birds in Kanabec County, you could just con-tinue on to the Northeast Region, where all those sought-af-ter birds are easier to find. And where the counties are easier to pronounce. Read on.

PRINCIPAL BIRDING LOCATIONS BY SEASON

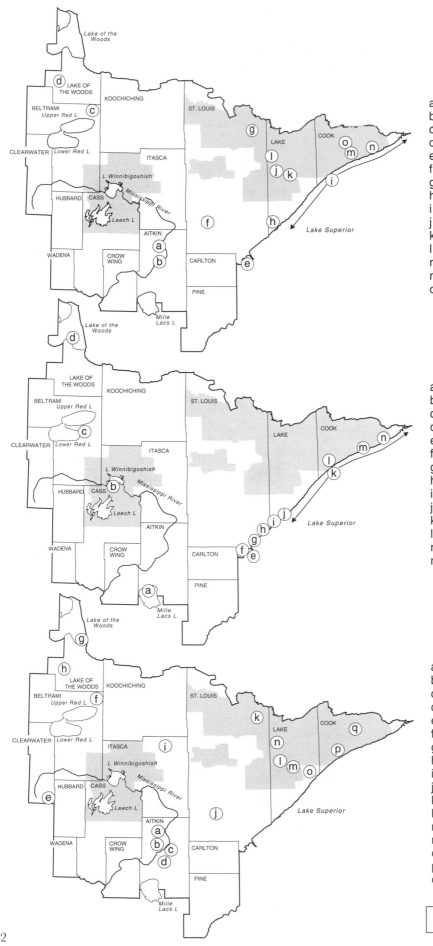

WINTER

a – Pietz's Road / County Road 18
b – Township Road 380
c – Highway 72 and vicinity
d – Beltrami Island State Forest
e – Duluth harbor area
f – Sax-Zim Bog
g – Echo Trail
h – Knife River / Two Harbors and vicinity
i – North Shore of Lake Superior
j – County Road 2
k – Stony River Forest Road / Whyte Road
l – Spruce Road
m – Grand Marais and vicinity
n – Paradise Beach and vicinity
o – Gunflint Trail and vicinity

MIGRATION

a – Mille Lacs Lake
b – Lake Winnibigoshish
c – Upper and Lower Red Lakes
d – Lake of the Woods
e – Park Point
f – Erie Pier
g – Hawk Ridge (fall)
h – Stoney Point
i – Knife River
j – Two Harbors and vicinity
k – North Shore of Lake Superior
l – Tofte-Lutsen area
m – Grand Marais and vicinity
n – Paradise Beach and vicinity

SUMMER/BREEDING

a – Pietz's Road / County Road 18
b – Township Road 380
c – McGregor Marsh
d – Rice Lake NWR
e – Itasca State Park
f – Highway 72 and vicinity
g – Pine and Curry Island SNA
h – Beltrami Island State Forest
i – Scenic State Park
j – Sax-Zim Bog
k – Echo Trail
l – County Road 2
m – Stony River Forest Road / Whyte Road
n – Spruce Road
o – Tettegouche State Park / County Road 7
p – Oberg Mountain
q – Gunflint Trail and vicinity

See Notes and Abbreviations on page 53.

Pine County

Hinckley. Tobie's. These two words practically say all there is in Pine County, as far as most Minnesotans are concerned. It's long been a virtual requirement for travelers between the Cities and Duluth to take the Hinckley exit, the halfway point on Interstate 35, and stop at Tobie's Restaurant — arguably the best-known restaurant in the state. My advice as you approach Hinckley? Get in the left lane, avoid the backup caused by those trying to exit, bypass the amusement park atmosphere at Tobie's and its adjacent businesses (which, indeed, include an amusement park -- a.k.a. Grand Casino Hinckley), and keep going.

As you drive by, though, be sure to note the significance of Hinckley as the dividing line between North and South. South of town, witness the farm fields, birds more characteristic of the Southeast Region, and the more moderate weather. Abruptly, it seems, the boreal forest of pine and aspen and alder swamps closes in north of town, ravens begin replacing crows, and cooler temperatures predominate. It would be tempting to abandon the county-line structure of this guide when it comes to Pine County. The true boundary between the Southeast and Northeast regions lies not at the Chisago-Pine County line, but along Highway 48.

Basically, since its most interesting birding potential lies in its northern half, Pine County well qualifies as a Northeast county. And you'll find plenty of boreal habitat in the **Nemadji State Forest (inset A)**, a relatively unknown area of aspens, alders, and tamarack bogs that spills over into Carlton County. The logging roads (labeled "S.F.R.") penetrating this forest look intriguing, but remember that many forest roads are not plowed in winter and are sometimes poorly mapped. If you're among the cartographically challenged, there are basically three easy-to-find roads to check (**A1**):

• The road **north of Kingsdale**, which dead ends in a large

tamarack bog.

• **Park Forest Road**, which heads west just north of Kingsdale and eventually comes out on County Road 171 east of Kerrick. And, as you drive the roads between the forest boundary and Kerrick or Bruno, watch for things like resident Sharp-tailed Grouse and wintering Snow Buntings in any fields and open tamarack bogs you pass.

• The road on the Carlton County line through the so-called **Nickerson Bog**. This spruce-tamarack bog has a few Connecticut Warblers nesting at the southern edge of its range, along with Northern Saw-whet Owl, Yellow-bellied and Alder flycatchers, Golden-winged and Mourning warblers, and Le Conte's and Lincoln's sparrows. Year-

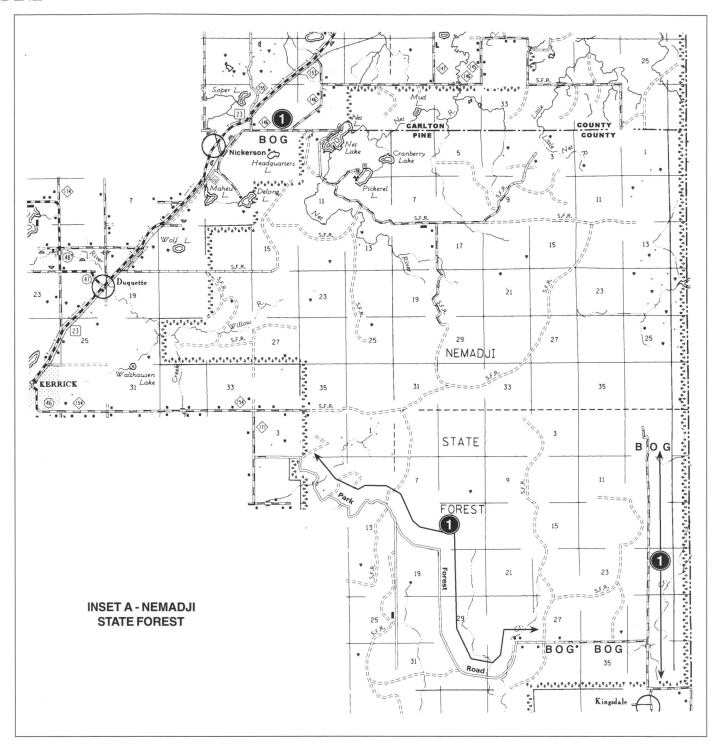

**INSET A - NEMADJI
STATE FOREST**

round possiblilities here and along other back roads near Nickerson include Northern Goshawk (especially fall-winter), Sharp-tailed Grouse, Great Gray Owl (rare), Black-backed Woodpecker (also rare), Gray Jay, and Boreal Chickadee (uncommon).

Scattered elsewhere in Pine County are some other birding places to be aware of, primarily in summer. From north to south:

• Sturgeon Lake is the largest lake in the county, and, as such, would be one spot to check during waterfowl migra-

tion for loons, grebes, and diving ducks more typical of Lake Superior. It is easily scanned from its south side along County Road 46.

• The Louisiana Waterthrush has been found in summer at the northern edge of its range along the Lower Tamarack River just upstream from St. Croix State Park. Without a canoe, though, this river is hard to access. You can approach its mouth at the St. Croix River by turning north off Highway 48 on County Road 173 just west of the state line, then going 1 mile north and 1.3 miles east. This river can also be accessed in Duxbury, and at four spots along the first 5 miles of County Road 25 (turn east off County Road 24, 2 miles south of Duxbury).

• Another place for Louisianas is along the equally hard-to-reach Kettle River. About the only way to access its habitat is to launch your canoe from Highway 48, 4.4 miles east of Interstate 35. Either drift downstream towards the state park, or paddle north for 3 miles along the west side of the Kettle River Scientific Natural History Area.

• St. Croix State Park itself (entrance on Highway 48) has lots of deciduous woods along the river of the same name for breeding Broad-winged Hawk, Barred Owl, Whip-poor-will, Veery, Scarlet Tanager, and the like. More interesting to check, perhaps, would be the park's pine stands: besides Pine Warblers, Black-backed Woodpecker nests have been found in recent years.

• Downstream, and adjacent to the park, is the Chengwatana State Forest. Besides woods birds, you might find something of note at its water impoundment. From downtown Pine City, take County Road 8 to the east side of town, go north on County Road 9 along Cross Lake for about 3.5 miles to County Road 10, then east 4.7 miles to where 10 turns north, and continue east 2 more miles.

• And farther south is a good sedge marsh on the south side of Highway 70, 7 miles east of Highway 361. Surprisingly, Yellow Rails and Le Conte's Sparrows have been found at this unusually-far-south location in wetter years.

The largest and best-looking sewage ponds in the county are at Sandstone: from downtown, go east 1.1 miles on Highway 123, 1 mile south on Prison Road, then take County Road 20 1 mile east and 1 mile south. (By the way, don't miss the turn east on 20 or you'll end up in federal prison! Also, by the way, if you continue south beyond the ponds another 0.7 mile, you'll come to a sign for the alleged Sandstone National Wildlife Refuge. Some maps show it, others don't, and no one knows why it's there.)

There are also larger-than-average sewage ponds at Pine City: from downtown, go north 1 mile on County Road 61, and east 0.2 mile to the gated ponds on County Road 55. And Hinckley has smaller ponds: from the junction of Interstate 35 and Highway 48, go 0.2 mile east to County Road 140, then 1 mile north, 0.7 mile east, and 0.2 mile south.

Carlton County

Not only are this county's birds ignored by most birders, but Carlton County itself could almost try the patience of some. After all, it is the only thing separating Duluth from Aitkin County, two of the most heavily birded areas in the Northeast Region, and those driving from one place to the other on Highway 210 probably wish this county were smaller. Similarly, Twin Cities birders eager to get to Duluth to chase the latest vagrant probably grow impatient at times along this county's portion of Interstate 35.

Be aware, however, that Sharp-tailed Grouse have been occasionally spotted along both these highways. Of course, it usually takes a quieter back road to spot this highly-sought grouse, which has been declining in numbers and re-

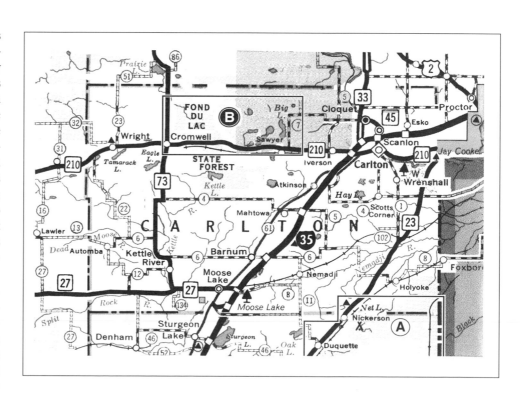

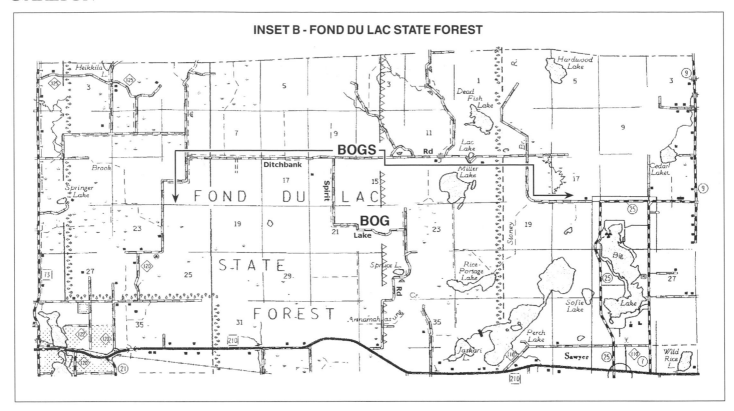

INSET B - FOND DU LAC STATE FOREST

liability for decades. One good spot to look recently has been west of Moose Lake: from downtown, go 4.5 miles west on Highway 27/73, then south and west 1.5 miles on County Road 134. I also recommend contacting the state's Department of Natural Resources for lek sites where there are blinds for spring viewing: their local office is in Cloquet at 1604 S. Highway 33; telephone (218) 879-0883.

In addition, such nesting species as Ruffed Grouse, American Woodcock, Barred and Northern Saw-whet owls, Alder Flycatcher, and Golden-winged and Mourning warblers occur widely through much of this county's landscape of woods (mostly deciduous), lakes, alder swamps, and scattered meadows. In winter, as in every other Northeast county, watch for raptors (like goshawks and Rough-leggeds), a Snowy or Great Gray owl (both rare here), Northern Shrike, Bohemian Waxwing, Snow Bunting (watch especially along Highway 210 between Sawyer and Wright), and winter finches.

There are a few specific places to be aware of in Carlton County, especially a couple of spruce-tamarack bogs worth checking in summer or winter. The possibilities of the Nickerson Bog on the Pine County line have already been covered under Pine County's inset A, but there are even more and better bogs in the **Fond du Lac State Forest (inset B)**. Almost the entire length of the Ditchbank Road

is worth birding, along with the 1.5-mile east-west section of Spirit Lake Road. Look especially in this under-birded area for Great Gray Owl, Black-backed Woodpecker, Gray Jay, Boreal Chickadee, Connecticut Warbler, and crossbills.

About the only other specific site to recommend might be Jay Cooke State Park, on Highway 210 east of Carlton, an especially scenic and hilly area along the St. Louis River. In winter here, the river is partly open upstream as far as the paper mill in Cloquet (easily found by following your nose). But of primary interest in these deciduous woods would be nesting Whip-poor-will (possibly), Yellow-throated Vireo, Wood Thrush, Scarlet Tanager, Eastern Towhee, and Indigo Bunting — all species uncommon to absent elsewhere in the Duluth area.

Incidentally, if you need Eastern Hemlock for your Minnesota list, ask at park headquarters for directions (and a permit) to the Hemlock Ravine Scientific and Natural Area. Probably fewer than 100 hemlocks exist in the state, and some 25 percent of them are in the Ravine.

The Moose Lake sewage ponds are better than most in the Northeast (which isn't really saying much — this region seems to excel at everything except sewage ponds). From downtown, go west 2 miles on Highway 27/73, then south 1 mile.

Aitkin County

I heard once that Aitkin County ranks last among all 87 Minnesota counties in per capita income. No matter. After all, it certainly stands among the top few ornithologically. There may not be any Spruce Grouse, Boreal Owls, Three-toed or Black-backed woodpeckers breeding in this county, but just about every other boreal specialty of the Northeast Region occurs regularly here, and there is simply no other county where Sharp-tailed Grouse, Yellow Rail, Great Gray Owl, and Le Conte's and Nelson's Sharp-tailed sparrows are seen more often. It is little wonder so many out-of-state birders have been attracted here over the years.

In addition, this is one of the few counties worth birding at all times of year. Migrant waterfowl flock to its wild rice paddies in spring as grouse and owls are in full display and full voice. In summer, numerous sought-after passerines nest in the extensive bogs and forests. Mille Lacs is one of the state's premier lakes for fall migrant water birds, and in winter there are owls, winter finches, and other northern specialties to look for.

Throughout the **inset A** map, in the vicinity of **Palisade**, there are any number of back roads which pass by hayfields, sedge meadows, alder thickets, spruce and tamarack bogs, and deciduous woodlands of aspen and black ash. Perhaps the most famous of these roads is the dead-end which turns north off County Road 18, 4 miles east of Highway 169, or 2 miles west of the County Road 5 intersection. You won't find a road sign at the corner, but the Pietz family lives at the end of this road, and thus the name

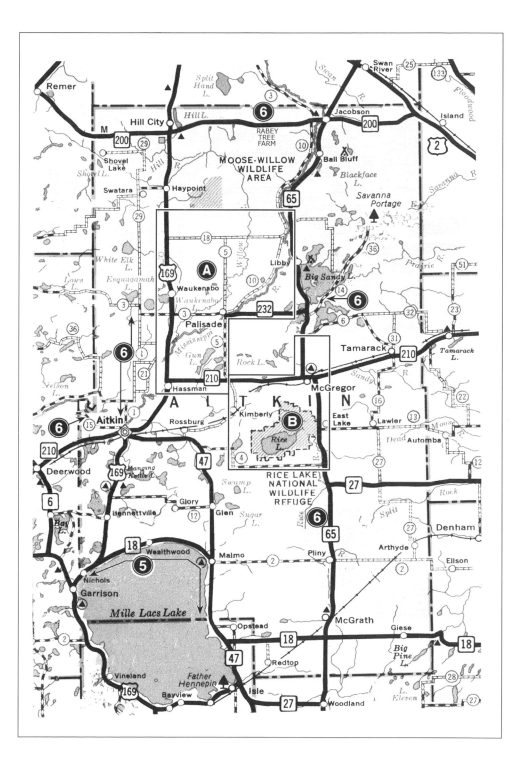

Pietz's (pronounced "Pizzas") **Road (A1)**.

Over the years, this could be considered the most consistent single location in Minnesota to find a Great Gray Owl.

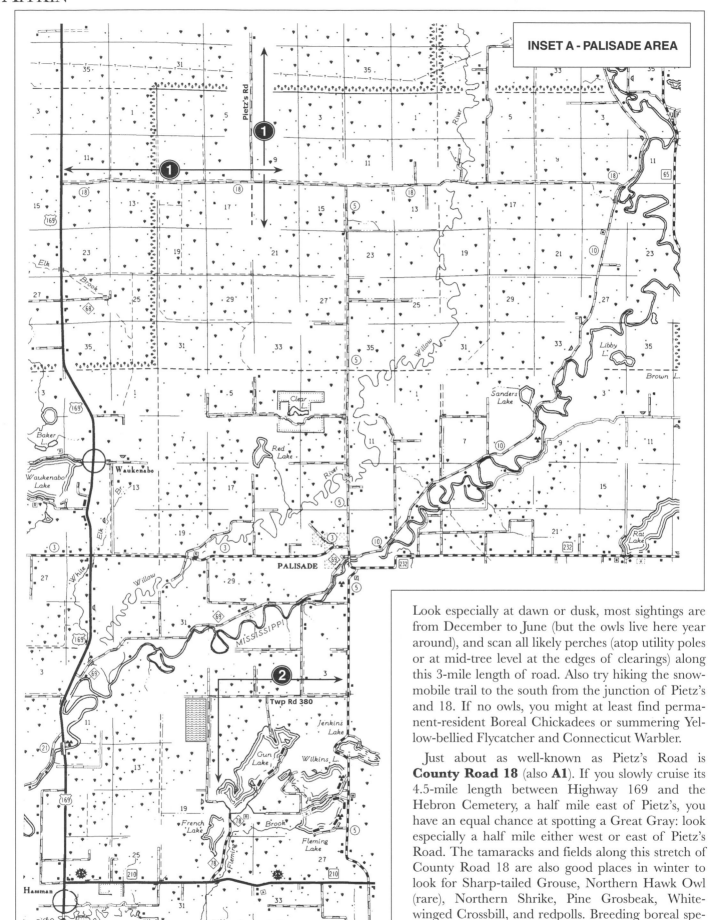

INSET A - PALISADE AREA

Look especially at dawn or dusk, most sightings are from December to June (but the owls live here year around), and scan all likely perches (atop utility poles or at mid-tree level at the edges of clearings) along this 3-mile length of road. Also try hiking the snow-mobile trail to the south from the junction of Pietz's and 18. If no owls, you might at least find permanent-resident Boreal Chickadees or summering Yellow-bellied Flycatcher and Connecticut Warbler.

Just about as well-known as Pietz's Road is **County Road 18** (also **A1**). If you slowly cruise its 4.5-mile length between Highway 169 and the Hebron Cemetery, a half mile east of Pietz's, you have an equal chance at spotting a Great Gray: look especially a half mile either west or east of Pietz's Road. The tamaracks and fields along this stretch of County Road 18 are also good places in winter to look for Sharp-tailed Grouse, Northern Hawk Owl (rare), Northern Shrike, Pine Grosbeak, White-winged Crossbill, and redpolls. Breeding boreal specialties are also plentiful, but even more numerous in this part of the county are mosquitoes.

A half mile east of Pietz's Road, the habitat along County Road 18 opens up for the next 3.5 miles, and farther east more ordinary deciduous woods close in. Around the intersection with County Road 5 are large sedge meadows and hayfields, a good area to scan for wintering Northern Goshawk, Rough-legged Hawk (or, with luck, perhaps a Gyrfalcon), Sharp-tailed Grouse (year around), Snowy and Northern Hawk owls in some winters, Short-eared Owl (rare but possible in all seasons), and Snow Bunting. In wet years, these meadows have had nesting Yellow Rails, but it's been a few years since any have been heard. More reliable in this habitat in summer are Sedge Wren and Le Conte's Sparrow.

Keep looking for Great Grays along the last 4 miles of County Road 18: try especially the side road going north, 3 miles east of County Road 5; owls are sometimes seen as well on County Road 10, within a mile or so south of the end of 18. If you follow County Road 10 as it leads north out of inset A to Highway 200, you'll pass fields where Sharp-tailed Grouse are sometimes seen.

In addition to Great Gray Owls, inset A maps the way to one of the most reliable Sharp-tailed Grouse roads in the state, **Township Road 380 (A2)**. It turns west off County Road 5, 3 miles south of Palisade. There has long been an active lek on the north side of 380, 1.5 miles west of County Road 5; watch for displaying grouse early in the morning from March through May. If you're here at the wrong time of day or year, you still have a fair chance to see grouse by walking through this field, or by driving 380 north and west of Gun Lake and scanning the roadside fields, alders, and tamaracks. Birders seem to have the best luck near the junction with County Road 5 and within a half mile east or 1 mile south of the corner where 380 turns south.

Even if there are no grouse to be seen, look at least for Sedge Wren, Le Conte's Sparrow, Bobolink, and Eastern Meadowlark in summer; in winter, scan for the same birds listed above for County Road 18. This road is also noteworthy as one of the farthest east locales in Minnesota where Black-billed Magpies regularly occur.

* * *

Inset B maps the way around the small but famous town of **McGregor**. Just as Pietz's Road is The Place for Great Gray Owls, so is the **McGregor Marsh (B3)** the location where birders have traditionally headed to add Yellow Rail to their lists. Indeed, over the years, McGregor and its sedge marsh south of town literally has been visited by hundreds of birders from throughout the U. S. and several foreign countries.

The main part of the marsh extends for 1.5 miles along both sides of Highway 65 from Highway 210 south, and a smaller (but often better) half-mile-long section of marsh along 65 begins at the County Road 8 junction. As mentioned earlier, the traffic on Highway 65 can be heavy and distracting as you're trying to listen for rails, so avoid weekends if possible, and use care as you bird along the shoulder. Or hope the rails are where you can hike away from the highway noise and listen. One good choice is Township Road 101, the dead-end road which turns east off 65, 0.2 mile south of the County Road 8 junction (but note the No Parking signs). Or try walking the Soo Line Recreational Trail, the abandoned railroad grade which crosses 65, 1.1 miles south of 210.

Listen for their rhythmic ticking calls (mostly at night), grab a strong spotlight and mosquito repellent, plunge into the marsh (note the water can be a few feet deep in places), and with lots of patience and careful stalking this rail can actually be seen. One group strategy is to stand shoulder-to-shoulder, facing the spot where the rail is thought to be, have the person in the center start tapping stones (or whatever), and see if the rail comes walking into view at your feet. If that doesn't work, get the group to form a circle around the rail's suspected location, and slowly close in. As you approach, the rail will probably fall silent; it will then either flutter off into the darkness, escape unseen between your legs, or — if you're lucky — freeze in place until spotted in your flashlight beam.

Note especially as well that a few Nelson's Sharp-tailed Sparrows, along with several Le Conte's, can also be found in this marsh, which is the only consistent location for this sparrow known in the Northeast Region. Unfortunately, these sharp-taileds are erratic and unpredictable singers (and if not singing they are seldom seen), and they usually hang out far from the road. There are nights they seem to sing all night long, there are some mornings they don't sing at all, and some days they will sing at high noon. (For reasons unknown, the Yellow Rails can be equally erratic, staying entirely silent on some nights or, conversely, calling away in broad daylight.)

Other possibilities in the McGregor Marsh include American Bittern, Sandhill Crane, Common Snipe, Sedge and Marsh wrens, Le Conte's Sparrow, and Bobolink. Be aware, as you search for sparrows, the two most common ones here are Savannah and Swamp.

Also located within inset B is **Rice Lake National Wildlife Refuge**. While there is nothing in the refuge that can't be found just as easily elsewhere, it has a nice mix of habitats and nesting species. The entrance road and refuge headquarters **(B4)** are on the west side of 65, 4.7 miles south of Highway 210. After stopping in the headquarters for maps and checklists, continue west and listen within the first half mile for the likes of Black-billed Cuckoo, Alder Flycatcher, Sedge Wren, Golden-winged Warbler, and Clay-colored and Le Conte's sparrows.

Denser deciduous woods follow and line much of the next 3.5 miles of the road where Ruffed Grouse, Barred Owl, Pileated and other woodpeckers, Least and Great Crested flycatchers, Yellow-throated Vireo, Veery, Wood Thrush, Mourning and other warblers, and Scarlet Tanager all occur. Four miles west of Highway 65, the one-way portion of the auto tour begins. It passes through more open areas (keep listening for Clay-colored and Le Conte's sparrows) and leads to the shore of Rice Lake itself (also marked **B4**). Scan for Common Loon, Ring-necked Duck, Sandhill Crane, and Black Tern. October duck concentrations on this lake have been censused at 100,000 individuals or more, with most of them Mallards and Ring-necked Ducks. The auto tour eventually loops back east to the beginning through more good woodlands.

Elsewhere in inset B is the largely inaccessible but interesting Grayling Marsh Wildlife Management Area, worth birding during the nesting season from May to July, as long as you don't mind the company of mosquitoes, deer flies, and wood ticks. The mile-long road into the large marshy water impoundment at Grayling turns east off County Road 73, 2.6 miles north of Highway 210. Virginia Rails, Soras, and Sandhill Cranes breed here.

*   *   *

As mentioned in the Mille Lacs County chapter, the large lake of the same name annually attracts good numbers of fall migrants from August to November, and the Aitkin County portion includes several of the best locations for scanning the lake. Concentrations of Common Loons by the hundreds have been documented in October (record high: 1,688 on 20 October 1998), lots of diving ducks annually occur, and there are fall flocks of Bonaparte's Gulls by the hundreds to sort through (record high: 1,217 on 27 October 1998).

The list of rarities and vagrants recorded on Mille Lacs is a long one. Red-throated, Pacific, and Yellow-billed (twice!) loons have been recorded, and Eurasian Wigeon, King Eider, Harlequin Duck, Long-tailed Duck, scoters (all three), and Barrow's Goldeneye have turned up among the ducks. Red Phalaropes (twice), Pomarine and Parasitic jaegers, Franklin's (probably annual), Little and California gulls, and Black-legged Kittiwake have all been sighted.

Starting at the Aitkin-Mille Lacs County line on Highway

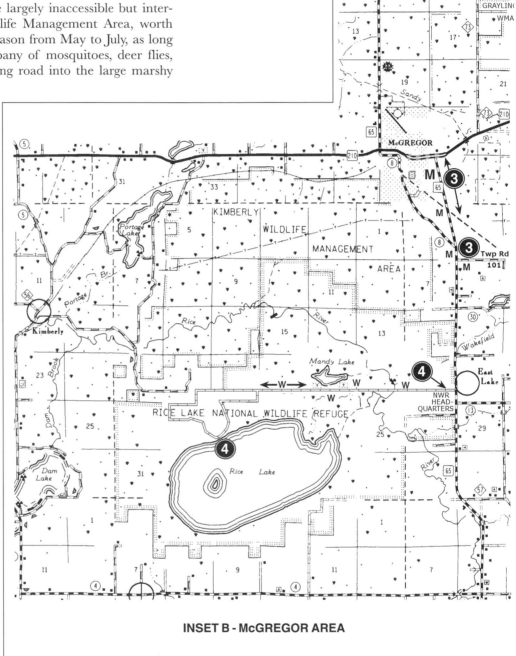

INSET B - McGREGOR AREA

18 and working counter-clockwise along the shore, there are nine areas which provide the best views of **Mille Lacs Lake (5)**:

• West of the junction of Highway 18 and County Road 80, 1 mile north of the county line.

• Fisher's and Castaway's Resorts, 4.2 and 4.5 miles respectively north of County Road 80, or 0.7 and 0.4 mile south of Malmo.

• The Malmo public access: follow the side road west from Malmo along the shore; just north of here there is also a lake view at the small campground at the mouth of the creek.

• Carlsona Beach Restaurant, about 3 miles northwest of Malmo.

• The so-called Wealthwood Beach, a 1.5-mile open stretch beginning just west of Carlsona's.

• Angler's Inn Resort, 0.8 mile east of Wealthwood.

• The community of Wealthwood: turn south off Highway 18 on Township Road 49.

• The wayside rest about 3 miles west of Wealthwood, and the next 1.5-mile portion of Highway 18 west of the wayside (careful: the highway shoulders are narrow to nonexistent).

• Along the 2-mile stretch of County Road 37: where Highway 18 turns north temporarily away from the lake, turn left on 37, which rejoins 18 by a public access wayside. From here, it's a mile and a half to the Aitkin-Crow Wing county line.

*   *   *

Beyond the confines of insets A and B, there are five roads which offer access to a variety of birding possibilities, and these areas are all marked **6**. From north to south:

• Along **Highway 200** between Hill City and Jacobson, there are spruce-tamarack bogs where wintering Northern Hawk and Great Gray owls have occasionally been seen, and where Northern Shrike, Gray Jay, Pine and Evening grosbeaks, White-winged Crossbill, and redpolls winter with some regularity. The best of these bogs is 8-10 miles east of Hill City or 6-8 miles west of Jacobson.

Be sure to stop as well at the Rabey tree farm at the eastern end of this bog, 10 miles east of Hill City or 6 miles west of Jacobson. These planted spruce trees on the south side of the highway have been consistently attractive for years to Boreal Chickadees (all year) and breeding Cape May Warblers. The best way to bird this area is to hike south from 200 on the snowmobile trail, just west of the signed Elliot Forest Road.

• In May-June, turn northeast on County Road 14, opposite the junction of Highways 75 and 232, 7 miles north of McGregor. Along this road to Savannah Portage State Park are pine stands for Pine Warblers; check especially around the **Savannah State Forest field station**, 3.1 miles from Highway 65. Adjacent to these forestry buildings is a good but inaccessible tamarack bog, where Yellow-bellied Flycatcher and Connecticut Warbler can at least be heard.

• **County Road 1** leads north from downtown Aitkin for 14 miles to its end at County Road 3. Along 1 and its connecting side roads are several hayfields and meadows with some tamaracks and alders in between. In winter, watch for owls (you know which ones!), Northern Shrike, Snow Bunting, both redpolls, and perhaps even a Gyrfalcon. During migration, look for Short-eared Owls, and in spring you might find Tundra Swans and other waterfowl if there are still any rice paddies around (most in this county have gone out of business). This is also one of the better roads in the county for spotting Sharp-tailed Grouse: in recent springs there have been active leks along County Road 1, 5 and 7 miles north of Aitkin.

• In springs following a heavy snow melt, the Mississippi River sometimes overflows its banks west of Aitkin to create flooded fields for ducks, shorebirds (records include both godwits, Red Knot, phalaropes, and Ruff), and other water birds. To reach this so-called **Cedarbrook area** from Aitkin, turn west on 4th Street / County Road 15, 2 blocks north of Highway 210, and follow the river for about the next 6 miles.

• Another good spruce-tamarack bog lies along a 2.5-mile section of **Highway 65** in southern Aitkin County, extending from 2 miles south of the Highway 27 junction to 3.5 miles north of Pliny. There are winter Great Gray and Northern Hawk owl records here; in summer, listen for rails and sparrows in the sedge marshes, and for Alder Flycatcher and Golden-winged Warbler in the alder thickets.

Of final note in Aitkin County, as if you needed somewhere else to bird, are small sewage ponds at McGregor (see inset B; foot access only) and at Hill City (0.2 mile west on Highway 200, 0.2 mile south).

Crow Wing County

There certainly must be a lot to see in Crow Wing County, and, judging by the amount of traffic, most of it seems to be on weekends from May to September. But don't ask me what it is, since I've never been able to find much there. To find out, the next time you're stuck in traffic in Brainerd, open your window and ask the guy in the motor home towing a boat in the next lane where he's headed. Chances are he'll name some tourist trap on the way to Nisswa. My favorite is the one with the statues of Paul Bunyan and Babe that actually offers helicopter tours of Brainerd (the best way to spot traffic jams, I guess). Or, he'll mention The Cabin on The Lake where he plans to catch

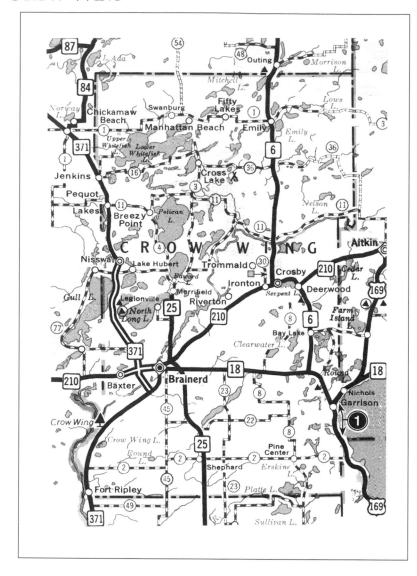

Grebes, and its red pine stands do have Pine Warblers, which, like pine trees, tend to be uncommon and local farther northeast in Minnesota. Also nesting in its deciduous woodlands are Red-shouldered Hawk (a few), Ruffed Grouse, Barred and Northern Saw-whet (listen in April) owls, Whip-poor-will (one place to listen is around the abandoned iron mines north of Ironton along County Road 30), and Golden-winged and Mourning warblers.

In winter, a goshawk might happen by, Bohemian Waxwings sometimes flock to mountain ash and crabapple trees in Crosby (or other towns — even Brainerd!), Red Crossbills occur erratically in pine stands, while Evening Grosbeaks and Common Redpolls frequent favored bird feeders. And in February be sure to check the shoulders of Highway 371 near Fort Ripley — for Ancient Murrelets! Back in 1969, one of the oddest birds ever found in the state somehow collided with a car in this most unlikely month and location.

In fall, you will certainly want to check Crow Wing County's share of **Mille Lacs Lake (1)**. There may be only a few miles of lake shore within the county, but most of the rarities seen on this lake have been here. (See the Aitkin County chapter for the list of migrants to watch for.) There are basically three areas from which to scan the lake:

• Starting in the town of Garrison itself, the lake is continually in view along Highway 18/169, between the marina at the northeast edge of town and the stone wall overlook (site of the shrine to the Almighty Walleye) in the center of town.

• Just south of town on 169 is a large wayside rest and boat ramp. Be sure to check the pine stand behind the rest rooms where migrant saw-whets have roosted and where a Worm-eating Warbler once turned up — in November! Continue south on the side road along the lake shore from the rest rooms, and in a half mile you'll loop back to Highway 169.

• Next is the St. Alban's Bay portion of Mille Lacs, which extends south for 2 miles along Highway 169 to the Mille Lacs County line. Though the highway shoulders are wide, use caution as you bird along this very busy road.

By the way, I have a suggestion for that guy stuck in traffic with you in Brainerd: tell him to launch his boat at the Ironton sewage ponds (1.5 miles north on County Road 30).

The Walleye (and ends up with Da Bullhead).

Clearly, this is the place where fishermen and other tourists come in search of the solitude of Minnesota's wooded lake country. The woods and lakes are there, but good luck finding any solitude. My advice? Head east on 210 back into Aitkin County where there are plenty of bogs and marshes to bird and get lost in. There are times when insects make better company than humans.

To be fair, though, some of Crow Wing County's lakes are good places to see Common Loons and Red-necked

Cass County

It goes without saying that the northern half of Minnesota includes most of this state's best birding areas, with birders attracted primarily to the coniferous forests of Aitkin, St. Louis, Lake, and Cook counties or to the prairies of northwestern Minnesota. Counties in between in the north central portion of Minnesota, therefore, tend to be somewhat neglected.

However, partly by virtue of its size alone, Cass manages to be a better-than-average county, including within its borders many lakes (with two of them among the largest in Minnesota), a vast amount of state and federal forest land, extensive marshes, and even a few interesting hayfields and pastures. So there is plenty to see, and the general birding possibilities — along with the summer traffic on the highways and lakes — are described in the Crow Wing County chapter.

The southern half of the Chippewa National Forest lies within northern Cass County, and this region of lakes, pines, and aspens is best known for its population of breeding Bald Eagles. Recent surveys have turned up over 700 active nests in Minnesota, and the majority of these are in and around this national forest. Other species characteristic of northern Minnesota's wooded lake country are also present here, though just about all the birds are found just as easily, or more so, elsewhere.

Besides eagles, there are Osprey nests to see, Common Loons and Red-necked Grebes summer on several of the lakes, and Pine Warblers can be found in almost any stand of piney woods. There is also evidence that the Northern Goshawk, whose summer status is poorly known, is one boreal forest specialty breeding more often in north central Minnesota than farther northeast, and some of the more remote sections of the Chippewa might be places to find some. For maps and other information, stop in at national forest headquarters in Cass Lake on Highway 2 on the west side of town.

Leech Lake and Lake Winnibigoshish (better and more easily known as Lake Winnie) are two of the largest lakes in the state, which, by virtue of their size, often attract good numbers of migrant water birds. Late fall (October-November) tends to be the best time to search for those relatively rare "big lake" species like Long-tailed Duck and scoters that are more characteristic of Lake Superior. **Lake Winnie (1)** is clearly the better of these two lakes, and it is just about as good as Mille Lacs. Fall records include the state's first Yellow-billed Loon, its second Mew Gull, an Ancient Murrelet shot long ago by a hunter, both Red-throated and Pacific loons, Little Gull, and Black-legged Kittiwake.

Lake Winnie also has Mille Lacs-like peaks of Common Loons in late September and October, with high counts in late October of over 1,600 in a day. Similarly, several hundred Bonaparte's Gulls congregate here, usually peaking in late October, with the record one-day census of 3,175 on 11 November 2001. On the Cass County half of the lake are these six vantage points from which to scope things out:

• On County Road 9, by the dam on the Mississippi River outlet at the Itasca County line; also note the fish hatchery ponds below the dam.

• At the Birches public access: watch for the sign on Forest Road 2163, which turns north off County Road 9, 3.5 miles southwest of the dam.

• From the nearby Tamarack Point campground and public access at the end of Forest Road 2163.

• In Bena: turn north off Highway 2 to the campground on the east edge of town.

• At Richard's Townsite campground and public access west of Bena: turn north off Highway 2 on County Road 91 / West Winnie Road, 2.7 miles west of Bena, go 0.2 mile, and turn right at the sign on Forest Road 2074.

• And at the public access about 5 miles farther up West Winnie Road.

Though **Leech Lake (2)** is not birded as often, a large Common Tern colony is located here (formerly Minnesota's largest), and it was the site of the state's only Caspian Tern breeding record. Most of this lake's shoreline is difficult to reach, and finding all its accesses is probably not worth the time, but there are three easy-to-find vantage points on the south side of the lake:

• The public access near Brevik: turn north off County Road 39, 2.2 miles north of Highway 200.

• The Highway 200 wayside rest, 0.5 mile east of Whipholt.

• Stony Point's campground and public access: turn east to the lake from County Road 13 on Forest Road 3797, 4.3 miles north of Highway 200.

Just west of Leech Lake, and probably more interesting, are the sedge marshes of **Swamp Lake (3)**, where Yellow Rails (and probably Nelson's Sharp-tailed Sparrows) have been heard consistently for several summers, at least through 1999. This location is along the west side of busy Highway 371, 11 miles south of Cass Lake or 6 miles north of the Highway 200 junction.

A quieter place for these two highly-sought birds is on the other side of Leech Lake, in the marshes along the **Boy**

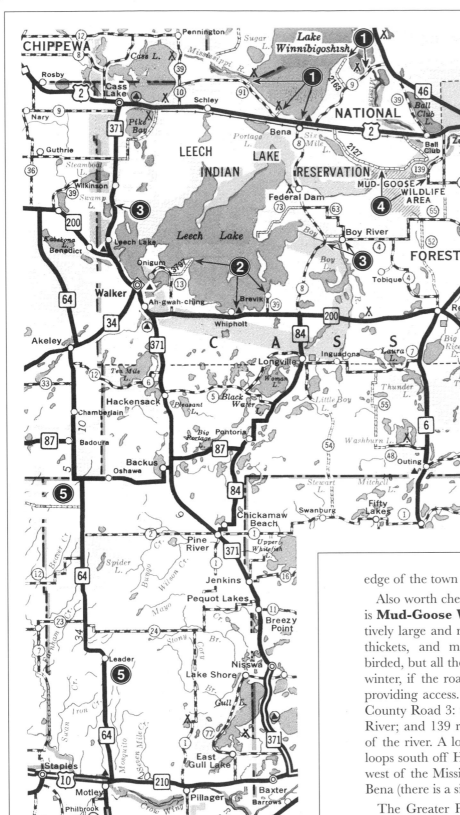

edge of the town of Boy River.

Also worth checking in summer in northern Cass County is **Mud-Goose Wildlife Management Area (4)**, a relatively large and remote area with a mix of tamarack bogs, thickets, and marshes. This interesting area is seldom birded, but all the more reason to go there (perhaps even in winter, if the roads are plowed). There are two loop roads providing access. County Road 139 loops into the area off County Road 3: turn west 0.4 mile south of the Mississippi River; and 139 returns to County Road 3, 3.4 miles south of the river. A longer route is on Forest Road 2127, which loops south off Highway 2: the east end of 2127 is 0.7 mile west of the Mississippi, and its west end is 4.1 miles east of Bena (there is a sign here for Six Mile Lake Road).

The Greater Prairie-Chicken may not be a species normally thought of as a specialty of the Northeast Region, but there may still be a small population in southern Cass County and adjacent portions of Wadena and Hubbard counties. Some **prairie-chicken leks (5)** were known to still be active near the towns of Leader and Oshawa in 1995, when 5 leks and 18 males were censused. Some of these may now be gone, since these pastures and meadows

River (also **3**). Access is more difficult, but you could at least listen from County Road 8 (about 6 miles south of Federal Dam), or 2.5 miles farther east from the southwest

are marginal habitats fragmented by trees and brush.

But if you like to explore back roads, turn east off Highway 64 on any of the four roads between Leader and 4 miles south of town. Or, from Oshawa, go 3.8 miles west on Highway 87, then turn southwest on the gravel road where 87 curves north. Besides prairie-chickens, these areas might also be good places to look for wintering raptors (perhaps even a Gyr, which likes to prey on gallinaceous birds),

Northern Shrikes, Snow Buntings, and redpolls. In summer, you might find Yellow Rail (in wet years), Sandhill Crane, Short-eared Owl (most likely in migration), and Le Conte's Sparrow.

Cass County also has small sewage ponds at Remer (0.9 mile southeast on Highway 200 from Highway 6, then south 0.2 mile, and west 0.2 mile) and Longville (0.2 mile east off Highway 84 on Forest Road 2309).

Wadena County

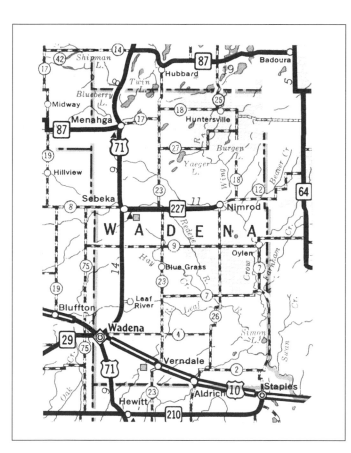

As one comedian would say, Wadena County gets no respect. After all, what kind of a county would have one of its principal towns named Nimrod? An earlier edition of the official Minnesota state map even managed to misspell "Wadena."

This is the smallest county in the Northeast Region, birders spend little time here, and as a result this chapter will be among the briefest in the book. Yes, many out-of-state birders would be interested in the Ruffed Grouse, American Woodcocks, Alder Flycatchers, Sedge Wrens, Golden-winged Warblers, Clay-colored Sparrows, and other widespread species nesting here and elsewhere in this region. And good migrants can show up anywhere (even in Wadena County), and I'll bet there are Northern Shrikes, Snow Buntings, redpolls, and other wintering species of interest.

But this is one of those counties that pales in comparison with its neighbors. Those to the north have more boreal specialties, counties farther south include better woods for southern birds, and West Region counties have prairie specialties. The northeastern corner of Wadena County may still have some Greater Prairie-Chickens, as mentioned in the Cass County chapter. But the population is marginal, if not gone (2 leks / 9 males censused in 1995), and it would be easier to look for them elsewhere.

Last but not least (or is it first and foremost in a county like this?), are two sets of sewage ponds. One is at Sebeka (1.5 miles east from Highway 71 on 227, then 0.5 mile south, and 0.2 mile west); the other at Verndale (1 mile west on County Road 104, then 0.2 mile north).

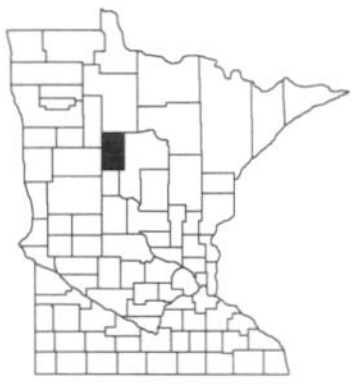

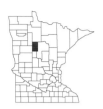

Hubbard County

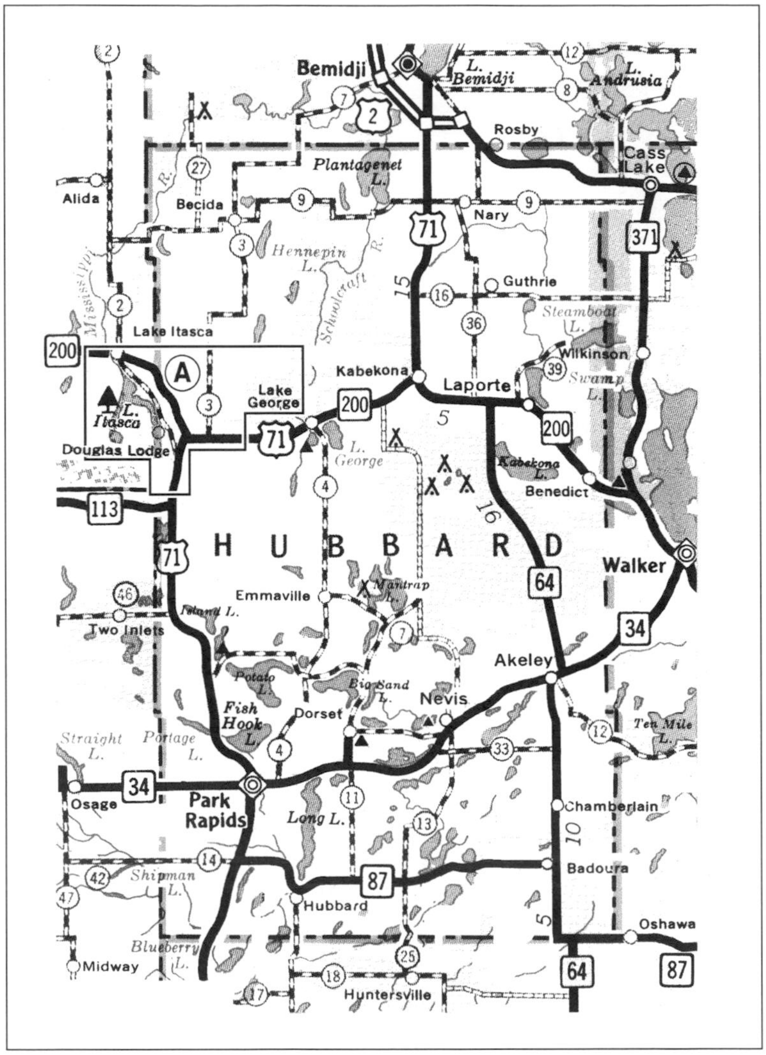

Like Wadena County, Hubbard may still have some prairie-chickens (3 leks / 9 males censused in its extreme southeastern corner in 1995). But, if not, there are at least a lot more lakes and coniferous forests here than in Wadena. This chapter, however, won't be any longer than the previous one, partly because its most interesting area, Itasca State Park, is delegated to Clearwater County's inset A. And partly because there aren't even any sewage pond directions to give.

Some of this county's lakes have Common Loons and Red-necked Grebes, but none are known to be specifically worth going out of your way for during migration or summer. The same is true of Hubbard County's boreal forests, since just about all their nesting species can be found more easily elsewhere. Note, however, this is as good a county as any to look for at least some winter specialties in the conifers and at feeders: e.g., Northern Goshawk, Northern Shrike, Gray Jay, Bohemian Waxwing (especially in towns with mountain ash and crabapple trees), Pine and Evening grosbeaks, crossbills (Reds are more likely in pines), and redpolls.

And that's about it, as far as I know. But don't just take my word for it. Relatively unknown counties like Wadena and Hubbard offer prime opportunities for exploration on your own. By now, readers must be tired of me telling them where to go birding. Get out there and find some good birds and areas on your own, and prove me wrong when I treat these counties so superficially. Tell me where to go for a change.

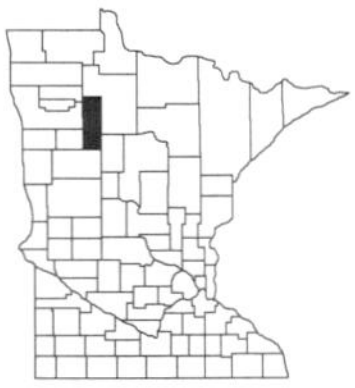

Clearwater County

Some may shake their heads in disbelief — a few may even be enraged — at the following statement, but the truth must prevail. Itasca State Park is just an average place for birding. True, Minnesota's oldest and most famous park is the source of the Mississippi River, and its lakes and pines and other woodlands are certainly pretty enough. And, yes, there is a decent variety of birds here, especially in summer, including some of the specialties of the Northeast Region. But, no, it cannot be said this park specializes in any of them. If you miss Itasca, you probably won't miss any birds.

Remember, however, to call a place in this region "average" is not an insult. It only means you can still see such widespread birds as Common Loon, Bald Eagle, Broad-winged Hawk, Ruffed Grouse, Barred Owl, Alder Fly-

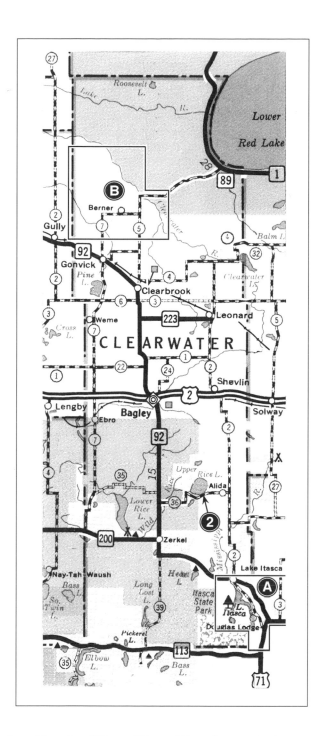

Boreal Chickadee, and Connecticut and other warblers. If you have the time and an abundance of optimism, continue north and east along 95 into a drier area of jack pines where the elusive Spruce Grouse is occasionally seen.

Within Itasca itself, there is another good spruce-tamarack bog marked on inset A along Highway 200 at the northeast corner of the park. But probably the best birding in the park is around the stands of larger coniferous trees at the **University of Minnesota's Field Station** (formerly named the Forestry School) and at **Douglas Lodge**, both marked **A1**, and both worth checking in fall and winter for grosbeaks or crossbills.

Time permitting, you should also take the so-called **Wilderness Drive** (also **A1**) west and south of Lake Itasca, which will at least lead you away from most of the tourists. True to its name, it actually passes by the west and south sides of the 1,580-acre Itasca Wilderness Scientific and Natural Area, where there is a large stand of virgin red and white pines. Try especially the Bohall and Nicollet trails for Black-backed Woodpecker and other boreal specialties.

While Lake Itasca may be more picturesque, a more interesting lake for birding lies a short distance north of the park. **Upper Rice Lake (2)** has long been known for its nesting Red-necked Grebes, in recent years Western Grebes have also been noted, and this lake has a summer record for a stray Pacific Loon. County Road 36 west of Alida provides the best view of the lake.

Wooded lake country mixed with farmlands predominates in most of the county, but more interesting is the landscape in relatively remote **northern Clearwater County (inset B)**, a mixture of grain fields, sedge meadows, wild rice paddies, brushlands, tamarack bogs, and aspen parklands. Much of this country is roadless, inaccessible, and part of the Red Lake Indian Reservation (where, at best, the residents tolerate birders and other visitors).

Inset B maps the roads in the more accessible portion of this area, where Northern Goshawk, Rough-legged Hawk, Sharp-tailed Grouse, Sandhill Crane, Marbled Godwit, Black-billed Magpie, Northern Shrike, Sedge Wren, Clay-colored, Grasshopper and Le Conte's sparrows, Snow Bunting, and Common Redpoll could be expected in season. Here, as well, it is worth searching for rarities such as Gyrfalcon, Yellow Rail, Snowy, Northern Hawk, Great Gray and Short-eared owls, Nelson's Sharp-tailed Sparrow, and Hoary Redpoll.

In particular be sure to check to see if any of the the wild rice paddies on inset B are still in business. Like other rice paddies, these are best scanned in April for waterfowl, especially swans (both migrant Tundras and summering Trumpeters), and in May for shorebirds. Whether or not you find any, be sure to check the large and impressive **water impoundment (B3)** along the Clearwater River. Besides swans and shorebirds, when the water levels are right, check the sedge meadows here for Yellow Rails and Nelson's Sharp-tailed Sparrows.

Elsewhere in northern Clearwater County, Highway 1/89 provides a few good vantage points for scanning Lower Red

catcher, Gray Jay, Winter Wren, Mourning and other warblers, and Evening Grosbeak. Note that birders have long been coming to Itasca, and over the years this coverage has turned up such impressive strays as Magnificent Frigatebird (a first state record), Swallow-tailed Kite, and Williamson's Sapsucker (Minnesota's second record).

Itasca State Park and vicinity (**inset A**) overlaps into Hubbard County, and some of the best birding spots in this area actually lie in that county outside the park boundary. Probably the most interesting of these is the so-called **Lake Alice Bog (A1)**, which can be accessed from County Roads 3 and 95. Over the years, these spruce, tamaracks, and alders have had nesting Black-backed Woodpecker, Olive-sided, Yellow-bellied and Alder flycatchers, Gray Jay,

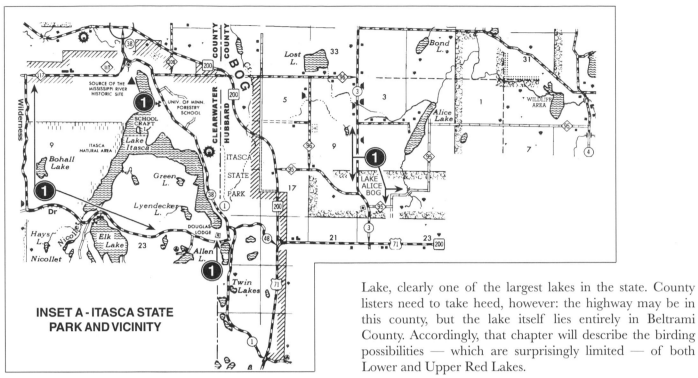

INSET A - ITASCA STATE PARK AND VICINITY

Lake, clearly one of the largest lakes in the state. County listers need to take heed, however: the highway may be in this county, but the lake itself lies entirely in Beltrami County. Accordingly, that chapter will describe the birding possibilities — which are surprisingly limited — of both Lower and Upper Red Lakes.

Finally, there are two sets of sewage ponds. One is at Clearbrook: from County Road 5, go 2 miles west on County Road 4, and 0.3 mile south to the gate. And in Bagley, turn east from Highway 92 on County Road 19 at the Baptist Church, follow 19 for 1.1 miles, then go 0.5 mile north.

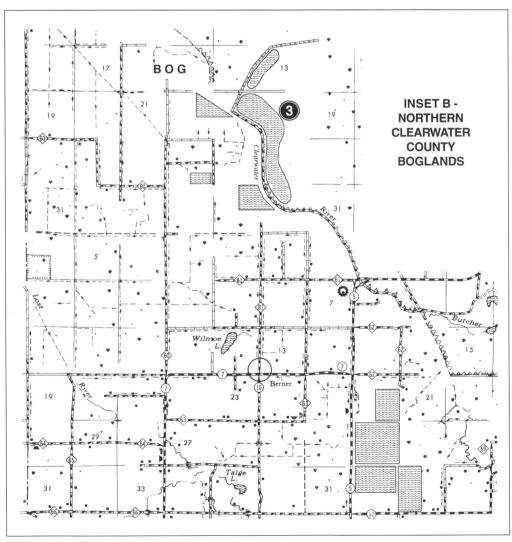

INSET B - NORTHERN CLEARWATER COUNTY BOGLANDS

Beltrami County

If you want to go fishing or simply relax among lakes and pines, southern Beltrami County is for you. If you want to see birds, however, head for the northern half. This relatively remote country, which includes the southern third of the nearly 600,000 acres of Beltrami Island State Forest and Red Lake Wildlife Management Area, extends from the Red Lakes north into Lake of the Woods County and east into Koochiching County. It is often and quite appropriately referred to as the Big Bog.

Roads in much of this area are few and far between, leaving literally hundreds of square miles quite inaccessible. While parts of this wilderness are fragmented by a mix of grain fields and aspen groves, much of it consists of miles of tamarack bogs, alder swamps, and sedge marshes. The birding possibilities, therefore, include those listed in the previous chapter under Clearwater County's inset B, which is a similar landscape.

Northern Beltrami County also includes a denser coniferous forest dimension of spruce, white cedar, and balsam fir. Accordingly, you could find such species as Black-backed Woodpecker, Olive-sided and Yellow-bellied flycatchers, Gray Jay, Boreal Chickadee, Cape May, Connecticut and other warblers, and crossbills. Rarities such as Gyrfalcon, Northern Hawk and Great Gray owls would be more of a possibility here than in northern Clearwater County, and with luck you would even have a chance of seeing a Spruce Grouse, Boreal Owl, or Three-toed Woodpecker.

Those with an urge to explore and test their navigation skills might want to wander first along those roads shown in northwestern Beltrami County. Note there aren't that many roads here, and a few navigational notes might be helpful. Dick's Parkway, the forest road north of Fourtown, comes to the Lake of the Woods County line in about 19 miles. In 3 more miles you can turn east to enter Lake of the Woods County's inset B; or continue north another mile and then west into Roseau County's inset D. Another choice is to turn east on County Road 704, 3 miles north of Fourtown, which becomes the Rapid River Forest Road and enters the southwest corner of the Lake of the Woods County's inset C map, about 27 miles from Fourtown.

There are also good roads to explore east of the two Red Lakes in **northeastern Beltrami County (inset A)**. If you are short of time, the three best roads on this map are Highway 72 and County Roads 40 and 111. This latter road parallels 72 and passes through some good bogs northwest of Kelliher. County Road 40 leads north and east from Waskish, exits the inset A map, and becomes a forest road at the Koochiching County line; in about 26 miles, this road eventually connects with Koochiching County Road 30 and ends at Big Falls. Note the inset A map also marks the locations of some wild rice paddies which, if still there, are always worth checking in spring.

Even more interesting is the country north of inset A, where there are two roads which are particularly interesting — primarily because they are literally the only roads in the county north of Upper Red Lake. **Highway 72 (1)** traverses miles of beautiful open tamarack bogs and sedge marshes which extend into Lake of the Woods County. Here you will see the true meaning of the term "Big Bog," as many of the inaccessible miles on both the east and west sides of 72 comprise the 80,000-plus acres of the Red Lake Peatland Scientific and Natural Area.

Look especially in winter for a Gyrfalcon or Northern Hawk Owl (both rare), Snowy Owl, Northern Shrike, Snow Bunting, and both redpolls; note that Hoarys, though always outnumbered by Commons, tend to prefer relatively open country such as this. In summer, listen for Yellow Rails and Nelson's Sharp-tailed Sparrows, while Sharp-tailed Grouse, Great Gray and Short-eared owls, and Black-billed Magpie are possible any time of year.

Equally interesting is the 13-mile-long road along the **north side of Upper Red Lake** (also marked 1), which turns west off Highway 72, about 5 miles north of Waskish. This dead-end road provides a few views of the lake, passes some wild rice paddies, and is one of the best places in the county to look for Sharp-tailed Grouse. In addition, Spruce Grouse, Black-backed Woodpecker, Boreal Chickadee, and other boreal specialties have been found in the denser conifer stands. One place to try for these is along the trail going north from the road, 3 miles west of Highway 72.

* * *

Of course, Upper and Lower Red Lakes comprise the most prominent feature on the Beltrami County map. As might be expected, the vast size of these lakes might occasionally attract birds more characteristic of Lake Superior: e.g., un-common loons, Long-tailed Duck, scoters, Barrow's Goldeneye, a jaeger, or unusual gulls. More likely in summer or migration would be any of the grebes, pelicans, swans, ducks, Franklin's and Bonaparte's gulls, and Caspian and other terns. Despite all these possibilities, however, the birding on these lakes tends to be surprisingly dull much of the time.

During periods of lower water levels, check any sand bars for shorebirds, and the considerable length of shoreline of these lakes at times will funnel through numbers of hawks

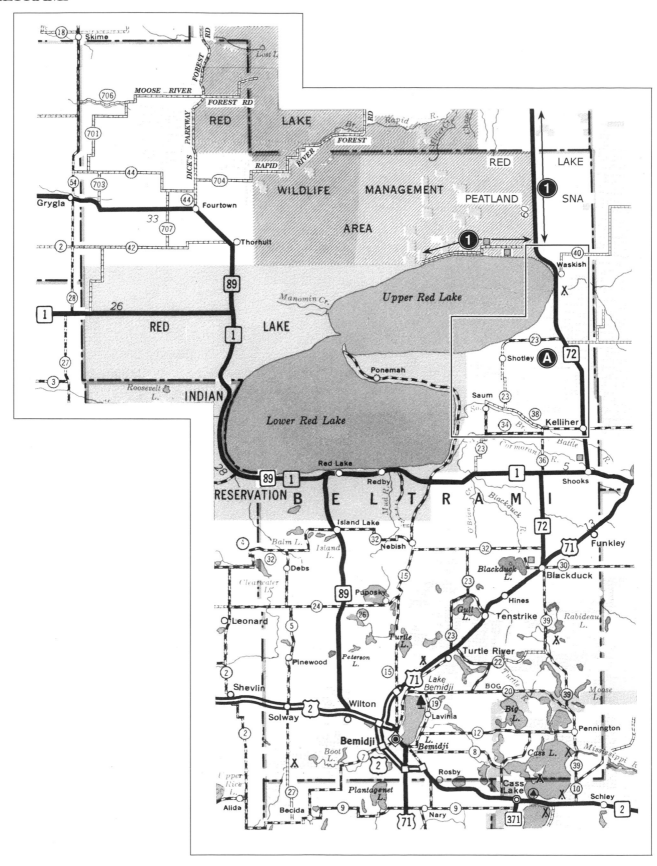

and passerines during migration. A good portion of the shorelines of these lakes is inaccessible, however, making them relatively difficult to scan. Besides that road along the

north side of Upper Red Lake mentioned above, this lake is most visible from four spots shown on the inset A map:

• In Waskish at the public accesses at the mouth of the

Tamarac River.

• Just south of Waskish, from the end of the road which turns west off Highway 72, 1.3 miles south of the river.

• The campground on County Road 23, 2 miles north of Shotley.

• The public access north of County Road 108, 3 miles west and 1 mile north of Shotley.

It may look on the county map that Lower Red Lake would be accessible along Highway 1 and from the road through Battle River (see inset A) and Ponemah. Actually, the lake is only visible intermittently from these roads, and the best views are from the Clearwater County parts of Highway 1/89 on the west side, and on that reservation road on the east side of the lake just north of the Blackduck River. Also note the entire lake lies within the Red Lake Indian Reservation, including that most intriguing-looking point between the lakes near Ponemah. If you venture that far, however, avoid the vicinity of the cemetery which is off-limits to non-natives.

(Use discretion if you choose to bird anywhere within the reservation. I know of no unpleasant incidents, but some

INSET A - NORTHEASTERN BELTRAMI COUNTY BOGLANDS

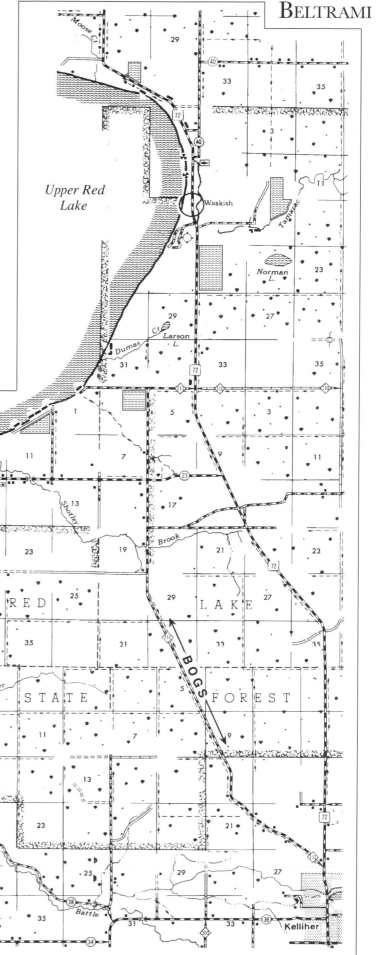

birders report never feeling entirely comfortable on these roads that, after all, are not ours.)

The southern half of Beltrami County includes numerous lakes of more modest size. The best of these might be Lake Bemidji, which is good for ducks and other water birds in early spring and late fall since it tends to freeze later and thaw earlier than most. Birding tends to be best where the Mississippi River flows into the lake along Highway 197 just southeast of downtown Bemidji. Also check where the river flows out of the east side of the lake: continue southeast on 197 to 1st Street, go 1 mile east to County Road 12, then north 1.5 miles on 12, and north another half mile on County Road 19.

While you're in the neighborhood, continue north on 19 to County Road 20 and the entrance to Lake Bemidji State Park. The best woods birding in the park, summer or winter, would probably be along the Bass Creek Trail and the boardwalk trail which passes through a nice spruce-tamarack bog. Another good bog is along County Road 20, 8 miles east of the park entrance, where Black-backed Woodpecker, Boreal Chickadee, and other coniferous forest specialties have been found.

If you're in Bemidji during late fall or winter, be sure to watch for Bohemian Waxwing flocks in residential areas, especially where there are mountain ash trees and berries. Note as well that stands of red and jack pines are widespread in southern Beltrami County. Crossbills, especially Reds, should occur some years in fall and winter, Pine Warblers are present during summer, and Connecticuts should be in some of the jack pine flats.

There are sewage ponds at Blackduck, west of town on County Road 30, 0.2 mile north of the Pine Tree County Park entrance.

Lake of the Woods County

It is said you can't tell a book by its cover. Take this guide, for example. Note the look of assurance and focus in the Great Gray Owl's eyes. Then turn to the counties inside, which seem only vaguely familiar to the author as he advises readers to wander around on their own. A parallel maxim might be you can't tell a county by its chapter length. That is certainly true of Lake of the Woods County, one of the best in the state. The lake itself and this county's portion of Beltrami Island State Forest / Red Lake Wildlife Management Area have already been discussed in the chapters on Roseau and Beltrami counties, leaving this chapter to be of only moderate length.

To begin with, while all of **Lake of the Woods (inset A)** this side of the Canadian border lies within this county of the same name, some of the lake's best vantage points are along Roseau County's portion of the shoreline, and that county's chapter describes its excellent birding potential. Although this lake is a long way from where most birders live, the coverage here has been good enough to at least turn up strays like a mid-summer Harlequin Duck, Little Gull, and multiple records of both Parasitic Jaeger and Sabine's Gull.

One vantage point on the lake is at **Arnesen (1)**, and on inset A are four other **accesses (A1):**

• From the dead-end roads in and around Lude.

• In Zipple Bay State Park (the woods in the park are mostly deciduous and not that interesting).

• Along the 2-mile length of County Road 4, between the state park and Morris Point.

• And especially at Morris Point, on nearby Pine Island, and the now-contiguous Curry Island. (The latter island, spelled Currys or Curry's on some maps, was formerly a separate island.)

The beaches in this last area, now protected as the Pine and Curry Island Scientific and Natural Area, often are good for migrant shorebirds (there is even a Snowy Plover record), but more significant is the small population of nesting Piping Plovers. This is now the only site in Minnesota where this endangered species breeds, although their numbers and the undisturbed beach acreage seem to dwindle every year.

The best way to see them is to rent a boat from Morris Point Resort and circumnavigate the island(s). But it's also OK to park at the resort and walk east along the beach towards Morris Point, where the plovers are often seen, as they were in 2001, and where you can try scoping out the island. However, do not walk on the point beyond the signs posted April-September to protect the plovers from disturbance; similarly, do not land on the island where posted.

There is another part of the lake on the map that might arouse some curiosity, but I don't recommend the birding there. True, the Northwest Angle is the most northerly point in the 48 contiguous United States, but the woods along the road to Angle Inlet are pretty ordinary, and there is nothing much to see from the end of the road (except a couple of marinas and the ubiquitous Walleye Fisherman). But if

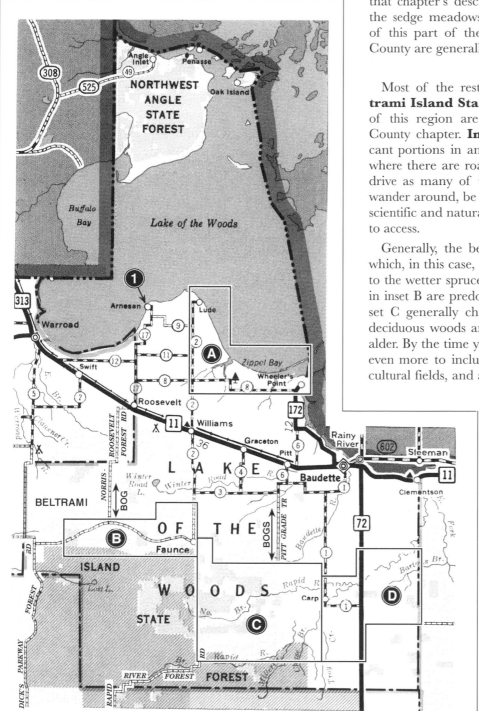

that chapter's description of the birding possibilities in the sedge meadows, brushlands, pastures, and hayfields of this part of the state; those in Lake of the Woods County are generally found north of Highway 11.

*   *   *

Most of the rest of the county lies within the **Beltrami Island State Forest**, and the habitats and birds of this region are discussed in the previous Beltrami County chapter. **Insets B, C, and D** map the significant portions in and around this vast boreal forest (i.e., where there are roads), and it is recommended that you drive as many of these roads as possible. And, as you wander around, be aware there are six large and roadless scientific and natural areas in the forest you won't be able to access.

Generally, the best roads to try are marked "BOG," which, in this case, includes upland jack pines in addition to the wetter spruce and tamarack bogs. Note the woods in inset B are predominantly coniferous. Farther east, inset C generally changes from denser conifer stands to deciduous woods and more open bogs of tamarack and alder. By the time you reach inset D, the landscape opens even more to include sedge meadows, brushlands, agricultural fields, and a few wild rice paddies (two especially large ones are marked on the inset D map). Be sure to follow Highway 72 south from inset D towards the Beltrami County line to experience the "Big Bog" at its best.

If you're short of time, there are two areas where you would probably have the best luck. One is in inset B in the vicinity of the **Norris Camp game refuge headquarters (B2)**. There are extensive jack pines west of here along the Faunce-Butterfield Forest Road for the next several miles where Connecticut Warblers are actually common and quite approachable in these drier uplands. Be sure to bird as well in the spruce-tamarack-white cedar bogs along the same road for the first 3 miles east of headquarters. Fairly reliable here are birds such as Black-backed Woodpecker, Olive-sided Flycatcher (curiously hard to find in Minnesota in summer), Yellow-bellied Flycatcher, Boreal Chickadee, and Cape May Warbler.

The other road especially favored by birders for both winter and summer residents is in inset C, the **Pitt Grade Forest Road (C3).** This road traverses a variety of habitats, from deciduous woodlands at its south end near the Rapid River, through some good spruce bogs and jackpine stands farther north, to the tamarack and alder swamps

you're still curious: take Highway 310 or 313 from Roseau County into Canada and to Manitoba Highway 12; at the town of Sprague turn north on 308, and follow the signs to Highway 525, which leads to Lake of the Woods County Road 49 in the Northwest Angle.

As previously noted in the Roseau County chapter, the wooded areas along the Lake of the Woods shoreline should also serve at times as concentration points for migrant passerines trying to find their way around the lake. Also note

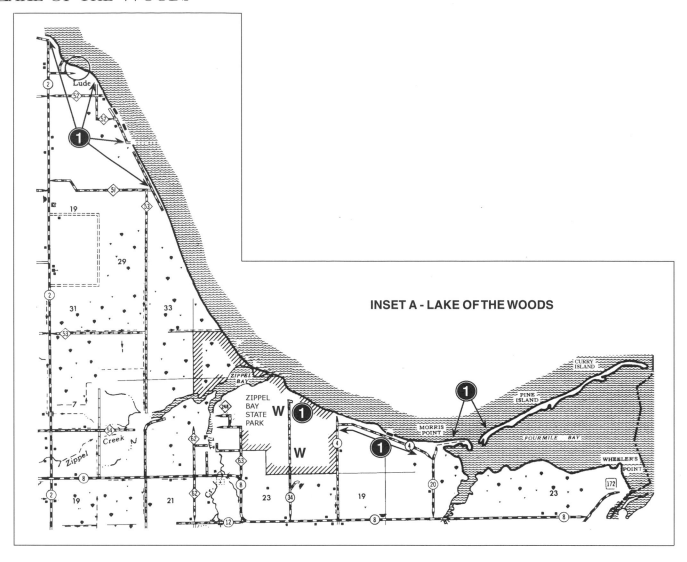

INSET A - LAKE OF THE WOODS

where the road emerges out of the north side of the state forest. Another good road through lots of coniferous areas for boreal specialties is the Faunce Forest Road farther west: it forms the west edge of the inset C map and the east edge of the inset B map.

Besides the presence of Connecticut Warblers (also found in the tamarack bogs), birders should be particularly aware that Spruce Grouse are reportedly widespread in this forest's jack pines. Like everywhere else, though, they are difficult to find. Northern Hawk and Great Gray owls are both possible, mostly in winter, but there are a few hawk owl breeding records in this part of the state. The rare Three-toed Woodpecker is possible at any time of year in the conifers. Less glamorous perhaps, but still noteworthy, is the presence of Pine Warblers and Red Crossbills in the jack pines, while Palm Warblers (mostly uncommon and local in summer in Minnesota) nest commonly in this forest's open tamarack bogs.

Time now to pass on some navigational hints for the truly adventurous:

• The road leading west off the inset B map comes to a T in 3 miles. A left here on Dick's Parkway leads south some 22 miles to Fourtown in Beltrami County; a right at the T goes a mile north and a mile west into Roseau County's inset D via the Winner Forest Road.

• The Rapid River Forest Road leads from the southwest corner of inset C and in about 27 miles eventually goes to Fourtown and Highway 89 in Beltrami County.

• The road leading east from the southeast corner of the inset D map goes into Koochiching County, eventually joins County Road 32 in about 20 miles, and continues to Loman.

• Be sure to note as well that some of the back roads in this and other state and national forests are only minimally maintained and may not be passable in winter or wet weather. Some also defy the cartographers' best efforts: even the most current maps fail to show when old logging roads are abandoned or new ones are built.

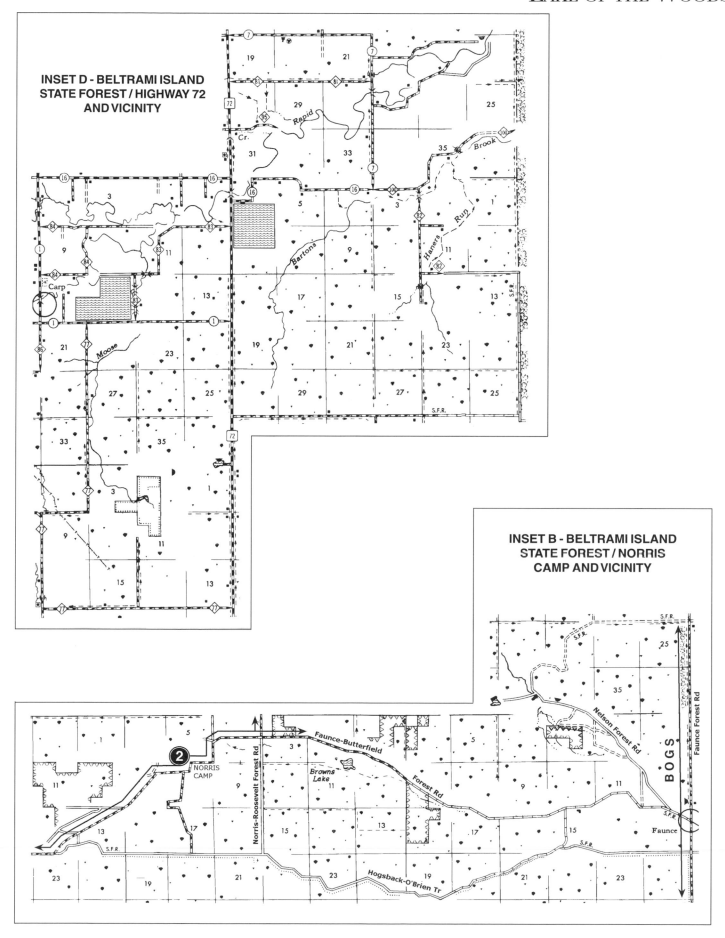

INSET D - BELTRAMI ISLAND STATE FOREST / HIGHWAY 72 AND VICINITY

INSET B - BELTRAMI ISLAND STATE FOREST / NORRIS CAMP AND VICINITY

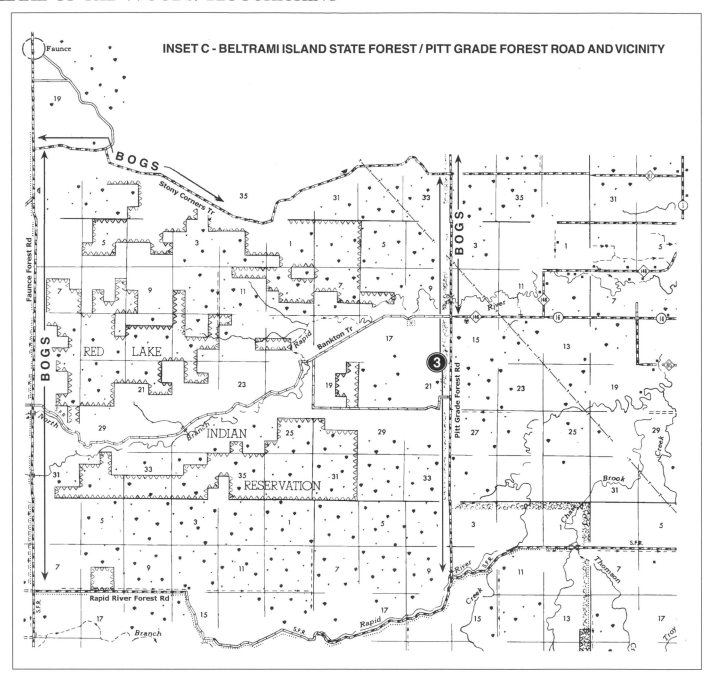

INSET C - BELTRAMI ISLAND STATE FOREST / PITT GRADE FOREST ROAD AND VICINITY

Koochiching County

As stated in previous editions of this guide, Koochiching has long been one of the most remote, inaccessible, and poorly known of Minnesota's 87 counties. It still is. While there are other counties whose birds and birding areas are only superficially known, in those cases we're pretty sure we're not missing much. Either their habitats or geographi-

cal position suggests there wouldn't be that much to see even if they were thoroughly covered.

Koochiching County, however, is another story. There certainly are Northeast Region specialties in the extensive coniferous forests that predominate through most of the county. In this case, we know we're missing a lot. So find

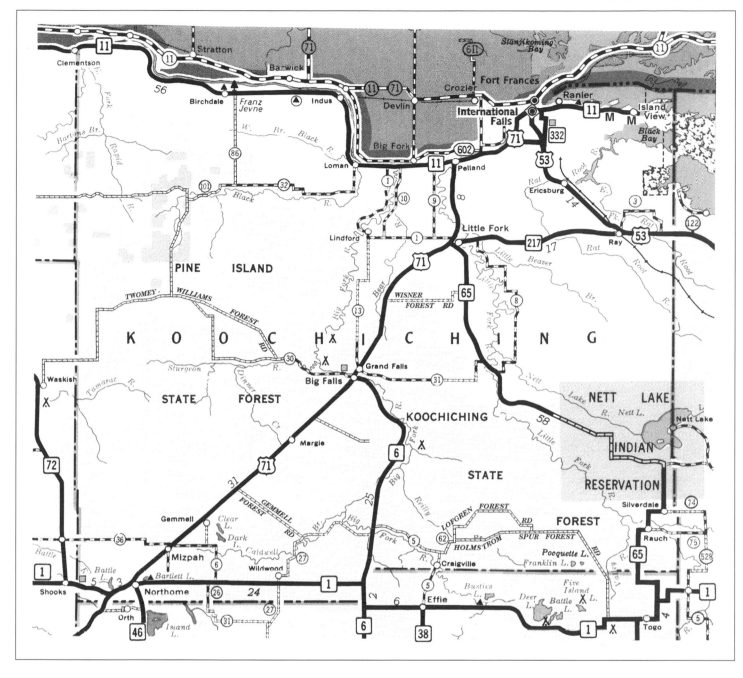

yourself a county map, make the effort to get up there (it's only a five-hour drive from the Twin Cities), and start exploring those back roads. These roads are relatively few and far between in this remote region, but they mostly go for many miles, so it might take a while to cover them.

One time to visit would be between late May and early July for passerines: at least 22 species of warblers nest in the county, including lots of Connecticuts. Or try November through March to search for owls and winter finches — though you won't find all the back roads plowed and passable then. Or come at any time of year for Spruce Grouse, Great Gray and Boreal (best heard in late March) owls, Three-toed (rare) and Black-backed woodpeckers, Boreal Chickadee, and other permanent residents.

Since much of eastern Koochiching County is predomi-

nantly deciduous woods (generally east of a line from Loman to the Valley River), exploration would be most worthwhile along the roads in the Pine Island and Koochiching state forests in the western half and south central part of the county. There are 11 roads I'd recommend trying first, all shown on the county key map, where you would probably find the most bogs and birds. So, get out your county map and begin in the center of the county at Big Falls:

• County Road 13, from Grand Falls north to Lindford.

• County Road 101, which continues west from the end of County Road 32, about 17 miles from Loman; where 101 ends at a T intersection, a forest road jogs north for a mile and continues west into Lake of the Woods County's inset D.

- County Road 86, between the west end of County Road 32 and Highway 11 (its north end is 1 mile east of Birchdale).

- The forest road, which turns south at the T at the end of 101, and leads about 11 miles to the Twomey-Williams road.

- County Road 30, which ends about 15 miles west of Big Falls; from here, turn north on the forest road which ends in about 8 miles at the Twomey-Williams road.

- The Twomey-Williams Forest Road, the west end of which begins off County Road 30, about 9 miles west of Big Falls; this road heads generally west into Beltrami County, becomes County Road 40, and comes out at Waskish.

- Highway 71, from Big Falls southwest to Mizpah; also try the dead-end road turning east off 71, about 7 miles southwest of Big Falls.

- The Gemmell Forest Road, which turns southeast off 71, 17 miles southwest of Big Falls, and forks in 8 miles: the left fork goes east and comes out on Highway 6, 1.3 miles south of County Road 5; the right fork goes south to Wildwood and Highway 1.

- The Holmstrom Spur Forest Road which turns east off

County Road 62, 2 miles from Craigville; this road eventually curves south into Itasca County, ending at Highway 1, 3 miles west of the Highway 65 junction. Also check the Lofgren Forest Road, which turns east from the north end of County Road 62 and loops south to the Holmstrom road.

- County Road 31, between Grand Falls and Highway 65.

- And the Wisner Forest Road, which turns east from Highway 71, 6.5 miles north of Big Falls, and comes out on Highway 6, about 6 miles south of Little Fork.

For a change of pace, try some water birding during migration. There are wild rice paddies on Highway 1 just east of the Beltrami County line, down in the southwestern corner of the county. Or check the sewage ponds at Big Falls (1.2 miles west on County Road 30) and International Falls (1.7 miles south on Highway 332). And, at or near Ranier on Rainy Lake east of International Falls, there have been records of Harlequin Duck and Little and Glaucous gulls.

For a real change, there are two marshes on Highway 11, about 8 and 11 miles east of International Falls. Virginia Rail, Marsh Wren, and Yellow-headed Blackbird — all quite local or absent in this part of the state — have been reported here in summer. Perhaps a Least Bittern, Yellow Rail, or Nelson's Sharp-tailed Sparrow could also occur.

Itasca County

The birding coverage in Itasca County isn't any better than in Koochiching, even though just about all of the Northeast specialties can occur here in habitat and in season. But there aren't really any specific locations that specialize in the things most birders are looking for; in a way, there is more quantity than quality in Itasca County's habitats. There are a couple of hundred lakes, lots of deciduous and mixed woods, numerous pine stands, and several scattered spruce and tamarack bogs, any of which could be worthwhile at times.

Probably the best coniferous woods in the county are in and around **Scenic State Park (1)**, just southeast of Bigfork off County Road 7. True to its name, this park is scenic, and it's a good place to see some of the specialties of the Northeast Region. In particular, Spruce Grouse have been seen several times over the years along the old road which leads to the fire observation tower in the northern part of the park. This road is currently open to vehicle access before Memorial Day Weekend and after Labor Day, and the best grouse area is reportedly east of the tower, more than 2 miles up the road. There have even been nesting records for Three-toed Woodpecker, though a Blackbacked would be more likely.

A big chunk of the Chippewa National Forest lies in Itasca County, though, as described in the Cass County chapter, its birding potential is limited. But one good place discovered in a recent summer by researchers doing bird surveys is the bog along the Alder Road, where Great Gray Owl, Yellow-bellied Flycatcher, Boreal Chickadee, and Connecticut Warbler were all located. From Marcell, turn south off Highway 38 on County Road 262, go 2.7 miles to a T, and here the Alder Road / County Road 253 goes southwest for 5 miles through the bog.

As described in the Cass County chapter, the best birding lake in this part of the state, especially during migration, is **Lake Winnibigoshish (2)**. The most accessible vantage points are in Cass County, but there are three accesses on the Itasca County side from which to scan:

- Plug Hat Point campground and public access is reached by turning north off County Road 9, just east of the dam on the Mississippi River.

- To reach another public access, go east on 9 to Highway 46, north on 46 for 4 miles, then west on County Road 148; in a half mile, follow the left fork to the lake.

- And on the west side of the lake is the Winnie camp-

ground / public access, but you'll need a county or national forest map to follow the directions: go west off Highway 46 on County Road 33, after several miles go south on Forest Road 2171, then east on Forest Road 2168 to the lake.

And finally, though there are no known sewage ponds in the county, there are at least some fish hatchery ponds that might have shorebirds when water levels are drawn down in the fall. Turn east off Highway 46 to Island Lake, 1 mile south of the Koochiching County line.

St. Louis County

As mentioned in the introduction, there are entire states smaller than this county, a place large enough that its key map doesn't fit on a single page. Not only is St. Louis County larger by far than any other county in the state, but ornithologically it is also better than any other. Of the 427 species currently on the Minnesota list, at least 360 have been recorded in this county. But the vast size of the county isn't the reason for its long list. Rather, it is the presence of Duluth situated at the western tip of Lake Superior. Indeed, of the birds on the St. Louis County list, all but about 30 of these have been found within Duluth's corporate limits.

DULUTH

Like St. Louis County, Duluth is also large, over 23 miles in length, and there is plenty of room in its city limits for birds in its range of habitats: extensive deciduous woodlands, stands of conifers, alder thickets and fields on the outskirts of town, residential areas with feeders and mountain ash trees, marshes in the backwaters of the St. Louis River, a large harbor with sandbars and mudflats, Lake Superior's beaches and rocky shorelines, and, of course, the lake itself — which is even open in most winters.

Most importantly, Duluth's geographic location on the lake attracts a long list of migrants concentrated along the North Shore of Lake Superior and at such famed locations as Park Point and Hawk Ridge. Accordingly, Duluth is not only a place to see Northeast Region specialties, but several birds which are local or rare on a statewide basis turn up here regularly. And sightings of Casual and Accidental species are almost routine.

During either spring or fall migration on Lake Superior or the harbor, watch especially for loons (three species seen annually), Horned and Red-necked grebes, Greater Scaup, scoters (uncommon to rare), shorebirds, gulls, and other water birds. Olive-sided, Yellow-bellied and other flycatchers, Philadelphia and other vireos, warblers (26 species annually, including the elusive Black-throated Blue and Connecticut), American Tree, Harris's, and other sparrows, and many passerines funnel through down the North Shore and along Park Point.

Migrants more partial to spring include Red-throated Loon (rare but annual on the lake), Tundra Swans and other waterfowl, raptors along West Skyline Parkway or at Park Point (in fall, of course, they're at Hawk Ridge), rarer shorebirds (such as Piping Plover, Willet, Whimbrel, Hudsonian and Marbled godwits, and Red Knot), and Bonaparte's Gulls in the harbor (often by the hundreds, sometimes with

a Little Gull among them).

Spring is also the best time to hear — and therefore to see — such breeding species as Ruffed Grouse, American Woodcock, Barred, Long-eared (rare), and Northern Saw-whet owls. Other nesting species of note in Duluth and vicinity include Peregrine Falcon, Upland Sandpiper, Common Tern, Black-billed Cuckoo, Yellow-bellied and Alder flycatchers, Winter and Sedge wrens, Veery, Wood Thrush, Golden-winged, Mourning, Canada and many other warblers, Clay-colored and Le Conte's sparrows, and Evening Grosbeak.

Fall is generally much more interesting, primarily due to the number of migrants attracted to Lake Superior or trying to find their way around lake. Noteworthy species more evident in fall than spring: Pacific Loon (now annual), Harlequin Duck (one or two each fall-winter), Parasitic Jaeger (a few annually at Park Point; records of Pomarine and Long-tailed also exist), hawks by the thousands (including Northern Goshawks, Golden Eagles, and Peregrines) and banded Northern Saw-whet Owls by the hundreds at Hawk Ridge, Buff-breasted Sandpipers in early fall at Park Point, American Pipit, Lapland Longspur (and sometimes a Smith's), Snow Bunting, Rusty Blackbird, and Red and White-winged crossbills (which sometimes disappear by winter).

Fall is also the time when rarities tend to be seen at the feeders, mountain ash trees, or coniferous trees in town: Black-backed Woodpecker (and sometimes a Three-toed), Gray Jay, Boreal Chickadee, Mountain Bluebird, Townsend's Solitaire, Varied Thrush, Northern Mockingbird, and Summer Tanager.

Additionally, several Northeast Region specialties usually thought of as winter birds can be seen as migrants: Gyrfalcon (not every year, but worth looking for in the harbor), Thayer's and Glaucous gulls (uncommon), Snowy Owl (regularly on the harbor ice and around the grain elevators), Northern Hawk and Great Gray owls (easy in some winters; rare or absent in others), Boreal Owl (rare most winters; best listened for elsewhere in early spring), Northern Shrike, Bohemian Waxwing (in residential areas), Pine and Evening grosbeaks, and both Common and Hoary (uncommon most winters) redpolls.

In case anyone still needs convincing that Duluth is the premier birding location in Minnesota, that almost anything is possible here, following are some more impressive Accidentals recorded: Yellow-billed Loon (twice), Black Vulture, Wilson's Plover (twice!), Glaucous-winged and Ivory gulls, Sandwich Tern (!), Band-tailed Pigeon, White-winged Dove, Common Ground-Dove, Western Wood-Pewee, Vermilion and Fork-tailed flycatchers, Clark's Nutcracker,

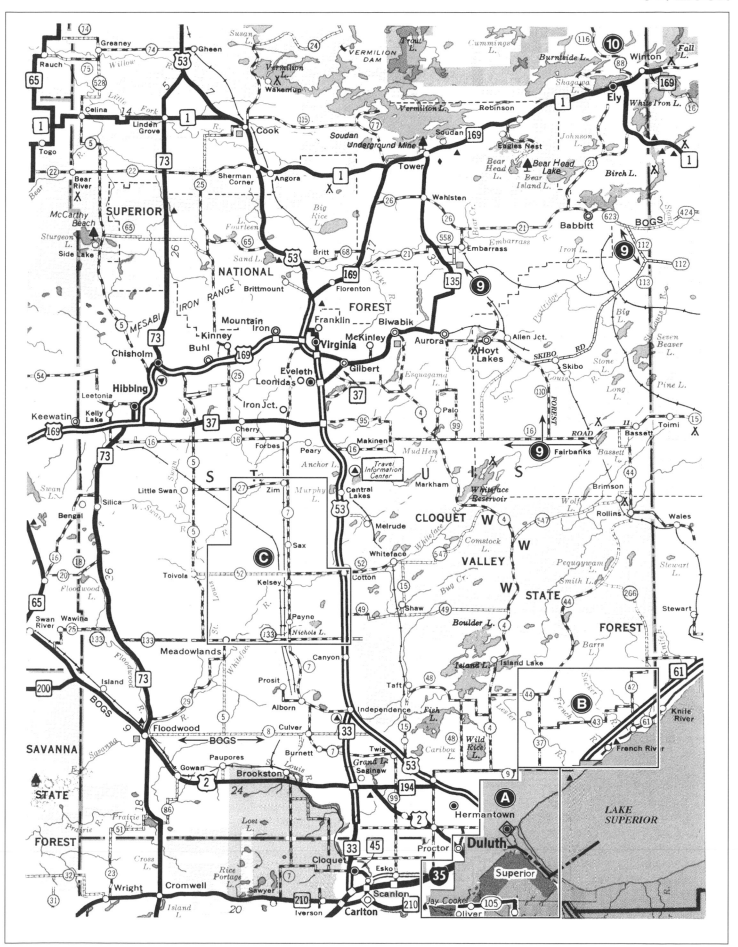

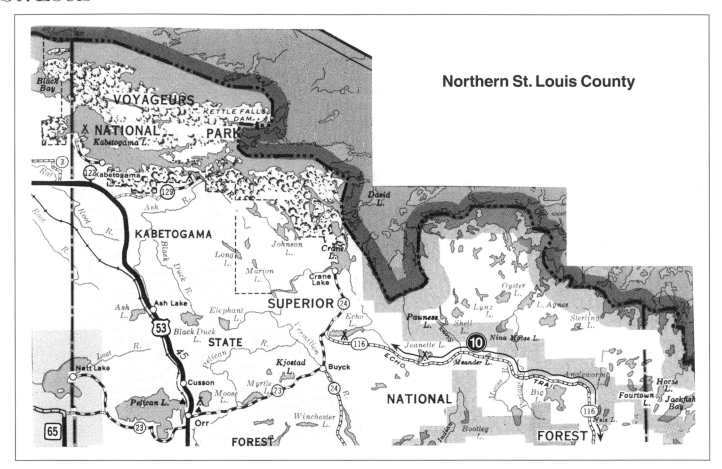

Northern St. Louis County

Northern Wheatear, Green-tailed Towhee, Black-throated (twice) and Golden-crowned sparrows, McCown's Longspur (twice), Scott's and Bullock's orioles, Gray-crowned Rosy-Finch, and Cassin's Finch.

Note that the entire list of vagrants is much longer (offhand, I can remember records for all but seven of the state's Casuals), and note most of these in Duluth and farther up the North Shore in Lake and Cook counties have turned up in fall.

CANAL PARK / PARK POINT / LAKE SUPERIOR

The **Inset A** map covers **Duluth** proper, and downtown is the natural place to begin. From the corner of Superior Street (Duluth's "main street") and Lake Avenue (the "zero avenue" separating Duluth's numbered avenues, east from west), follow Lake Avenue across Interstate 35 to the stoplight at Railroad Street. Here, if it's late October though mid-May, continue straight on Canal Park Drive into **Canal Park (A1)**. (Or, if you prefer to head directly out to Park Point, turn right on Railroad Street, go one block to another stoplight, turn left, and you're back on Lake Avenue en route to Park Point via the Aerial Lift Bridge.)

The shops, hotels, and restaurants in Canal Park are overrun with tourists and locals in summer and early fall, but at other times of year it's worth checking around the breakwaters by the Lift Bridge for loons, ducks, jaegers, and gulls.

There are also continuous views of the lake along the popular Lakewalk, which runs from Canal Park north to downtown, and then curves northeast to its end at 26th Avenue East. The habitat along the Lakewalk may look like it would be attractive to migrant passerines, but I've never seen much here.

From Canal Park Drive, head over one block to Lake Avenue, cross the Aerial Lift Bridge, Duluth's most famous landmark, and continue to Park Point. This 6-mile-long peninsula (also called Minnesota Point), actually starts after you cross the bridge, and includes some 40 blocks of residences, the Recreation Area, the Sky Harbor Airport, and continues to its end at the Superior Entry shipping channel.

Before heading directly out to the Recreation Area, note that migrants can be seen along any of the residential blocks. Also, to scan Lake Superior for water birds and the beach for shorebirds, you can stop at the public access points at 12th, 16th, 22nd, 31st, and 36th streets. Or, to check the other side of Park Point for ducks, the bay is visible by turning right at 8th, 15th (it's been OK to scan from the Army Reserve parking lot), and 19th streets, and it is almost continually visible from 33rd to 40th streets.

The best of these accesses is via 19th Street: turn right at the stop sign, bear left around the apartment buildings, and follow public access path to the bay next to the marina. From here, you can scope the sandbars on the back side of **Hearding Island (A1)**, where ducks, shorebirds, and gulls often loaf. This spot is best in May, when you can often find flocks of Bonaparte's Gulls, and Caspian and Common terns — sometimes with a Little Gull or two among them. Note there is usually a sandbar on the south side of the island, which can be seen between houses at 24th Street. Also, Hearding Island can be distantly scanned from the Port Terminal across the bay (see below).

When most refer to Park Point, this generally means the **Park Point Recreation Area (A1)** between the bus turn-around at 43rd Street and the airport. I admit it can be dull here in summer (when it crowds with tourists), in winter (unless there is a Snowy Owl on the bay ice), and during migration if

INSET A - DULUTH

migrant passerines; the beaches on the Lake Superior side for shorebirds (watch for rarities like a Piping Plover, Whimbrel, Buff-breasted Sandpiper, or Red Knot); the lake itself for loons, scoters, jaegers, and gulls; the ballfields for loafing gulls (on stormy days), Black-bellied and golden-plovers (if the fields are wet), pipits, and longspurs); and the bay side for scoters and other ducks.

If time permits, walk through the gate to the left of the airport buildings, and hike **beyond Sky Harbor Airport (A1)** where there are two more miles worth of migrants in the trees, on the beach, and in the weedy field along the airport runway. Unless fenced off (a new fence is planned in 2002), be sure to check this latter area in fall for Horned Larks, American Pipits, Lapland Longspurs (and sometimes a Smith's), and Snow Buntings; sometimes a Short-eared

the weather has been too nice for too long. But, as indicated earlier, the Recreation Area has often been the best single spot for birding anywhere in Minnesota, especially when there is rain or fog to ground migrant warblers or northeast winds to blow in jaegers and rare gulls.

The best times are early May to early June in spring and mid-August through mid-October in fall, and just about anything is possible. Check the trees along the dunes for

Owl flushes from the grass.

Time permitting, continue hiking on the beach or on the hiking trail through the pines and other trees all the way to the **Superior Entry** (also **A1**), the shipping channel separating the southern tip of Park Point from the northern tip of Wisconsin Point. Around these breakwaters is probably the best place on Park Point to spot a jaeger or rare gull (Sabine's Gull has been almost annual in recent falls), and in spring watch for Red-throated Loons and Whimbrels.

(You could also reach the Superior Entry by driving around through Superior, Wisconsin, and out to the end of Wisconsin Point — see the SUPERIOR section below. This saves you a 4-mile round-trip hike, and it's easier from there to scan the lake and breakwaters on the Minnesota side.)

DULUTH HARBOR

Winter is perhaps the most interesting time in the harbor area, especially around the grain elevators and railroad tracks along **Garfield Avenue (A2)**, where spilled grain attracts mice and rats and Rock Doves. These in turn annually attract a few Snowy Owls, and this is the most consistent place in the state to find this species. Typically, one or two individuals are present for the season (November to March) on the Duluth side of the harbor, and a few additional owls are temporarily seen as they pass through the area. (There are actually more rats and habitat in Superior on the other side of the harbor; see the SUPERIOR section below.)

The best time to look for owls is at dawn or in late afternoon when they are most actively hunting, perched on just about any structure. During the day, especially when sunny, they tend to sit on the frozen bay and can be difficult to spot among the ice chunks. Most individuals wintering here are immatures and often appear darker than their white surroundings; most also eventually become banded, color-marked, and wing-tagged by local owl researchers. It's not a pretty sight.

To reach Garfield Avenue from Canal Park, take Railroad Street southwest as it parallels Interstate 35 and ends at Garfield by the first grain elevator. Or, take Interstate 535 towards Superior, just before the bridge take the Garfield Avenue / Port Terminal exit, then loop back left under the bridge, and get in the right lane to go on Garfield. Check any of the connecting side streets into the railroad yards along 535, or those which lead towards the grain elevators. Keep clear of the trucks and trains, and stay back from the grain elevators themselves. The best places to scan the bay ice are from the Port Terminal and near Interstate Island (see below).

A few Red-tailed Hawks normally winter in the harbor as well, occasionally a Rough-legged, Merlin, or Peregrine has also overwintered. Yes, there are records of Gyrfalcons subsisting on the harbor's pigeon population. When present, Gyrs tend to arrive for the season in late December and be most active in late morning and early afternoon. A flock of Rock Doves exploding into flight might indicate a Gyr (or another raptor) is after them, and remember that the pigeons on the Superior side are just as tasty. Note, however, the Gyrfalcon is not an annual event here, and overly optimistic birders have misidentified other things as Gyrs.

One of the best places to scan the buildings and bay ice for Snowys and Gyrs is from the **Port Terminal** (also marked **A2**). From the Garfield Avenue - Port Terminal exit off Interstate 535, go straight and then bear left past the United Parcel Service building, bear right at the T, and drive to the edge of the bay opposite Hearding Island. Also be sure to take the road to North Star Steel: turn right at the sign just west of the UPS building, and you'll shortly come to good places to scan the bay ice and a spot from which to scope **Interstate Island** (also marked **A2**).

In summer on Interstate Island, a few Common Terns still nest among hordes of Ring-billed Gulls, and during migration rarities are sometimes spotted among the shorebirds, Bonaparte's Gulls, and Caspian Terns loafing on the sandbars.

During migration, there is one other spot in the harbor area worth checking. To reach this **Erie Pier area** (also **A2**), better known as just "40th," take the 40th Avenue West exit off Interstate 35, cross over to the frontage road on the bay side of the freeway, and park by the large gate just beyond the frontage road. (Even if the gate is open, it can be locked without notice while you are inside, so it's best not to drive in.) Grab your scope and walk up the gravel road which leads to the levee surrounding a large pool where dredge material from the harbor comes and goes.

The water levels here are constantly changing: the pool can be dry and overgrown with weeds, or filled with water, or with low water and mudflats. If you have the time, walk the levee around the entire perimeter of the pool. Watch for water birds of all kinds (including marsh birds in the ponds to the right between the railroad tracks and the freeway), and check the wooded areas for warblers and other migrants. The weedy areas are great places for Horned Larks, American Pipits, sparrows (every Regular species except Henslow's has been seen), Lapland Longspurs (plus an occasional Smith's), and Snow Buntings. Such vagrants as Burrowing Owl, Fork-tailed Flycatcher, Northern Wheatear, and McCown's Longspur all have been found at 40th in recent years.

ST. LOUIS RIVER / WEST SKYLINE PARKWAY

Upstream from the harbor area beyond 40th Avenue West, the St. Louis River becomes more of a river and less of a bay. In this western part of Duluth are the marshes and backwaters of the St. Louis River, an area of primary interest during April when water birds (including flocks of Tundra Swans some years), hawks (especially Bald Eagles), and a variety of other migrants first arrive in Duluth each spring. Unless you have a boat or can walk for miles, there are three areas (all marked **A3**) which provide the best access and birding along the river: Indian Point, Mud Lake and vicinity, and Fond Du Lac.

• To reach **Indian Point Campground**, turn off Grand Avenue / Highway 23 at the sign on 75th Avenue West. This small peninsula is often a good spot for warblers and similar migrants, and there have been days with better warbler waves here than at Park Point. The Western Waterfront Trail also begins just northeast of here, loops around Indian Point, and provides bicycle and hiking access for a couple of miles upstream as far as the Spirit Lake Marina. (This trail will eventually extend farther, but in the meantime you can hike along the railroad tracks beyond the marina, past the Morgan Park and Gary-New Duluth neighborhoods, and all the way to Fond Du Lac.)

• Continuing southwest on Grand Avenue / Highway 23, there is river access at Clyde Avenue (the sign is a quarter mile before the stoplight at Morgan Park Entrance Road) and in Morgan Park (turn left on Beverly Street to the ballfield). A better area is just south of Morgan Park in the Gary-New Duluth section of Duluth. Turn east off Grand Avenue on McCuen Street / Highway 39 (also well-marked) which leads to the **Mud Lake area**. First, pull into the WWJC radio station parking lot just before the bridge to Oliver, Wisconsin, and scan the marshy backwaters. Then backtrack a short distance, park by the gate under the railroad bridge (where there is a meaningless no-trespassing sign), and walk north a short distance to the tracks which lead out into Mud Lake.

If you have time for only one spot on the river, this is normally the best place to look for Tundra Swans and other waterfowl and for Bald Eagles in April. The marshes at Mud Lake (especially at the north end) are also worth birding from May into summer for American Bittern, Green Heron, Virginia Rail, Sora, Marsh Wren, and perhaps Yellow-headed Blackbird — note these species are generally rare or local elsewhere in Duluth. Rarities found at Mud Lake in past years have included Least Bittern, Yellow-crowned Night-Heron, and King Rail.

In this same area are two other places to scan the river. Return to Grand Avenue / Highway 23; at this corner turn left downhill to the so-called Boy Scout Boat Landing. And just west on 23 at the top of the hill is an overlook that offers a wide view of the river.

• Continue west on Highway 23 into **Fond Du Lac** (which, by the way, is still within the city limits), and this is where the river first opens up each spring. Turn left on 131st Avenue West, which becomes Water Street and leads to a nice backwater area and shortly dead ends. Return to 23, continue to the bridge over the St. Louis River and give it one last scan. Just before the bridge, you can turn right on Highway 210 which leads into the hills and deciduous woodlands of Jay Cooke State Park and the St. Louis-Carlton county line.

In the western part of Duluth are two widely separated spots on Skyline Parkway: one is worthwhile for breeding woods birds; the other of note in spring to observe hawk migration.

• Most significant, but under the threat of development, are the beautiful and extensive deciduous forests of **Magney-Snively Park (A4)**, which runs along Skyline Parkway above Morgan Park and Gary-New Duluth. Take the Boundary Avenue / Skyline Parkway exit off Interstate 35 in Proctor, and follow Skyline south past the Spirit Mountain Recreation Area and through the woods. Unless gated for the winter season, the parkway winds its way south and west and eventually comes out on County Road 3 / Becks Road.

Of interest in this seldom-birded area would be a few nesting species that are mostly rare or local elsewhere in Duluth: e.g., Eastern Wood-Pewee, Wood Thrush, Yellow-throated Vireo, Scarlet Tanager, Indigo Bunting, and Eastern Towhee. The habitat also seems right for the possibility of finding a Yellow-billed Cuckoo, Eastern Screech-Owl, Whip-poor-will, or Black-throated Blue Warbler in summer.

• While the fall hawk migration at Hawk Ridge is much more famous, since 1997 there has been a significant spring raptor movement documented from **Enger Tower** on West Skyline Parkway (also **A4**). From 1st Street West, turn up the hill on 11th Avenue West, at 6th Street turn left to Skyline Parkway, and continue west a short distance on Skyline to the first pull-out just below Enger Tower. (On some days, depending on the wind direction, the count site is switched farther west on Skyline to the Thompson Hill Travel Information Center, near the junction of Interstate 35 and Highway 2 in Proctor.)

The raptor count usually starts in early March and ends in mid-May, with the best flight days late March through April. Over 20,000 raptors (vultures included) have been counted each of the past two springs, and in five years a Mississippi Kite and two Gyrfalcons have been recorded. Some of the more significant season totals have been: over 2,200 Turkey Vultures, 271 Ospreys, 2,800+ Bald Eagles, 12,500+ Broad-wingeds, over 6,300 Red-tailed, and 66 Golden Eagles.

HAWK RIDGE

A place like Hawk Mountain in Pennsylvania may have more fame, money, and visitors — too many, some would say. But **Hawk Ridge Nature Reserve (A5)** is the place to go if you want to see hawks in fall. From Highway 61 / London Road, turn up 45th Avenue East (43rd or 47th also will work) to its end at Glenwood Street, turn left on Glenwood and go a half mile to Skyline Parkway at the top of the hill, then turn right on Skyline for a mile to the Main Overlook.

During the past 10 years, an average season's total has been over 88,000 individuals. In 1993, a record 148,000-plus were counted. Other impressive totals include one-day records of 799 Turkey Vultures, 743 Bald Eagles, 1,229 Northern Goshawks (!), 48,000 Broad-wingeds, 3,991 Red-tailed, 204 Rough-leggeds, and 26 Golden Eagles.

Some season-long totals include: 4,368 Bald Eagles in

1994, 5,819 Northern Goshawks in 1982, 110,000-plus Broad-wingeds in 1993, 15,448 Red-taileds in 1994, 133 Golden Eagles in 1994, and 111 Peregrines in 1997.

Sixteen species of hawks are seen annually, while five others are less than annual. Over the years, these have included former-raptor Black Vulture (Minnesota's first in 2001), five Mississippi Kite records, Ferruginous Hawk (once), a few Prairie Falcons, and about a couple of dozen Gyrfalcon sightings.

The counting and banding usually start in mid-August and end around Thanksgiving. The migration is relatively slow in August and November; the bulk of the movement occurs from the second week of September through the third week of October. So, why so many birds? Southbound hawks (and other migrants) are stopped by Lake Superior, funneled down a couple of hundred miles of the North Shore, and all eventually fly past Hawk Ridge as they detour around the lake.

The best days tend to accompany cold fronts with winds from the northwest or west. On most days, hawks tend to start flying a couple of hours after sunrise and to slow down by mid-afternoon. Please don't make the mistake of so many who arrive in the late afternoon, expecting to see hawks after work or school.

Despite the numbers cited above, don't expect to see hundreds or thousands of hawks on every day. There is little or no appreciable movement in fog, during rain, or when the winds are calm or from the south or east. There are also those frustrating days with apparently favorable weather when, for reasons unknown, nothing is flying.

October is usually the most interesting month, as Northern Goshawks, kettles of Red-taileds, and both Bald and Golden eagles are moving through. This is also when most of the owls are netted at the Hawk Ridge Banding Station (generally off-limits without prior arrangement). Most are Northern Saw-whets: 500-1,000 per season on the average, mostly late September to mid-October. Typically, 20-50 Long-eareds are netted in October, and at least one Boreal Owl is banded most years. In 1995, no fewer than 1,402 saw-whets were banded, and on a single night in 1989 there were 292 netted!

With careful searching, a "countable" Northern Saw-whet or Long-eared can sometimes be found roosting by day in conifer groves, or whistled or squeaked in at night. However, avoid walking through the pines adjacent to the Banding Station, since this may disturb the banding operation. Better places to look would be in the thicker conifers along the North Shore, or in the large pine grove along Skyline Parkway at the Ridge (best access is from the Pinewoods Trail, 0.7 mile beyond the Main Overlook).

October is also the best time to watch for other migrants that are often spotted at Hawk Ridge: e.g., Snow Goose, Sandhill Crane, Black-backed Woodpecker (virtually annual in the pines along the Pinewoods Trail, from mid-September into October), Northern Shrike, Gray Jay, Boreal Chickadee, Bohemian Waxwing, Harris's Sparrow, Lapland Longspur, Snow Bunting, Rusty Blackbird, and winter

finches. More unusual species such as Short-eared Owl and Townsend's Solitaire fly by almost every year.

SUPERIOR, WISCONSIN

Before leaving Duluth and heading up the North Shore or to Sax-Zim, there are a few things to be aware of on the Superior side of the harbor. Remember, though, this section is not for the faint-hearted provincial Minnesota lister: you might see something good in Wisconsin you need for your Minnesota list!

• As previously noted, the Superior Entry is probably the best area to spot jaegers and rare gulls on Park Point. Also, from the Wisconsin side you can actually get a better view of the Minnesota side of the lake and breakwaters.

Follow Highway 2/53 south all the way to the far edge of Superior, where you will see an obvious sign for Moccasin Mike Road / Wisconsin Point / Lake Superior just before the large wayside rest. Turn east, and in 1.4 miles (just before the road ends at the dump), turn left and drive 3.1 miles almost to the north end of Wisconsin Point. Just before the stop sign at the T at the end of the road, turn right on a short side road which ends at the sand dunes, set your scope up at the top of the rise, and hope that what flies by passes through Minnesota air space.

• Duluth's landfill attracts no gulls, but Superior's does. Follow the directions above to Moccasin Mike Road, and the dump entrance is 0.2 miles beyond where you turn north to the Superior Entry. The landfill workers almost welcome the company of birders, so feel free to drive in. The landfill's limited hours are currently posted as 8:30 a.m. to 6:45 p.m. on Tuesdays and Thursdays only, but don't be surprised to find the gate closed or open when it isn't supposed to be, and you can still walk in if the gate's closed. If you're looking for a Glaucous, Thayer's, Iceland (rare), or Great Black-backed (rarer) in Duluth-Superior, this would be your best bet from November to March.

• Typically, as mentioned earlier, there are more Snowy Owls to be seen on the Superior side of the harbor on the bay ice, in the railroad yards, and by the grain elevators. And if a Gyrfalcon is around, it's just as likely to be seen in Superior. Check all the likely-looking areas along Highway 53, just west of the Interstate 535 bridge along 3rd Street, and just west of downtown (go west from Tower Avenue on either Winter Street / 9th Street or on Belknap Street / Highway 2).

NORTHEAST OF DULUTH

After the Lakewalk ends at 26th Avenue East, it's not easy to see the lake for the next 34 blocks. But when you reach the mouth of the Lester River just beyond 60th Avenue East, the lake becomes almost continually visible along the way to Lake County. Starting at the Lester River, refer to **inset B**, the map which covers the North Shore and inland

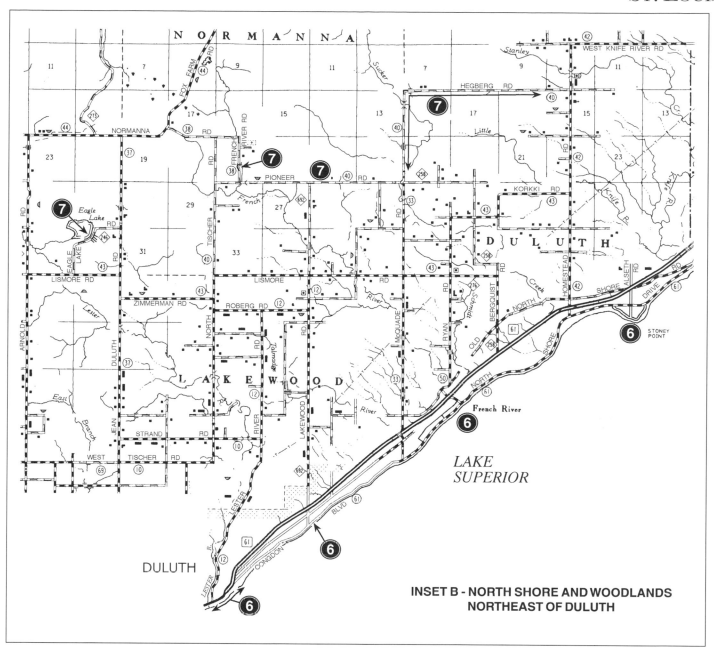

INSET B - NORTH SHORE AND WOODLANDS NORTHEAST OF DULUTH

areas just **northeast of Duluth**. The excellent potential for fall migrant land birds and for northern winter specialties have all previously been discussed, and from here into Lake County you could literally stop anywhere along the North Shore and potentially see something of interest.

There are, however, four places in particular where most birders usually stop: Lester River-Brighton Beach, the Lakewood Pumping Station, French River, and (especially) Stoney Point.

• Start at the **Lester River and Brighton Beach (B6)**, scanning both the lake and trees along the shore. The Brighton Beach Road bears right just after the visitor information booth, and, for reasons unknown, there's a sign here for Kitchi-Gammi Park (even though everyone calls it Brighton Beach). This road, which is unplowed and closed in winter, shortly joins County Road 61 / North Shore Sce-

nic Drive / Congdon Boulevard / North Shore Drive and continues up the North Shore along the lake.

If the road to Brighton Beach is closed, you will come to the Scenic Drive 0.6 mile beyond the Lester River. Here, the main four-lane version of Highway 61 continues straight up the North Shore, and it eventually rejoins the Scenic Drive at Two Harbors in Lake County. Also note that Superior Street runs between these two roads for 3.5 miles as far as McQuade Road. While birders generally prefer the Scenic Drive, it's also worth birding along Superior Street for migrant land birds or along main Highway 61 for raptors in fall-winter.

• About two miles farther along the Scenic Drive is the Lakewood Water Treatment Plant, two large brick buildings birders usually refer to as the **Lakewood Pumping Station (B6)**, or simply "Lakewood." Not only are the lake

227

and trees around the buildings worth a careful check for migrants, but there are some small settling ponds behind the main building — though nothing of special note has ever been seen on them, probably because they're too full of chemicals.

This is also the site of some systematic and impressive counts of fall migrants from the late 1980s into the mid-1990s. Daily coverage from August through October began at dawn, lasted an average of two hours per morning, and about a quarter of a million individuals were counted each year. There were several dates with totals over 10,000, two of these counts exceeded 33,000, and no fewer than 96,000 migrants were counted/estimated on October 1, 1988. There also was that amazing August evening in 1990 when no fewer than 43,690 Common Nighthawks flew by in less than 3 hours!

Other one-day counts included: 14 Black-backed Woodpeckers, an estimated 9,000 Northern Flickers, 103 Gray Jays, 3,415 Blue Jays, 2,051 Black-capped Chickadees, 40 Boreal Chickadees, 62,700 robins, 3,882 Cedar Waxwings, 29,300 warblers (mostly Yellow-rumpeds), 5,370 blackbirds (mostly Red-wingeds), 1,190 redpolls, 7,110 Pine Siskins, and 917 Evening Grosbeaks. Certainly nowhere else in Minnesota is there a migration of land birds which even remotely compares with that along Duluth's North Shore each fall.

• In two more miles you finally reach Duluth's city limits (only some 23 miles from Fond Du Lac at the opposite end of town), Scenic 61 / Congdon Boulevard becomes North Shore Drive, and just beyond is the Lakeview Castle Restaurant. This would easily be the ugliest building in Duluth except for two things: 1) it's not in the city limits; and 2) Duluth's Public Library is uglier.

About a mile after the Castle, watch for gulls in fall-winter by an old fishing boat ramp. Though the flock sometimes attracted here is generally small, both Thayer's and Glaucous have been seen. In another half mile is the mouth of the **French River (B6)**, a popular spot for fishermen and a good spot to scan the lake. Also check the river itself under the road for Harlequin Duck, which has been here or nearby several times in fall-winter.

• Four miles beyond the French River, watch for the large Tom's Logging Camp sign on the left, and turn right here to **Stoney Point** (also **B6**), easily one of the best spots for migrants on the entire North Shore. Stoney Point Drive follows the shore around the point (spelled "Stony" on some maps), returns to North Shore Drive in 0.7 mile, and its entire length is worth hiking. Half way around, Alseth Road also leads north back to the main road, and this is often an even better road to walk in fall. As evidenced by its records of Yellow-billed Loon, Pomarine Jaeger, Laughing and Sabine's gulls, Black-legged Kittiwake, Lark Bunting, Black-throated Sparrow, and other strays, watch for just about anything in the fields, brushy edges, spruce trees, and on the lake itself.

These many possibilities include: Red-throated (spring) and Pacific (fall) loons, Long-tailed Duck, all three scoters, migrating hawks, a roosting Long-eared or Northern Saw-whet owl, Great Gray Owl (or even a Boreal, hunting at dawn or dusk during invasion winters), Black-backed Woodpecker, Gray Jay, Boreal Chickadee (fall or winter), a lost Mountain Bluebird or Townsend's Solitaire or Northern Mockingbird, Bohemian Waxwing, Northern Shrike, migrating warblers (and other woods birds), Lapland Longspur, Snow Bunting, and all of the winter finches (both fall and winter).

Inset B also includes some inland roads northeast of Duluth. The habitats and birds here are nothing special, and this map could have been omitted, but this area is included since so many birders pass by this area. There are small bogs, meadows, and mixed woods here to find many of the Northeast Region's nesting specialties: e.g., Ruffed Grouse, American Woodcock, Black-billed Cuckoo, Barred and Northern Saw-whet owls, Alder Flycatcher, Winter and Sedge wrens, Golden-winged, Blackburnian, Mourning, and other warblers, and Clay-colored and Le Conte's sparrows. In addition, these roads have been good during some past winters to search for Great Gray Owls or an occasional Northern Hawk Owl.

Probably the most interesting **wooded areas** to check if you have the time are these (all marked **B7**):

• Eagle Lake Road and the dead-end streets east of the lake have lots of coniferous trees and feeders for winter specialties like winter finches; Black-backed Woodpecker, Gray Jay, and Boreal Chickadee also appear at times.

• The mixed woods at the jog on the French River Road where 15 species of warblers are possible in summer (including Mourning and Canada warblers some years).

• The spruce-tamarack bog at the junction of Lakewood and Pioneer roads (listen for Yellow-bellied Flycatcher and Lincoln's Sparrow); also check the alder swamp 0.6 mile to the east (Alder Flycatcher, Sedge Wren. and Golden-winged Warbler).

• The mixed woods along the last 2 miles of McQuade Road and the 3.5-mile length of Hegberg Road (several warblers, including a Northern Waterthrush swamp on McQuade, a mile north of Pioneer).

SAX-ZIM BOG

But is there life in St. Louis County after Duluth? Yes, some good birding areas do exist elsewhere in the county, but not as many as you might expect within an area this large. In most places, deciduous and mixed woods predominate over more interesting coniferous forests, and none of the county's lakes is better than any other for water birds.

But one of Minnesota's best known birding areas is found just northwest of Duluth. It has long been called the **Sax-Zim Bog (inset C)**, even though Sax is nothing more than a house or two, and Zim has a highway department garage and little else. However, these two place names have long been familiar to birders, and with good reason. In addition

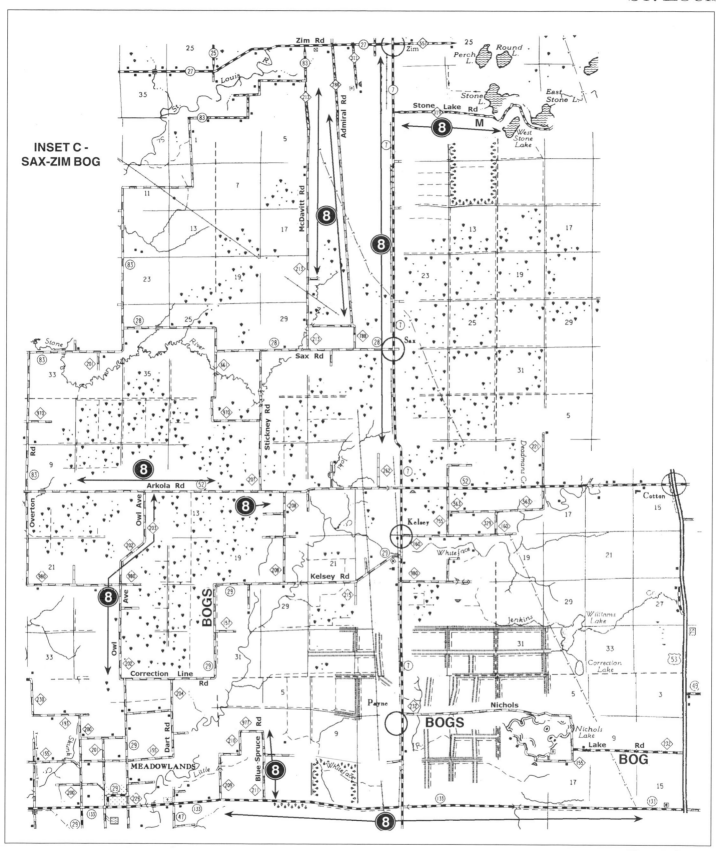

INSET C - SAX-ZIM BOG

to its miles of spruce, tamarack, and northern white cedar bogs, there is also a mix of extensive alder thickets, aspen and black ash woodlands, hayfields, and sedge meadows with a nice variety of breeding and wintering species.

Year-round specialties include Ruffed and Sharp-tailed (easiest in April-May on the lek described below) grouse, Great Gray Owl (almost common in Sax-Zim some years; best looked for November-June), Black-backed Woodpecker (rare), Gray Jay, Black-billed Magpie (at the extreme edge of its range), Boreal Chickadee, and Evening Grosbeak.

In late May-early July also look and listen for nesting species such as Sandhill Crane (rare), Upland Sandpiper, Northern Saw-whet Owl (more vocal in April), Black-billed Cuckoo, Yellow-bellied and Alder flycatchers, Winter and Sedge wrens, Golden-winged, Cape May, Palm (locally), Connecticut (almost common) and Mourning warblers, Le Conte's and Lincoln's sparrows, Bobolink, and both meadowlark species.

Winter possibilities include Northern Goshawk, Rough-legged Hawk (absent some winters; more consistent in fall), Snowy (one most winters) and Northern Hawk (not every year, but there are many records) owls, Northern Shrike, Snow Bunting (a few; especially west and north of Meadowlands along County Roads 133 and 5), Pine Grosbeak, White-winged Crossbill (absent some winters), and Common and Hoary (uncommon to absent) redpolls.

Virtually all the roads within the inset C map are worth traveling, but there are eight **boglands** in particular to bird (all marked **C8**). From north to south:

• County Road 319 / Stone Lake Road: Great Gray Owl; Yellow Rail possible in wet years on south side of the road, 1.5 to 2 miles east of County Road 7.

• County Road 7 between County Road 52 and Zim: Great Gray Owl; sometimes Snowy or Northern Hawk owls, Rough-legged Hawk, and Snow Bunting; Buff-breasted Sandpiper on sod farms late July-early September.

• The parallel County Roads 213 and 788: Great Gray Owl, and sometimes Northern Hawk Owl, Sharp-tailed Grouse, or Black-backed Woodpecker.

• County Road 52 between County Roads 83 and 207: Boreal Chickadee, Connecticut and Palm warblers.

• The small Sharp-tailed Grouse lek southwest of the junction of County Roads 52 and 208. Sometimes a Snowy or Northern Hawk owl, Rough-legged Hawk, and Snow Buntings winter in this and nearby fields; in summer, look for Upland Sandpiper, Le Conte's Sparrow, Bobolink, meadowlarks, and Brewer's Blackbird. Also be sure to look for grouse along County Road 29 and adjacent roads just north and northeast of Meadowlands.

• County Roads 202 and 203 (a.k.a. Owl Avenue!): Great Gray Owl, Boreal Chickadee, Connecticut and Palm warblers; look especially for chickadees 0.5-1.0 mile south of County Road 52.

• County Road 211 / Blue Spruce Road: Boreal Chickadee on the south half; Black-billed Magpie at the north end.

• Almost all of County Road 133, between Highway 53 and County Road 209: Great Gray Owl, Boreal Chickadee, and Connecticut Warbler.

There are two other general areas not far from Sax-Zim that are also worth trying for boreal forest specialties of the Northeast Region: the spruce and tamarack bogs near Floodwood and the extensive mixed woods in Cloquet Valley State Forest.

• The best road in the Floodwood area is County Road 8, which passes through an 8-mile stretch of boglands, 4-12 miles east of town. This area is centered at the junction of County Road 5, which leads north to Meadowlands in inset C. Also check the more open tamarack bogs along the 3-mile stretch of Highway 2, 4-7 miles northwest of Floodwood. The traffic is often heavy, but Great Grays nest in the area, and in winter watch for Northern Shrike, Snow Bunting, and perhaps Northern Hawk Owl.

• The Cloquet Valley State Forest east of Sax-Zim is an area of upland woods mixed with some nice looking bogs along County Road 4 and its side roads between Boulder Lake and Whiteface Reservoir. Look and listen for just about anything, although this area is seldom birded, there are few places on County 4 to park safely, and even fewer specific places known to be particularly good for birds. There are even a few Spruce Grouse somewhere in this forest, although Ruffeds are far more likely.

CENTRAL AND NORTHERN ST. LOUIS COUNTY

Everything said so far in this chapter — and it is considerable! — has only covered the southern third of the county. But this chapter is nearly over, since there are surprisingly few significant areas in the central and northern thirds of St. Louis County. Even the beautiful lakes and vast boreal forests of Voyageurs National Park and the Boundary Waters Canoe Area Wilderness are only worth mentioning in passing, since these remote, roadless places are inaccessible to canoe-less birders and have no species that can't be found more easily elsewhere. If you're looking for a wilderness experience, by all means get out the canoe and camping gear and go there. (And if you're heading for the Boundary Waters, you'll need an entry permit: call 877-550-6777 or go to their website, <www.bwcaw.org>.)

If you're looking for birds, however, I have four other suggestions: three in east-central St. Louis County, and one farther north.

• For a change of pace from woods birding, check the former **Embarrass wetlands (9)**, especially from April to June. Habitat for migrant waterfowl and nesting marsh birds is scarce in this part of the state, so it is worth checking these former wild rice paddies in summer for Sora, Virginia Rail, and Yellow-headed Blackbird. There is even a recent spring record for Cinnamon Teal. From the town of Embarrass, go 1 mile west on County Road 21, then south on County Road 558 for 1.7 miles to the pools.

• Not far south of Embarrass is Hoyt Lakes, and just south of there is a large area of **spruce bogs** (also marked **9**), a good place to search for a variety of boreal nesting birds and for Great Gray Owl, Three-toed or Black-backed woodpecker, and Boreal Chickadee at any time of year. Look and listen along County Road 110 / Forest Road 11 as it heads east out of Hoyt Lakes as Kennedy Drive, curves south, and after 14 miles comes to a T-intersection with County Road 16. County 16 actually offers better habitat for woodpeckers and is one of the best roads in the state to look for Three-toeds. There is an 8-mile stretch with bogs and snags extending from 4 miles west of the 16/110 junction to 4 miles east of this corner.

• Another good stretch of **spruce bogs** (also **9**) for these same possibilities lies just southeast of Babbitt. From the east side of town, follow County Road 623 east and southeast for about 5 miles to a junction with two forest roads. The left fork is Forest Road 424, which leads east through more bogs and comes out on Highway 1 (see Lake County's inset C). The right fork is Forest Road 112, which continues southeast through the boglands and comes to another fork in about 4 miles. The left fork, still numbered 112, eventually goes east to Lake County Road 2 (see Lake County's inset B). The right fork is Forest Road 113 / Skibo Road: though usually not plowed in winter, it winds southwest and leads to County Road 110 southeast of Hoyt Lakes.

• The **Echo Trail (10)** is not a hiking trail, but a road which begins just east of Ely and extends for miles through predominantly coniferous forest. Most Northeast Region specialties can be found along this road; some of the more interesting possibilities include Spruce Grouse (especially between Big Lake and the Portage River, about 20-25 miles from Ely), Boreal Owl (listen in March and early April), Black-backed Woodpecker (or a Three-toed), and at least 20 species of breeding warblers.

Turn north from Highway 169 on County Road 88, 1 mile east of the Highway 1 junction, and after 2.2 miles you will come to the start of the Echo Trail or County Road 116. At first the road is paved, but it soon turns to gravel and is narrow and winding until it reaches the Portage River. Here the road widens and straightens, but the coniferous habitat continues for another 15 miles or so. The last 8 miles of the Trail to its junction with County Road 24 goes through predominantly deciduous woods, so if you're still looking for grouse and woodpeckers you might want to turn back towards Ely and try again. Also check any of the dead-end side roads that look inviting.

*　　*　　*

Finally (at last!), St. Louis County has a small lake with open water in winter and four sewage ponds. Silver Lake, just west of downtown Virginia, is kept partly open most winters by a steam plant. Though overwintering ducks are few to nonexistent, the lake can be good in late fall or early spring when everything else is frozen.

The sewage ponds, from north to south:

❑ Cook; turn south off Highway 53 on County Road 25, and where 25 turns west continue south 0.5 mile on County Road 912.

❑ Biwabik; the largest of the four; 1.2 miles south of Highway 135 on County Road 4.

❑ Meadowlands; 0.2 mile south on County Road 227 (see inset C).

❑ Floodwood; turn west off Highway 2 on Floodwood Road, go 0.7 miles, then 0.2 mile south, and 0.2 mile east.

Lake County

Once the Duluth area is left behind and you head up Highway 61 into Lake County, almost all of the excellent fall and winter birding possibilities discussed in the St. Louis County chapter for Lake Superior and its North Shore stay with you. Unfortunately, though, this county has relatively few good places from which to scan the lake, there are no raptor concentrations to compare with Hawk Ridge, Snowy Owls are not as consistent here as in the Duluth-Superior harbor, and Park Point has much more potential for shorebirds, jaegers, rare gulls, and grounded warbler waves.

Birders also tend to find Cook County more interesting, and they may think of Lake County as only something they need to drive through en route to Grand Marais for the latest fall vagrant or to the Gunflint Trail for coniferous forest specialties. However, I do not recommend you pass through Lake County too quickly. Numerous vagrants have been discovered along the North Shore at Knife River and Two Harbors, mostly in fall, with some of these yet to be

recorded at Duluth or Grand Marais. And, in recent years, Lake County's portion of the Superior National Forest could arguably be considered better for summer and winter birding than the Gunflint Trail.

NORTH SHORE / KNIFE RIVER AND TWO HARBORS

As you cross the Lake County line on the North Shore Scenic Drive / County Road 61, you enter the **inset A** map of the **Knife River - Two Harbors area.** If you're wondering if the town of **Knife River (A1)** is worth a stop, consider that this is the site of no fewer than four first state records (King Eider, Red Phalarope, Black-legged Kittiwake, and Mew Gull). In addition, there are recent fall sightings of Scissor-tailed Flycatcher, several Townsend's Solitaires, Varied Thrush, Northern Mockingbird, Summer

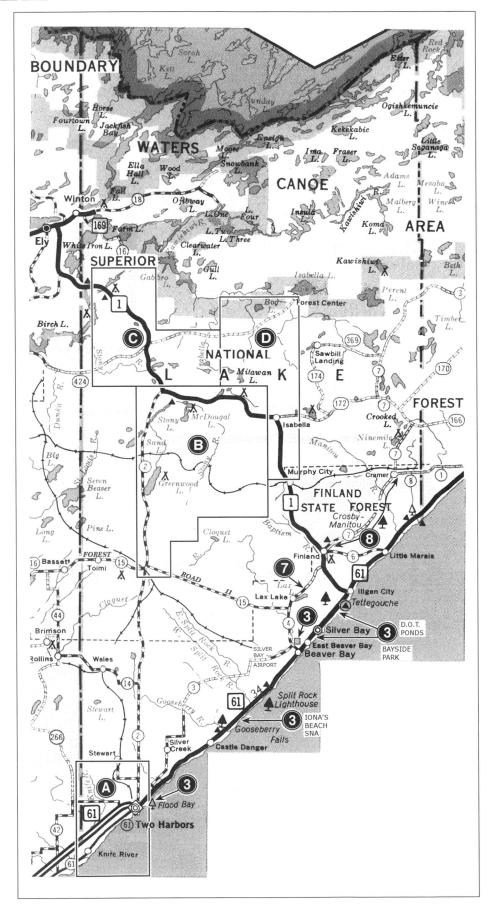

Tanager, and even a Black-throated Sparrow.

There are three places in Knife River to check during migration and winter:

• After entering town on Scenic 61, turn right on Marina Drive, cross the tracks, and bear slightly left to continue straight on a short gravel road which dead ends at the lake next to the harbor. From here, you can scope the lake and Knife Island, where there is a nesting colony of Herring Gulls with a few cormorants among them. Also, be sure to hike through the small peninsula to your right between the harbor and the lake, where several interesting migrants have occurred.

• Next, continue up Scenic 61 a short way and park at Emily's General Store, Inn and Deli. Just beyond Emily's, walk along Skiff Landing Road as it crosses the railroad tracks and dead ends in a couple of blocks. This is usually the best place to find rarities. Just after Skiff Landing Road crosses the tracks, there is a driveway leading to the gravel and weedy beach near the mouth of the river, often a spot where numbers of gulls are loafing.

• Finally, as time permits, walk any of the residential streets north and west of Emily's, and you might turn up some interesting migrants or a fall-winter flock of Bohemian Waxwings, crossbills, or redpolls.

Continue northeast on Scenic 61, and in about 7 miles you'll merge with Highway 61 and enter **Two Harbors (A2)**, a much larger town with even more birding potential during migration and winter. While Knife River may take only a few minutes to check, Two Harbors will take a few hours to thoroughly cover its birding areas:

• The easiest way to reach Agate Bay, the main harbor, is to turn right (south) off Highway 61 on Waterfront Street, 3 blocks east of the railroad viaduct. Waterfront Street ends at the Edna G. tugboat dock, where you can scope one side of the harbor for loons, grebes, ducks, and gulls. Also be sure to explore the open areas to the west by the iron ore docks for birds like Northern Shrike, Lapland Longspur, Snow Bunting, and an occasional Snowy Owl. To the east of the Edna G., between the railroad tracks and the harbor, are some good weedy areas for sparrows and other migrants.

• Backtrack on Waterfront to 1st Avenue, go east 3 blocks to 3rd Street, and then south to the large parking lot by the lighthouse and main breakwater. Here you'll have a better view of the Agate Bay harbor, where records include Yellow-billed Loon, King Eider, Black-legged Kittiwake, plus several sightings of Pacific Loons, Harlequin and Long-tailed ducks, and all three scoters. While fall may be more interesting than spring in Two Harbors and elsewhere on the North Shore, be aware there are two rare-Regular migrants which tend to be absent in fall. Look especially for Red-throated Loons and Whimbrels in May, this latter species preferring to rest on breakwaters, rocky points, and small islands.

• At the south side of the parking lot, watch for the Harbor Walk trailhead. This trail curves around behind the lighthouse, past some flat rock ledges along the lake shore (sometimes good for shorebirds), and through some nice dense woodlands. Look for warblers and other migrant passerines here (there was a Black-throated Gray Warbler in May 2000!), and the cedars and other conifers are good potential roosts for Long-eared and Northern Saw-whet owls in fall. Where the Harbor Walk splits, either take the left fork back to the parking lot, or bear right along the less developed part of the trail leading to the city water plant on the east side of town.

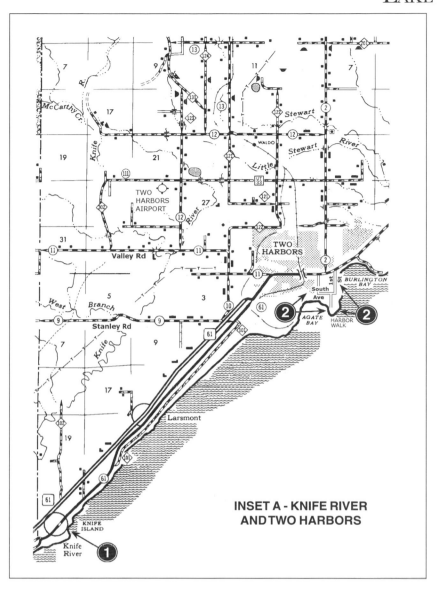

INSET A - KNIFE RIVER AND TWO HARBORS

• To drive to the water plant at the corner of South Avenue and 1st Street, backtrack on 3rd Street, take the first right on South Avenue, and go 2 blocks. It is worth parking here (or anywhere nearby) and walking through the eight-square-block area bordered by 1st and 3rd streets and by South and 4th avenues. There are lots of spruce trees, mountain ash trees, and feeders, and this is usually the best neighborhood in Two Harbors in fall-winter to look for small owls, Townsend's Solitaire, Varied Thrush, Bohemian Waxwing, and winter finches. In fall 2000, both an Ash-throated Flycatcher and a Black-headed Grosbeak even appeared here.

Along 1st Street, between the water plant and Highway 61, there are several spots from which to scan Burlington Bay (i.e., the second harbor) on the east side of Two Harbors. It is just as good as Agate Bay. There is also a good weedy field for sparrows and things to the west of 1st Street, just south of Highway 61. Also note the sign for the golf course on the north side of Highway 61, just west of 1st Street. If it's early morning or a rainy day in August or

September, when golfers unlikely to be out, and you're looking for Buff-breasted Sandpiper and other shorebirds, there are two small ponds to check near the golf course parking lot. One is along the cart path to the first tee and the other is by the ninth green.

One last area to check in winter before leaving Two Harbors behind is the set of back roads shown on inset A north and west of town. During some owl "invasion" winters, Great Grays have been particularly fond of this area, as evidenced by one afternoon when 19 individuals were spotted here during a three-hour period, 10 of these in 40 minutes within a four-square-mile area. Certainly, such numbers of Great Grays are not present every winter, but it is worth looking along these roads (or those in adjacent St. Louis County — see that county's inset B), especially in late afternoon when Great Grays tend to most actively hunt. Watch as well for Northern Hawk and Snowy owls, which have been attracted to these fields in some years.

Be aware of a couple of other birding possibilities northwest of town in inset A. In spring or fall, you might want to check for water birds at the ponds shown near the north end of County Road 122 and along UT33. From this latter pond, continue west 0.7 mile to the Two Harbors Airport. Even without permission (though, after the September 11 events, you should probably ask), birders and others have always been welcome to wander around here. In August-September you can sometimes find Buff-breasteds and other shorebirds along the runway; later in fall, watch for Horned Larks, American Pipits, Lapland Longspurs, and Snow Buntings.

NORTH SHORE / BEYOND TWO HARBORS

At Two Harbors you have a choice to make. Either turn up County Road 2 to look for summer or winter birds of the boreal forest, or continue up the North Shore on Highway 61 for migrant land birds (especially in fall) and Lake Superior specialties (in winter as well as during migration).

If you choose the latter, consider that many list Highway 61 as one of the most scenic in all the United States. Oh yes, there is certainly lots to see: deer standing in the road at night, narrow to nonexistent road shoulders in many places, the limited passing opportunities on this relatively narrow and winding highway, slow tourist traffic competing for space with speeding semis, and all those trees between you and the mostly invisible lake. Until recently, when parts of this highway have been improved, this was rated the most dangerous highway in the state. Those who like driving this road would also probably enjoy the summer weekend traffic in Brainerd.

Following are the locations of interest during migration in Lake County along the North Shore beyond Two Harbors, with the best birding spots marked **3**. These places (and those along Cook County's portion of the North Shore) are referenced by the mile markers posted on Highway 61. Mile 0 is the corner of London Road and 10th Avenue East in Duluth, the Lake/Cook county line is mile 71, and the Canadian border is mile 150. If a location is given as mile 52.4, for example, it is 0.4 mile northeast of mile 52 or 0.6 mile southwest of mile 53.

Keep in mind that rarities can occur literally anywhere during migration along the North Shore, so stops at places other than those included below might well be rewarding. Note as well that conventional birding wisdom has always held that fall is better than spring. The dynamics are that a couple of hundred miles worth of southbound migrants are stopped by Lake Superior and then funneled down and concentrated along its North Shore. However, though mostly overlooked by birders, spring migrations here have produced several eye-opening vagrants over the years.

• **Flood Bay State Wayside** (mile 27.6) is your first stop, 1.3 miles northeast of the County Road 2 stoplight in Two Harbors. Besides scanning the lake, be sure to hike to the right towards the Superior Shores Resort and carefully check the marshy pond, its shrubby edges, and the weedy area along the beach. As evidenced by a recent Tricolored Heron sighting, this spot can be good for just about all sorts of migrants.

At mile 28.5 you'll come to the mouth of the Stewart River (another place to scan the lake), Betty's Pies Restaurant (probably the most overrated pies in the state), and the start of County Road 3. This road is an alternate inland route to Beaver Bay to check for Great Grays and other owls in winter. Also, Buff-breasted Sandpipers have been found in August-September at the Silver Bay Municipal Airport, about 5 miles before the road ends at County Road 4.

• Gooseberry Falls State Park (mile 39.4) may be a popular stop for birders and other tourists, but little of note has ever been reported at this scenic park.

Instead, continue another 2.6 miles, and at mile 42 turn into parking lot at the new public access boat ramp. From here, you can walk to the left through the planted conifers (check for roosting owls) to **Iona's Beach Scientific and Natural Area** (though the beach itself is nothing special). Or, hike a short way past the boat ramp to the point, where you might find warblers and other migrants. A short trail also connects the beach and point.

Split Rock Lighthouse State Park (mile 45.9) is next, but, like Gooseberry, the scenery is better than the birding potential.

• Five miles after Split Rock, you'll enter Beaver Bay, and turn up County Road 4 on the northeast edge of town (mile 51.1). Follow County 4 for 0.8 mile to the top of the hill and turn right into a small parking lot on the Superior Hiking Trail. (Note that Black-throated Blue Warblers breed locally at many places along this trail, southwest as far as Castle Danger, and northeast through Cook County into Canada.)

This parking area is a good vantage point to scope the **Beaver Bay sewage ponds**. It's also OK — and recommended — to walk from here through the opening in the fence and hike around all three ponds. With shorebird habitat so limited in this part of the state, the potential here is obvious, but just as interesting are the open and grassy surroundings, another habitat in short supply in this heavily wooded region. As a result, also watch especially for migrant American Pipits, a variety of sparrows, Lapland Longspurs, Snow Buntings, Rusty Blackbirds, and other field birds.

(In summer, if you're looking for Black-throated Blue Warblers or Philadelphia Vireos, you could also continue beyond the ponds on County Road 4 to the back side of Tettagouche State Park and to County Road 7 beyond Finland; see pages 239-240.)

• Continuing northeast a mile from Beaver Bay, you might want to see if there's a rarity among the gulls which sometimes congregate by the docks at the bottom of the hill on Fish House Road in East Beaver Bay (mile 52).

Usually more interesting is **Bayside Park** (mile 52.4): turn right at the sign, and check both sides of this new harbor and marina. During migration or winter, you might turn up something around the rock jetties (every time I stop here I expect to see a Harlequin Duck, Purple Sandpiper, or

Red Phalarope), in the adjacent open area of weeds and gravel (a Smith's Longspur is found among Laplands almost every fall somewhere on the North Shore), or in the mountain ash and other trees.

The town of Silver Bay is next, home of the Northshore Mining Company (mile 54) and its piles of taconite. Taconite pellets are high-grade iron processed from low-grade ore, which now is all that's left in the ground on the Iron Range in central St. Louis County. Some plants process their ore into taconite up on the Range, but in Silver Bay the ore is brought in by rail, processed at Northshore Mining, and then shipped out.

Silver Bay is the site of a famous environmental controversy in the 1970s when Reserve Mining Company owned this operation. It used to deposit the tailings processed from the ore, which included asbestos-like fibers, into Lake Superior. Reserve was eventually forced to dump the tailings into inland settling ponds, and it went out of business a few years later.

During this hiatus, before Northshore Mining took over, you could bird this unique expanse of grass, gravel, and large water impoundment. Whimbrels, Buff-breasted Sandpipers, Snowy and Short-eared owls, and flocks of pipits, sparrows, longspurs, and Snow Buntings used to be found here. These birds still occur, but without special permission this area is off-limits to birders. However, given the depressed mining economy, this plant could again close. So, for future reference, note that East Lakeview Drive (mile 55.4) leads from Highway 61 to a water treatment plant at the edge of the property.

• After Silver Bay, Palisade Head (mile 57.1) is the next point of interest, a site where Peregrine Falcons have been nesting. The signed road leads to a parking lot at the top of the cliff and a spectacular view of Lake Superior. The Peregrine's nesting ledge below is difficult or impossible to see, but if you stand around long enough a falcon will probably fly by eventually.

A half mile beyond Palisade Head are the small but interesting **Department of Transportation ponds** (mile 57.6). Turn at the "Truck Station Illgen City" sign, the ponds are behind the garage, and, whether or not any workers are around, it's always been OK to bird here. Since marshy ponds and relatively open areas are not found much along the North Shore, this site has attracted several interesting migrants.

In another mile you'll come to a large wayside rest and the main entrance to Tettagouche State Park (mile 58.6). You can pick up a park map at the visitors center, but, as mentioned previously, the best birding is at the west side of the park, best accessed from County Road 4 north of Beaver Bay.

There aren't any other specific birding spots along the rest of Lake County's portion of Highway 61, but note the junction with Highway 1 (mile 59.3), which leads into inset D and to County Road 7 — see below.

INLAND LAKE COUNTY

There may not be many spring or fall migrants concentrated in Lake County away from Lake Superior, but there is certainly a long list of significant species to see during summer and winter within insets B, C, and D. These maps include most of the roads in this county's share of the Superior National Forest — or, more accurately, since logging interests always seem to predominate, the Superior National Tree Farm.

If you're wondering why the northern third of the county is not included on an inset map, it's because there's nothing accessible to include. Except for the Fernberg Trail / County Road 18, which mostly traverses deciduous and mixed woods east of Ely, there essentially aren't any roads up there — and none at all in the vast and beautiful Boundary Waters Canoe Area Wilderness. And between inset D and the Cook County line, the habitat is generally not as interesting as in west-central Lake County, with no specific birding areas of interest.

Almost any of the roads shown on the three insets are worth exploring for coniferous forest specialties, but keep in mind that some of these roads are not plowed in winter, and they may be treacherous or impassable from March to mid-April when comprised of mud and melting snows. Also, during your explorations, be prepared to encounter new logging roads not on any maps, to discover that an alleged road shown on the map has been abandoned, or to find road numbers changed.

Year-around residents you might find along almost any of these forest roads include Northern Goshawk, Ruffed Grouse, Barred Owl, Black-backed Woodpecker, Gray Jay, Common Raven, Boreal Chickadee, Red-breasted Nuthatch, and Evening Grosbeak. In winter, add Northern Shrike, Pine Grosbeak, both crossbills (also possible some summers, but both can be absent some winters), and redpolls to the list of possibilities.

The list of widespread nesting specialties includes Common Loon, Bald Eagle, American Woodcock, Black-billed Cuckoo, Northern Saw-whet Owl, Yellow-bellied and Alder flycatchers, Winter Wren, and some 20 species of warblers (including Cape May, Northern Waterthrush, Mourning, and Canada). Additionally, some more local summer possibilities would include Whip-poor-will, Long-eared Owl, Olive-sided Flycatcher, Philadelphia Vireo, Bay-breasted, Wilson's and Connecticut warblers, and Rusty Blackbird.

Of special note, of course, are these rarer and sought-after residents of central and northern Lake County: Spruce Grouse, Northern Hawk (mostly winter), Great Gray and Boreal owls, and Three-toed Woodpecker.

If you have time for no other road in the Superior National Forest, be sure to at least make the 46-mile drive up **County Road 2 (inset B)** from Two Harbors to Highway 1. This road turns north off Highway 61 at the stoplight by the Holiday gas station (mile 26.3). It enters the inset B map about 25 miles north of town, and in another mile or so it

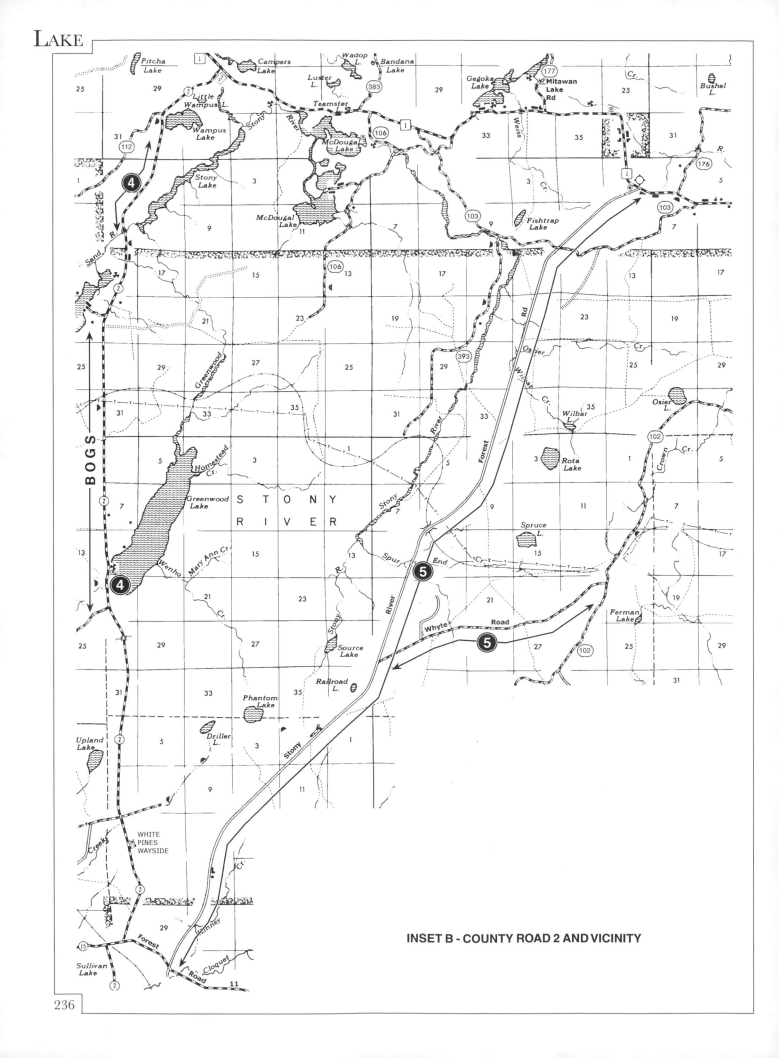

INSET B - COUNTY ROAD 2 AND VICINITY

intersects with County Road 15 / Forest Road 11. Currently, you have to jog east a short distance at this junction to continue north on 2, but this will change once the construction here is completed.

(Forest Road 11 is a piece of work! Considering there are more Moose than vehicles in this part of Lake County, it's a mystery why it's as wide as any interstate and paved its entire length, from Hoyt Lakes in St. Louis County to Silver Bay. Recently completed, this road passes through miles of habitat for grouse, owls, woodpeckers, and winter finches, although birders have yet to pinpoint any specifically productive areas.)

The birding along County Road 2 can be worthwhile in places south of 11, but start seriously looking for both birds and mammals north of here. You have perhaps a 50-50 chance of spotting a Moose, this is where I had my lifer Lynx, and I have seen Gray Wolf along this road at least twice. A couple of miles north of Forest Road 11 is the White Pines Wayside located within an island of virgin white pines that somehow managed to escape logging. This is a very pretty area worth a brief stop, but nothing out of the ordinary is usually present.

Continue north, and listen for Northern Saw-whet Owls, which are widespread and quite vocal on April nights along this and other roads in the Superior National Forest. A whistled imitation of its call will often bring a saw-whet close to the road and into view. While you're at it, listen as well in spring for Barred, Great Gray, and Long-eared owls. The latter two species don't call much and are thus hard to find, and you almost have a better chance of hearing a Boreal Owl, especially in March or early April.

About 6 miles north of the White Pines Wayside, watch on the right for the public access parking lot at **Greenwood Lake (B4)**. The lake itself isn't particularly special, but there are good bogs for a mile or so both south and north of here, a better-than-average stretch to find Northern Hawk and Great Gray owls, Black-backed Woodpecker, Boreal Chickadee, and nesting warblers (including Cape May, Wilson's, and Northern Waterthrush).

One real attraction on County Road 2 is the Spruce Grouse, which in winter is more reliable here than anywhere else in Minnesota. This elusive species is present year around, but the best time to look is in winter, late December-early March, when they come in the road to pick at salt and grit. Most sightings are between dawn and an hour or so later, before too many logging trucks and other vehicles go by and scare them off.

Although they have been seen at random locations farther south on County Road 2 (careful: there are also Ruffed Grouse here), the most consistent spot by far is just beyond the **Sand River** (also **B4**). Look for the Sand River sign 7.5 miles north of Greenwood Lake (some 41.5 miles north of Two Harbors), and the grouse are most often seen within the first few hundred yards north of the river, or in the stretch 1.2 - 2.0 miles north of it. With luck, some observers have found a dozen or more individuals in one flock (the record is 27!). If unlucky, you may find one hit by a truck.

This same area is also good for those same owls, woodpeckers, chickadees, warblers, and other birds you looked for near Greenwood Lake and elsewhere. County Road 2 ends at Highway 1, 4.5 miles north of the Sand River, or about 46 miles north of Two Harbors. If you come to Highway 1 without having seen a Spruce Grouse, it's worth turning around and making another drive or two back and forth to the Sand River.

Another excellent road in inset B for just about everything is the 20-mile-long **Stony River Forest Road (B5)**. Its south end is at Forest Road 11, 1.5 miles east of County Road 2, and it goes north to intersect Highway 1, 2.7 miles west of Isabella. Equally good for birding is the so-called **Whyte Road** (also marked **B5**), which turns east from the Stony River Road about 8 miles north of Forest Road 11, or 12 miles south of Highway 1. About 5 miles east, the Whyte Road turns north, becomes Forest Road 102, and comes out on Highway 1, 5 miles south of Isabella (see inset D). Among other things, Great Gray Owl is a good possibility along these roads at any time of year, and Connecticut Warblers can be heard singing from the spruce and tamarack bogs.

These roads, along with the inset B portion of County Road 2, are perhaps the best ones in the county from which to listen for Boreal Owls calling on territory. They are most vocal during mid-March to early April, although they sometimes call in winter on milder nights; later in April is also good if it's a late spring. Their preferred habitat is a mixed stand of trees within predominantly coniferous areas, the nests are in tree cavities (usually in mature aspens), and their roosting sites and hunting territories tend to be in spruce bogs (which may be several hundred yards away from the nest cavity).

The male's territorial call, which closely resembles the winnowing of a snipe, is usually given from the cover of a spruce tree near a potential nest cavity. When a female is attracted, he flies to the cavity and his song is lengthened into a prolonged phrase. Once heard, the calling male is typically a challenge to reach, since the call you hear may be a mile or more away, and your hike in the dark after him may be through deep snow and difficult terrain. If you manage to get near a calling male but can't spot him on his singing perch, try giving a short whistle. This may actually fool the male into thinking a female has come in, and he might then fly to a visible perch at his nest cavity. Recordings are relatively ineffective in attracting Boreal Owls to roadsides.

* * *

If you had no luck with Spruce Grouse on County Road 2, turn east on Highway 1 towards Isabella, and some birders have seen them at various locations on this road. Or, turn west from 2 on Highway 1, which leads northwest to the **Spruce Road** in **inset C**. Grouse have been also spotted along this stretch of 1, especially between mile markers 302 and 300. This part of Highway 1, though, is mostly narrow, winding, and without shoulders, with few places to stop safely. It's usually best to continue directly to the

LAKE

Spruce Road, which is well-marked and turns right (north-east) just before mile marker 297, 14.1 miles from County Road 2.

While Spruce Grouse can be seen on this road, the primary attraction would be the two **Three-toed Woodpecker bogs** (both marked **C6**). Though hardly a sure thing, in recent years this rare-Regular permanent resident has been found more consistently along the Spruce Road than anywhere else in Minnesota. The best time to look and listen is February to mid-June, when the birds are drumming on territory and often responsive to recordings. Of course, Black-backeds are also possible here.

One area to concentrate on is the vicinity of the corner with Endless Waters Road, the gated drive 0.4 miles up the Spruce Road. It is currently OK to walk this road, which dead ends in less than a mile at some houses. But do not

drive on Endless Waters Road, even if the gate is open; also be sure to park on the Spruce Road so you are not in the way of vehicles using either road. The other good woodpecker area is 3.5 miles up the Spruce Road: hike left (north) on the snowmobile trail, and a woodpecker can often be found within the first couple of hundred yards. Also try along the Spruce Road itself, between the trail and the parking area 0.6 mile farther up; in winter, this is as far as the road is normally plowed.

Once you return to Highway 1, you can continue northwest to Ely in St. Louis County. In about 3 miles you will come to a bridge and dam at the Kawishiwi River. In winter, there is almost always a flock of goldeneyes present in the open water.

If you're returning southeast towards County Road 2, watch for the Tomahawk Trail / Forest Road 377 signs, 7.7 miles from the Spruce Road (or 6.4 miles from County 2).

If you have the time to explore, this road heads east into inset D through predominantly coniferous areas where Boreal Owls have been heard. Later in the spring, also listen in the drier clearings for Whip-poor-will, an uncommon and quite local species in this part of the state.

As shown on the **inset D** map, the Tomahawk Trail dead ends at Isabella Lake, but before it does you can turn south towards **Isabella and vicinity** on either Forest Road 173 or 373. These roads connect with 396, and all three roads pass through some good spruce bogs, more places to look for those two elusive woodpeckers, Boreal Chickadees, and winter finches.

There tend to be more red and jack pines in the vicinity of Isabella, especially along Highway 1 and

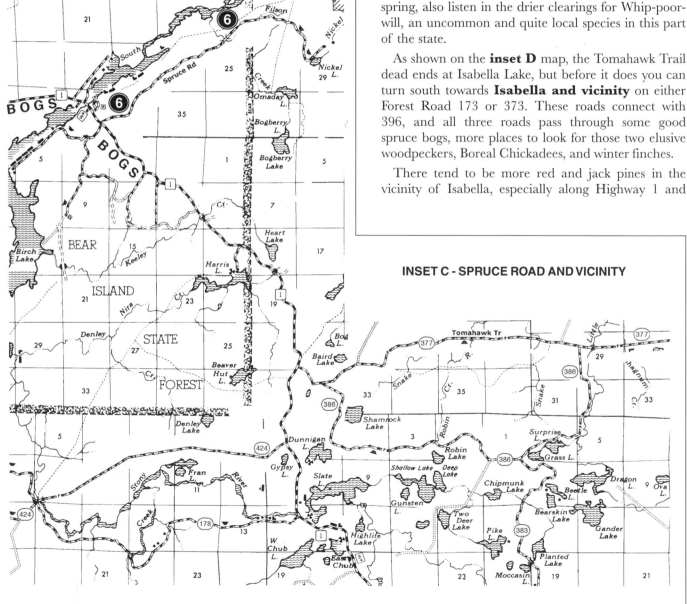

INSET C - SPRUCE ROAD AND VICINITY

238

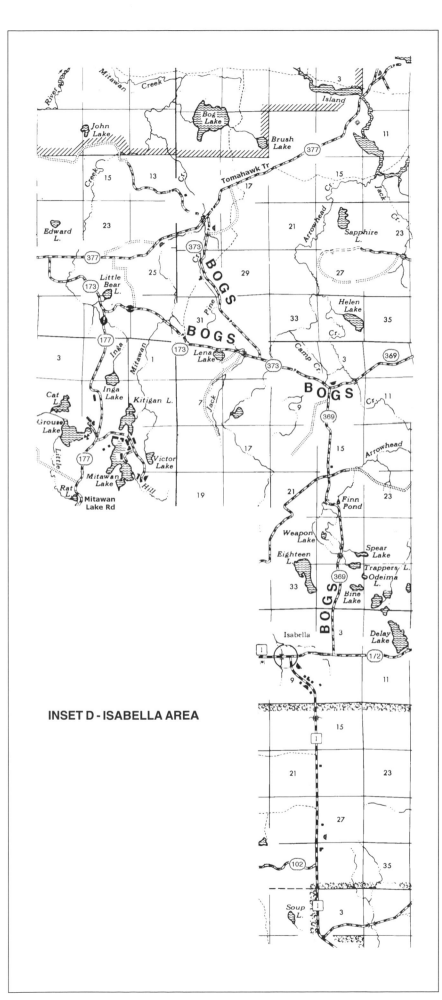

INSET D - ISABELLA AREA

the Mitawan Lake Road / Forest Road 177 (which turns north off Highway 1, 6 miles west of Isabella). Such habitat is particularly attactive to Red Crossbills, mostly in winter. Also in winter, check any feeders you find for grosbeaks and red-polls. One consistent feeding station in recent years has been at the Superior National Forest ranger station on Highway 1, a mile west of Isabella. Another good feeder has been at Grouse Lake: turn west off the Mitawan Lake Road at the sign for Grouse Lake, which is at the end of the plowed section of road.

* * *

There is some additional woods birding to do in Lake County south of the Superior National Forest, especially if it's between late May and early July and you're looking for Philadelphia Vireos and Black-throated Blue Warblers.

One good place to start is along the west side of **Tettegouche State Park (7)**. From Beaver Bay, follow County Road 4 beyond the sewage ponds and the County Road 3 junction, and in about 8 miles from Highway 61 watch for the public access sign at Lax Lake. In another 0.7 mile, park in the small parking lot on your right, the access point for Tettegouche. If you're coming from the north, this lot is 3 miles south of the County Road 4 - Highway 1 junction.

Hike up the gated service road which reaches the top of the hill in 0.8 mile, but in less than a half mile stop by the bench on the left side of the trail and start listening. This area, along with Oberg Mountain in Cook County, is perhaps the easiest Black-throated Blue spot to reach in Minnesota. (This warbler also nests at many places along the Superior Hiking Trail in Lake and Cook County, but it typically involves a long hike to reach them. For trail maps and more information, contact the Superior Hiking Trail Association: telephone 218-834-2700; website <www.shta.org>).

If you hear none near the bench, continue listening to the trail junction top of the hill. Turn right or left or continue straight here if you still haven't found one — the trail to the right is probably your best choice. This warbler's preferred habitat is a deciduous woodland on a slope predominated by maples, with a closed canopy, lots of shade, a shrubby understory, and a few balsam firs mixed in. This trail is also good for several other breeding warblers, including Golden-winged (sometimes in the swamp by the parking lot), Black-throated Green (careful: one of its songs is similar to the Black-throated Blue's), Blackburnian, Black-and-white, Mourning, Canada, and Ovenbird.

Finding a Philadelphia Vireo is more of a challenge since its song is so similar to the ubiquitous Red-eyed's, and who chases down every Red-eyed song which sounds a bit higher-pitched and slower? Its breeding habitat and range are also poorly understood, but it seems to prefer birch snags to aspens, especially in semi-open areas in a cut-over woods or alder swamp. Their breeding range seems to be limited to the area along or near the North Shore of Lake Superior, mostly between Beaver Bay and Grand Marais. But this vireo has also been found in summer elsewhere in northeastern Minnesota and in mature aspen woodlands.

There are good areas to look and listen for Philadelphias (and Golden-winged Warblers at the edge of their range in Lake County) along County Road 4 between Lax Lake and Finland. Another road to try is **County Road 7** northeast of Finland (**8**). This beautiful road follows the Baptism River and other watercourses lined with alder swamps, birch snags, tall aspens, and spruce stands. Beyond Crosby-Manitou State Park and the "town" of Cramer (at the junction with County Road 8), the road eventually enters the more closed-in woodlands of the Superior National Forest.

En route, stop and listen for vireos and Golden-wingeds wherever the habitat looks right, and chase down every vireo song whenever you have a hunch. If nowhere else on 7, be sure to try along the road 0.4 mile north of Cramer, a consistent spot for both Philadelphias and Golden-wingeds for several years.

Cook County

"Last but not least" is a cliche which is certainly appropriate for Cook County, easily one of the best birding counties in Minnesota. Of all the places to look for the nesting specialties of the Northeast Region's boreal forests, the Gunflint Trail and vicinity has long been a favored destination for birders. During migration, especially in fall and particularly in Grand Marais, Cook County's portion of the North Shore of Lake Superior has recorded a long list of unusual strays that rivals the array of vagrants found in the Duluth area. Spring birding up the North Shore has additional potential for turning up rarities, and it is the time to hear Boreal and other owls up the Gunflint and other roads in the Superior National Forest. Birders can also find most of what they're looking for in winter in Cook County, although these specialties are generally easier to reach in Aitkin and Lake counties and around the Duluth area.

NORTH SHORE OF LAKE SUPERIOR

As you bird up the North Shore along Highway 61, watch for most of the same species listed previously for Duluth and Lake County. Winter birding is probably best earlier in the season (i.e., December) when more gulls and other water birds are still lingering, and when the Bohemian Waxwing flocks tend to be larger. In spring, look especially for the rare Red-throated Loon and for Whimbrels on rocks and breakwaters as you scan the lake for Long-tailed Ducks and scoters. Summer specialties along the North Shore include Whip-poor-will, Philadelphia Vireo, and Black-

throated Blue Warbler. In fall, of course, look literally for almost anything, with mid-October into November tending to be the most interesting time.

As mentioned in the Lake County chapter, you need to watch for things other than birds on Highway 61: too many deer, weekend traffic, narrow road shoulders, and limited visibility all present potential difficulties. Also, as covered previously, Cook County's North Shore birding spots are referenced with Highway 61's mile markers, but remember that vagrants can and do turn up anywhere along the Shore, so don't necessarily limit yourself to the locations included below. On the other hand, however, if your time is really limited you may want to head directly to Grand Marais, which is always the best single place for migrants.

Between the Lake County line and the Grand Marais area mapped on inset A, the most interesting birding sites are all marked **1**:

• The Lake-Cook county line is well-marked at mile 71, and just over a couple of miles later, at mile 73.3, watch for a parking area on the right. A gated road here leads to the right to Sugar Loaf Cove, which includes an old boat landing where you can scan the lake, some stands of conifers for perhaps a roosting owl, and a small scientific and natural area interpretive center of potential interest to history buffs and botanists.

But a better area for birding is **Taconite Harbor** (mile 76.9), formerly a small community for mining company employees. The houses have been removed and the ore docks in the harbor are now idle, but there is a signed road which

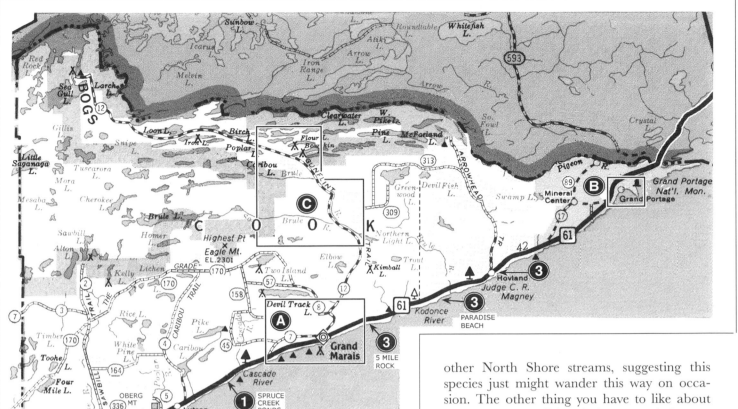

leads down to the harbor and a small boat landing.

Of special interest would be the grassy clearing along the road where the houses used to be and the large gravel parking lot just before the boat dock. Since openings in this heavily wooded part of the state are few and far between, they have the potential for attracting and concentrating migrant Short-eared Owl (rare), Horned Larks, American Pipits, sparrow flocks, Lapland Longspurs (there are also North Shore records for the other three species, the Smith's probably annual), Snow Buntings, and meadowlarks (in fall, of the unidentified variety). While you're at it, you might as well check the woods too: a Williamson's Sapsucker actually turned up here in October 1999.

• Two miles farther northeast is the town of Schroeder, and at mile 79.2 on the east side of town you can turn right to scan the lake at Father Baraga's Cross Wayside. Temperance River State Park (mile 80.2), like other North Shore parks, offers a nice place to camp, a view of the lake, and scenic trails past the rapids and falls of an often spectacular river. The birding, though, is only average — unless, that is, an American Dipper decides to return. Since one was discovered here in 1970, there have been several rumors and reports (some more credible than others) from this and other North Shore streams, suggesting this species just might wander this way on occasion. The other thing you have to like about the Temperance River is its name: it has no bar at its mouth!

The town of **Tofte** follows at mile 82.5. Turn right at the post office on Tofte Park Road, which curves back to the right, parallels Highway 61, and leads to a park on the lake and to some yards with bird feeders and mountain ash trees. There are even more mountain ash trees for waxwings and things around the Bluefin Bay restaurant and condos, just northeast of the post office. Besides looking for Bohemian Waxwings and winter finches, note this is probably the best town besides Grand Marais to check for such rarities as Mountain Bluebird, Townsend's Solitaire, Varied Thrush, Northern Mockingbird, and Summer Tanager in fall or winter.

Also in Tofte is the beginning of the Sawbill Trail / County Road 2, one of the main roads leading north into the Superior National Forest.

• The **Lutsen Sea Villas**, 4.5 miles after Tofte at mile 87, has even more mountain ash trees and other cover which are always worth birding during winter or migration, as evidenced by the lost White-eyed Vireo here in October 2001. Those in the condos or the registration office never seem to mind the presence of birders, so take the time to walk around both the west (units G to I) and east (units A to F) halves of the property.

• Just beyond the Sea Villas, watch for the brown Superior Hiking Trail sign at Forest Road 336 (mile 87.3) which leads to **Oberg Mountain**, one of the best places in the state for nesting Black-throated Blue Warblers. Go up 336 for 2.1 miles to the parking area on the left, and the signed trail to Oberg Mountain is on the east side of 336. At the

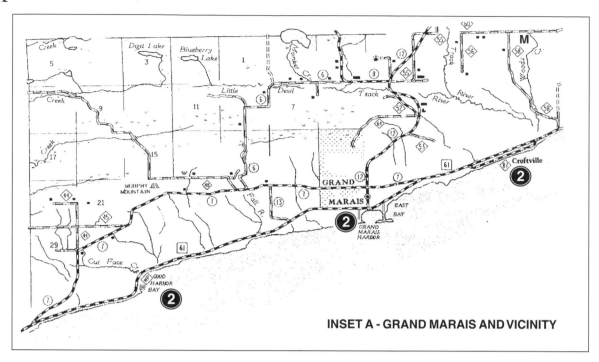

INSET A - GRAND MARAIS AND VICINITY

first fork in the trail, where the main Superior Hiking Trail goes left, bear right at the Oberg Mountain sign up the hill through the maples.

Near the top of the mountain, a half mile or so from the road, you'll reach the trail loop. Take the left fork and start listening for the next few hundred yards. Try not to let the more common Black-throated Greens fool you with their similar song, and there are also Canada and other warblers to listen for at Oberg. Even if the birds don't cooperate, the view from the loop trail is terrific.

As mentioned in the Lake County chapter, remember there are Black-throated Blues to be heard at several points along Cook County's portion of the Superior Hiking Trail (telephone 218-834-2700; website <www.shta.org>).

• Return to Highway 61 and continue 2.7 miles to the Lutsen Resort on the Poplar River at mile 90, where there are feeders and a view of the lake. Then return to the highway and immediately northeast of the river turn north on County Road 5 towards the ski area. Go 1.1 miles up 5, turn left at the wooden Homestead Stables gate, bear left around the stables, and park by the ski hill's equipment garage. From here, it's a short walk to the **Lutsen sewage ponds**, a better-than-average spot because of the mud shorelines and open grassy surroundings, and because there are so few such ponds up the North Shore. Minnesota's most recent Groove-billed Ani was found at these ponds in 1995 — in October, of course.

A couple of miles farther up Highway 61 is the community of Lutsen and the junction with the Caribou Trail / County Road 4, another road leading north into the Superior National Forest.

• The next birding spot is easy to miss. Watch carefully at

mile 97.3 for the small parking area on the north side of the highway, where there is a gated road which leads to the so-called **Spruce Creek ponds**. Hike past the gate, and the old road bears right into a large clearing with grass, gravel, and a few small ponds. Again, such habitat is scarce in this part of the state, and thus worth checking for shorebirds (Buff-breasted and White-rumped sandpipers have appeared in fall), American Pipit, sparrows, Lapland Longspur, Snow Bunting, mystery meadowlarks (in fall), and Rusty Blackbird.

At mile 100 is the mouth of the Cascade River, where there is a wide view of the lake and several mountain ash trees to check for waxwings and the like.

* * *

Not far beyond the Cascade River you enter the **inset A** map, which shows **Grand Marais and vicinity**. Unless you want to turn up County Road 7 to look for Philadelphia Vireos (see below), continue to mile 104 and the overlook for **Good Harbor Bay (A2)**. For reasons unknown, this is arguably the most reliable place on Lake Superior for finding Long-tailed Ducks from October to May. Since they are usually far from shore, scan the bay carefully with a spotting scope, especially around the rocky islands where Whimbrels sometimes pause in May. Be sure to look for all three scoters here during migration, especially October-November, since this is an especially consistent spot for these as well.

You can also check the bay from the Cutface Creek Rest Area at the bottom of the hill, and at mile 105.6 there is a closer vantage point from which to scope the islands.

Four miles beyond Good Harbor Bay at mile 108, you enter the city limits of **Grand Marais** itself (**A2**), easily the best spot on the North Shore of Lake Superior beyond

Duluth. If you only have time in fall to bird only one spot in this part of the state, especially in October-November, this is the place to be.

Among the many strays which have turned up in Grand Marais and vicinity in fall: Brant, King Eider, Barrow's Goldeneye, Purple Sandpiper, Laughing, Ivory and Glaucous-winged gulls, Black-legged Kittiwake, Ancient Murrelet, Anna's Hummingbird (!), Say's Phoebe, Scissor-tailed Flycatcher, Carolina and Rock wrens, Fieldfare (!), Hooded Warbler, and Black-headed Grosbeak.

But don't overlook the potential for spring vagrants in Grand Marais and vicinity, as evidenced by records then of Rock Ptarmigan (!), Lewis's Woodpecker, Say's Phoebe, Fork-tailed Flycatcher (!), Sage Thrasher, Painted Bunting, Lazuli Bunting, and McCown's Longspur.

Even if rarities of this magnitude aren't around, Grand Marais is an especially favorable place to try for such uncommon to rare migrants as Harlequin and Long-tailed ducks, scoters, Whimbrel, Thayer's, Iceland, Glaucous and Great Black-backed gulls, Snowy Owl, Black-backed Woodpecker, Mountain Bluebird, Townsend's Solitaire, Northern Mockingbird, Summer Tanager, and Smith's Longspur.

In addition to Lake Superior itself, there are several places in town to check, all easily found and walked to since Grand Marais isn't that big:

• The open areas and mountain ash trees in the campground to the west of the harbor; turn south off Highway 61 at W. 8th Avenue to access this and the following three areas.

• The thickets, rocky shoreline, and west breakwater behind the power plant, and the west side of the harbor.

• The wooded areas around the swimming pool and campground office.

• The inner harbor by the boat docks, just east of the campground office, where a fish processing operation has been attracting gulls in October and November.

• The east side of the harbor, Artists Point, and east breakwater behind the old Coast Guard station; to access these areas, turn south from downtown on Broadway.

• The woods and brush along the shoreline of East Bay on the east side of town between the Shoreline and Aspen Lodge motels.

• The feeders, mountain ash trees, and conifers along the residential streets north of the highway.

Just east of Grand Marais at mile 111.7, look for the sign for **Croftville Road** / County Road 87 (also **A2**). No fall-winter trip to Grand Marais would be complete without checking this road, which parallels the lake side of Highway 61 past good bird feeders, mountain ash, and spruce trees. It's worth hiking or slowly driving its 1.5-mile length to look for Townsend's Solitaire, Bohemian Waxwing, winter finches, and other fall migrants and winter residents.

Also on the inset A map, there are two locations to be aware of for some breeding birds of possible interest. The Croftville Road rejoins Highway 61 just west of the Devil Track River, and a half mile farther east is County Road 58. Turn north up 58, in about 3 miles you'll come to a T at County Road 60, and 0.5 mile east is a marshy pasture where American Bittern, Sora, and Sedge Wren are all possible. Such habitat and birds are hard to come by in Cook County, and two calling Yellow Rails even found their way to this marsh in 1993.

Just as interesting is the consistent spot west of Grand Marais for nesting Philadelphia Vireos found by the Hoffmans, Cook County's resident bird experts. Follow County Road 7 west out of town for about 5 miles, and bear right (west) on County Road 45. Go 1 mile, and turn north on County Road 44 for a half mile to the corner with several mail boxes. These aspens and birch may look no different to us, but they must look good to Philadelphia Vireos, which have nested around this corner for several years. As previously mentioned, the status of this species in Minnesota is poorly known since no one knows how many of those presumed Red-eyed Vireo songs heard almost everywhere actually come from Philadelphias.

* * *

From Grand Marais, some birders choose to head north up the Gunflint Trail to look for coniferous forest specialties during summer or winter (see inset C). But there are still a few more birding places along the North Shore beyond the Grand Marais area.

• At mile 114.5 on Highway 61, about 5 miles northeast of Grand Marais, there is the sign for **Five Mile Rock (3)**, an island with nesting Herring Gulls and occasional flocks of Whimbrels in May. Along this stretch of 61 and up County Roads 58 and 67, which are just west and east of Five Mile Rock, listen in summer for Whip-poor-wills at night and Philadelphia Vireos by day. Both these local species also occur along other roads in the Grand Marais area, and possibly along the entire length of Cook County's shoreline.

• After Five Mile Rock, the lake is visible from the highway almost continually for the next several miles, and at mile 123 you will come to **Paradise Beach** (also marked **3**). Look from this gravel beach towards the small offshore islands where Long-tailed Duck, all three scoters, and occasional Harlequin Ducks and Whimbrels are often seen during migration. This may be, in fact, the single most consistent spot in the state for scoters, and it is almost always worth the drive here from Grand Marais in May, October, and November. (At this point, rather than continuing up the North Shore, many weekend birders turn around and head for home.)

• Not far past Paradise Beach is Naniboujou Lodge on the Brule River (mile 124.2), which has both a wide view of the lake and open grassy surroundings. And in about another 4 miles is the town of **Hovland** (also **3**) and its Chicago Bay (mile 128.3), where scoters are often seen. On the east side of Hovland at mile 129, the Arrowhead Trail / County Road 16 heads north into the Superior National Forest.

Farther northeast on 61, the lake is also worth scanning from Horseshoe Bay (mile 130.1) and at Big Bay (mile

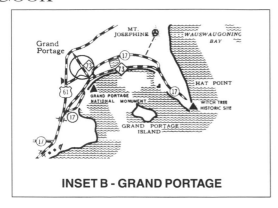

INSET B - GRAND PORTAGE

133.3). In another mile or so, watch for the sign for County Road 17, which turns away from the lake and leads to Mineral Center and County Road 89. If you turn north on 89, you'll be following the former route of old Highway 61, and this interesting road now dead ends at the dismantled bridge and abandoned customs station at the "town" of Pigeon River.

All that remains to bird on the North Shore this side of the Canadian border is **Grand Portage** on **inset B**. As shown on this map, the system of roads in this community is a bit complex. The west side of the bay can be scanned from the Grand Portage Lodge and Casino: follow the signs where County Road 17 turns east off Highway 61 at mile 144. Then continue on 17 past the reconstructed fort and national monument, and turn right off 17 on Bay Road / County Road 73 which goes east along the edge of the bay. Where 73 rejoins County 17 / Upper Road, turn right to the marina to scan the east side of the bay — or to catch a boat to Isle Royale National Park.

The road ends shortly near the famous Witch Tree, an ancient and gnarled white cedar, but you won't be able to see it without a boat. Finally, follow the Upper Road back west towards town and be sure to scan the large and better-than-average sewage ponds on the south side of the road.

About 5 miles beyond Grand Portage, you'll come to the border crossing at mile 150.5, and you'll see the sign for Grand Portage State Park just before the border on the north side of Highway 61. While the birding here may not be anything special, it's worth the half-mile hike to see High Falls on the Pigeon River, Minnesota's highest accessible waterfall.

INLAND COOK COUNTY

To find out what to see and when to look for it in the extensive boreal forests of Cook County's share of the Superior National Forest, simply see the previous Lake County chapter. Accordingly, this present account on the Superior National Forest will not be as lengthy as Lake County's, even though there is plenty of boreal forest habitat for those permanent and summer resident specialties in Cook County. As you refer to Lake County's account, also be sure to keep in mind the comments on the condition of back roads in winter and early spring, and their occasional tendency to appear or disappear or be renumbered, despite what the maps show.

Note the eastern portion of the roadless Boundary Waters Canoe Area Wilderness lies in Cook County, although, as mentioned previously, the birding in this vast and beautiful area is essentially no different than more accessible areas in the Superior National Forest. Again, if you're heading into the Boundary Waters, you'll need an entry permit: for information, call 877-550-6777 or go to their website (www.bwcaw.org).

About the only Lake County birds you probably won't be able to find nesting in Cook County are Golden-winged and Connecticut warblers, and Great Gray Owls tend to be harder to find. Otherwise, everything else is possible here, especially such permanent residents as Northern Goshawk, Ruffed and Spruce (good luck!) grouse, Barred and Boreal (good luck!) owls, Black-backed and a few Three-toed woodpeckers, Gray Jay, Boreal Chickadee, Evening Grosbeak, and both crossbills (often absent in summers). Additionally, watch for Northern Hawk Owl (rare), Northern Shrike, Pine Grosbeak and redpolls during winter months.

In summer, add Long-eared and Northern Saw-whet owls, Yellow-bellied and Alder flycatchers, Blue-headed Vireo, Winter Wren, both kinglets, Swainson's Thrush, several warblers (including uncommon and local breeders such as Tennessee, Cape May, Bay-breasted, and Wilson's), Lincoln's Sparrow, and many others to the list of possibilities. There are also a few Rusty Blackbirds at the southern periphery of their breeding range, and Solitary Sandpipers have nested here. Also keep an eye open for Moose and Black Bear as you drive around — with luck, a Gray Wolf might even stroll by.

From Highway 61, most birders head up into the woods via the "trails" (actually county roads): the Sawbill out of Tofte, the Caribou out of Lutsen, the Gunflint out of Grand Marais, or the Arrowhead out of Hovland. Except for the Gunflint, though, none of these roads leads to any specific spots or other roads of particular favor among birders, and it is recommended you obtain a Superior National Forest or Cook County map to explore them on your own (see the maps section of References and Resources in the introduction).

You will certainly find spruce bogs and other good boreal habitats during your wanderings, and one road to try would be Forest Road 170, also called The Grade. It can be accessed from the Sawbill and Caribou trails, and it extends from Lake County Road 7 all the way northeast to its end by Two Island Lake.

But everyone's favorite road is the **Gunflint Trail**, or County Road 12, which begins as W. 5th Avenue in Grand Marais and ends some 55 miles later at Sea Gull Lake. Along the way, the Gunflint and its connecting side roads pass through lots of good coniferous forest habitat, and **inset C** includes the most worthwhile areas.

The best section of the Gunflint Trail, where birders

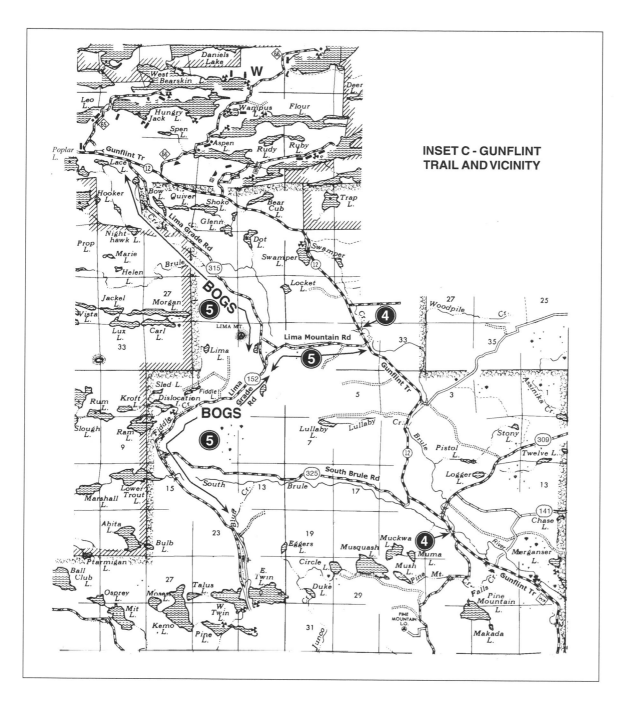

spend the most time, is between the South Brule River and Poplar Lake (where there is a small store and nice cafe at Trail Center Lodge). There is less coverage by birders farther up the Gunflint, where the birds and habitat have generally not been as interesting — until recently.

A wind storm a couple years ago leveled a huge section of the forest, including areas along the Gunflint beyond Poplar Lake, creating lots of snags and habitat for Northern Hawk Owls (two nesting pairs were found in 2001, in the stretch between 44 and 49 miles from Grand Marais) and Three-toed and Black-backed woodpeckers. Also, the last 8 miles or so of the Gunflint passes through some excellent spruce bogs. At the end of the road there is a campground and popular access point for the Boundary Waters.

Within inset C, birders often make their first stop where

the road crosses the **South Brule River (C4)**, 15.7 miles from Grand Marais. There is a parking area on the east side of the road, and just north of here it's worth hiking the old road on the west side of the Gunflint which cuts back south and crosses the river. Try especially for Three-toed Woodpecker, which has been found more than once here in recent summers, and it's as good a place as any to find such breeding birds as Black-backed Woodpecker, Yellow-bellied and Alder flycatchers, Boreal Chickadee, and warblers (at least 15 species regularly nest around this area).

After the South Brule River, in 1.2 miles, note where the South Brule Road / Forest Road 325 turns west off the Gunflint Trail. But continue north for now, in 4 more miles the Lima Mountain Road turns west (more on this later), and just north is the **North Brule River** (also marked

C4). There are good places here to park and hike off the road just north and just south of the river, on the east side of the Gunflint, good spots to look and listen for whatever you couldn't find by the South Brule River.

The first confirmed Boreal Owl nest in the lower 48 United States was found in 1978 in a balsam fir snag by the parking area on the north side of the North Brule River. The snag is no longer standing, but Boreals are still in the area and, as described in the Lake County chapter, tend to be most vocal in March and early April. Surveys in Cook County since the 1980s have turned up territorial pairs each year, with over 30 calling males and six nests actually found one year. Along the Gunflint Trail and its side roads, especially from the South Brule River north, has been as good an area as any in the state for this highly-sought owl.

Actually, the best places to bird in the Gunflint Trail area are west of the Gunflint, and the best of these is along the **Lima Mountain Road (C5)** / Forest Road 152. You'll see the sign for it just south of the North Brule River, and it's worth spending as much time as possible along its 2.2-mile length. Watch especially for Spruce Grouse, those two elusive woodpeckers, Boreal Chickadee, nesting warblers and other passerines, and winter finches. You might have the best luck with grouse in late summer and fall (careful: Ruffeds are also present); this road might offer your best chance at finding a singing Cape May or Bay-breasted war-bler, two quite uncommon and local breeding species.

The Lima Mountain Road ends at the spot we call the triangle. Here, the right fork becomes Forest Road 315 and goes north, and the left fork continues as Forest Road 152 and goes south. Both forks are also named the **Lima Grade Road** (also **C5**), and it's worth birding this road in both directions.

If you turn north, in about 6 miles the road comes out to the Gunflint Trail, a mile east of Trail Center Lodge or 28 miles from Grand Marais. There are good coniferous stands en route, but also be sure to look for owls and woodpeckers in the open burned area which starts a couple of miles up the road.

If you turn south at the triangle, the Lima Grade Road continues through more spruce bogs. The first mile or so of road southwest of the triangle includes the bog where Minnesota's first Three-toed Woodpecker nest was found. The road eventually crosses the South Brule River, passes through more bogs, and dead ends at Twin Lake.

A half mile north of the South Brule River, watch for the junction with Forest Road 325 / South Brule Road, which heads east for about 6 miles back to the Gunflint Trail, 17 miles from Grand Marais. Just west of the Gunflint, the road passes by an extensive alder swamp where both Wilson's Warbler and Rusty Blackbird have been found in summer.

APPENDIX A

MINNESOTA ORNITHOLOGISTS' UNION RECORDS COMMITTEE REQUEST FOR DOCUMENTATION

Species ______________________________

Observer ______________________________

Please return to:
MOURC c/o Kim R. Eckert
8255 Congdon Blvd.
Duluth, MN 55804

Date(s) ______________ Location ______________________________

Reason Observation is Unusual ______________________________

____

Because your observation is significant, please provide us with as much information as possible for the permanent file of Minnesota bird records. If you have **photos**, **tape recordings** of vocalizations, **sketches**, written or taped **field notes**, please include them with this form. It would also be appreciated if you could incorporate this information into a Note of Interest for possible inclusion in ***The Loon.*** Thank you for your cooperation!

I. **DESCRIPTION OF THE BIRD** as it appeared in the field. Please type if possible, and attach extra sheets if necessary. In addition to the bird's appearance, also describe its size, any vocalizations heard, and include any relevant information on its behavior.

____

____

____

____

____

____

____

____

____

____

____

____

____

____

____

____

(See other side)

II. SPECIES SIMILAR TO THIS BIRD and how eliminated from consideration.

_____

_____

_____

_____

III. YOUR EXPERIENCE with this and similar species.

_____

_____

_____

IV. OTHER OBSERVERS; if they have additional information regarding this record, please include with this report, or list their addresses so they can be contacted.

_____

V. CHECK APPLICABLE STATEMENTS:

___ You were aware at the time of the observation that this record was unusual

___ Photos or tape recordings were taken of bird (PLEASE INCLUDE WITH THIS REPORT)

___ Field guides were not used nor needed to make identification

___ Field notes or sketch made during observation, before/after (circle one) field guide was consulted (PLEASE INCLUDE WITH THIS REPORT)

___ Field notes or sketch made ___ minutes/hours/days (circle one) after observation, before/after (circle one) consulting field guide (PLEASE INCLUDE WITH THIS REPORT)

___ Identification made by consulting field guides while bird was in view

___ Identification made from memory after consulting field guides___minutes/hours/days later
(circle one)

Field guides and other references consulted: _____

VI. LIGHT CONDITIONS; bird–observer–sun orientation; time of day _____

_____

Length of observation _____ Distance from bird _____

Optics used _____

Habitat _____

VII. NAME AND ADDRESS of person completing this form _____

_____ Date: _____

248

APPENDIX B

CHECKLIST OF MINNESOTA BIRDS: 427 Species recorded as of January 2002

REGULAR SPECIES (313)

- Red-throated Loon
- Pacific Loon
- Common Loon
- Pied-billed Grebe
- Horned Grebe
- Red-necked Grebe
- Eared Grebe
- Western Grebe
- Clark's Grebe
- American White Pelican
- Double-crested Cormorant
- American Bittern
- Least Bittern
- Great Blue Heron
- Great Egret
- Snowy Egret
- Little Blue Heron
- Cattle Egret
- Green Heron
- Black-crowned Night-Heron
- Yellow-crowned Night-Heron
- Turkey Vulture
- Greater White-fronted Goose
- Snow Goose
- Ross's Goose
- Canada Goose
- Mute Swan
- Trumpeter Swan
- Tundra Swan
- Wood Duck
- Gadwall
- American Wigeon
- American Black Duck
- Mallard
- Blue-winged Teal
- Cinnamon Teal
- Northern Shoveler
- Northern Pintail
- Green-winged Teal
- Canvasback
- Redhead
- Ring-necked Duck
- Greater Scaup
- Lesser Scaup
- Harlequin Duck
- Surf Scoter
- White-winged Scoter
- Black Scoter
- Long-tailed Duck
- Bufflehead
- Common Goldeneye
- Hooded Merganser
- Common Merganser
- Red-breasted Merganser
- Ruddy Duck
- Osprey
- Bald Eagle
- Northern Harrier
- Sharp-shinned Hawk
- Cooper's Hawk
- Northern Goshawk
- Red-shouldered Hawk
- Broad-winged Hawk
- Swainson's Hawk
- Red-tailed Hawk
- Ferruginous Hawk
- Rough-legged Hawk
- Golden Eagle
- American Kestrel
- Merlin
- Gyrfalcon
- Peregrine Falcon
- Prairie Falcon
- Gray Partridge
- Ring-necked Pheasant
- Ruffed Grouse
- Spruce Grouse
- Sharp-tailed Grouse
- Greater Prairie-Chicken
- Wild Turkey
- Northern Bobwhite
- Yellow Rail
- Virginia Rail
- Sora

- Common Moorhen
- American Coot
- Sandhill Crane
- Black-bellied Plover
- American Golden-Plover
- Semipalmated Plover
- Piping Plover
- Killdeer
- American Avocet
- Greater Yellowlegs
- Lesser Yellowlegs
- Solitary Sandpiper
- Willet
- Spotted Sandpiper
- Upland Sandpiper
- Whimbrel
- Hudsonian Godwit
- Marbled Godwit
- Ruddy Turnstone
- Red Knot
- Sanderling
- Semipalmated Sandpiper
- Least Sandpiper
- White-rumped Sandpiper
- Baird's Sandpiper
- Pectoral Sandpiper
- Dunlin
- Stilt Sandpiper
- Buff-breasted Sandpiper
- Short-billed Dowitcher
- Long-billed Dowitcher
- Common Snipe
- American Woodcock
- Wilson's Phalarope
- Red-necked Phalarope
- Parasitic Jaeger
- Franklin's Gull
- Little Gull
- Bonaparte's Gull
- Ring-billed Gull
- Herring Gull
- Thayer's Gull
- Iceland Gull
- Lesser Black-backed Gull
- Glaucous Gull
- Great Black-backed Gull
- Caspian Tern
- Common Tern
- Forster's Tern
- Black Tern
- Rock Dove
- Mourning Dove
- Black-billed Cuckoo
- Yellow-billed Cuckoo
- Eastern Screech-Owl
- Great Horned Owl
- Snowy Owl
- Northern Hawk Owl
- Barred Owl
- Great Gray Owl
- Long-eared Owl
- Short-eared Owl
- Boreal Owl
- Northern Saw-whet Owl
- Common Nighthawk
- Whip-poor-will
- Chimney Swift
- Ruby-throated Hummingbird
- Belted Kingfisher
- Red-headed Woodpecker
- Red-bellied Woodpecker
- Yellow-bellied Sapsucker
- Downy Woodpecker
- Hairy Woodpecker
- Three-toed Woodpecker
- Black-backed Woodpecker
- Northern Flicker
- Pileated Woodpecker
- Olive-sided Flycatcher
- Eastern Wood-Pewee
- Yellow-bellied Flycatcher
- Acadian Flycatcher
- Alder Flycatcher
- Willow Flycatcher
- Least Flycatcher
- Eastern Phoebe
- Great Crested Flycatcher

- Western Kingbird
- Eastern Kingbird
- Loggerhead Shrike
- Northern Shrike
- Bell's Vireo
- Yellow-throated Vireo
- Blue-headed Vireo
- Warbling Vireo
- Philadelphia Vireo
- Red-eyed Vireo
- Gray Jay
- Blue Jay
- Black-billed Magpie
- American Crow
- Common Raven
- Horned Lark
- Purple Martin
- Tree Swallow
- Northern Rough-winged Swallow
- Bank Swallow
- Cliff Swallow
- Barn Swallow
- Black-capped Chickadee
- Boreal Chickadee
- Tufted Titmouse
- Red-breasted Nuthatch
- White-breasted Nuthatch
- Brown Creeper
- Carolina Wren
- House Wren
- Winter Wren
- Sedge Wren
- Marsh Wren
- Golden-crowned Kinglet
- Ruby-crowned Kinglet
- Blue-gray Gnatcatcher
- Eastern Bluebird
- Mountain Bluebird
- Townsend's Solitaire
- Veery
- Gray-cheeked Thrush
- Swainson's Thrush
- Hermit Thrush
- Wood Thrush
- American Robin
- Varied Thrush
- Gray Catbird
- Northern Mockingbird
- Brown Thrasher
- European Starling
- American Pipit
- Bohemian Waxwing
- Cedar Waxwing
- Blue-winged Warbler
- Golden-winged Warbler
- Tennessee Warbler
- Orange-crowned Warbler
- Nashville Warbler
- Northern Parula
- Yellow Warbler
- Chestnut-sided Warbler
- Magnolia Warbler
- Cape May Warbler
- Black-throated Blue Warbler
- Yellow-rumped Warbler
- Black-throated Green Warbler
- Blackburnian Warbler
- Pine Warbler
- Palm Warbler
- Bay-breasted Warbler
- Blackpoll Warbler
- Cerulean Warbler
- Black-and-white Warbler
- American Redstart
- Prothonotary Warbler
- Worm-eating Warbler
- Ovenbird
- Northern Waterthrush
- Louisiana Waterthrush
- Kentucky Warbler
- Connecticut Warbler
- Mourning Warbler
- Common Yellowthroat
- Hooded Warbler
- Wilson's Warbler
- Canada Warbler
- Yellow-breasted Chat

- Summer Tanager
- Scarlet Tanager
- Western Tanager
- Spotted Towhee
- Eastern Towhee
- American Tree Sparrow
- Chipping Sparrow
- Clay-colored Sparrow
- Field Sparrow
- Vesper Sparrow
- Lark Sparrow
- Savannah Sparrow
- Grasshopper Sparrow
- Henslow's Sparrow
- Le Conte's Sparrow
- Nelson's Sharp-tailed Sparrow
- Fox Sparrow
- Song Sparrow
- Lincoln's Sparrow
- Swamp Sparrow
- White-throated Sparrow
- Harris's Sparrow
- White-crowned Sparrow
- Dark-eyed Junco
- Lapland Longspur
- Smith's Longspur
- Chestnut-collared Longspur
- Snow Bunting
- Northern Cardinal
- Rose-breasted Grosbeak
- Blue Grosbeak
- Indigo Bunting
- Dickcissel
- Bobolink
- Red-winged Blackbird
- Eastern Meadowlark
- Western Meadowlark
- Yellow-headed Blackbird
- Rusty Blackbird
- Brewer's Blackbird
- Common Grackle
- Brown-headed Cowbird
- Orchard Oriole
- Baltimore Oriole
- Pine Grosbeak
- Purple Finch
- House Finch
- Red Crossbill
- White-winged Crossbill
- Common Redpoll
- Hoary Redpoll
- Pine Siskin
- American Goldfinch
- Evening Grosbeak
- House Sparrow

CASUAL SPECIES (26)

- Tricolored Heron
- White-faced Ibis
- Eurasian Wigeon
- King Eider
- Barrow's Goldeneye
- Mississippi Kite
- King Rail
- Ruff
- Red Phalarope
- Laughing Gull
- California Gull
- Sabine's Gull
- Black-legged Kittiwake
- Least Tern
- Burrowing Owl
- Say's Phoebe
- Scissor-tailed Flycatcher
- White-eyed Vireo
- Rock Wren
- Sprague's Pipit
- Yellow-throated Warbler
- Prairie Warbler
- Lark Bunting
- Baird's Sparrow
- Black-headed Grosbeak
- Lazuli Bunting

ACCIDENTAL SPECIES (88)

- Yellow-billed Loon
- Magnificent Frigatebird
- Neotropic Cormorant
- White Ibis
- Glossy Ibis
- Black Vulture
- Black-bellied Whistling-Duck
- Fulvous Whistling-Duck
- Brant
- Garganey
- Common Eider
- Smew
- Swallow-tailed Kite
- White-tailed Kite
- Crested Caracara
- Willow Ptarmigan
- Rock Ptarmigan
- Black Rail
- Purple Gallinule
- Whooping Crane
- Snowy Plover
- Wilson's Plover
- Black-necked Stilt
- Eskimo Curlew
- Long-billed Curlew
- Western Sandpiper
- Purple Sandpiper
- Curlew Sandpiper
- Pomarine Jaeger
- Long-tailed Jaeger
- Black-headed Gull
- Mew Gull
- Glaucous-winged Gull
- Ross's Gull
- Ivory Gull
- Sandwich Tern
- Arctic Tern
- Dovekie
- Ancient Murrelet
- Band-tailed Pigeon
- Eurasian Collared-Dove
- White-winged Dove
- [Passenger Pigeon]
- Common Ground-Dove
- Groove-billed Ani
- Barn Owl
- Common Poorwill
- Chuck-will's-widow
- White-throated Swift
- Magnificent Hummingbird
- Anna's Hummingbird
- Calliope Hummingbird
- Rufous Hummingbird
- Lewis's Woodpecker
- Williamson's Sapsucker
- Western Wood-Pewee
- Black Phoebe
- Vermilion Flycatcher
- Ash-throated Flycatcher
- Fork-tailed Flycatcher
- Clark's Nutcracker
- Violet-green Swallow
- Pygmy Nuthatch
- Bewick's Wren
- American Dipper
- Northern Wheatear
- Fieldfare
- Sage Thrasher
- Curve-billed Thrasher
- Black-throated Gray Warbler
- Townsend's Warbler
- Hermit Warbler
- Kirtland's Warbler
- MacGillivray's Warbler
- Painted Redstart
- Green-tailed Towhee
- Brewer's Sparrow
- Black-throated Sparrow
- Golden-crowned Sparrow
- McCown's Longspur
- Painted Bunting
- Great-tailed Grackle
- Bullock's Oriole
- Scott's Oriole
- Brambling
- Gray-crowned Rosy-Finch
- Cassin's Finch
- Eurasian Tree Sparrow

249

INDEX TO BIRDING LOCATIONS

Page references refer only to the text in the three regions; locations on the maps and those cited in the Annotated List of Minnesota Birds (p. 14-49) are not indexed. The county chapters are also not indexed here; these are shown on the inside front and back covers. Note that lakes and sewage ponds are indexed under "Lake" and "sewage ponds" respectively. Also note the following abbreviations: Co. = County; NWR = National Wildlife Refuge; SNA = Scientific and Natural Area; WMA = Wildlife Management Area.

253

INDEX TO BIRDS

In the introduction, only the primary entries of each species in the Annotated List of Minnesota Birds section (pages 14-49) are indexed. Note that bird groups such as shorebirds, owls, warblers, etc. are also indexed; therefore, when looking up White-winged Crossbill, for example, also refer to the "crossbills" and "finches, winter" entries.